BISEXUALITIES

BISEXUALITIES:
THE IDEOLOGY AND PRACTICE OF SEXUAL CONTACT WITH BOTH MEN AND WOMEN

Erwin J. Haeberle and Rolf Gindorf, Editors

With Contributions by
Philip Blumstein, Eli Coleman, John P. De Cecco, Milton Diamond,
Richard C. Friedman, John H. Gagnon, Rolf Gindorf, Julian Gold,
Cathy Stein Greenblat, Erwin J. Haeberle, Gert Hekma, Gilbert Herdt,
Michael Kimmel, M. E. Miller, John Money, A. X. van Naerssen, Jay P. Paul,
Douglas W. Pryor, Michael W. Ross, Pepper Schwartz, Alan Warran,
Martin S. Weinberg, Colin J. Williams, Alex Wodak, Joseph Wong

BISEXUALITIES

THE IDEOLOGY AND PRACTICE OF SEXUAL CONTACT WITH BOTH MEN AND WOMEN

Erwin J. Haeberle
and Rolf Gindorf
Editors

CONTINUUM • NEW YORK

1999
The Continuum Publishing Company
370 Lexington Avenue
New York, NY 10017

Copyright © 1994 by Gustav Fischer Verlag
English texts Copyright © 1998 by The Continuum Publishing Company

Printed in the United States of America

Library of Congress Cataloging-in-Publication Data

Bisexualities : the ideology and practice of sexual contact with both men and women
  / Erwin J. Haeberle and Rolf Gindorf, editors ; portions translated by Lance W.
Garmer.
    p.   cm.
  Bisexualitäten. English
  Includes bibliographical references and index.
  ISBN 0-8264-0923-7 (alk. paper)
  1. Bisexuality—Cross-cultural studies. 2. Bisexuality–Philosophy.
I. Haeberle, Erwin J.   II. Gindorf, Rolf
  HQ74.B575   1998
  306.76 5—dc21   96-40051
                                                                         CIP

CONTENTS

FOREWORD

This book reprints some of the papers presented at the first scientific congress on human bisexual behavior. It was held at the Reichstag in Berlin in July 1990 and was organized by the German Society for Social-Scientific Sex Research (DGSS) as its tenth national congress. We were quite mindful of the fact that Berlin had seen the world's first sexological congresses in 1921 and 1926, and that the latter had opened in the plenary hall of the very same Reichstag, which at that time, had still been the working Parliament of the Weimar Republic. Therefore, deliberately counting these first pioneering congresses, we called our own meeting the Third International Berlin Conference for Sexology. After all, it was only in 1933, when Hitler and the Nazis came to power, that the German sexological movement was suddenly, deliberately, and thoroughly destroyed. Most of its pioneers were Jewish: Magnus Hirschfeld, Albert Moll, Arthur Kronfeld, Max Marcuse, Felix Theilhaber, Ludwig Levy-Lenz, Eugen Steinach, Wilhelm Reich, Charlotte Wolff, Ernst Gräfenberg, Hans Lehfeldt, and many others. They were no longer welcome in the country of their birth, and almost all of them were forced to flee into exile. Thus, within a very short time, they found themselves dispersed in many countries: France, England, Denmark, Norway, Sweden, Switzerland, Palestine, Egypt, the Soviet Union, and the United States.

After Hitler's defeat, even those sexologists who had survived did not return to Germany, and thus their work was eventually forgotten. Their scientific heritage was never claimed, and especially Berlin made no effort, on either side of the Wall, to reestablish the world's first Institute for Sexology, which had been founded by Hirschfeld in 1919.

When the Wall finally came down in the fall of 1989, it was again possible to plan an international sexological congress in a newly united Berlin and, indeed, the International Academy of Sex Research proceeded to organize its annual meeting in this city.

Unfortunately, because of a dispute about the program, the planned meeting in Berlin was canceled on short notice and moved to Sigtuna in Sweden. The essence of this dispute never became clear to all Academy members, but it seems to have had something to do with incompatible views on homosexuality research. Apparently, on this issue there were two hostile camps within the Academy, with several natural scientists taking one side and quite a few social scientists taking the other. (See also the following Introduction under "The Current Discussion: Essentialists vs. Constructionists.")

However, it seemed to us that a continued dialogue between these two camps was urgently needed and therefore we decided to seek the cooperation of the Berlin endocrinologist Günther Dörner (a member of the "essentialist" camp) for a two-part, large conference. The second part on "Bisexualities" was to be entirely organized by us. The first part was devoted to various other topics, but was also meant to give Dörner and other essentialists ample opportunity to make their case with regard to the causes of homosexuality.

To our pleasant surprise, this "joint venture" went very well, our organizational cooperation functioned smoothly, and thus we were able to welcome a great number of sex researchers from all over the world to our congress, including many members of the Academy. This was, in part, also due to the fact that they had made firm travel arrangements for Berlin long in advance and were unable to change them in time for Sigtuna.

Thus, our Third International Berlin Conference for Sexology turned into a great success. For the first time after the end of the Nazi and communist dictatorships a large international meeting of sexologists returned to the newly united city. Not only that, the second part on "Bisexualities" could be held at the Reichstag, to the great satisfaction of our many Jewish colleagues. They felt very strongly, as we did, that, by reclaiming this historical site after sixty-four years for a scientific meeting, sexology once more took up where it had been forced to leave off, and that thereby the evil spirit of Nazism had finally been exorcized. In order to honor our greatest sexological pioneer, our society also, for the first time, presented its Magnus Hirschfeld Medals for Outstanding Contributions to Sexual Science and Sexual Reform to two distinguished Jewish colleagues who had personally suffered from Nazi persecution: Ernest Borneman (Austria) and Herman Musaph (Netherlands), both now deceased. Since then, on the occasion of three subsequent congresses (1992, 1994, and 1997), we have awarded the medals to six more recipients: John De Cecco (USA), Imre Aszódi (Hungary), Dalin Liu (China), Ruth K. Westheimer (USA), Jonathan Ned Katz (USA), and Maj-Briht Bergström-Walan (Sweden). Moreover in 1994, the renewed sexological activity in Berlin encouraged the Robert Koch Institute, a federal research institution, to open an Archive for Sexology in the future German capital. This Archive thus became the first permanent and publicly accessible sexological institution in Berlin since 1933. Located in the very center of the city, it now houses a research library and various collections, among them many original documents relating to the work of our scientific pioneers.

THE PRESENT VOLUME is a modest record of the historic meeting of 1990. Some lengthy, but very interesting German-language papers could not be translated for this volume, but are contained in the German edition (Gustav Fischer Verlag, Stuttgart 1994). However, as is common today not only in sexology, but also in many other fields, the most important literature is written in English. In the present case, the contributors are leading sex researchers from Germany, the Netherlands, Australia, and Hong Kong. In addition, the USA is especially well represented, including three prominent researchers who formerly worked at the Kinsey Institute (Gagnon, Weinberg, and Williams). Among experts, the names De Cecco, Coleman, Diamond, Green, Herdt, Money, Schwartz, and Blumstein are also well known worldwide.

Our volume deals with the biological as well as the sociological aspects of bisexual behavior. It contains fundamental, critical historical, and methodological discussions, transcultural comparisons, and new empirical findings, and it also covers clinical aspects. In short, the most recent and complete introduction to one of the most interesting areas of today's sex research is contained between the covers of this book. We sincerely hope that it will not only entertain and instruct many readers, but that it will also prove to be but the first sign of the renewed strength of our science in the city of its birth.

Berlin and Düsseldorf, Fall 1997
ERWIN J. HAEBERLE AND ROLF GINDORF

Addresses of the Editors:
Prof. Dr. phil. Erwin J. Haeberle, Ed.D.
Robert Koch-Institut
Archiv für Sexualwissenschaft
Hannoversche Str. 27
10115 Berlin
Germany
website: http://www.rki.de/GESUND/ARCHIV/HOME.HTM
e-mail: HaeberleE@rki.de

Rolf Gindorf
DGSS
Gerresheimer Str. 20
40211 Düsseldorf
Germany
website: http://www.sexologie.org
e-mail: Rolf.Gindorf@sexologie.org

1. The First International Conference for Sexual Reform on a Sexological Basis. September 15–20, 1921. Langenbeck-Virchow-Haus, Berlin. Organizer: Magnus Hirschfeld.

2. First Congress of the International Society for Sex Research. October 10–16, 1926. Opening ceremony in the plenary hall of the Reichstag. Organizer: Albert Moll.

3. International Berlin Conference for Sexology (on "Bisexualities"). July 13–15, 1990. Reichstag. Shown are some participants during a conference break. First row from the left: Rolf Gindorf, Erwin J. Haeberle, John Gagnon, Milton Diamond, Richard Green, Martin Weinberg, Günther Dörner, John Money, standing behind him: Eli Coleman. Also standing, between Diamond and Green: Reinhard Wille, behind him: Theo Sandfort, sitting before him; Rob Tielman. Sitting next to him, behind Weinberg: Gunter Runkel. Sitting between Haeberle and Gagnon: A.X. van Naerssen. *InterAction Stock.* Copyright ©1990 M. Diamond

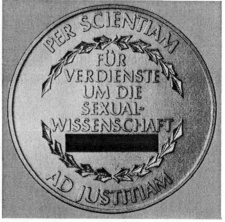

4. The Magnus Hirschfeld Medal awarded by the DGSS since 1990 for outstanding contributions to sex research and sexual reform. Left: front; right: back. The name of the recipient is engraved in the place of the black rectangle. So far, the following sexologists have been honored: Ernest Borneman (Austria), Herman Musaph (Netherlands), John P. De Cecco (USA), Imre Aszódi (Hungary), Dalin Liu (China), Ruth K. Westheimer (USA), Jonathan Ned Katz (USA), and Maj-Briht Bergström-Walan (Sweden).

INTRODUCTION

Bisexuality: History and Dimensions of a Modern Scientific Problem

Erwin J. Haeberle

When someone falls in love with a woman today and with a man tomorrow, when he first finds a member of one and then of the other sex erotically attractive and has "carnal knowledge" of both, this in itself was and is not considered a problem in many cultures. Nor was it one in our own Western antiquity. Neither religious nor secular authorities nor medical experts regarded it as a topic worthy of discussion. On the contrary: as seriously as even then everyone took love and carnal desire, the sex of the lovers involved was not something to which one paid much attention. For the Greek Stoics, it was one of the *Adiaphora*, the indifferences of life. It was well understood by everyone that wanton Eros caused all of love's desires according to his whim and inspired all sorts of strange and sometimes unhappy pairings. People knew that this god answered to no one, and thus they made no attempt to explain or justify his willful and often cruel jokes. As a matter of principle, every person was a possible object of another person's love, just as it happened to please divine caprice.

The Christian Middle Ages, which condemned love between members of the same sex as sinful, were also convinced that every person was capable of such a sin—as well as of all other sins. All men were sinners, and the Devil never rested, but constantly lay in waiting everywhere. He could cause the fall of anyone who was not on guard—a belief that was also shared by all Protestant reformers and especially the British (and later American) Puritans.

In short, even our own culture assumed well into the modern age that people could have same-sex as well as other-sex desires. The community may have disapproved of some or all of these desires from time to time, but their ubiquitous existence, that is, man's ambierotic potential, was never doubted.

Such doubts first awoke in the course of the eighteenth century with the growth of the bourgeoisie and the "scientification" of life until, during the mid- and late nineteenth century, the doubters began to believe the opposite of what humanity had always believed before: Now everyone was convinced that men and women "normally" could love only the other sex. Any broadening of this spectrum and especially a strong inclination to one's own sex was sick or at least "abnormal." Erotic variety became suspect. It was a cancerous growth in the healthy body social, a sign of degeneration, of confusion and disorder, a dangerous atavism, a reversion to a primitive, animalistic level that hindered every predicted social progress.

Therefore, when we approach the topic today, we must become familiar with this first, far-reaching paradigm change and endeavor to understand how and why it came about. If we do not, we run the danger of being duped and overwhelmed by its unquestioned assumptions and of ending up in complete confusion. Indeed, our modern concepts "homosexuality," "heterosexuality," "bisexuality," and, indeed, the very word "sexuality" itself are creations of the nineteenth century and carry with them that century's particular interests and concerns. Woe to the researcher who fails to keep this in mind and who takes such concepts at face value! He will notice too late that his frock-coated ancestors' brilliant insights and flashes of genius are in reality will-o'-the-wisps that today cannot provide any illumination at all. Utterly disoriented, he will finally sink into an intellectual morass, for the thicket of empty formulae at which he may grasp in his desperation no longer offers him or anyone else any support.

"Homosexuality": From Conduct to Condition — Twice Going and Coming Back

THE MODERN WORD *bisexuality* (sometimes also *ambisexuality*) in the sense of "erotic interest in both sexes" could not come into existence until after the words *homosexuality* and subsequently *heterosexuality* (as a counter-concept to homosexuality) had been coined. *Bisexuality* then offered a link, as it were, between them, a sort of transition as well as a combination, a logical third possibility. The concept thus did not arise until after people had understood that the simple opposition "homosexual—heterosexual" did not suffice to describe human erotic reality. Yet the key concept that first made the entire triad possible, indeed actually forced it into existence, was the concept of "homosexuality," which has become all too familiar to too many of us today.

This concept is just over one hundred twenty-five years old, and yet it now so completely dominates every discussion of same-sex love that one must ask oneself how humanity managed to do without it for thousands of years. When biblical prophets, Greek philosophers, Roman lawgivers, medieval theologians, "enlightened" pedagogues, or Romantic poets talked about the topic, they had to do so without the word "homosexuality," because it simply did not exist.

Strictly speaking, three different ideas can inhere in the word *homosexuality* today, although speakers and listeners are often quite unaware of this.

(1) If, for example, someone says, "There is a great deal of homosexuality in prison," he is speaking of homosexuality as a behavior, a particular kind of **conduct**. He is actually saying, "There is a great deal of homosexual behavior in prison." He does not mean to say that there are many "homosexuals" in prison or that many people there become "homosexual." Rather, the sentence merely states that many prisoners, lacking partners of the other sex, have sexual contact with one another.

(2) An entirely different idea is behind the question, "Is homosexuality a sickness?" The word here does not mean a kind of behavior or conduct, but rather a **condition**. Depending on the answer, this condition may be good or bad, but, in any case, it is a condition, a character trait, a type of quality inherent in certain persons. "Homosexuality" is something that some people have, not something that they do.

(3) Finally, when researchers speak of different "homosexualities," they indicate that they think of "homosexuality" neither as a behavior nor as a condition but rather as a **social role**, that is, of different homosexualities as a spectrum of such

roles. They do not mean different forms of same-sex contacts or different subdivisions of the same diagnosis, but rather different types and ways of how people live in society as "homosexuals."

Indeed, the noun *homosexual* itself can have three meanings: either someone who engages in a particular kind of conduct; or someone who has a particular condition; or someone who plays a particular social role.

In most Western countries, though, there is now a tendency to lump all three meanings together and to see conduct, condition, and social role as different aspects of the same phenomenon: "Homosexuals do what they do because they are what they are, and so they can always be recognized by their typical lifestyle."

This modern view, however, immediately becomes blurred once we turn our gaze to the past—that is, to a time before the word *homosexuality* had been invented. Our distant ancestors had, of course, a whole range of terms for same-sex eroticism. Of these, *Greek love, pederasty, sodomy,* and *buggery* are still known today. Yet none of these expressions can be correctly translated as "homosexuality," since they were meant to express entirely different notions. First of all, they referred only to men. There was a special word for same-sex female eroticism: *tribadism.* (The word *lesbianism* for love between women was first introduced toward the end of the nineteenth century. Prior to that, already in antiquity, it had meant "oral intercourse," regardless of the sex of the persons involved.) There was no expression that would have applied to both sexes.

Second, the older terms referred only to sexual acts that, theoretically, could be performed by anyone; they did not suggest a particular type of person. A devotee of "Greek love," a pederast, a sodomite, or "bugger" (*bougre* in French) was someone who did certain things, not someone who suffered from a particular condition. Sodomites committed sodomy as thieves committed theft; both were very well capable of behaving correctly like everyone else. Thus, sodomy was no more a condition than was theft. Instead, these were acts committed wickedly and willfully, crimes that the community had to prevent or at least punish. It would therefore have been both pointless and impossible to call someone a "pseudopederast" or a "latent sodomite." It was just as inconceivable that adolescents should go through a purely psychological "sodomitic phase." There simply could be no thief without theft, no adulterer without adultery, no murderer without murder, no pederast without pederasty, and no sodomite without sodomy. In short, the old terms referred only to people who had actually performed certain acts. If there was no such act, the terms could not be applied.

It is also important to understand that *sodomy* and *buggery* were very negative terms—after all, they had been first introduced to describe religious "abominations," i.e., the sins of Sodom and the heresy of the Bulgarians (*bugger* is a corrupted form of *Bulgar*[ian]). Indeed, even the word *pederasty* became a term of reprobation as soon as people took it out of its original, ancient Greek context. *Greek love* was somewhat more neutral, but whoever wanted to say something positive about love between men had to forego all traditional terminology and try, with the help of amicable verbs, to formulate new, complete sentences avoiding the traditional loaded substantives.

Yet as long as the Occident was dominated by Judeo-Christian moral ideas, it would have been utter folly for upright citizens to say anything positive about same-sex eroticism. The few who dared to do so were quickly silenced and their works publicly burned. It was not until the Age of Enlightenment, the subsequent French Revolution and Napoleon's reforms that the religious influences on the penal law were removed, at least in parts of Europe. For the first time since antiquity, sexual contact between men lost its "criminal" character and could thus again be openly defended.

The Invention of the Homosexual in the Nineteenth Century

THE FIRST IMPORTANT defense of this still widely condemned behavior was written during the early nineteenth century by the Swiss milliner **Heinrich Hössli** (1784–1864). Under the title *Eros: Die Männerliebe der Griechen—ihre Beziehungen zur Geschichte, Erziehung, Literatur und Gesetzgebung aller Zeiten* (Eros: The man–male love of the Greeks—Its relationships to the history, education, literature, and legislation of all time), the autodidact published a two-volume work whose subtitle hinted at a new idea: *The Undependability of External Marks in the Sex Life of the Body and the Mind.* This idea becomes clearer in an opening quote on the title page of the first volume. In it, Hössli's own comprehensive text is anticipated:

> Rabbinical teachings about the soul have a peculiar trait, namely, they explain the contradictions in the character of the sexes and their often strange sympathies and antipathies by appealing to reincarnation such that, as homonymous poles, female souls in male bodies are repelled by women and male souls in female bodies are repelled by men, yet, conversely, they attract one another despite the same corporeal sex due to the different sex of the souls. A fabulous, yet quite refined and ingenious explanation of some matrimonial contrarities. . . . (Literatur-Blatt, edited by W. Menzel, June 4, 1834.)

So here it is, two years after the death of Goethe, the future explanation of sodomy! For the first time in occidental apologetic literature, some strange creatures make their long-lasting, ill-fated appearance—the "female souls in male bodies," the particular, as yet unrecognized and unclassified human beings, the mysterious, outwardly masculine non-males who are only acting in accordance with their female nature when they love men.

Hössli's entire work consists in showing that same-sex lovers have no choice. They have an entirely particular character of their own and are thus "different from the others." For this reason, it is unjust and a crime against nature to oppress or persecute them. After all, the ancient Greeks, as was well known, had never done this either. Modern laws that call for the punishment of such lovers must be abolished.

Hössli's two volumes had no measurable influence during his lifetime. A planned third volume did not appear, the work was banned altogether, and the remaining copies, stockpiled in an attic, were burned in an accidental fire. Yet a German forensic authority soon had ideas of his own that were similar to Hössli's. From 1852 on, **J. L. Casper** wrote various articles in his *Vierteljahrsschrift für gerichtliche und öffentliche Medizin* (Quarterly for forensic and public medicine) and distinguished in them between acquired and congenital pederasty. He also found that the act of "sodomy" (anal intercourse) did not take place in all same-sex contacts, and that some such contacts were actually quite legal. In any case, most of the contacts could be proven in court only with difficulty, and it would therefore be best to let them all go unpunished.[1]

Similar conclusions had been drawn by others in the meantime, and so the laws against "unnatural fornication" were abolished in several German states in imitation of the *Code Napoléon.* In Bavaria, Württemberg, and Hanover, for example, consensual sexual relations between men were no longer punishable. Unfortunately, though, the old laws in Prussia continued to stand, and it turned out that, in the course of the expected founding of the German Reich, Prussian law was to be extended to all German jurisdictions, including those already reformed.

In the face of this worrisome development, a man-loving legal assessor from Hanover, Karl Heinrich Ulrichs, set out on a lonely crusade. As early as 1864, under the pseudonym *Numa Numantius,* he had published two broshures: "Vindex" and "Inclusa." The subtitle of the latter clearly summarized its content: "Proof that sexual love of men is hereditary in a class of anatomically male individuals."[2] Laws against this love were therefore unjust and had to be abolished. After all, an absolutely fundamental principle was involved: The state may punish people only for what they *do*, not for what they *are.*

Both pamphlets were banned in several states and then allowed to be published again, attracting much attention in the process. They were soon followed by additional writings from the same pen and, in the course of the next thirteen years, the author produced exactly a dozen titles that elaborated his fundamental thesis. After some initial hesitation, he also abandoned his pseudonym and signed his real name. Indeed, Ulrichs went even further and appeared before a German lawyers' congress in 1867 in order to call for the decriminalization of love between men. However, his enraged colleagues shouted him down, and he had to leave the podium without having finished.

In spite of the great public interest in his work at the time, Ulrichs remained completely unsuccessful in reaching his goal. Impoverished and forgotten, he died in Italy in 1895. Nevertheless, in retrospect one can say that he was and still is one of the most influential figures in sex research. More than anyone else, he propagated same-sex love as a particular condition, a special way of being, and even researchers who rejected his conclusions accepted—sometimes unconsciously—his premises. For this reason, we quote Ulrichs's basic idea here in detail:

> At all times and among all peoples, the observer of the human race notices among anatomically male individuals expressions of sexual passion vis-à-vis anatomically male individuals. . . . The question then becomes pressing to him: "Is this phenomenon, which seems to be so abnormal, natural, genuine, sexual love?" The answer does not seem easy at first sight. For, on the one hand, a firm conviction tells him that a man *cannot* love a man. "Thus," he might conclude, "this phenomenon can *not be* genuine natural love." On the other hand, though, all those expressions really bear the mark of unartificed true sexual longing. Thus, a seemingly inextricable entanglement. . . . And, yet, there is a solution. All difficulty disappears as soon as one reasons the other way around: "That love directed toward men is obviously true sexual love; a man can not love a man: therefore, the loving part can not be a true man."[3]

This "untrue," i.e., "false" man belongs to a special group of people who had been hitherto unrecognized or overlooked. This was also the reason why there had not been any word for them, no term for their peculiarity. Thus, Ulrichs had to invent a new terminology and make it acceptable to all parties:

> Those men who, as a result of their congenital nature, feel attracted exclusively to male individuals, I call Uranians. I call their love Uranic and the entire phenomenon Uranism. The Uranian is a riddle of nature. He is a man only in regard to anatomy, not to amorous drive. Indeed, his amorous drive is that of a female.[4]

This means that, in the case of a Uranian, anatomy and psyche, body and soul, are not in agreement. As a "half-man," he is therefore the representative of a "third sex." His case is best described as a "female soul in a male body," or, as Ulrichs, the accomplished Latinist, put it: "*Anima muliebris virili corpore inclusa.*" He derived the term "Uranism" for this state from a passage in the text of Plato's *Symposium* where a distinction is made between two Aphrodites or love goddesses: (1) the "common" Aphrodite, the daughter of Zeus and Dione and (2) the "Uranic" Aphrodite, the motherless daughter of Uranos who came into the world entirely without female participation. She is the goddess of love between men and of the Uranians. In contrast, the "common," "Dionic" Aphrodite is responsible for the love between man and woman and for the men who love women. Ulrichs calls them Dionians.

If one now applied this distinction not only to men but also to women, then the well-known two sexes turned into four: Male and female Dionians (old) and male and female Uranians (new). In addition to the complete, genuine, total men and women, one now had to recognize hybrid forms—previously unsuspected pseudo-males and pseudo-females in whose bodies dwelled the souls of the other sex.

Unfortunately, however, Ulrichs was not able to enjoy the brilliance of his ingenious insight for very long, because a disturbing reality soon began to intrude and to dim its original luster. He received a large number of letters from enthusiastic readers who praised his basic idea but claimed certain exceptions, modifications, and additions for themselves. Some men, for example, did indeed feel attracted to the same sex, yet could not discover anything feminine in their own souls. Instead, they considered themselves masculine through and through. Others reported a persistent love for both sexes, and still others, in contrast, told of episodic changes between their desires for women and men.

Thus, Ulrichs had no choice but to modify his original thesis and to make room for variations. After much thought he therefore introduced a new scheme that, instead of the initially postulated four sexes, now presented a total of ten.[5]

The male (not the female!) Uranians now appeared in three variants: Masculinians, Intermediate Stages, and Femininians, and there also was a new category—the Uranodionians, who were attracted to both sexes and were themselves again divided into two subgroups—the conjunctive (persistent) and disjunctive (episodic) Uranodionians. Ulrichs was tentative about the female version of this category, the female Uranodionians, because, while he saw them as theoretically necessary, he had apparently not yet received any information about their real existence.

> I. Men. II. Women. III. Uranians, male. IV. Uranians, female.
>
> ⌒
>
> 1. Masculinians. 2. Intermediate Stages. 3. Femininians.
>
> V. Uranodionians, male. VI. Uranodionians, female (?). VII. Hermaphrodites.
>
> ⌒
>
> 1. conjunctive. 2. disjunctive.

Figure 1. *English version provided by E. J. Haeberle*

Ulrichs's original, simple idea has already become quite complicated at this point. Moreover, further possible differentiations are contained in the outline of his new scheme. After all, if—just as in the male parallels—one should also admit three variants of the female Uranians and two variants of the female Uranodionians, one would already arrive at a new grand total of thirteen sexes instead of the ten actually outlined here.

Yet a scheme that, instead of the traditionally accepted two sexes, now proposes thirteen, some of which are very fuzzily defined, no longer has anything in common with a brilliant idea, a simple explanation of otherwise inexplicable phenomena. On the contrary, it carries this explanation *ad absurdum.*

At this point, one might have expected that Ulrichs, corrected and instructed by reality, would have looked for another hypothesis, but far from it! It never occurred to him to doubt his own unquestioned assumption that "a man cannot love a man." Indeed, he did not understand that his entire theory had become necessary and possible only on the basis of this modern, quite arbitrary assumption that no ancient Greek or Roman would ever have made. Actually, no Arab, Polynesian, Chinese, or Japanese would have made it either or did make it during Ulrichs's lifetime. What appeared to him, a German lawyer, as a problem of natural science was, in reality, nothing more than a culturally defined, sociopolitical and ideological, i.e., "artificial" question, and a meaningful answer could have been expected only from a cultural science that critically reflected on itself. But such a science was still far away in the age of imperialism and the belief in unlimited progress.

In spite of his personal lack of success, Ulrichs's writings continued to have a growing long-term effect. True, people soon abandoned his poetic-literary terms *Uranian* and *Uranodionian* and replaced them with various expressions that sounded more medical or technical, but his naive association of same-sex erotic inclinations with a reversal of gender roles or identities was just as naively perpetuated. In the case of men, same-sex interests were somehow associated with a physical or mental "femininity," and, in the case of women, with a corresponding "masculinity." In 1869, for example, an Austro-Hungarian writer and journalist, **Karoly Maria Kertbeny** (originally Karl Maria Benkert), coined the Greco-Latin hybrid word *der Homosexuelle* (the substantive "homosexual") and, within a few years, the correlate *der Heterosexuelle* ("heterosexual") also found wide acceptance. [6]

One year later, the Berlin psychiatrist **Carl Westphal** introduced the concept of "contrary sexual feeling" that was now supposed to designate a psychopathological condition.[7] A patient fitting this diagnosis was a "contrasexual." Translated into Italian as *amore invertito*, it then became the English and French *inversion*. This, in turn, finally produced the German retro-translation *Inversion.* The patient suffering from this deplorable condition was an "invert." All this meant what Ulrichs had also meant—a reversal or transposition of masculine into feminine erotic feeling in the case of men and of feminine into masculine erotic feeling in the case of women. The word *contrary* signalled that such a reversal went against nature and health, in short, that it was wrong, and that, ideally, there should be only complete "total men" and complete "total women" in whom everything "fit together."

As one can see, the Uranians, homosexuals, contrasexuals, or inverts disturbed a sense of psychiatric order. Female souls or feelings in male bodies (or vice versa) simply were not to be accepted as normal. This was some "psychic hermaphroditism," a psychosomatic hybridism in need of correction for the benefit of the hybrid patient. His or her soul had to be brought back into harmony with the obvious physical appearance.

The new scientific "experts" simply did not recognize that tying a particular erotic behavior to a particular gender role or identity was an arbitrary decision, an intellectual fad of the times, a typically modern scientific error. If one had instead, just as in antiquity, seen gender role and sexual behavior as two different, often mutually independent factors, one would never have been able to talk of hybridism. It would never have occurred to anyone to look for a sort of femininity in the same-sex desires of a man or for a sort of masculinity in those of a woman. Indeed, these problematic alleged characteristics of the other sex in persons having same-sex erotic feelings were simply psychiatric projections. Had one avoided or abandoned these projections, then the disturbance or "mismatch" would also have disappeared with them. Therefore, in the final analysis, it was an ignorant and arrogant psychiatric sense of order that here created the problem for itself.

One may note, however, that the nascent psychiatry of the time was very grateful for the great number of patients produced by its projections. The hidden femininity of so many men was to be rooted out, and so many women were to be delivered from their unbefitting masculinity that a growing guild of psychiatrists was kept busy with the respective therapies. It would have been asking a great deal if one had pleaded with them to ignore this new source of income.

And almost no one in the medical profession dared to utter such a plea, except the Berlin "physician for nervous disorders" **Magnus Hirschfeld.** As he himself had same-sex erotic inclinations, he refused to find anything wrong with them. (Incidentally, Ulrichs had not done so, either.) Rather, Hirschfeld took up Ulrichs's concept of "intermediate stages," albeit in a much broader sense. According to Hirschfeld, in real life there was nothing but a large spectrum of intermediate stages between the "total man" and the "total woman." In the actual world, most people fell somehow between these extremes, in their anatomy as well as in their psychology. It was thus no wonder that there were masculine as well as effeminate homosexuals and heterosexuals. In either case, in fact in almost all cases, one was simply dealing with natural variations such as had to be expected among living creatures. (At most, anatomical deformations, i.e., the various forms of genuine, somatic hermaphroditism, could be pathological.)

In May 1896, Hirschfeld first introduced this idea that he had borrowed from Ulrichs. However, he was smart enough to put forth only two simple scales (Fig. 2 and 3) instead of his predecessor's confusing groupings and bracketed sub-groupings of ten or more different sexes.[8]

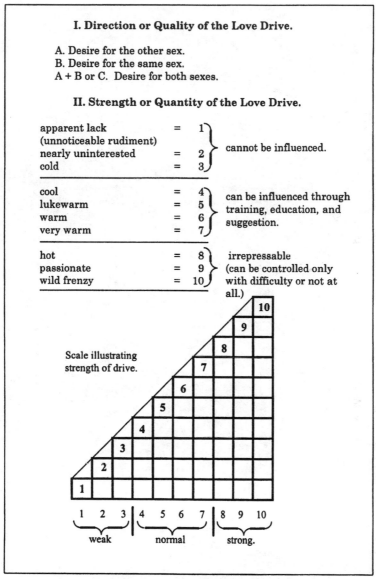

I. Direction or Quality of the Love Drive.

A. Desire for the other sex.
B. Desire for the same sex.
A + B or C. Desire for both sexes.

II. Strength or Quantity of the Love Drive.

apparent lack	=	1	
(unnoticeable rudiment)			cannot be influenced.
nearly uninterested	=	2	
cold	=	3	

cool	=	4	can be influenced through
lukewarm	=	5	training, education, and
warm	=	6	suggestion.
very warm	=	7	

hot	=	8	irrepressable
passionate	=	9	(can be controlled only
wild frenzy	=	10	with difficulty or not at all.)

Scale illustrating strength of drive.

1 2 3 | 4 5 6 7 | 8 9 10
weak   normal   strong.

Figure 2. *English version provided by E. J. Haeberle*

The first scale (Fig. 2) measures the "drive" in ten levels from 1 (apparent total lack) to 10 (wild frenzy); the second scale, (Fig. 3) likewise in ten levels, measures the degrees of "attraction" to the other sex or to one's own. There are three examples given for the second scale:

(1) In the case of a "total man" and a "total woman," a ten-level column of heterosexual inclinations stands opposed to a merely three-level column of same-sex inclinations. The latter are thus insignificant in comparison to the former.

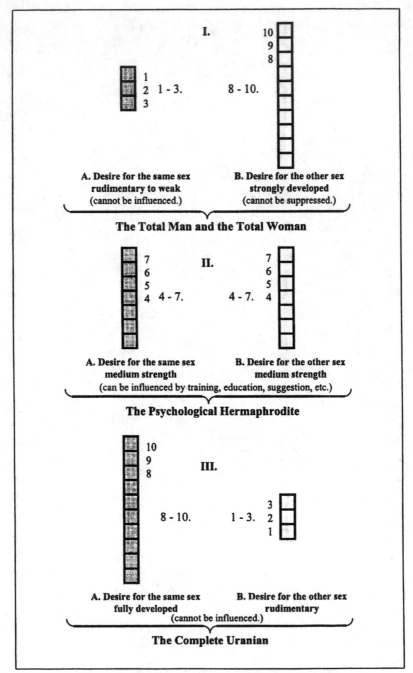

I.

1
2   1 - 3.   8 - 10.
3

10
9
8

A. Desire for the same sex
rudimentary to weak
(cannot be influenced.)

B. Desire for the other sex
strongly developed
(cannot be suppressed.)

The Total Man and the Total Woman

II.

7   7
6   6
5   5
4   4 - 7.   4 - 7.   4

A. Desire for the same sex
medium strength

B. Desire for the other sex
medium strength

(can be influenced by training, education, suggestion, etc.)

The Psychological Hermaphrodite

III.

10
9
8

8 - 10.   1 - 3.   3
                        2
                        1

A. Desire for the same sex
fully developed

B. Desire for the other sex
rudimentary

(cannot be influenced.)

The Complete Uranian

Figure 3. *English version provided by E. J. Haeberle*

(2) In the case of "psychicological hermaphrodites," both columns have seven levels and are therefore equal.

(3) In the case of a "complete Uranian," we find a constellation showing the exact reverse of the "total man" (ten-level same-sex and three-level heterosexual columns).

Hirschfeld excludes any possibility of therapeutic influence on (1) and (3) and believes in a limited possible influence only on (2).

In fact, though, the three illustrated cases are only examples of the two extremes and of the exact middle. In real life, an infinite variety of possibilities lie between them and must be taken into account.

With these variable, ten-level columns, Hirschfeld broke free from the previous, confusing proliferation of petrified categories and made a differentiated view possible. This was also gratefully taken up by other authors, such as **Ludwig Frey**, who, under the title *Men of the Enigma*, spoke of homosexuals as "transitional human beings" and elaborated:

> The law of unnoticeable transition also obtains in the broad realm of sexual life. . . . Just as no person is entirely identical to another physiognomically, so might he be similar to another sexually, but he will never be entirely identical to him. . . . One can rightly say: There are as many sexual predispositions as individuals.[9]

Frey then supplied completely fluid scales in which "virility," i.e., manliness, very gradually gives way to "muliebrity," i.e., womanliness (Fig. 4). The Uranian (German: *Urning*) is then to be situated somewhere in the midsection of the transition.[10]

The progress in comparison to Ulrichs is clear, but his original error is yet again uncritically perpetuated by Hirschfeld and Frey. The arbitrary linkage of erotic inclination and gender role continues to be maintained: Men who feel same-sex erotic attractions are somehow feminized and their female counterparts are somehow masculinized. Homosexuality somehow has to do with a defective gender role or identity. Homosexual men are somehow lacking in real maleness and homosexual women are somehow lacking in real femaleness. Instead, the typical sensibility of the other sex, even if diluted a thousand times over, is in them somewhere, perhaps in their brains.

Now, Hirschfeld in particular knew very well that there were completely virile men who were attracted to other completely virile men, and this observation alone should have been enough to falsify the entire hypothesis. However, like Ulrichs and all the others, in these cases he resorted to circular logic: The inclination itself was an expression of femaleness and this was proof enough even if no other trace of it was found. Loosely based on Ulrichs: "A man cannot love another man. If he does, then it follows he is not a real male, but rather has a female or, at least with regard to this point, a feminized soul."

A man's psychological "femaleness" was thus always proven *per definitionem* and *a priori* by the mere existence of his same-sex inclinations, and any other proof was therefore unnecessary. All the better, though, if, in many men, feminized body forms or effeminate gestures also came into play. This could only support the original thesis.

Curiously enough, it was to be Hirschfeld's fate as a researcher to discover and name a sexologically new category of human beings—*the transvestites.* These were men

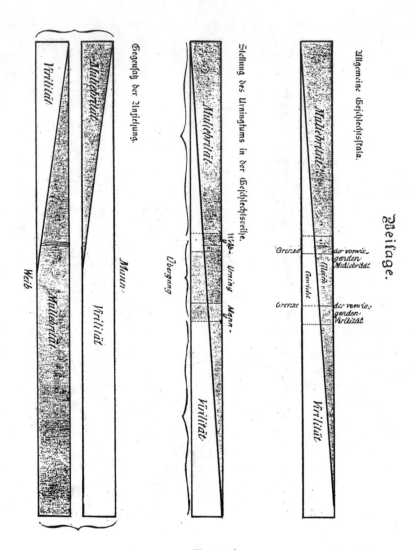

Figure 4.

and women who preferred to dress in the clothes of the other sex and to mimic that sex in speech and gesture as well. Unexpectedly, though, a great many of these very effeminate men and masculine women felt an erotic inclination to the *other* sex; indeed, many of them were married and wanted to remain so.

Nevertheless, even this did not faze Hirschfeld and his contemporaries. They simply talked of "miscellaneous psychological characteristics" that came into play here. On the other hand, one did recognize that male transvestites could, in turn, not only be more or less feminine or masculine, but also more or less homosexual or heterosexual. Feminine behavior in males and masculine behavior in females could thus become manifest independently of their homosexuality or heterosexuality.

At this point, then, gender role and erotic predilection were finally beginning to be perceived as separate phenomena, and nothing more would have stood in the way of genuine conceptual progress. But this line of reasoning was not pursued long enough before the Nazi dictatorship put an end to German and then to other European sex research. Hirschfeld's last word in the matter is probably the outline from his *Geschlechtskunde (Sexology)* of 1926, which very adroitly and cogently summarizes all his ideas concerning this topic (Fig. 5).[11]

Male and Female

Sex Differences are Differences of Degree.

> I. The sex organs,
> II. the other physical characteristics,
> III. the sex drive,
> IV. the other psychological characteristics.

Intersexual Variants

> I. *Hermaphroditism as an intersexual formation of the sex organs,*
> II. *Androgyny as an intersexual mix of the other physical characteristics,*
> III. *Metatropism, i.e. Bisexuality and Homosexuality as an intersexual formation of the sex drive,*
> IV. *Transvestism as an intersexual expression of the other psychological characteristics.*

Figure 5. *English version provided by E. J. Haeberle*

Later, the matter came to be seen somewhat differently, but Hirschfeld's outline in this general and abstract form remains essentially correct according to our present-day understanding. It covers a number of somatic and psychic factors that are important for an individual's gender and sexual life, and it rightly maintains that there are only differences of degree. It also shows that the different factors, being independent of one another, can produce many combinations and variations.

A comparable overview in accordance with the state of today's research could still follow Hirschfeld's basic design. One would classify the phenomena somewhat differently and give them different names, but their graduated character and their possible independence from one another would be preserved.[12]

This is a present-day outline based on Hirschfeld's model. Despite many similarities, a decisive difference is clear: physical sex, gender role, and sexual orientation are recognized as factors potentially independent of one another. In particular, no automatic linkage of same-sex behavior to a reversal of gender role or identity is being made.

After all, the main problem with Hirschfeld's overview had been the two assumptions in his accompanying text that all of this was somehow innate and that a homosexual orientation somehow had something to do with a deficient, imbalanced, or transposed masculinity or femininity. Thus, in the final analysis, homosexuality remained something somatic, something biologically determined like the sexual hybrids of hermaphroditism and physical androgyny with which they were also implicitly compared. On the other hand, the comparison with transvestism implies an innate gender role-reversal or role-conflation. In short, for Hirschfeld, homosexuality remains a biological

---

Human Sexuality: Basic Aspects

Sex

Sex is defined as a person's maleness or femaleness. It is determined on the basis of five physical criteria: chromosomal sex, gonadal sex, hormonal sex, internal accessory reproductive structures, and external sex organs.
People are male or female to the degree in which they meet the physical criteria for maleness or femaleness.
Most individuals are clearly male or female by all five physical criteria.
However, a minority fall somewhat short of this test, and their sex is therefore ambiguous (hermaphroditism).

Gender

Gender is defined as a person's masculinity or femininity. It is determined on the basis of certain psychological qualities that are nurtured in one sex and discouraged in the other.
People are masculine or feminine to the degree in which they conform to their genders.
Most individuals clearly conform to the gender appropriate to their physical sex.
However, a minority partially assume a gender that contradicts their physical sex (transvestism), and for an even smaller minority such an inversion is complete (transsexualism).

Sexual Orientation

Sexual orientation is defined as a person's heterosexuality or homosexuality. It is determined on the basis of preference for sexual partners.
People are heterosexual or homosexual to the degree in which they are erotically attracted to partners of the other or same sex.
Most individuals develop a clear erotic preference for partners of the other sex (heterosexuality).
However, a minority are erotically attracted to both men and women (ambisexuality), and an even smaller minority are attracted mainly to partners of their own sex (homosexuality).

Figure 6.

Gender

When examining a person's gender, one has to distinguish two aspects:

- **Gender Role**, i.e. the social role as male or female, and

- **Gender Identity**, i.e. the self-identification as male or female.

The term "Gender Role" refers to the outward manifestation of gender, i.e. to how the role is played. However, like any other role, the gender role can be played with or without conviction. The term "Gender Identity" refers to this inner conviction, i.e. to how far the player identifies with the role.

Figure 7.

Human Sexuality: Examples

Male-Masculine-Heterosexual

A person of male sex usually adopts the masculine gender role and develops a heterosexual orientation. Such an individual then conforms to our image of the "typical" male.

Male-Masculine-Homosexual

A person of male sex who has adopted the masculine gender role may very well develop a homosexual orientation. Such an individual may then look and behave like any other "typical" male in all respects but one - his choice of sexual partner.

Male-Feminine-Heterosexual

A person of male sex may adopt the feminine gender role and even a feminine gender identity. In the latter case he may then even try everything possible (including a "sex change operation") to make the body conform to the feminine self-image. In this case, an erotic preference for males, would, of course, have to be considered heterosexual.

Male-Feminine-Homosexual

A person of male sex may adopt the feminine gender role and identity and try everything possible to make the body conform to the feminine self-image. If such an individual then also developed an erotic preference for females this sexual orientation could only be called homosexual.

Figure 8.

category that, like the other three categories he names, refers to an intermediate stage between the total male and the total female.

Yet in Hirschfeld's time there were already critics who vehemently contradicted him. In 1929, for example, the physician Erich Meyer wrote:

> A double danger also lies in Hirschfeld's idea of intermediate stages. First for the homosexual himself: he comes to believe that he is a special type of person. This leads to separation and to the feeling of isolation, which then can all too easily be associated with the feeling of inferiority. . . . Yet, even if the opponents of homosexuals do not see born criminals and inferiors in such intermediate stages, then they do see museum specimens that they do not have to take seriously.

> We are of Hirschfeld's view that homosexuality is characteristic of the homosexual, i.e., that it is rooted in his personality and arises entirely from it—that it is determined by his constitution, insofar as the psyche is determined by constitution. But I refuse to see the psychic functions as completely and finally explained by the function of the anatomical-chemical structure of the body.[13]

Meyer no longer speaks of a homosexual's masculinity/maleness or femininity/femaleness, nor does he accept a somatic explanation for his sexual orientation. Indeed, he points out occasional, spontaneous changes in this orientation:

> I already hear the objection that bisexuality is the real issue here. I do not want to argue about words. But one thing is certain in such cases: these people had a decidedly homosexual orientation. This later changed into a heterosexual one. The opposite also occurs. In the end, these cases can be explained only by purely psychological processes. The doctrine of a physical determination of homosexuality will never explain these cases.[14]

The Abolition of the Homosexual by Kinsey

INTERESTINGLY ENOUGH, twelve years later, it was left to a trained biologist to prove Dr. Meyer right and Dr. Hirschfeld wrong. In 1941, the American Alfred C. Kinsey had already conducted 1,600 of his interviews and examined the "criteria for a hormonal explanation of the homosexual" in a first publication. In it, Kinsey presented thirty cases from his collection that demonstrate thirty different shadings and combinations between exclusively heterosexual and exclusively homosexual behavior (Fig. 9).[15] From these examples, the zoologist Kinsey concluded that a hormonal explanation of "the homosexual" is extremely difficult at best, but probably impossible:

> Any hormonal or other explanation of the homosexual must allow for the fact that something between a quarter and a half of all males have demonstrated their capacity to respond to homosexual stimuli; that the picture is one of endless intergradation between every combination of homosexuality and heterosexuality; that it is impossible to distinguish so-called

acquired, latent, and congenital types; and that there is every gradation between so-called actives and passives in a homosexual relation.

Any hormonal or other explanation of the homosexual must allow for the fact that both homosexual and heterosexual activities may occur coincidentally in a single period in the life of a single individual; and that exclusive activities of any one type may be exchanged, in the brief span of a few days or a few weeks, for an exclusive pattern of the other type, or into a combination pattern which embraces the two types.

Any explanation of the homosexual must recognize that a large portion of the younger adolescents demonstrates the capacity to react to both homosexual and heterosexual stimuli; that there is a fair number of adults who show this same capacity; and that there is only a gradual development of the exclusively homosexual or exclusively heterosexual patterns which predominate among older adults.[16]

Case No.	Age	Estimated frequency		Percentage homosexual	
		Homosexual	Heterosexual		
0104	24	0	450	0	
2697	22	4	550	1	HETEROSEXUAL
7099	19	30	1,000	3	
2153	22	15	200	7	
6246	24	30	266	10	
2433	31	200	1,200	14	
8306	22	2,400	10,000	19	
7009	25	150	600	20	
9053	22	30	100	23	
7031	34	800	2,250	26	
0892	19	150	300	33	
0640	27	1,400	2,400	37	
8817	26	350	475	43	
3367	26	150	150	50	
2463	21	200	200	50	
6983	22	200	150	57	
7434	24	3,000	2,000	60	
6369	26	1,200	700	63	
3599	22	100	50	67	
8153	21	500	150	77	
2777	29	15,000	4,200	78	
8460	21	800	200	80	
7864	31	1,000	200	83	
9924	25	700	100	88	
3687	27	1,250	100	93	
7841	29	2,000	100	95	
8837	41	3,000	100	97	
0168	19	500	4	99	HOMOSEXUAL
4047	24	1,600	0	100	
2432	29	4,000	0	100	

Figure 9.

This first essay, initially published in an endocrinological journal, attracted no serious attention despite its provocative statements. Their true implications were probably first understood by only very few readers. However, when Kinsey and his associates presented their famous first "Report" in 1948, it caused an international sensation. The text was now based on more than 11,000 interviews and presented its findings about homosexual behavior on a seven-part scale.[17]

Of course, Kinsey's second scale was basically a simplified version of his first, tilted ninety-degrees to the left. Theoretically, he could already have divided his first scale into only seven sections from 0 to 6 rather than into thirty. Indeed, this realization once again makes it clear that the important thing in the Kinsey scales is not the number of (arbitrarily determined) subgroups, but rather the fluid transition from one group to another which the scales are making obvious. As Kinsey himself stated:

> Males do not represent two discrete populations, heterosexual and homosexual. The world is not to be divided into sheep and goats. Not all things are black nor all things white. It is a fundamental law of taxonomy that nature rarely deals with discrete categories. Only the human mind invents categories and tries to force facts into separated pigeonholes. The living world is a continuum in each and every one of its aspects. The sooner we learn this concerning human sexual behavior the sooner we shall reach a sound understanding of the realities of sex.[18]

For Kinsey, then, nature was too varied to be forced into the picayune contrast "homosexual/heterosexual." Man as a species possessed the capability to react to same-sex as well as to other-sex stimuli, since he was heir to a corresponding mammalian heritage. If anything at all had to be explained here, then it was the exclusivity of behavior

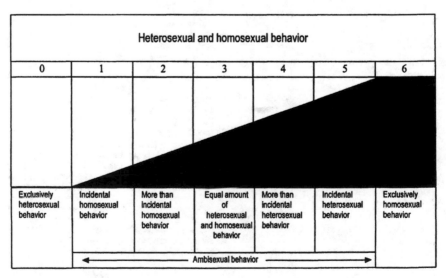

Figure 10. *English version provided by E. J. Haeberle*

at both ends of the spectrum. Undoubtedly, this had to be attributed mostly to cultural influences. In any case, from the standpoint of biology, homosexual behavior as such was just as "natural" as heterosexual behavior.

Kinsey's second, seven-part scale subsequently acquired a certain degree of international renown and was reprinted in many textbooks and reference works. Unfortunately, however, it was often incorrectly interpreted, because few people bothered to read Kinsey's own directions and explanations. Specifically, he expressly emphasized that his scale represented both overt and covert experiences, i.e., not only actions performed but also purely psychic reactions that did not lead to any sexual contacts at all. Thus, for example, a married man without any real homosexual contacts who regularly fulfilled his "marital duties" yet, while so doing, fantasized primarily about males, was not rated at 0, but rather at 2 or 3, according to how strong or frequent his homosexual wishes and fantasies were. On the other hand, a male prostitute who had only one girlfriend but thousands of homosexual contacts could receive the same rating of 2 or 3 if his actual sexual wishes were directed toward this girlfriend and he served his male clients without any erotic desire of his own and "only for the money."

In view of the enormous, statistically documented discrepancies between wish and deed, in view of the enormous scope of variation between exclusively heterosexual and homosexual behavior, and in view of the many changes—indeed reversals—between them, Kinsey no longer saw any justification to speak about "the homosexual" as he had still done, albeit ironically, seven years earlier. He now drew the logical conclusion:

> It would encourage clearer thinking on these matters if persons were not characterized as heterosexual or homosexual, but as individuals who have had certain amounts of heterosexual experience and certain amounts of homosexual experience. Instead of using these terms as substantives which stand for persons, or even as adjectives to describe persons, they may better be used to describe the nature of the overt sexual relations, or of the stimuli to which an individual erotically responds.[19]

Once this usage was adopted, it also became clear that the question about the number of homosexuals in a certain population had, as a matter of principle, no scientific answer. It was only possible to state how many people were to be assigned to which section of the Kinsey scale at any given time.

With his radical suggestions, though, Kinsey marched too far ahead of his contemporaries. They remained quite incapable of leaving their now familiar beaten track. The compulsion to classify was simply too deeply ingrained. The German physician **Walter Bräutigam**, for example, expressly referred to Kinsey's research, but then nevertheless started to make a list of different "forms of homosexuality": developmental homosexuality, pseudo-homosexuality, inhibited homosexuality, and preferential homosexuality.[20]

Whether wanted or not, such clinical typifications led many minds back to the idea that one was dealing with different types, hybrids, or intermediate stages of more or less distinct "homosexuals." It was not at all easy to distinguish between development in one instance and inhibition in the other, between real and pseudo-preference. Apparently, in case of doubt, some expert had to explain whether "genuine" homosexuality was present in a certain person. In any case, "preferential homosexuality," by implication once again referred to a distinguishable, particular group.

Yet, it was not only clinicians who saw merit in clearly distinguishing between heterosexuals and homosexuals. Indeed, prepared not least by Kinsey's enormous public effect itself, a homosexual liberation movement gradually arose, which also wanted a clear distinction. It fought for an end to social discrimination and for the reform of the penal law directed against homosexuals, and the demands seemed much more easily attainable if one postulated the existence of homosexual people who would then organize themselves as a large sociopolitical pressure group and "sexual minority."

The Rebirth of the Homosexual in the Modern Gay Movement

IN VIEW OF THE necessary "gay" liberation struggle, Kinsey's abolition of "the homosexual" seemed to be of little help, indeed, it seemed retrogressive. Therefore, this old-fashioned psychiatric Golem, who, in the Kinsey reports, had already crumbled to statistical dust, was quickly resurrected as the modern *gay man*, clad in a stylish "Castro clone" costume—a modern, strong, and healthy fighter for the Good. Moreover, he was soon joined on the front lines by the *lesbian woman*, and thus there arose a new social group that, in pursuit of its goals, cultivated a separate identity of its own.

Of course, this process was set in motion and maintained by sociopolitical forces, not scientific discoveries. In the daily struggle for power and influence, science first had to take a back seat. Eventually, though, the burgeoning gay movement also led to a growing acceptance of gay research and this, in turn, brought long-forgotten historical and ethnological facts to light that did not jibe with the initial, naive gay self-image. In 1974, for example, there appeared the first issue of a special scientific journal, the *Journal of Homosexuality*, that became increasingly self-critical under its openly gay editors. Among other things, Kinsey's work was also rehabilitated; indeed, his ideas were again taken up and pursued much further than he himself had dared to pursue them at the time; but more about this later.

At first, the postulate of a "gay or lesbian identity" led to a dichotomization that was useful for the gay movement. One either belonged or one didn't. One was either gay or not, and if one was, even in secret, then one had the moral duty to strengthen the ranks of the oppressed brothers and sisters by "coming out" openly, i.e., by admitting to "being gay."

In fact, more and more men and women soon decided to take this step. The movement grew and won an increasing number of rights for itself. With success, though, there appeared unexpected signs of fragmentation as well. For example, a new, hitherto unknown group began to organize because it found itself oppressed by both dichotomized camps—the bisexuals.

They refused to join either side, established their own organizations and journals, and finally held their own national and international congresses with the expressed goal of bringing together bisexuals for the representation of their own interests. Indeed, some demanded a special bisexual identity for themselves and their lovers of both sexes.

This also followed the logic of the new sociopolitical developments. Indeed, there had already been similar self-identifications for some time. Thus, some men and women took the seven stages of the sliding Kinsey scale, entirely against the intentions of the author, as a fixed designation of types and then typified themselves as a "Kinsey 3" or a "Kinsey 2," for example. This again shows how much Kinsey's suggestion went against the intellectual climate of the times, how difficult it was for most people to understand him at all, and how stubborn the urge to categorize still remained. The classified as well as their classifiers simply could not break free from the old way of thinking, the old concepts, the old ideas. Only a few of them were aware that these ideas had first been introduced by Ulrichs and were thus little more than one hundred years old.

With their deliberate self-organization, the bisexuals also began to require a dichotomization that would help them to draw clear lines. They wanted to be able to distinguish between themselves and others and therefore invented the new term "monosexual" for them. The former "heterosexuals" and the former "homosexuals" were thus united under a overarching concept, as they were always erotically interested in only a *single* sex (regardless of whether it was the other or the same one). Compared with this, then, the bisexuals now appeared as the actual fully rounded personalities, the only real "total men" and "total women." (This witty terminological move was not completely new, however, as Hirschfeld's contemporary **Benedikt Friedländer** had already mocked nonbisexuals as "stunted" or "morally stunted.")[21]

Predictably, all of these polemical and combative ideas contributed little to rational insight, and they did not stand up to critical examination over time. As Ulrichs and all his disciples after him had also had to learn, things are not quite so simple, and, in their zeal, neither the old psychiatrists nor the new gay and bisexual liberators did justice to the complexity of the issue.

A well-known author on the topic of bisexuality realized this early on. The American therapist **Fritz Klein** followed Kinsey's lead and constructed a "sexual orientation grid" that divided up seven variables in three dimensions (past, present, and ideal). One number from 1 to 7 (corresponding to the numbers 0 to 6 in Kinsey's scale) was to be entered into each of the resulting twenty-one spaces. Completely filled out, the grid gives a very differentiated, individualized picture that hardly ever repeats itself exactly even in larger groups, such as among the male and female students in a classroom.[22]

Klein Sexual Orientation Grid

Variable	Past	Present	Ideal
A. Sexual Attraction			
B. Sexual Behavior			
C. Sexual Fantasies			
D. Emotional Preference			
E. Social Preference			
F. Self-Identification			
G. Straight/Gay Lifestyle			

1	2	3	4	5	6	7
Other sex only	Other sex mostly	Other sex somewhat more	Both sexes equally	Same sex somewhat more	Same sex mostly	Same sex only

Figure 11.

At best, Klein's grid is again nothing more than a simple teaching aid to illustrate the complexity of what is today usually called "sexual orientation." The scientific discussion about this has since developed much further, as it received a powerful impetus from sociology at the end of the 1960s, contemporaneous with the growing gay movement.

The Renewed Deconstruction of the Homosexual by Critical Sociologists

THE CLOSER STUDY of "deviance" and "stigma" to which critical sociologists turned in the 1960s, sooner or later also had to lead to different approaches in sex research. On the topic of homosexuality, one of the first signs of this was the essay "The Homosexual Role" by **Mary McIntosh** (1968).

This author again denied—and more clearly than Kinsey—that "homosexuality" was a condition, an essence, or exclusive character trait of certain people. After all, there were still the "bisexuals," who made any clear distinction impossible. In addition, it was obvious that "homosexuals" voluntarily or involuntarily played a deviant and stigmatized social role and that other people, certain "non-homosexuals" in particular, did not play this role despite *de facto* identical sexual behavior. Therefore, any attempt to contrast a "clean" random sampling of homosexuals with an equally "clean" control group of "heterosexuals" was scientific nonsense and purely arbitrary. For this reason, it was also pointless to investigate the genesis of the supposed character trait "homosexuality": "One might as well try to trace the etiology of 'committee chairmanship' or 'Seventh-Day Adventism' as of 'homosexuality.'"[23]

Instead, she proposed that researchers should investigate why and how the incorrect notion of homosexuality as an essence had developed in the first place.

This proposal was indeed taken up by several "gay" historians who showed that the role of the "homosexual," as we know him today, first arose in the course of the eighteenth century with the beginning industrialization in Europe. Soon, though, they were contradicted by other "gay" historians who, at least in isolated instances, believed to have discovered examples of this role, indeed, genuine "gay communities," already in antiquity and the Middle Ages. Initially, this dispute among experts confused many observers.[24]

Additional impetus from the sociological side was thus more important for the continued debate. The Americans **John Gagnon** and **William Simon**, both associates of the Kinsey Institute, for the first time interpreted sexual behavior as "scripted behavior."

According to them, human sexual behavior is not the natural expression of a universal inner drive, but rather the result of individuals processing and appropriating different (in part competing and even mutually exclusive) "scripts" furnished by society. Here, the word *script* is to be understood like a screenplay or a theatrical text telling one how to act. It also tells us when and how to react to other people's "cues" and what the entire drama means. Since everyone of us is offered an entire bundle of different sexual scripts from different sources (parents, siblings, friends, church, school, mass media, and so forth), we must choose from among them or, more particularly, we must piece together our own script over the course of time from the various scripts according to our own preferences and abilities. Armed with this personal script, we then meet male or female partners who also follow their own scripts, and these scripts can either be reconciled with ours or not. Or a mutual accomodation results: Both partners change their scripts a little in order to arrive at a new, common script they can live with as a couple.[25]

However, scripting has not only the just mentioned *intrapsychic* and *interpersonal* aspects, but also a general *cultural* one: Scripts also determine what is considered "sexual" in a particular culture and what sexual behavior is conformist or deviant and under what circumstances. In this sense, "homosexuality" as a concept and its positive or negative connotations are also culturally determined constructs. Such constructs determine the bounds within which couples and individuals experience and help to create—as well as misunderstand—their own conformity or deviance.

For example, an old and, despite all scientific progress, long-lived misunderstanding is the equation of reproductive behavior, gender behavior, and sexual behavior. If researchers do not keep these three behaviors separate, they will unavoidably go astray. As John Gagnon explains:

> Appropriate patterns of reproductive, gender, and sexual conduct are all products of specific cultures and all can be viewed as examples of socially scripted conduct. Western societies now have a system of gender and sexual learning in which gender differentiated scripts are learned prior to sexual scripts, but take their origins in part from these previously learned gender scripts. . . . There are two important points: The first is that both gender and sexuality are learned forms of social practice, and the second is that looking to "natural differences" between women and men for lessons about sexual conduct is an error.[26]

Yet, apparently, this error is very hard to correct. For example, the *gender role reversal* among feminized male rats and their subsequently changed postures, movements, and gestures in attempted *reproductive behavior,* have led some hormone researchers to false conclusions about *sexual behavior* between men.[27]

Such conclusions are inadmissible on logical grounds alone, to say nothing of the fact that rats are not people. (It goes without saying that so-called homosexuals reproduce in exactly the same way and with the same gestures, movements, and body language as heterosexuals, a fact that many lesbian mothers and gay fathers will gladly confirm.) Or, to take another example, the researchers Ulrichs and Hirschfeld saw a reversal of gender in homosexual behavior, e.g., a female or feminized psyche in men. Not only that, many of their readers, thanks to the massive suggestion of their environment, actually *experienced* this in themselves. Following the script handed to them by their culture, they thought that homosexuals were somehow feminized, and therefore they devoloped all sorts of feminine mannerisms, often up to the point of "going drag," i.e., wearing dresses, even if they did not have any transvestite inclinations. Lesbian lovers, on the other hand, made an effort to simulate a division of gender roles like those between a man and a woman. One played the "active" masculine role (*butch*) and the other the "passive" feminine role (*femme*). Among both gays and lesbians, these stereotypes often determined the minutest details of sexual contact.

For example, in the late 1960s, i.e., before the successes of the modern gay movement, it was obvious to every visitor that the San Francisco "scene" was dominated by "drag queens," effeminate "Marys" and "sissies," and even the other, outwardly inconspicuous gays had a repertoire of feminine, "limp-wristed" gestures which they used, often emphatically and ironically, among themselves. They addressed one another with female first names, not infrequently giggling and shrieking like school-girls. When sexual contact occurred, a distinction was often made between "active" and "passive" roles. Gay bars competed for customers with "female impersonators," "male actresses," and "drag shows."

Fifteen year later, after the almost complete victory of gay liberation in San Francisco, the drag shows had disappeared from the bars. Customers were no longer concerned with the distinction between "active" and "passive"; instead, "everybody did everything." Almost no one believed any longer in the old T-shirt inscription: "It's a bitch to be butch!" On the contrary, a great majority now cultivated a decidedly masculine appearance with deep voices, short-cropped hair, mustaches, lumberjack shirts, blue jeans, and thick-soled hiking boots. This then became fashionable in the other gay scenes of the U.S. and Europe as the "Castro clone look" (named after Castro Street in San Francisco).

In both cases, however, these were mostly the *very same people* who now, by the late seventies, had grown fifteen years older.

This dramatic change in the appearance and self-perception of gays can best be explained by new internal and external scripting. This change also once and for all laid to rest the old theories from Ulrichs to Hirschfeld that had linked homosexual behavior to a reversal of gender roles. Indeed, as now had become clear, this linkage had not been "given by nature," but rather had been imposed by culture. It now revealed itself as an instrument of oppression and self-oppression, as the way of living up to a cliché, as a type of self-fulfilling prophecy. As soon as the oppression was lifted and a sufficient measure of gay self-determination had been attained, the old cliché lost its force.

Needless to say, the "Castro clone look" itself was also a cliché, albeit a historically necessary one. It was a deliberately developed "counter-cliché," as it were, that finally destroyed all the old prejudices not only in society but also in one's own head. Not until gays had convinced themselves through their own experience that they by no means had to be feminine but could, on the contrary, be supermasculine, was it possible for them to bring about for themselves the dissociation of sexual behavior from a reversal of gender roles. After that, it was only the broad, "unenlightened" public—including the political and religious "gay bashers"—and some researchers who still believed in the old stereotypes. Whether intentionally or unintentionally, they simply failed to notice the great "turnaround" in the gay scene.

The basic assumptions of the scripting theory were thus once again confirmed:

(1) Sexual behavior varies according to culture and historical period.

(2) The significance (in the double sense of importance and meaning) of sexual behavior varies according to culture and historical period.

(3) The definition of what is "sexual" and its experience vary according to culture and historical period.

(4) The linkage of sexual behavior, gender behavior, and reproductive behavior varies according to culture and historical period.

(5) The academic study of all this (i.e., sex research or sexology) is itself culturally and historically determined with respect to both subject and method.[28]

Thus, scripting theory was able to become critical also of its own conclusions (and those of all other theories). These conclusions were not "eternal truths," but rather intellectual conventions acceptable here and now. All explanations of the cause of homosexuality, for example, are never more than "culturally plausible reports," regardless of whether they are given by scientists or ordinary "gay people." It is important only that the reports come from "authorized explainers." According to the cultural environment in question, these can be priests, lawyers, psychiatrists, endocrinologists, neurologists, geneticists, sex researchers or early "gay" thinkers, or other "authorities." Today, though, not everyone accepts all authorities, if only because they vehemently contradict one another. In fact, various older or more recent reports appear plausible to different academic schools or sexual-political groups, and thus even the "scientific" discourse now presents us with a "simultaneity of the unsimultaneous."

Furthermore, such reports or, to put it more precisely, justifications of motivation, are generally offered only for same-sex behavior. Heterosexual behavior is largely seen as unproblematic and requiring no explanation. Only when it, too, violates social norms, (as in the cases of adultery, sex with minors, or rape) is a search for the causes made. The decisive motive for this search, however, is always the wish to prevent the violation of norms in the future. The "explanation" that is then finally offered must be plausible in this sense for the culture concerned: "Such ways of explaining conduct should be understood as cultural conventions rather than scientific truths."[29]

Applied to the supposed scientific problem of explaining homosexual behavior, this means for John Gagnon that:

> From the perspective of scripting theory, same-gender erotic preferences are elicited and shaped by the systems of meaning offered for conduct in a culture. What is usually construed as culture against "man" or culture against nature is thus actually conflict among differently enculturated individuals or groups.[30]

> What is required is a constant recognition that acts of usage and explanation are acts of social control in the strong sense, that "homosexual" and "homosexuality" are names that have been imposed on some persons and their conduct by other persons—and that this imposition has carried the right of the latter to tell the former the origins, meaning, and virtue of their conduct.[31]

This is true, although, on the face of things, it was initially men-loving authors like Ulrichs, Kertbeny, and Hirschfeld themselves who had propagated labels like "Uranian," "homosexual," and "third sex." They had done this, however, only as a reaction to concrete social oppression which they hoped to escape through the postulate of a special class of people. Indeed, the legal context in which these neologisms arose irrefutably proves this (the struggle for the abolition of the Prussian penal paragraph 143, the corresponding paragraph 152 in the North German Federation, and finally paragraph 175 of the new German Reich).

Since the topic of homosexuality ultimately always has to do with social disputes, Kinsey the biologist was also naive when he justified the great breadth of variation between exclusively heterosexual and exclusively homosexual behavior by pointing to the diversity of nature. According to him, erotically exclusive behaviors are deliberately cultivated in repressive societies just as plant monocultures are in modern factory farming or the so-called agribusiness. If human nature were simply left alone, its great erotic diversity would also remain apparent for all to see.

Gagnon holds against this that scientific considerations of this sort play virtually no role in the social reality of our Western industrial world and that, on the contrary, clear delineations are the order of the day. Heterosexuals, homosexuals, and bisexuals constitute themselves as groups and fight over their "appropriate" position in society. In so doing, they develop their own respective scripts and paradigms, which are never anything more than ideological instruments of struggle. For several sex researchers, Kinsey's biological explanation sufficed to dissolve the traditional dichotomy of heterosexuality/homosexuality, but it was not plausible enough to modern Western culture in general to succeed politically.

Nor did the ideological critique by openly "gay" researchers accomplish anything in this regard. For the German-speaking countries, for example, **Rolf Gindorf** criticized Ulrichs's, Kertbeny's, and Hirschfeld's teleological and biologistic concepts of sexuality already in 1977 and pointed out the dangers immanent to those concepts. Instead of the classical sexual theory of a universal (and uniquely "healthy") heterosexuality on the one hand and of its "homosexual counter-ideology" of a specific biological-genetic "predisposition" on the other hand, he called for an "overcoming of the dichotomization":

> The dilemma of traditional sex research lay in the unconscious, but unquestioningly assumed division into opposing *drives* and *hereditary factors*. . . . The division into heterosexuality and homosexuality, into heterosexuals and homosexuals, is also an artefact that rests on a grave error, namely, on the assumption that a fundamentally different model is necessary to explain heterosexual and homosexual behavior. The entire investigation of etiology was ideologically loaded beforehand because it separated a segment of the sexual continuum and attempted to make analyses with the help of fundamentally different concepts.[32]

Here, too, heterosexuality, homosexuality, and bisexuality were already characterized as "virtual realities,"[33] a view that later came to be called "social constructionism."

But it was all in vain: The discriminators and the discriminated, the researchers and their objects, maintained—albeit for opposite reasons—the postulate that "homosexuals" were identifiable as a group. Therefore all of them also continued the search for the cause of that identifiability.

The Current Discussion: Essentialists vs. Constructionists

THE SEARCHERS FOR causes are today referred to by the umbrella name "essentialists." They are mostly natural scientists who believe in an essence, special quality, character trait, or condition called "homosexuality." On the opposing side are the "constructionists," mostly social scientists. For them, "heterosexuality," "homosexuality," and "bisexuality" are nothing more than sociopolitical constructs which are misunderstood as natural phenomena.

The essentialists seek the cause of homosexuality somewhere in given biological factors, in a person's physical constitition: in prenatal hormonal influences, certain brain structures, or in the genes.[34] The essentialists believe that these physical/biological factors, individually or in combination, explain the inclination to same-sex contacts. This explanation, in turn, is then supposed to relieve homosexuality of all moral blame, because it would stand revealed as a somatically determined and diagnosable condition—like skin color, hair color, and left-handedness, for example.

If homosexuality, like skin color, should finally turn out to be a physical characteristic, then, it is hoped, there would no longer be any reason for discrimination. Homosexuals would have to be given their full civil rights, and natural science would once again have liberated a prematurely judged, oppressed class of people by means of clear identification and value-free classification.

However, instead of reaping universal gratitude for their efforts, the essentialists find themselves mocked and ridiculed by the constructionists at every turn, and a flood of arguments rains down upon them:

(1) Natural science has never liberated anyone. On the contrary, its findings have all too often been misused for the worst kind of oppression. Social Darwinism, racism, forced "eugenics," and psychiatric torture are only the most obvious examples. Proof of a biological predisposition toward homosexuality would only be cause for further discrimination. Hirschfeld's thesis of congenital homosexuality, for example, was by no means a barrier for the Nazis' persecution of homosexuals, but rather served as a welcome justification. After all, "Reichsführer SS" Heinrich Himmler, without scientific proof and soleley on the basis of his "Germanic spleen," also firmly believed that homosexuality was congenital. For exactly that reason, he had homosexuals, including his own nephew, killed by the thousands as "racially inferior."

(2) Obvious congenital biological characteristics like skin color and sex have by no means protected blacks and women from disenfranchisement. Indeed, even left-handed and redheaded people have occasionally been oppressed and disadvantaged.

(3) It is quite naive to assume that prejudiced people who are eager to discriminate can be stopped by scientific arguments. Thus, the real question is not "What biological condition do we find?" but rather "What social consequences should follow from the condition once we find it?" The answer to this question is always a value judgement. Value judgements, however, are a moral issue, not a scientific one.

(4) Moreover, proof of a physical trait that "excuses" homosexual behavior would lead to yet another, very interesting question: "How should the homosexual behavior of persons be judged who have not been shown to possess this trait?" Since they are not biologically excused and thus act "unnecessarily" and "willfully" should they be condemned? If yes, should those found guilty be able to claim another, unknown, as yet undiscovered somatic cause? Should society then set up an entire system of experts in order to distinguish "real" from "fake" homosexuals according to the most recent scientific findings? But if the "fake" ones would not be condemned, i.e., if society intends to tolerate even "willful" homosexual actions anyway, then what was the purpose of all that previous, allegedly exculpating research?

(5) In the age of genetic manipulation, proof of a "gay gene" is a rather nightmarish idea. Were such evidence to become available, one might well fear that people would soon try to locate the gene in unborn fetuses. Then the parents could decide whether they wanted to have a "gay" son or a "lesbian" daughter. If not, an abortion could be offered. How many people would take advantage of this? How many could pay for it? In which countries could a prenatal diagnosis be offered? To which citizens? At what prices? Should health insurance companies pay for it? Should a "medical indication" for it be introduced? In the end, would there be homosexuals only in poor countries and in poor segments of the population? But isn't it exactly there, where the birth rates are highest? Would homosexuality, like rickets in earlier times, ultimately become a new mark of poverty? Conversely, could the birth of homosexuals one day be consciously and intentionally promoted? Who could have an interest in this, and under what circumstances? Lesbian mothers, for example, who would pay for artificial insemination by a gay man? Or "normal," nonconformist parents who thereby want to protest against the government? Would the birth of a homosexual child thereby become proof of its parents' political unreliability? Or, on the contrary, could governments become active, wanting to compensate for a shortage of women by offering premiums for homosexual progeny?[35] Could and should "gay" soldiers be bred for special elite troops, similar to those in ancient Greece? Could the widespread implantation of "the gay gene," especially in third-world countries, ultimately be the only way to prevent the world population explosion? [36] Such questions and many others have not even been asked yet, let alone thought through.

(6) In all this, the criteria set up by the biologist Kinsey as early as 1941 for an explanation of "the homosexual" continue to be completely disregarded (see above). For example, do scientists also want to discover a large number of variably distinct "bisexual genes"? And if such genes were found, what would this accomplish? Are they really needed in order to justify the existing sexual diversity? But if they are not needed for that purpose, would simple proof of a "gay gene" be enough? After all, one could claim that this gene was sometimes or often modified or weakened in its effect by various social influences. But if social influences could, through this back door, again have a determining and exculpating effect, then what is the reason for all that ongoing natural scientific research?

Summa summarum: It would be wrong to see only an old pattern in the debate between essentialists and constructionists: nature vs. nurture, innate vs. acquired traits. This by now entirely obsolete debate existed already in the eighteenth century between "preformationists" and "epigenesists." The former believed that every future organism was already "preformed" at the beginning of its growth and thus already contained all visible future developing traits *en miniature.* The latter, on the other hand, believed in a postnatal shaping by the environment.

But this is no longer the point of contention today. Everyone agrees that innate as well as acquired factors have an effect on human behavior. Much more important now are the fundamentally different scientific assumptions in the definition of the scientific object. One group claims to study a concrete object existing in reality, "the homosexual." However, exactly this "natural" existence is disputed by the other group. Any agreement between the two hostile camps on what exactly is to be studied is therefore impossible. They use the same terms, and both speak of homosexuality, but with very different implications, and thus they simply talk past each other. It is like the case of tunnel drillers who begin working simultaneously on opposite sides of a mountain (here called "homosexual behavior") but who, in the middle, miss one another by miles. They simply worked on different levels.

The constructionists do not deny that homosexual behavior exists, but they do deny that this behavior defines a certain type of person. Rather, it is a behavior that occurs rarely, occasionally, frequently, or constantly in many people; it grows stronger, weakens, or disappears, and, in many cases, it exists concurrently or intermittently with heterosexual behavior. This observation alone invalidates every attempt to localize any sort of physical predisposition to homosexuality in certain individuals. For example, the selection of a "homosexual" random sample as well as an appropriate (opposite) control group raises considerable methodological problems. However, with an astonishing naivité, these are simply ignored by most natural scientists.

When a biologist, endocrinologist, neurologist, or geneticist looks for "homosexuals," he usually finds them among volunteers from "gay" organizations, bars or clubs, among readers of "gay" magazines, in correctional institutions, or in various patient collectives. Their own claim that they are "gay" or "homosexual" is usually taken at face value. Hardly anyone asks about their actual (and not infrequently bisexual) behavior. Indeed, neurologists have even compared the brains of supposed "homosexual" and "heterosexual" corpses that could no longer be questioned. If questions are asked at all, the Kinsey scale is often used, but never as its author intended. On the contrary, the scale is misapplied as a means to place the subject, as a type, on one of the levels from 0 to 6 according to the frequency of his homosexual contacts. It is then also left to the discretion of the investigator where he draws the line for heterosexuality. At 6 or 5 or 4? Or even at 3? Investigators themselves sometimes also decide without further questions whether a particular subject is homosexual. They simply judge according to appearance or body language or even according to information from third parties. But even if there could be general agreement on strict criteria for a "homosexual" random sample, and even if these criteria could then also actually be met, there would still be the question about the necessary size of that sampling, i.e., about how representative it was or could be of all persons with predominantly homosexual behavior. Any claim to universal validity founders on to this question alone.

Conversely, control groups frequently consist of participants in other, nonsexological studies, and these participants are often simply classified as heterosexuals without any background checks whatsoever, especially if they come from the same work group or are even colleagues of many years. It is just simply inconceivable that such people and other acquaintances should be homosexual or even bisexual! For that reason, an exhaustive questioning of control groups is even rarer than that of the original samples.[37]

The strength of the evidence presented in many homosexuality studies is correspondingly minimal. Different investigators proceed from entirely different definitions of who their subjects are and then also constitute their differently sized random samples according to completely different criteria. Some American critics once took the trouble to analyze two hundred twenty-eight articles about homosexuality from fort-seven different scientific journals. The fundamental definitions of "sexual orientation" diverged so far from one another that, in the end, "nothing could be compared with anything" and there was no appreciable overall result. The critics came to the conclusion that all such investigations would remain unfruitful as long as they assumed the existence of a homosexual identity or a clearly definable homosexual orientation. They also concluded that, in the future, it would make more sense to investigate only sexual relationships, not homosexual, heterosexual, or bisexual individuals.[38]

But even if, against Kinsey's advice, one were to "divide the world into sheep and goats" and were to study only "pure" random samplings and control groups from the extremes of 0 and 6 on his scale, what would it prove, since all others, some of whom repeatedly move back and forth between 1 and 5, would remain unconsidered? What could be learned about them, and how?

Indeed, it was no accident that even the inventors and propagandists of "the homosexual" from Ulrichs to Hirschfeld sooner or later, for better or worse, had to concern themselves with "transitions" as well. All of their parentheses, columns, bars, and sliding scales, all their subgroups, special forms, and "intermediate stages" were surely enough indication that, upon closer view, the "third sex" itself dissolved into a multitude of new sexes. Thus, in the end, the "bisexuals" always ruined even the most ambitious theory of homosexuality.

In spite of this, or perhaps because of it, attempts to bring the diversity somehow into a simple system of classification never ceased. Still, eventually, investigators learned from past mistakes and no longer tried to classify individuals, but rather their behavior, and this in such a way that a single conceptual key would open all secret doors.

An interesting attempt of this sort was made by **John Money**, who thereby hoped at the same time to mediate in the debate between essentialists and constructionists. His new magic formula was called "Nature—Critical Phase—Culture"; that is to say, biological predispositions are formed in a critical early phase of fetal or child development in such a way that subsequent cultural influences have an effect primarily in a particular direction and no longer in another. He sees homosexual and bisexual behavior (as well as several other types of otherwise puzzling behavior) as being explained by an early "gender cross-coding."[39]

Gender Cross-Coding (Transposition)

	Continuous or Chronic	*Episodic or Alternating*
Total	Transsexualism	Transvestophilia (fetishistic transvestism)
Partial unlimited	Gynemimesis Andromimesis	Transvestism (nonfetishistic transvestism)
Partial limited	Male Homophilia Female Homophilia	Homo/heterophilia (bisexuality)

Figure 12.

The overview is self-explanatory. The concepts of gynemimesis (imitation of women) and andromimesis (imitation of men) are new, as is the concept of transvestophilia, which, being fetishistic, is distinguished from simple transvestism.

No problem need arise from the fact that homosexuality is referred to as homophilia here. But something else does create a problem: Once again, same-sex behavior is explained as a cross-coded or transposed gender role or identity, as if in men it somehow had something to do with femininity and in women it somehow had something to do with masculinity. On this point, Money's "gender cross-coding" is all too reminiscent of Westphal's "contrary sexual feeling." Therefore, after everything that has been said so far, our esteemed colleague's presumed new insight can only give the impression of being a rehash of long outmoded ideas. After critical examination, his entire scheme thus seems like a procrustean bed into which he, for the sake of diagnostic order, forces all sorts of phenomena that are actually independent of one another. It is simply too nice and too good to be true.

Some Practical Consequences

THE REPEATED AND now probably final deconstruction of the categorical triad "Homosexuality—Bisexuality—Heterosexuality"; the disappearance of this concept and of all concepts derived from it in the recent sex research literature; the current attempts to address the old questions differently and with a different vocabulary, must sooner or later also have consequences for scientific and professional practice. This can be shown most easily with an example from epidemiological research.

In view of the AIDS threat, anonymous surveys were designed in many countries in order to determine the actual or possible risk of infection among persons willing to be tested or who had already been tested. Initially, the questionnaires were often very naive. A man, for example, might simply be asked before a test, "Are you gay?" If he answered "yes," then "homosexuality" was checked in a box on the form as a risk factor. If he said "no," it automatically meant the box "heterosexuality." Only gradually did epidemiologists understand that not all self-defined gays are sexually active and that many men with same-sex contacts do not define themselves as gay. So the question was changed to "Have you had homosexual contacts?" Yet all too many persons who were questioned still did not think that their own same-sex activities were being referred to, especially if they simultaneously also had heterosexual relationships. Having become somewhat cleverer, the questioner then asked, "Have you had homosexual or bisexual contacts?" According to the answer, one of three boxes was then checked: "Patient is heterosexual" or "Patient is homosexual" or "Patient is bisexual." But here, too, the questioners had to learn that many men did not associate the word "homosexual" with their own same-sex activities and that others rejected the label "bisexual" for their behavior despite proven or admitted sexual contacts with both women and men. Therefore, one finally asked them separately and even more simply, "Did you have sexual contact with men, with women?" If both were affirmed, the interviewer wrote, as usual, "Patient is bisexual." Not only that: the persons in question, together with "the homosexuals," were added to a new epidemiological category, "homosexual and bisexual men." (By the same logic, of course, one might also have lumped together "heterosexual and bisexual men," but this did not occur to anyone.) The new, combined category ("homo/bi") was then introduced all over the world under the influence of the American Centers for Disease Control (CDC).

However, it became clear to several epidemiologists, over time, that very different types of behavior were here being treated alike, and that, epidemiologically, they were of very different relevance. For a valid prognosis, it was obviously important to find out exactly what the bisexual behavior consisted of in each individua case. If a male prostitute, for example, served several male clients daily and had several girlfriends at the same time, he played an entirely different epidemiological role than an otherwise "faithful" husband who used the services of this male prostitute (and only of this male prostitute) as a client once per year. This crucial distinction was needlessly obliterated by the blanket categorization "bisexual patient." Other types of bisexual behavior, long known to sexologists, were also discovered, such as that of dyed-in-the-wool gays who sometimes had sex with women, even with lesbians, or that of "heterosexual swingers" who sometimes also "accepted same-sex partners into the bargain," or that of sexually experimenting teenagers, or of prisoners, and so forth.

The epidemiologists' original short-sightedness was even greater in the case of women who had sex with women. Thus, the CDC, for example, defined a woman as a lesbian "if she has sexual contact with women and has not had sexual contact with men since 1977."[40]

This even excluded the majority of those who called themselves lesbians, to say nothing of the large number of women who, despite identical sexual behavior, did not so define themselves. Even the comparatively "worldly wise" Department of Public Health in San Francisco did not recognize until ten years after the beginning of the AIDS epidemic that the mutually exclusive terms "homosexual" and "bisexual" led to false conclusions about the risk of infection among women. (The sexologists working in San Francisco could have told the officials this right from the start, but they were not consulted.) So it was not until 1993 that the previously ignored insight was officially announced:

> Women who have sexual contact with women exhibit a diversity of sexual identities, personal traits, and manners of behavior that put them at risk of HIV-infection. The concepts "lesbian" or "bisexual" are usually used to refer to these women, but their choice of partners and their sexual behavior no longer always accord with such descriptions of identity. There are self-defined lesbians who have sexual contact with men, even for money, and there are women who define themselves as heterosexual but have female sexual partners. Women who have sexual contact with women might have few or many partners, they can be mothers, drug addicts, college graduates, street prostitutes, homeless persons, or prisoners. Despite these differences, current HIV statistics can lead them to believe that they run no or only a minimal risk of infection.[41]

Suddenly worried, the office thus came to the following conclusion:

> The facts described here show that it is problematic to use broad categories of identification instead of concentrating on specific types of behavior that carry a risk of HIV infection. Our attempts to reduce HIV infection and other sexually transmitted diseases as a part of public health will be inadequate as long as we remain unable to speak plainly and clearly about specific behaviors with all segments of the population.[42]

In view of such belated insights, the traditional questionnaires did indeed seem somewhat too simple. There were thus attempts in several countries to allow for more differentiation. These attempts essentially tried to avoid historically and culturally loaded (that is, ideological) concepts such as "homosexual" and "bisexual" and to ask only about the number of sexual contacts with the one or the other sex. As a model for such a procedure, a simplified, anonymous (albeit never used) form I myself designed years ago is reproduced below.

Risk of Infection

Sex [ ] male
[ ] female

1. Sexual Contacts

	Sex and number of partners since 1990	
	Number of males	Number of females
	___	___
of these were:		
i.v. drug users	___	___
paid (prostitutes)	___	___
paying (johns)	___	___
hemophiliacs or transfusion recipients	___	___
from an area with a high infection rate	___	___

2. i.v. Drug use [ ]

3. Blood and blood products

Coagulation factor [ ]
Transfusion [ ] Date of Transfusion:_______

4. Pre- und perinatal [ ]

5. Cannot be determined [ ]

Figure 13.

The trouble spent in filling out such a form is basically no greater than before. But the form offers several advantages:

- It supplies numerical *relations* between the various possible sexual contacts and thus a clearer idea of possible "promiscuity."

- It also gives an approximate idea of the *total number* of sexual contacts.

- It completely avoids the adjective "homosexual" and the substantives "homosexual" and "homosexuality," yet describes same-sex contacts all the more precisely.

- It describes contacts with both sexes according to the differing preponderance of those contacts (balance of heterosexual and homosexual contacts).

- It distinguishes between prostitutes (male and female) on the one hand and "johns" on the other.

- It documents the character and the extent of sexual contacts outside of "stable" sexual relationships.

- It forces the physician, counselor, or questioner to come at least one step closer to the sexual reality of the questioned person, who possibly deviates significantly from the commonly assumed "normality." This can become a very valuable aid in counseling.

In spite of these undeniable advantages, considerable and probably insurmountable difficulties stand in the way of the universal introduction of such a survey form, even if the strictest anonymity could be guaranteed. They range from political reservations to the problems and costs of organization. In addition, there is also justified mistrust on the side of those questioned and insufficient training in the techniques of questioning on the side of the questioners. Nevertheless, independently, and as a first step, the forms of some countries (such as those of Switzerland and the U.S.) have since come to follow some of the ideas presented here.

My questionnaire should therefore not be taken as a proposal for immediate, concrete action, but rather as an illustration of how inadequate the traditional categories are when it comes to capturing the diversity of real life. Moreover, it forces one to look more closely at the individual and to choose simple, precise language that admits of no misunderstandings and does not run up against ideological reservations.

This is especially important when taking a patient's sex history before medical treatment (such as for sexually transmitted diseases). Nonmedical sex therapists and marriage counselors also sometimes need to gain a realistic picture of the sexual behavior of a client or couple in order to be able to help at all. It is precisely in these situations that terms like "homosexual" and "bisexual" often meet with some inner resistance and even rejection. Ultimately, they hinder effective communication. The only certain way to success here is the avoidance of all clichés, stereotypes, and ideologically loaded concepts. Only simple, precise questions about the gender and the number of sexual partners can be helpful here. In addition, the questioner must make it known through his entire demeanor that he himself is entirely free of stereotypical ideas, that he knows about and accepts the actual diversity of human sexual behavior, and that he has no inclination whatsoever to label or denigrate people, no matter what they tell him. Only then does he have some chance to obtain truthful information.

Of course, all this is also true of any kind of sex research, whether by questionnaire or by personal interview. Concepts like "homosexual" and "bisexual" would only cause unnecessary confusion here and therefore are always scrupulously avoided by today's sexologists. In other words: The nineteenth-century concepts are today no longer used in either epidemiological or sexological research. Neither are they used in sexual counseling or sex therapy, and they should also be abandoned in sex education, sexological training, and continuing medical education. On the contrary, it is precisely the training of experts that should sharpen the critical consciousness about the dubiousness of traditional labels. Not until physicians, psychiatrists, psychologists, educators, sociologists, lawyers, criminologists, epidemiologists, theologians, and science writers have broken the habit of using these labels will a much-needed sense of reality with regards to human sexual behavior return to our society.

These considerations once more throw a helpful light on the preceding scientific debate. It is now clear that this debate had been too abstract, "academic," and divorced from life, and that, for more than a century, its terminology had painted the picture of a neatly ordered reality that never existed. To that extent, sexology today once again finds itself in the ungrateful role of a spoilsport vis-à-vis medicine and other established disciplines. It disturbs the beloved old siren songs of reductionism with an obstinately dissonant *basso continuo* of doubt and thus seems to live up to its reputation as the perpetual academic outsider. This, too, contributes to the well-known, ongoing rejection it meets from universities the world over. The messenger is shunted aside, because no one is eager to hear his message that, in all matters sexual, "nothing is ever simple."

Translated by Lance W. Garmer
with revisions by Erwin J. Haeberle

Endnotes

1. Johann Ludwig Casper, "Über Notzucht und Päderastie und deren Ermittelung seitens des Gerichtsarztes" (On rape and pederasty and its investigation by the forensic physician), *Vierteljahrsschrift für gerichtliche und öffentliche Medizin*, Vol. 1 (1852). Additional articles are in subsequent issues.

2. Karl Heinrich Ulrichs, *Inclusa*, 1864. Reprinted by Max Spohr in Leipzig in 1889.

3. *Prometheus*, 1869. Reprint by Max Spohr in Leipzig, 1889, 10–11.

4. Ibid., prefatory remark.

5. Karl-Heinrich Ulrichs, *Memnon*, 1868. Reprint by Max Spohr in Leipzig, 1889, 50.

6. Karoly Maria Kertbeny (as anonymous author), "Section 143 of the Prussian Penal Code of April 14, 1851, and its upholdng of Paragraph 152 in the draft of a penal

code for the North German Confederation. Open, expert letter to His Excellence Herr Dr. Leonhardt, Royal Prussian Minister of State and Justice, Berlin 1869." Reprint in the *Jahrbuch für sexuelle Zwischenstufen* (Yearbook for sexual intermediate stages), 7:1, i–iv and 3–66.

7. Carl Westphal, "Die conträre Sexualempfindung, Symptom eines neuropathischen (psychopathischen) Zustandes," (Contrary sexual feeling: Symptom of a nuropathic [psychopathic] condition), in *Archiv für Psychiatrie und Nervenkrankheiten* (Archives of psychiatry and nervous diseases), Vol. 2:1, 73–108.

8. Magnus Hirschfeld, *Sappho und Sokrates: Wie erklärt sich die Liebe der Männer und Frauen zu Personen des eigenen Geschlechts?* (Sappho and Socrates: How is the love of men and women to persons of their own sex to be explained?) 2d ed. (Leipzig: Max Spohr, 1902), (1st ed., 1896), 9 and 16.

9. Ludwig Frey, *Die Männer des Rätsels* (Men of the enigma) (Leipzig: Max Spohr Verlag, 1898), 65.

10. Frey, *Männer*, Appendix.

11. Magnus Hirschfeld, *Geschlechtskunde* (Sexology), Vol. I: *Die körperlichen Grundlagen* (Physical fundamentals), (Stuttgart: Julius Püttmann Verlagsbuchhandlung, 1926), 481 and 547–48. (The diagram pictured here is a summary of statements made by Hirschfeld.)

12. The following diagrams are modifications of those in E. J. Haeberle, *The Sex Atlas* (New York: Seabury Press, 1978), 138–39.

13. Erich Meyer, "Vom Paidon Eros der Antike zur Homosexualität der Gegenwart" (From Paidon Eros of antiquity to homosexuality of the present), in *Zeitschrift für Sexualwissenschaft und Sexualpolitik* (Journal for sexual science and sexual policy), 16: 4 (August 1929), 233–34.

14. Ibid., 234.

15. Alfred C. Kinsey, "Homsexuality: Criteria for a Hormonal Explanation of the Homosexual," in *The Journal of Clinical Endocrinology*, 1: 5, 424–28.

16. Ibid., 428.

17. Alfred C. Kinsey et al., *Sexual Behavior in the Human Male* (Philadelphia: W. B. Saunders, 1948), 638. (The scale here is slightly modified in order to make clearer its similarity to Kinsey's preceding scale of 1941, Fig. 9.)

18. Ibid., 639.

19. Ibid., 617.

20. Walter Bräutigam, *Formen der Homosexualität* (Forms of homosexuality) (Stuttgart: Ferdinand Enke Verlag, 1976).

21. Benedikt Friedländer, *Die Renaissance des Eros Uranios* (The renaissance of Eros Uranois) (Berlin: Bernhard Zacks Verlag, 1908), 86.

22. The diagram is reproduced here with minor modifications. The original is in Fritz Klein, Barry Sepekoff, and Timothy J. Wolf, "Sexual Orientation: A Multivariable Dynamic Process," in *Journal of Homosexuality*, 2: 1/2, (1985), 39–42. (Klein himself has subsequently introduced various slight modifications.)

23. Mary McIntosh, "The Homosexual Role," in *Social Problems*, 16: 2 (Fall 1968), 182–92 (here, 183).

24. The most prominent gay historian on the essentialist side was John Boswell, who already signaled his position in the title of his large study: *Christianity, Social Tolerance and Homosexuality: Gay People in Western Europe from the Beginning of the Christian Era to the Fourteenth Century* (Chicago/London: University of Chicago Press, 1980). The most prominent person on the constructionist side was Michel Foucault, who placed the invention of the homosexual in the nineteenth century in his book *Sexualität und Wahrheit: Der Wille zum Wissen* (Sexuality and truth: The will to knowledge) (Frankfurt am Main: Suhrkamp, 1977) (see 58 in particular concerning the topic of "the homosexual"). Foucault's thesis is essentially shared by the Englishmen Plummer and Weeks, who, however, locate the genesis of the homosexual already in the eighteenth century. (See Kenneth Plummer, *Sexual Stigma: An Interactionist Account* [London/Boston: Routledge & Kegan Paul, 1975]; Kenneth Plummer, *The Making of the Modern Homosexual* [Totowa, N. J.: Barnes & Noble Books, 1981]; Jeffrey Weeks, *Coming Out: Homosexual Politics in Britain from the Nineteenth Century to the Present* [London: Quartet Books, 1977].) John Boswell later attempted to reconcile misunderstandings that had arisen between essentialist and constructionist historians of homosexuality in the essay "Revolutions, Universals, Sexual Categories," in *Salmagundi*, No. 58–59, (Fall/Winter 1982–83), 89–113.

25. The scripting theory was first applied by the authors to human sexual behavior more than twenty years ago. See John Gagnon, William Simon, *Sexual Conduct: The Social Sources of Human Sexuality* (Chicago: Aldine, 1973).

26. John Gagnon, "The Explicit and Implicit Use of the Scripting Perspective in Sex Research," in *Annual Review of Sex Research*, Vol. 1, (1990), 5.

27. Of these researchers, the Berlin endocrinologist Günther Dörner has long been the best known. Over the course of years, he has repeatedly clarified and expanded his findings. See, for example, Dörner et al., "A Neuroendocrine Predisposition for Homosexuality in Men," in *Archives of Sexual Behavior*, No. 4 (1975), 1–8; Dörner, "Hormones and Sexual Differentiation in the Brain," in *Sex, Hormones and Behavior*, ed. R. Porter and J. Whelen, Ciba Foundation Symposium 62 (new series), Amsterdam, 1979, 81–112; Dörner, "Sexual Differentiation of the Brain," in *Vitamins and Hormones*, Vol. 38 (1980), 325–81; Dörner et al., "Prenatal Stress as Possible Aetiogenic Factor of Homosexuality in Human Males," in *Endokrinologie*, No. 75 (1980), 365–68; Dörner et al., "Stress Events in Prenatal Life of Bi- and Homosexual Men," in *Experimental and Clinical Endocrinology*, Vol. 81 (1983), 83–87; Dörner et al., "Sexual Differentiation of Gonadotropin Secretion, Sexual Orientation and Gender Role Behavior," in *Journal of Steroid Biochemistry*, Vol. 27 (1987), 1081–87.

28. See John Gagnon, "The Explicit and Implicit Use . . . ," ibid., 1–43.

29. John Gagnon, "Gender Preference in Erotic Relations: The Kinsey Scale and Sexual Scripts," in *Homosexuality/Heterosexuality: Concepts of Sexual Orientation*, ed. D. P. McWhirter, S. A. Sanders, and J. M. Reinisch (New York/Oxford: Oxford University Press, The Kinsey Institute Series, 1990), 195.

30. Ibid., 194.

31. Ibid., 183.

32. Rolf Gindorf, "Wissenschaftliche Ideologien im Wandel. Die Angst vor der Homosexualität als intellektuelles Ereignis" (Scientific ideologies in change: Fear of homosexuality as an intellectual event) in D*er unterdrückte Sexus. Historische Texte und Kommentare zur Homosexualität* (The repressed sexus: Historical texts and commentaries on homosexuality), ed. J. S. Hohmann (Lollar: Achenbach, 1977), 129–44.

33. Ibid., 143.

34. Aside from the already mentioned endicronologist Günther Dörner, the (openly gay) neurologist Simon Le Vay, the twins researcher J. Michael Bailey, and the geneticist Dean Hamer have also come forward with biological models of explanation for human homosexual behavior. Le Vay believes that it is possible to pinpoint the organic cause of homosexual inclinations in a certain region of the brain (Le Vay, "A Difference in Hypothalmic Structure Between Heterosexual and Homosexual Men," in *Science*, Vol. 253 [1991], 1034–37). Bailey and Hamer believe in a genetic cause, and Hamer even thinks that he has localized a region for a corresponding gene on the end of the X chromosome (Hamer et al., "A Linkage Between DNA Markers on the X chromosome and Male Sexual Orientation," in *Science*, Vol. 261 [1993], 321–27). Hamer and his co-authors do indeed call "homosexual orientation" a "naturally occurring variation" and they expressly warn of misusing their discovery to determine or to change this variation (321 and 326), but it may well be doubted whether they themselves believe that the misuse can be avoided. Incidentally, it is also useful to remember in this context that geneticists have earlier believed to have discovered specific genes for violence, alcoholism, and even thalassophilia (love of seafaring). Little remains of these discoveries.

35. On this point, we include without commentary an excerpt from a recent newspaper article: "In China, It's Mostly a Boy—Thanks to Ultra-Sound."

> "Only one girl was born in our village last year—otherwise, there were boys everywhere," said Y. H. Chen. . . . He expained that, for a bribe of $35–50, a physician would reveal whether a pregnant women could expect a boy or a girl. "If it's a girl, then it's aborted." . . . Partially for this reason, the ratio of newborn boys to girls in China was 118 to 100 last year. . . . This means that more than 12% of female fetuses were aborted. . . . Worried about this development, the press is beginning to warn that today's male infants will not be able to find any women in 20 years. However, aside from vague warnings about the increase of "bachelor villages," no one is investigating what social consequences could result in a society that has a large surplus of men. China is not the only country with this problem. . . . Apparently due to prenatal ultrasound examinations, the ratio among newborns in South Korea is 113 boys to 100 girls.
> —*International Herald Tribune*, July 22, 1993, 1–2.

36. The reader is reminded that already Aristotle saw a means of birth control in homosexuality. He reports that the government of Crete had intentionally encouraged homosexual behavior in order to prevent an overpopulation of the island (*Politics*, II, 10).

37. See Wendell Ricketts, "Biological Research on Homosexuality: Ansell's Cow or Occam's Razor?," in *Journal of Homosexuality*, 9: 4 (1984), 65–93.

38. Michael G. Shively, Christopher Jones, and John P. De Cecco, "Research on Sexual Orientation: Definitions and Methods," in *Journal of Homosexuality*, 9: 2/3 (1983–84), 127–36.

39. John Money, "Agenda and Credenda of the Kinsey Scale," in *Homosexuality/ Heterosexuality: Concepts of Sexual Orientation*, ed. D. P. McWhirter, S. A. Sanders, and J. M. Reinisch (New York/Oxford: Oxford University Press, The Kinsey Institute Series, 1990), 54.

40. S. Y. Chu, J. W. Buehler, P. L. Fleming, and R. L. Berkelman, "Epidemiology of Reported Cases of AIDS in Lesbians, United States 1980–1989," in *American Journal of Public Health*, Vol. 80 (1990), 1380–81.

41. Department of Public Health, "HIV Risk Among Women Who Have Sex with Women," in *San Francisco Epidemiologic Bulletin*, 9: 4 (April 1993), 25.

42. Ibid., 27.

Bisexuality: A Biological[1] Perspective

Milton Diamond[2]

There is little doubt that much of the present impetus to study the human phenomena loosely called bisexuality stems from the AIDS epidemic and interest in the transmission vectors of HIV disease. While this attention is of value for itself and relatively new from the perspective of psychology, sociology, and the humanities, the broader study of bisexuality is a relatively classical subject in biology. This is particularly true when our discussion encompasses botanical and invertebrate species. Even were we to limit our discussion to mammalian forms, this holds true. And the broad study of sexual orientation and partner preferences, how an individual chooses another for mating, is certainly not a subject of interest limited to the human species.

The biological definition of bisexuality is relatively clear. Biological bisexuality refers to the presence in the same individual of male and female structures related to the production, delivery, or storage of gametes. This may be normal and typical for each individual of that species, a common or rare variation, or a condition of sequential or simultaneous hermaphroditism. When behaviors are referred to, the definition becomes somewhat more vague and complicated.

Behavioral definitions revolve around activities associated with insertion or use of a sperm delivery organ being classified as male and those behaviors associated with receiving sperm or egg fertilization being categorized as female. As the behaviors become more complicated and courtship is extended, the definitions are broadened. They enlarge to encompass those behaviors which somehow might be construed to facilitate these basic behaviors in a sex-linked manner that is typical for the species. When humans are the species in focus, the biological definition remains the same, but at core, bisexuality refers to activities or inherent interests of an individual for sexual/genital involvement with both male and female partners. And for humans, the behavioral definitions take on social and political significance which often prejudice interpretation.

Biological Diversity

LEAVING ASIDE THE huge diversity among botanicals, the different bisexual types found among animal species are legion. Some examples should suffice. Among the better known invertebrate species are *Crepidula fornicata* and *Anonymus virilis*. *Crepidula* is a clam-like mollusk which is often found, as its name might suggest, with individuals piled one atop each other. The first individual to secure a perch acts as a female for the individual that alights on it. This second individual attaches to the first and produces sperm which inseminates eggs produced by the one below. When individual number two is found by a third, number three attaches and becomes the male to the converted individual below which now produces ova. This succession of male to female changes continues in turn as each new individual joins the pile. Each new top member produces sperm to fertilize eggs produces by the previous top male which now produces eggs. The gonads to provide these gametes are mature and appropriately activated by the situation encountered by the individual *Crepidula* (Brusca and Brusca 1990).

Anonymus virilis is a flatworm member of the phylum Platyhelminthes with another colorful popular name: "twenty-four penises." This aquatic species creeps on different substrata and seemingly inserts its twenty-four penises (stylets) into anything soft. It continues until it eventually does so to a conspecific. In so doing, while vaginae are available, it may essentially puncture the other's skin and deposit sperm in a process called hypodermic impregnation. The recipient produces eggs for appropriate fertilization as a female. In another instance, however, the impregnated member may insert its own penises into a different individual and deposit sperm. Basically, each individual can function as a male and female (Hyman 1951). While self-fertilization cannot occur, simultaneous fertilization can. This is true for many species of this phylum. Some species of leeches also copulate in this manner (Najarian 1976).

With consideration of vertebrates there are still many examples of fascinating bisexuality. Perhaps fish best demonstrate this. Among fish there are true examples of bisexual characteristics (Demski 1987; Thresher 1984). Two groups exhibiting different evolutionary strategies will again serve as examples showing the great diversity in ways bisexuality is manifest.

The seas basses, fish of the family Serranidea, like the flatworms, are *simultaneous* hermaphrodites. Within seconds, members of this group can mate acting as a male and releasing sperm in one instance and then acting as a female releasing ova the next. *Hypoplectrus*, a species of fish called hamlets, are well known in this regard (Thresher 1984).

The reef-dwelling wrasse *Thalasoma duperry* (family Labridae) in contrast, is a species which demonstrates *sequential* hermaphroditism. Some few individuals start off life as males, but most are born as females. Then, depending upon those conspecifics with which it interacts, the female either remains a female or develops into a male (Ross, Losey, and Diamond 1983).

Typically, these fish mate promiscuously in quite sex-specific ways.[3] Their male or female behavior is definitely linked to the spawning process. With some fish species, sex change occurs in the largest individual present in the absence of an opposite-sexed individual (see Fishelson 1975, and Shapiro 1979), but in *Thalasoma* the female-to-male sex change requires visual clues from smaller conspecifics. A mature female alone will not become a male. When two females are placed together, however, the larger of the two will become a male in the absence of another larger fish (which is usually a male). This change is not dependent on the sex or color of the smaller fish, only on behavioral cues from a smaller conspecific. A smaller companion fish of a similar but not identical species won't serve as a proper stimulus to change.

The sex change of the larger of the two, however, can be inhibited by the presence of an even larger conspecific of either sex. Sex change not only involves behavioral shifts but replacement of developing oocytes with the development of active spermatogenesis (Ross, Losey, and Diamond 1983). The stimuli involved in these changes are visual, not pheromonal.

On the reef, a female probably changes sex when the relative numbers of larger and smaller conspecifics change within her home range. Considering the reef life of these fish, where many species cohabit and population densities may be relatively large, this flexible mechanism of insuring both fertile males and a large reproductively active female population is a good strategy. The crucial matter to be emphasized here is *the dual requirement for both a stimulus by one type of partner and the absence of another type.* This duality might be considered the basic principal of behavioral bisexuality. Such conditions will allow certain individuals, which already possess the potential, to dramatically switch their sex and behavior.

Among many birds, structural bisexuality has been reported as a rarity. Behaviorally, some species of gulls (western gulls, ring-billed gulls, and California gulls) have been reported to occasionally demonstrate female–female courting, mounting, and sharing of a nest site (Conover, Miller, and Hunt 1979; Hunt and Hunt 1977; Ryder and Somppi 1979). In these instances, however, there was a notable shortage of males, and this behavior is not considered routine. Some hand-reared domestic geese have also been reported to demonstrate homosexual-like activities (Lorenz 1967). Nevertheless, the phenomenon of homosexual or bisexual activities among birds is rare.

Mammals: Ungulates, Primates, and Rodents

THE PHENOMENON OF hermaphroditism or structural bisexuality becomes rarer as we probe higher in the evolutionary scale. Some examples, however, do exist. The common domestic cow provides one of the best illustrations, known to all cattle breeders. In the condition known as Freemartin (Lillie 1917), a female *Bovine* fetus, while in utero with a male twin, becomes "masculinized" by the gestational androgens present. These are sufficient to modify both her internal and external genitals. These females are almost always sterile, and in a manner similar to that induced in rats (discussed below), the female demonstrates male like behaviors. Twinning in cattle is a rare situation.

Even among normal cows, female–female mounting may occur when one is in estrus. This is a sexual mount to be sure and does not appear to be a displacement activity in the absence of a male. If a bull were present, however, he would mount the female and female–female mounting would be less likely to occur. A bull mounting a bull, however, is rarely seen.

In the sheep (*Ovine*), a closely related ruminant species, female–female mounting and the Freemartin condition are both rare. In this species, twinning is quite common. Interestingly, in the only known example of its kind in mammals, males reared together, without any experience with females, will occasionally develop a relationship in which they mount each other and then prefer mounting each other (without intromission) to mounting a female (Schein 1991).

In the field, primates seem heterosexual in almost all instances. Rarely does any activity occur which might be considered preferentially homosexual. While male–male or female–female mounting is not uncommon, it is almost always a demonstration of dominance or status in the primate hierarchy or appears to be a substitute behavior. With this in mind, some instances of homosexual-looking behavior have been reported. Hardy, cited in Weinrich (1982), claims that among languors (*Presbytis entellus*) male–male mounting occurs in situations of sexual excitement where the males do not have females available for mounting. Yamagiwa (1987) also cites male–male activity among wild gorillas as a result of a relative lack of females. Some male–male and female–female sexual-appearing activity has been reported for the Bonobo (*Pan paniscus*) (de Waal 1990). The Bonobo is a chimpanzee like primate with very human like activities including occasional ventral-ventral mounting and copulation. Their activities also include occasions of same-sex behaviors which can be considered mutual masturbation, kissing, genital play, and genital apposition. De Waal (1990, p. 387) explains these behaviors as serving not erotic, but important tension-regulating functions.

In all of these nonhuman mammalian situations it appears that homosexual or bisexual activities occur when, as mentioned, for *Thalasoma* above, there is present *the dual requirement of both a stimulus by one type of partner and the absence of another type.* Such conditions allow certain individuals, which already possess the potential, to switch from their preferred sex and behavior. This means both that the environmental situation must be conducive to the behavior and that only certain individuals and certain species will respond.

In contrast to *spontaneous* homosexual or bisexual behavior, there is a large literature on the *induction* of male-to-female and female-to-male behaviors among mammals. Starting with the classical paper by Phoenix, Goy, Gerall, and Young (Phoenix et al. 1959) working with the guinea pig, many have reported on paranatal influences on mammalian sex behavior development. While different from our normal understanding of bisexuality, some of these findings are instructive for the present discussion.

With good justification, much has been made of the fact that androgens given to neonatal *female* rats can result in these individuals, when adults, displaying *malelike* mounting behavior when placed with a receptive female. Similarly, *male* rats castrated paranatally, and thus having their endogenous androgens removed, will demonstrate *femalelike* lordoses when placed with a normal adult male (for reviews of this large area of research, see Whalen 1968; Feder 1981; and McEwen 1983).

Several features of these experiments warrant emphasis: (1) the individual test female is placed with a receptive female, which she mounts in a malelike fashion. She is not tested with a male. (2) The individual test male is not placed with a receptive female, to see if he will mount her or if he will lordose. He is instead placed with an intact adult male toward which he lordoses.[4]

Also worthy of note is that even androgens, when given neonatally to males, can adversely affect their male sexual behaviors. For instance Diamond, Llacuna, and Wong (1973) have shown that testosterone propionate can be as deleterious as estrogen in *decreasing* ejaculation, intromission, and mounting. But noteworthy for our present discussion, the treatment also resulted in a significant *increase* in oral-genital licking. This is a typical male-sex behavior and extremely rare for females.

The significance of all these findings is great in showing how behaviors can be reorganized by hormone manipulation during critical stages of development. Male and female rodents can, with relative ease, be experimentally induced to behaviors that are not typical for members of their sex. And this may indeed have theoretical relevance to how human behavior might be modified by endogenous idiophatic events.

However, for most direct relevance to human sexual orientation, the studies referred to, with comments (1) and (2) above, may be argued not to have demonstrated homosexual or bisexual behaviors since the test animals were not given a choice to see which type of partner, male or female, they might have preferred or if they would mate with both. They were shown only to have been given the ability, when placed in a research situation, to demonstrate behaviors typical of the opposite sex. Studies where the experimental animals were given a choice would be of value.

While it is now known that androgens convert to estrogens within the rat brain (for review, see Baum 1979) and this can produce the deleterious effects to mounting and ejaculation referred to above, it does little to explain the simultaneous increase in male oral-genital behavior. Also, there is little evidence to demonstrate that while these animals can be induced to show opposite-sex behaviors, they *prefer* same-sex sexual partners.

The point to be made is that definitions of opposite sex behavior and assertions of homosexuality and bisexuality have to be very clear and specific. If too broad, they obscure more than they reveal.

Comparable work to that in rodents has been done with other species including primates (e.g., Phoenix, Goy, and Resko 1968). Suffice it to say that males and females can be experimentally induced, with hormone manipulation, to show behaviors typical of opposite-sex individuals. The magnitude of the influence is dependent upon the time, duration, and size of the endocrine manipulation. With primates, much more of a biological push is needed to alter inherent tendencies.

One well-known set of primate studies is worth emphasis here, even though it does not involve hormonal intervention. The studies of Harlow and coworkers (Harlow 1961) are often cited to show how social input is crucial for sexual development. That issue cannot be denied, but another aspect of these studies bears emphasis. A normal rhesus monkey raised in isolation will not react appropriately enough to mate when placed with a willing partner. However, it is clear that such an isolated male will still try to mount or insert. While his mounting attempts will be aberrant, his behaviors will be male, not female. Similarly, a previously isolated female will show deviant female patterns, not male ones. She will try to "present" and "receive." The basic biological drives are intact in both sexes, but social learning is needed so males can learn where and how to "insert" and females where and how to "receive." The inherent male and female patterns are there to be augmented and refined by learning and practice. So-called preferential bisexual behavior has not been reported for primates.

Humans

KINSEY ET AL. (KINSEY, Pomeroy, and Martin 1948; Kinsey et al. 1953) clearly state they thought the term *bisexual* best reserved for nonhuman species with biological characteristics of both male and female. Although quite rare, true hermaphroditism or intersexuality, with both ovarian and testicular tissue present, does exist in humans and its presence has long been well known (for review, see Armstrong 1964 and Overzier 1963). Much more common are conditions of pseudohermaphroditism in which, judging from the appearance of the external genitalia, the impression rather than the actuality of hermaphroditism exists. The behavioral disposition of individuals with these hermaphroditic or pseudohermaphroditic conditions is usually in keeping with their genetic-endocrine heritage, although they may be reared erroneously (Diamond 1965, 1968, 1976/77, 1982).

Kinsey Scale

WITH THE USE OF their now classical "scale" for sexual orientation, Kinsey and colleagues (1948, 1953) evaluated individuals in terms of both behavior and psychic orientation. Determinant were the sex of the partners with whom the respondent had sexual experiences and the sex of the partner about whom the respondent was fantasizing. This seven-point Kinsey scale ranges from exclusive heterosexual behavior (0) to exclusive homosexual behavior (6). An individual with an equal number of male and female partners would be rated 3 on the scale (K=3). Someone with only incidental activity with someone of the same sex would be rated 1 (K=1). Someone with only incidental activity with someone of the opposite sex would be rated a 5 (K=5).

The Kinsey scale can be used to evaluate an individual's actual behavior or preferred behavior. In the latter mode it is an index of the sex of the preferred partner toward whom one might be attracted. This is seen as the prime measure of sexual orientation or sexual preference. Thus, heterosexuality, homosexuality, and ambi- or bisexuality are seen as terms of psychological sexual orientation or sexual preference.

Very few people in any society studied sustain anything like an equal balance of both same-sex and other-sex partners for a long period of time. Behaviorally, those warranting a 3 on the scale are rare. On the other hand, it is not rare for an individual to be married having sex with his or her spouse while fantasizing about a partner of his or her own sex. To smooth out this disparity, an individual's behavioral and psychological scores may be averaged to get a single composite index. This can result in an overall rating of K=3 but it's meaning might be misunderstood.

Behaviors rated 1 through 5 were termed ambisexual by Kinsey et al. Most individuals were found to be exclusively or predominantly heterosexually or homosexually active over years and decades; bisexual behavior over a lifetime was a minority practice. It is worth recalling that Kinsey et al. (1948, 1953), in addition to the 0 to 6 scale, also used an x in their ratings. This was for individuals, not at all rare, who were neither sexually aroused nor attracted to either males or females. These individuals were not erotically interested in sexual contact of any kind. They constituted some 2% of their male and about 5–18% of their female respondents.

Considering sexuality in humans, it should be clear that the terms *heterosexual, homosexual,* and *bisexual* refer better to behaviors than to people. Used in this context, the terms indicate the sex of the erotic/love/affectional partners a person prefers; whether these partners are of the same sex or opposite sex or either. Other than this, the labels may say very little about the person involved. A banker who prefers same-sex or opposite-sex partners, for example, might have more things in common with other bankers than with a plumber having similar erotic preferences. For just such reasoning, Kinsey et al. (1948, 1953) disparaged use of the terms *homosexual, heterosexual,* or *bisexual* as labels for their respondents.

While Kinsey and his colleagues did not label people by their "score" and use their ratings as nouns to refer to individuals, others were and are not so fastidious. The use of the terms as labels is actually common. The labels "homosexual" and "heterosexual" seem convenient to discuss individuals or populations of persons involved in same-sex or opposite-sex activity. Those who are labeled, however, are not always appreciative. First, the labels are often stigmatizing. Second, individuals who engage in homosexual behavior often find themselves caught in a crossfire. Politically active gays, and those who would discriminate against them, want such persons to identify as homosexual whether or not the individual identifies as such. More ambiguous has been the status and labeling of those with ambisexual behavior. Individuals who exhibit both same-sex and opposite-sex erotic activities or fantasies often see themselves as heterosexual or homosexual, not both or bi. On the other hand, many lay persons consider anyone with any homosexual experience, regardless of how infrequent, a "homosexual."

Some persons who feel strongly on this issue see individuals who exhibit ambisexual preference as "fence sitters" who should really belong to either the heterosexual or homosexual camp rather than as male or female bisexuals with their own arousal patterns. Others, cited by Rubin (1983), just as vociferously contend that those who engage in ambisexual activities would benefit from their own group identity, and call for being open as a bisexual, just as one might be open about being homosexual. This seems the present political *zeitgeist*.

Survey Data

This question of definition or label or self-identity, as used by either investigators or the people investigated, is of more than polemic interest. It affects the nature of the data collected and its validity.

As the term *bisexual* came more into general use and the nature of bisexuality more under scrutiny, various investigators established their own definitions. While Kinsey et al. (1948, 1953) considered ambisexuals as those demonstrating K=1 through K=5, Weinberg and Williams (1974, 1975), Bell and Weinberg (1978), and Green (1987) considered bisexuals as those whose behaviors and fantasies averaged K=2 through K=4. Haeberle (1978) categorized heterosexuals as K=0-2, homosexuals as K=4-6, and ambisexuals as K=2-5. All these investigators were coping with the reality that the term often obscures as much (if not more) than it reveals. It is extremely rare that an individual would both live and fantasize an erotic life with someone who was not sexually arousing, but an occasional or even prolonged "fling" might occur. Necessity might also force such behavior. Blumstein and Schwartz (1972) have written: "*Bisexuality* . . . gives a misleading sense of fixedness to sex-object choice . . . the preferable term, [is] *Ambisexuality*, connoting some ability for a person to eroticize both genders under some circumstances."

In this manner, in contrast with true erotic predilection, any individual may exhibit hetero-, homo-, or bisexual behaviors for many reasons which have nothing to do with sexual arousal or interest (see Diamond 1984, 11–12). Blumstein and

Schwartz (1977) discuss individuals' sex-object choice changing in many ways and many times over a life cycle, with the individuals often unaware of their ability to change, and early sexual experiences not being the final or even the strongest determinant of adult sexual expression.

With these ambiguities, among others, the size of the "true" ambisexual population—or heterosexual population, for that matter—is difficult to establish. The data on males is limited and the data on females even more so. Aside from the study by Kinsey et al. (1953) there is no known large-scale survey of females which documents bisexuality. And neither the male nor the female Kinsey studies were conducted among random samples, so they may be of little interest in this regard. To use them to identify groups, as has been done so often in the past, might misrepresent not only the size of this population, but that of any group extracted from the data set.

Kinsey et al. (1948) reported, in one of their most controversial findings: "it appears that nearly half (46%) of the [male] population engages in both heterosexual and homosexual activities, or reacts to persons of both sexes, in the course of their adult lives [p. 656]." By extension, with heterosexuals (K=0) representing 50% of the population and exclusive homosexuals (K=6) representing 4% of the population, ambisexuality should be considered almost as common as heterosexuality. Extracting from the original Kinsey data, even if we combine the K=1 behaviors with exclusive heterosexual behavior and K=5 with exclusive homosexual behavior, the size of the remaining ambisexual population remains significant. Indeed, these numbers have been challenged.

It has been said that, in contrast with the female volume, which was reissued, one reason the Kinsey et al. (1948) male volume was never reissued in paperback or later editions is due to concern with the statistical value of their sample and its lack of randomness. This was a major criticism at the time of publication (Terman 1948) and remains so today. Gebhard (1972), one of the co-authors of the 1948 and 1953 studies, discusses this and other shortcomings of the original study. He points out that the original study had a high percentage of prison inmates, particularly among the non-college-educated population, which tends to inflate the proportion of those with ambisexual experience in the total study population.

Figures given by Kinsey et al. (1953: table 142) for female ambisexual behavior, K=2–5, were something between 4 and 11% for those twenty to thirty-five years of age. Some 1 to 3% demonstrated exclusively homosexual, K=6, activities.

But even if the numbers are more or less a true reflection of the population having engaged in both same-sex and opposite-sex activity, we know nothing of the motivation for the behavior. What percentage represents true bisexual arousal compared with sexual experimentation or curiosity? Considering that many male respondents were prison inmates or had prison experiences, what percentage represents a forced sexual activity or purely displacement activity?

Suffice it to say, the actual representation of homosexuals or ambisexuals in any population is under dispute both scientifically and politically. Despite the AIDS epidemic as a prod to such research, attempts at a national U.S. study to obtain such data have been stymied by political and sexophobic considerations (Booth 1989). Attempts to similarly frustrate such research in Britain were successful for a period (Wellings et al. 1990) but were overcome.

Nevertheless, some information is available. A study of several thousand self-identified homosexual males in the United States, the Netherlands, and Denmark by Weinberg and Williams (1974) indicated that about 1 in 5 Americans were sexually active as K=2, 3, or 4 and about 1 in 10 Dutch or Danish gay men were similarly active. Their findings for Americans are at variance with three more recent studies: Bell and Weinberg (1978), McWhirter and Mattison (1984), and Diamond and Higa (in preparation). These newer studies are of U.S. males and their findings are relatively consistent (see Table 1).

For the newer studies of males who identify as engaging in homosexual behavior, about three out of four or more claim to be exclusively homosexual and fewer than one in ten claim they ever had more than incidental sex with a female. Unfortunately, all four of these studies also are nonrandom.

Table 1				
KINSEY RATINGS AMONG MALES SELF-IDENTIFYING AS GAY BEHAVIOR AND FANTASY				
Kinsey Scale	Weinberg and Williams (1974) [N=239][a]	Bell and Weinberg (1978) [N=575][b]	McWhirtier and Mattison (1984) [N=312][c]	Diamond and Higa (1988) [N=276][d]
Behavior				
6	51%	74%	82%	77%
5	30%	18%	11%	19%
4	13%	3%	7%	2%
3	4%	5%	0	2%
2	2%	0	0	0
1	0	0	0	0
0	0	0	0	0
Fantasy				
6	NR	58%	76%	64%
5	NR	28%	16%	25%
4	NR	8%	9%	8%
3	NR	6%	0	3%
2	NR	0	0	0
1	NR	0	0	0
0	NR	0	0	0

NR= Not Recorded
a= gay white U. S. males
b= gay white U. S. males
c= committed gay male couples only
d= gay multiracial males in Hawaii

Difference among the findings of the original Kinsey et al. (1948) study, the early Weinberg and Williams (1974) study, and the latter research offered in Table 1 may reflect behavior changes over time. The evolving so-called "Age of Aquarius" and movement toward decreased sexual restrictions might have fostered among homosexual oriented males or females a lessened feeling of obligation to engage in heterosexual activities, and for heterosexuals may have provided an increased availability of partners to more readily satisfy their erotic desires.

A recent probability sample household survey in Dallas (Dixon et al. 1991) by the Centers for Disease Control found only 7.3% of their male population (N=701) reporting having had any male–male sexual contact from 1978 to 1989 and a just-analyzed 1989 random sample of Hawaii residents found less than 3% of males (N=1,024) and 1.2% of females (N=987) as having engaged in same-sex or bisexual activity (Diamond, Ohye, and Wells in preparation).

Studies cited by Schover and Jensen (1988, 47) for a randomly selected population of Danish women found only 1 of 625 women from twenty-two to seventy years of age admitting to having had a homosexual experience.

A recent study by the Dutch research group NISSO (National Institute for Social Sexological Research) and Utrecht University has the first known national random sample data of male and female sexual behavior (Sandfort and Van Zessen 1991). It is worth considering in some detail. In a 1989 study using face-to-face interviews (N=421 males and 580 females), only about 13 in 100 males admitted to *ever in their life* having a homosexual experience and only about 3.3% would consider themselves homosexual (K=5–6) and an additional 4.5% of their male sample would self-label themselves as bisexual (K=2–5). *Only 1.2% of the males had bisexual activities in the preceding twelve months.*

Among females, only about 10 in 100 reported ever having had homosexual activity and only about 3% of the female population would consider themselves bisexual (K=2–5). Less than 1% of the female population had had bisexual activities in the preceding year. Fewer than 0.5% of the interviewed women considered themselves homosexual.

Most importantly in regard to these data, a follow-up study of individuals who initially refused to be interviewed found males not to differ significantly from the main sample on all relevant variables (lifestyle, sexual risk behavior, sexual preference). And while the females that were not in the original study, but found in the follow-up, reported more risk behaviors and were more likely to have had homosexual experiences and a current homosexual self-labeling, the number involved is too small to estimate how much the basic figures might be modified (Sandfort and Van Zessen 1991).

Lastly, findings from a most recent British national random study (Wellings at al. 1990) echo these findings. These researchers report only "9% of men and 4% of women reported some homosexual experience, and 5% of men and 1% of women reported ever having a homosexual partner."

These recent British, U.S., Danish, and Dutch reports appear fairly uniform in results and offer very different findings than would have been predicted by previous research. And the comparatively liberal attitudes toward homosexual or bisexual activity in Denmark or the Netherlands, if not in Britain or the U.S., must be considered strongly. These studies taken together certainly seem to indicate that bisexuality, and indeed homosexuality, may be less common than previously considered. This appears whether the group surveyed are self-identified gays or from random samples.

Looking at the phenomenon from another perspective, it is safe to say that most individuals, most of the time, and for most of their lives, have sex with only males or females, not both. On the other hand, some individuals, at least for a few years, engage in sex with both. Aside from that, with the exception of the Netherlands and the U.K., for the present we have no good data for any country on the actual size of its homosexual and bisexual population nor how diverse are its sexual interests. Without a reliable random study for the United States and other countries, we have to consider that a population of men—the size of which we do not know—do not associate with homosexual groups or consider themselves as such, but do demonstrate ambisexual activity. But adding consideration of the data from Dallas and Hawaii, we might anticipate that the number will be significantly smaller than previously thought.[5]

Polygraph Studies

SO FAR, WE have discussed assessment of sexual orientation by fairly obvious methods. Most studies directly ask subjects to self-identify on the basis of the type of partner—male, female, or both—with whom they experience sexual activities or to whom they are attracted. Or they ask respondents the number of male and female partners they have had in a specific time period. Since the advent of AIDS the interval of concern is usually from 1978 to the present. Field observers such as anthropologists might obtain such information by direct observations, and clinicians in their offices might, in their own way, learn how individuals select partners.

Another method is available: genital plethysmography. This is a laboratory technique of assessment believed to bypass an individual's possible attempt to either pretend or mask socially controversial homosexual or bisexual arousal or interest. In societies such as ours, personal reports may be self-serving or might even reflect biases of which the individual him or herself is unaware. Polygraph studies supposedly reveal a core orientation.

This technique utilizes the physiological phenomenon of genital vasocongestion which occurs when an individual sees or hears stimuli found sexually arousing. Essentially, these responses are measured by placing a vaginal photoplethysmograph probe in a female's vagina or a penile strain gauge or volume-measuring device around a male's penis and recording the subject's responses to different stimuli. The visual stimuli might be slides, movies, or video depictions of nudes or frank sexual activities. To such stimuli reflexive blood flow responses occur (vasocongestion and/or erection) with greater deflections of the recording device interpreted to indicate greater erotic interest to the stimuli. Pupillary responses (Hess 1968, Hess and Polt 1960) and other physiological measures have also been used to this end. Genital vascular responses however, seem to be better known and more reliable.

While pupillary and genital responses are probably a valid reflection of erotic interest, the responses might also be to novelty, shock, or something else. Nevertheless, practiced test givers can most usually differentiate the responses of erotic interest from other causes. Many studies have documented the heuristic and practical value of such measures.

This technique has been found valuable in differentiating those who find homosexual stimuli appealing from those who find heterosexual stimuli appealing, and vice versa, those who find homosexual or heterosexual stimuli unappealing.

In this area, where the work of many might be cited, e.g., Abel et al. (1975), Conrad and Wincze (1976), Mavisskalian et al. (1975), McConaghy (1967, 1978), Zuckerman (1971), and the work of Freund (1963, 1974, 1982, 1984, 1989) is classic. Basically Freund, in summarizing his years of experience (personal communication), feels that individuals, males or females, are best considered either gynephilic (attracted/aroused by females) or androphilic (attracted/aroused by males) rather than homosexual or heterosexual. His many investigations in this area lead him to conclude that, while individuals may engage in sexual activity with either males or females or both, very few actually show reflexive responses to both. His basic emphasis is in keeping clear the distinction between what arouses individuals and what they do. These two features may or may not be in concert. From the data presented in Table 1, it is interesting to note that among individuals who consider themselves homosexuals, more claim bisexual attractions than engage in bisexual behavior. Why this is so remains an intriguing question.

Social Background and Sexual Orientation

WHAT CAUSES THIS androphilia or gynephilia? One thing we can say for certain: It is not a simple matter of rearing. Three types of studies illustrate this. The first focuses on an individual's upbringing and family constellation. The second looks at cross-cultural research, and the third inspects those cases, rare but not unknown, where individuals are reared socially opposite to their biology. As with the animal data, due to space restrictions, calling attention to a few salient studies will have to suffice.

Upbringing and Sexual Rearing

TWO TYPES OF studies are important here. The first I will call "watching the children" and the second I will call "watching the family." The work of Green (1987) typifies the first type of study. Green followed prepubescent boys with obvious effeminate behavior (N=66) and boys who were masculine (N=56) for fifteen years, to see how they would develop. In U.S. culture being a "sissy" is socially difficult and stigmatized. Formal and informal forces are usually marshaled against the practice. How the boys would react to family, society, and establishment was the subject of the investigation. Of the families involved with the "sissy" boys, most tried on their own to discourage the effeminate behavior, and a minority of the parents even entered their sons into a formal treatment program. Nevertheless, the study found that, when interviewed as adults, out of "two-thirds of the original group of 'feminine' boys reveal that three-fourths of them are homosexually or bisexually oriented. By contrast, only one of the two-thirds of the previously 'masculine' boys is homosexually or bisexually oriented."

The second type of study is typified by the work of Bell, Weinberg, and Hammersmith (1981) in the United States and Siegelman (1981) in Great Britain. These investigators looked for features in the family constellation and background of adult heterosexuals, homosexuals, and bisexuals. Their basic finding was that no common parameter of family or upbringing could be linked causally to sexual orientation. These workers on both sides of the Atlantic basically concluded they could find no correlation between any aspect of an individual's childhood or adolescent experiences and their homosexual or bisexual activities. Most homosexuals are reared as heterosexuals in apparently conventional households.

Bell, Weinberg, and Hammersmith (1981) cautiously conclude: "Exclusive homosexuality seemed to be something that was firmly established by the end of adolescence and relatively impervious to change or modification by outside influences. For the bisexuals, by contrast, a homosexual preference seemed to emerge later and to be more tied to learning and social experiences." (p. 211) and "*our findings are not inconsistent with what one would expect to find if, indeed, there were a biological basis for sexual preference*" (p. 216; emphasis in original).

A study combining features of both types of research is also instructive. Mandel et al. (1980, 1979) followed the development of boys raised in households where the parental influence was openly lesbian. They concluded: "analysis of the children's data has not revealed any sexual identity conflict or homosexual interest. Relationships with fathers and other males do not differ significantly [from that of boys reared in heterosexually parented families]." In summarizing results on both boys and girls these authors state: there is "no evidence of gender conflict or poor peer relations" for samples of children reared by lesbian mothers (Hotvedt and Mandel 1982). Similar work has been done studying boys who grow up in households parented by openly gay males. These boys, when adult, like those brought up in lesbian households, also were heterosexually oriented without conflict or homosexual interest (Green 1978). Also, neither homosexuals nor heterosexuals perceived their parent's personalities differently (Newcomb 1985).

Cross-Cultural Studies

AGAIN, ONLY A FEW of the studies appropriate here will be mentioned. Three very different types will serve as examples. Whitam and Mathy (1986) studied, in detail, homosexuality in four different cultures: Brazil, Guatemala, the Philippines, and the United States. Across these quite diverse societies these sociologists found many similarities in how homosexual lifestyles were manifest. Examples of such behaviors included preferences in occupational interests, to involvement in entertainment and the arts, to cross-dressing, and use of their respective languages in effeminate ways. These researchers concluded that the similarities were not culturally instituted but were more likely the result of inherent biological tendencies manifest despite acceptance or rejection by the community. Whitam and Mathy conclude: "The view which emerges from cross-cultural research is that sexual orientation is not highly subject to redefinition by any particular social structural arrangement" (p. 31).

The well known work by Herdt (1981) and Stoller and Herdt (1985) is the second example of this group of studies. These researchers documented a New Guinea culture, the Sambia, where homosexual behavior is taught, encouraged, and institutionalized as a way to transfer masculinity from adults to adolescents; the young boys fellate the adult men to obtain there semen. Moreover, females' bodies are presented as not only unattractive and to be avoided, but poisonously dangerous. Nevertheless, these boys, upon reaching adulthood choose females as regular sexual partners, and are almost always heterosexual. Neither youths nor men report impulses to suck penises and they do not ever engage in anal intercourse.

Schiefenhovel (1990) reports on a similar New Guinea culture, the Kaluli, in which anal intercourse is used to transmit the masculinity-inducing semen between older men and younger boys. He too stresses that heterosexual, not homosexual or bisexual, behavior is the preferred and exclusive outlet for these males when they mature. And this is obtained, despite a severe shortage of adult women due to female infanticide.

A set of studies provide the third type of cross-cultural evidence supporting an inherent sexual orientation independent of upbringing. These are the reports from the Dominican Republic by Imperato-McGinley and colleagues (Imperato-McGinley, Guerrero, and Gautier 1974; Imperato-McGinley and Peterson 1976; Imperato-McGinley et al. 1979). These investigators found a population in which, due to a genetic defect, males were born without penises. They were assumed to be girls and raised accordingly, but at puberty they started to develop penises and respond to their own endogenous male hormones. Despite their rearing, all the boys rebelled against their female status and assumed male identities and life patterns. Occasionally, these studies have been criticized (e.g., Gooren et al. 1990) by calling attention to the fact that, at least for the last twenty years or so, this phenomenon has been understood by the natives in the population and the children have been reared appropriately from birth. Indeed that is true. However, prior to the 1970s this was not so and the sex role switch referred to above occurred before the problem was identified. In those earlier days, the boys were inadvertently and unambiguously reared as girls and then, on their own, switched to live as males.

Cross-Sex Rearing

THERE ARE NOW KNOWN to me three instances, two sets of male twins and one singleton, in which an individual was reared as a female, with surgery and endocrine treatment to alter the biology to facilitate the transformation. The first case involved a set of twins extensively reported upon in the literature (Diamond 1982; Money and Ehrhardt 1972). In this case, as a result of a surgical accident during circumcision, an unambiguously male child had his penis ablated. Believing that gender identity would be based upon the sex of rearing, the decision was made to rear this individual as a female (Money and Ehrhardt 1972). Originally, it was reported that the induced transition was a success (Money 1973; Money and Tucker 1975).

It is now known, more than fifteen years later, that despite subsequent surgical orchidectomy and treatment with female hormones, this individual never accepted the female status or role as claimed by the early investigators (Diamond 1982). Prior to puberty, the twin, without ever being told of his previous history, rebelled against the imposition of a female status. The twin, at his own request, wanted to live as a male.

It is now known that, at eighteen years of age, this individual, who was raised as a girl, sought and had phalloplastic and scrotal reconstruction surgery. He now, at the age of twenty-eight, lives as a male, and seeks females as sexual partners. His adjustment is not without its difficulties, but, to him, seems preferable to imposed life as a female.

The second set of identical twins involves two six-year-old Samoan children who were brought to my attention. It seems that one was causing a great deal of disorder at school. The "female" of this twin set was acting rowdy and picking fights, not only with female classmates but also males. The child's history revealed that, unbeknownst to him to that date, ambiguous genitalia at birth had prompted the surgeons then in attendance to reassign him as a female. With appropriate castration and hormonal follow-up, they convinced the parents to rear the child as a girl.

Despite the rearing as a female, even at this young age, the child rebelled against wearing girls' clothes and following the parents' and teachers' admonitions to "act like a girl." The twin's typical play patterns and demeanor were typical for a six-year-old rambunctious boy and such that the brother, in discussion with me, often slipped into using the male pronoun while referring to his twin; e.g., "*He*, I mean *she*, swims better than me." Asked to draw a child, the misassigned twin drew an ambiguous figure he identified as male. The child spontaneously expressed the desire to grow up as a boy.

The third case is similar. In the summer of 1990, I was called to review the behavior and condition of a four-year-old child. Here again, the history revealed that due to ambiguous genitalia at birth, the decision had been made to reassign the boy as a girl. The decision was followed with appropriate castration and hormonal therapy and the advice to rear the child as a girl. In consultation with Dr. Richard Green of U.C.L.A., it became apparent that by the age of four this individual was exhibiting marked boyish behavior sufficient to disturb the parents and attending professionals. The child was not easily accepting the female role. The fixedness of behavior patterns along male lines, and aversion to the female role, were strong despite the contrary upbringing.

In these last two instances, the individuals were too young to express erotic interest in a sexual partner. I predict in these cases, as I did in regard to the first twin mentioned above (Diamond 1976/77, 1978, 1979) that despite being reared as girls, they will be gynephilic (Diamond 1982). Despite the writings of some on the power of upbringing, role modeling, and learning, *there is no known case anywhere in which an otherwise normal individual has accepted rearing or life status in an imposed role of the sex opposite to that of his or her natural genetic and endocrine history.* The removal of penis and testes and imposition of a female rearing has never proven sufficient to overcome the inherent bias of the normal male nervous system.

Genetic Studies

PERHAPS THE STRONGEST evidence that sexual orientation has a biological basis involves genetic studies of human families and twins. In the middle of this century, research was done by F. J. Kallman (1952a, 1952b, 1963). Kallman studied forty monozygotic and forty-five dizygotic male twin pairs in which at least one of the co-twins, at the onset of the study, admitted to homosexual behavior. Among this sample

Kallman reported 100% of the monozygotic concordant for homosexuality. The dizygotic twins were seen essentially similar to the general male population. Although others found similar genetic components to sexual orientation, e.g. Schlegel (1962), these works were not accepted by many because they did not jibe with the societal preferences of the times. The mood of the 1950s and 1960s preferred to have human behavior a matter of social construction or free will rather than biological predisposition.

Kallman (1952a, 1952b) also reported finding that if one member of a monozygotic twin pair of brothers rated Kinsey=5 or 6, then the chance that his brother also rated K=5 or K=6 was better than 90%. He reported that if the brothers differed in concordance it was usually within one or two points on the Kinsey scale. The fact that Kallman's numbers seemed to come out so cleanly also encouraged skepticism. Several studies soon followed which reported monozygotic twins not concordant for homosexuality (Green and Stoller 1971; Klintworth 1962; Ranier et al. 1960), and theories which held to a genetic component to homosexuality lost support.

That situation essentially held until the 1980s. The work of Pillard and colleagues (Pillard, Poumadere, and Carretta 1982; Pillard and Weinrich 1986), and of myself with Whitam (1987), Whitam and Dannemiller (1987), and Whitam and Vacha (1988) began to reintroduce evidence supporting a major genetic component to sexual orientation.

Pillard and colleagues studied families and inquired of the sexual orientation of the male and female siblings in some 100 male and 86 female index families (Pillard, Poumadere, and Carretta 1982; Pillard and Weinrich 1986; Weinrich 1987). The index families were chosen for having a known heterosexual or homosexual adult. The brothers and sisters of these index individuals were interviewed or surveyed by mailed questionnaire. Their basic finding is that among brothers, if a family contained one index son who was homosexual, between 20 and 25% of the brothers would also be gay. If the index brother was heterosexual, the chance of other brothers being homosexual was only about 4 to 6%. They did not find any significant familial component to homosexuality among sisters. The data from cases where homosexual females were the index cases is still under review (Weinrich 1987). Eckert and colleagues (Eckert et al. 1986) reported similar findings even though they studied six pairs of monozygotic twins in which at least one member of each pair was homosexually active. They also found that the two male pairs were more or less concordant for homosexuality while the four female pairs were not.

It is interesting to also extract from the data offered by one of these study authors (Weinrich 1987). Weinrich reports that only 10 bisexuals were identified from the total study population of 178 men, 5 to 6% of the population. This is far fewer than would have been predicted from the Kinsey data but is in keeping with the later studies referred to in Table 1 and discussed above.

Some years ago, Frederick Whitam and I began to investigate the concordance of homosexuality and heterosexuality among twins. We reported briefly on our initial findings (Diamond and Whitam 1987a; Diamond, Whitam, and Dannemiller 1987b; Whitam, Diamond, and Vacha 1988) and our study is ongoing. By advertising in gay magazines and newspapers and by word of mouth, we sought twins of whom at least one was homosexual. We indicated we were interested in the twin set whether or not they were identical or fraternal and whether or not the second twin was also gay.

Table 2
HOMOSEXUAL TWIN STUDY
DIAMOND, WHITAM, AND DANNEMILLER

Totals

N=18 MZ pairs + 12 DZ pairs= 30 pairs= 60 men

Concordance for homosexual behvaior

MZ = 13/18 = 72%
DZ = 4–6/12 = 33–50%
All = 17–19/30 = 57–63%

	N	% of all 0–6	% of 3–6
K= 0	11	18%	
K= 3–4	2?	3%	4%
K= 5	13	22%	27%
K= 6	34	57%	69%

Among our initial respondents of 10 sets of monozygotic twin brothers we found 8 sets concordant for homosexuality. Of the 10 index twins where one rated a K=5 or K=6, 8 of the brothers also rated K=5 or K=6. Among 9 sets of dizygotic brothers, with most conservative analysis, we found 3 sets concordant. Now with 30 pairs of twins in our sample, 18 monozygotes and 12 dizygotes, our findings remain similar. There is a 72% concordance for homosexuality among one-egg twins and 33–50% concordance for homosexuality among our two-egg twins. Considering all our twins together (Tables 2 and 3), regardless of zygosity, there is approximately 60% concordance (Diamond, Whitam, and Dannemiller, in preparation). Our data for monozygotic twins are not as strong as that reported by Kallman (1952), but both studies find strong concordance for homosexuality. On the other hand, our findings for dizygotic twins are stronger than his. Concordance among our two-egg twins is in keeping with the 20–25% concordance reported for nontwin brothers by Pillard and colleagues (Pillard, Poumadere, and Carretta 1982; Pillard and Weinrich 1986). This is appropriate since two-egg twins have gene sets similar to regular brothers.

Of particular interest in looking at bisexuality is our finding, similar to those by Kallman, that when the brothers were concordant for sexual orientation, they were usually so within one rating on the Kinsey scale. For instance, a brother with a rating of K=6 would often be found to have a brother also rating K=6 or K=5. In our findings, when concordance was not found, however, the nonconcordant brother was most often seen with behavior rating K=0. In other words, homosexual brothers either have equally homosexual or heterosexual brothers rather than bisexual ones. Brothers exhibiting K=5 or K=6 behavior (Table 3) rarely have a brother with a rating of K=2 to K=4 (Diamond, Whitam, and Dannemiller, in preparation).

	Monozy		Dizy	
Table 3 HOMOSEXUAL TWIN STUDY DIAMOND, WHITAM, AND DANNEMILLER				
Twin	Index	Brother	Index	Brother
1	6	6	6	0
2	6	0	6	0
3	6	5	6	3–5
4	6	6	6	6
5	5	6	5	0
6	6	6	6	3–6
7	6	6	5	6
8	6	0	6	0
9	6	5	6	6
10	6	5	6	6
11	6	0	6	0
12	6	0	6	0
13	5	5		
14	6	0	Concordance = 33–50%	
15	5	5		
16	5	5		
17	6	6	Total males = 60	
18	6	6	Total pairs = 18 MZ = 12 DZ	
Concordance = 72%				
OVERALL CONCORDANCE = 57–63%				

Hirschfeld, early in our century, after reviewing his extensive records, reported: "Homosexuality runs in families in at least 35% of the cases." Homosexuality is congenital: "No outside influence, neither masturbation, nor impotence, nor yet disgust with the opposite sex, or seduction, or Binet's 'fortuitous shock,' can adequately explain the definite orientation of the homosexual impulse toward a certain sexual goal from the first awakening of the sexual impulse or from the first wet dreams."

Transsexualism

A FULL DISCUSSION of transsexualism here would be warranted if space permitted. Unfortunately this is not so. But a few comments are justified. I have personally and extensively interviewed more than 100 transsexuals over some thirty years in sex research. One of the more salient findings is that an individual's feeling about himself or herself, how he or she identifies, not as masculine or feminine, but as male or female, is independent of the sex of the erotic partner preferred. A transsexual believes he or she is of the opposite sex not because of the person's love or erotic object, but independent of it. Since sexual identity holds similarly so for heterosexuals and homosexuals as well, this should not be surprising. It reinforces the thesis that an individual's sexual preference or orientation is a separate level of sexuality and independent of his or her sexual or gender identity. One can be a transsexual who is heterosexually, homosexually, or ambisexually oriented. A more complete discussion of this is available (Diamond 1976/77, 1979, 1984, 1980). It might also be mentioned here that children brought up by transsexual parents do not develop as transsexuals (Green 1978).

Concluding Comments

SOME MATTERS SEEM simple. Among invertebrates, structural and behavioral bisexuality is quite common. And among fish and other lower vertebrates the combination is also not uncommon. For mammals, however, and humans in particular, the structural phenomenon is rare and the behavioral one a matter of definition.

Over the years certain terms have evolved in sexology to try to clarify such definitional problems. One speaks of *technical* virgins (they have done everything but . . .), of *core* gender identity (the inner voice which, independent of culture and rearing, says "I am a male" or "I am a female"), and also of *primary* or *true* bisexuality.

One can have sex with an erotically unarousing and unattractive partner for a nonsexual reason. We have seen this demonstrated among natives of New Guinea but people of all cultures exhibit sexual behaviors for nonerotic reasons in different circumstances and with different motives. One can of course accept that having sex without erotic interest in the sex of the partner may be another type of bisexuality. But the *primary* bisexual, or ambisexual, is one who is erotically *aroused psychologically* by both males and females, not necessarily one who will have sex with both males and females without being aroused by both.

Sometimes the distinction is made between *primary* and *secondary* homosexuality. The former are individuals oriented from the onset of their erotic inclinations, and the latter come to their homosexual interest after an initial and extensive heterosexual period or where the sexual behavior is serving nonerotic needs. Comparably, one might speak of primary or secondary bisexuality. In addition to "primary and secondary" terminology, "true" and "pseudo" or "false" are terms which are also used. In this vein it is possible to have true and pseudo or primary and secondary heterosexuality (feigned heterosexual activity by a primary homosexual) but that is rarely considered. Primary heterosexuality is most common, primary homosexuality less so, and primary bisexuality least common.

To be sure, both types of individuals (and more) exist. As Kinsey et al. (1948) have said: "the world is not to be divided into sheep and goats. Not all things are black nor all things white . . . nature rarely deals in discrete categories." The number or percentage of any group in the human population is not clearly known. The more recent evidence shows, however, that primary ambisexuality—sex with both males and females prompted by erotic arousal—is relatively rare. When it exists, while it is much less common than heterosexuality or homosexuality, it is nevertheless, no doubt, the result of the same biological biases which determine either distinct androphilic or gynephilic arousal.

Unlike those individuals in which bias to one arousal pattern predominates, however, the neural centers or programs organizing sexual object choice in the case of bisexuals have been sensitized to both. The more frequent displays of ambisexual behavior are, however, much more a response to social and interpersonal forces than manifest in genital interactions.

The strongest evidence of some biological underpinning to an individual's sexual object choice/partner preference comes from several areas. These were mentioned above: surveys which look for correlations and cause and effect, clinical findings, cross-cultural studies, physiological response research, transsexual cases, family genealogies, and twin studies.[6, 7] The genetic studies are firmly believed to be the most convincing, and along with the papers already mentioned many others exist (Puterbaugh 1990).[8, 9]

Having a biological underpinning doesn't mean these behaviors cannot be shaped by experience and learning. Studies from many disciplines make it clear that bisexual, homosexual, and heterosexual behaviors can be modified to conform to individual situations, social stereotypes, and mores. On the other hand, many individuals manifest ambisexual and homosexual activities against social dictates to the extent they might even put their social life if not their actual physical life in jeopardy. These behaviors, as with heterosexual ones, are often expressed as compulsive and self-generating and arising from within.

Sexual orientation, as are all other evolutionarily crucial behaviors such as mate selection, is a biologically organized phenomenon with the capacity for social modification and learning. A recent study (Ernulf et al. 1989) has found that a majority of self-identified homosexuals, as do heterosexuals, think their orientation is inherent and constitutional rather than learned or imposed. And they prefer to think of matters this way.

But so saying does not yet mean we have all the answers to the questions of sexual orientation or partner preference. It only means we have a better idea of where we might be more productive in looking for answers. And we must recognize that dealing with humans means we can expect some of the more complicated scenarios that nature can provide.

In ways we do not yet understand, not all sibs of homosexual index individuals show homosexuality even among monozygotic twins. There is obviously more than one set of genes involved. And they apparently interact with genes of other traits and social forces to organize how the final behaviors will be manifest. And why, among monozygotic twin brothers who are not concordant for homosexuality, do only a minority show bisexual behavior whilst the majority are heterosexual (K=0) instead? Intuitively one might expect a higher ratio of bisexuals to heterosexuals. Indeed, it may be that bisexuality is related to homosexuality and heterosexuality but quite different in its developmental pattern. And equally fascinating for us to know is how and why some social situations at some times seem capable of modifying these inherent biases yet seem ineffectual at other times and situations.

As first proposed some twenty-five years ago (Diamond 1965) and many times since, the available evidence indicates manifest sexual orientation is most probably the result of interacting inherent biological forces meshing with environmental and social pressures. The biology sets a predisposition, a bias, with which the individual interacts with his or her surroundings (Diamond 1965, 1976/77, 1978, 1979, 1980, 1982, 1984, 1987a, 1987b; Diamond and Karlen 1980). And particular stages or "critical periods" in development seem more significant than others in organizing these behaviors. Others, even though they once thought otherwise, e.g., Money (1963), are now coming to these same conclusions (Money 1988).

The biased predisposition is believed to lead to a cognitive frame or psychic symbolism which provides an internal standard against which possible behavior choices will be compared. This will hold for considerations of both sexual identity and partner preferences.[10] In identity, the only categories conceivable are male and female, but in object/partner choice a spectrum is realizable (Diamond 1976/77, 1979). This spectrum not only can encompass degrees of gynephilia or androphilia, which translate into homosexuality, bisexuality, and heterosexuality, but other attributes as well. Genetics underpins not only fixedness but flexibility as well. Genetic flexibility is no doubt related to the nonconcordance seen in female sibs of index homosexuals.

The internally imposed fixedness may or may not be in keeping with social prejudices. All individuals, going through life, are constantly forced to temper internal desires with external forces. Legal restrictions and social taboos or other motives can move an individual to exhibit behaviors and form sexual and emotional attachments to partners he or she would not otherwise desire, or refrain from relationships that would be preferred. But given a free pick and opportunity, an individual's choice will be manifest (Diamond 1978, 1979). Our biological heritage has given most humans the flexibility to adjust.

It is common in biological studies of behavior and structure to ask how this is adaptive for the species. What are the evolutionary origins or consequences of this feature? This is not unlike a sociologist asking what are the societal origins or consequences for any particular social practice. And if homosexuality or bisexuality has a biological basis, how has it evolved and is it adaptive? Many have, indeed, specifically considered evolutionary aspects of homosexuality from a biological perspective, e.g., Hutchinson (1959), Kirsch and Rodman (1982), Trivers (1971, 1974), and Wilson (1975). Their conclusions are divergent and speculative, and basically run to an advantage by balanced polymorphism where a combination of alleles for homosexuality, and related to homosexuality, provide an increased fitness (Hutchinson 1959) to a theory that clashes between parent and child may make it advantageous for the parents' ability to reproduce and transmit their genes if the offspring does not (Trivers 1974). While interesting to consider, anything said here is obviously speculative.

I would suggest, however, that humans, while having biases in their erotic preferences, are immensely flexible, and that bisexuality and homosexuality represent adaptive mechanisms for satisfying erotic and nonerotic needs and relieving sexual tension in a manner different from but analogous to heterosexuality. And nonheterosexual activities persist since they are no threat to the survival of the species. There are sufficient numbers of humans reproducing with many bisexuals and homosexuals among them.

A last word: For some persons the idea that sexual orientation is biologically biased toward heterosexuality or homosexuality and predisposed is threatening (see Ernulf et al. 1989). Some have expressed consternation that if the developmental biological forces for sexual orientation are known (or even suspected), some governmental, religious, medical, or social agency might use the knowledge to force conformity to a dictated ideal or otherwise modify a potential homosexual outcome, e.g., De Cecco (1987, 1990), Gagnon (1987), Schmidt (1984), Sigusch et al. (1982); see also Dörner (1983). Actually, the argument can more forcefully be made that knowing the social construction of sexual orientation might more easily lead to such a coercion and social manipulation. Even believing that it is social construction that leads to such is probably more dangerous since even despots know it is easier to modify the social arena than the biological. Unfortunately, groups who have the end of homosexuality or ambisexuality as their goal, I fear, need no scientific justification for their malignant ends. They are sufficient in their own ignorance and need no factual information to further their aims. Ignorance and prejudice, more than knowledge and acceptance, will work against humanity. Indeed, the truth is more likely than not to benefit us all.

Endnotes

1 This paper was scheduled as a keynote address as a memorial to Magnus Hirschfeld (1868–1935).

2. The paper, given on July 14, 1990, is dedicated to my daughter Leah Naomi Diamond and her husband, Gerd Harnisch, on the occasion of their wedding in Berlin on July 6, 1990, and to my wife, Grace Hope, deceased in 1989, whose birthday was July 15.

3. The term *sex* is used when referring to the biological characteristic of male or female. The term *gender* is only appropriate in a social context for humans. In this vein, a male living as a woman would have male sex and female gender.

4. The terms *malelike* and *femalelike* are not arbitrary evaluations. In the rat, as in all nonhuman mammalian species of which we know, the two sexes are quite distinct in their mating patterns. Under normal situations males rarely lordose and females rarely mount.

5. The research by Humphreys (1970) is probably the best-known study documenting that many married men engage in homosexual activities while maintaining heterosexual lifestyles and identities.

6. I have avoided dealing with much of the endocrinological evidence supporting a biological basis of sexual orientation. This is due both to lack of space and also to the controversies and unsettled issues which surround such studies. I think the bulk of evidence does indicate inherent male-female differences in the sensitivity of the CNS to hormonal stimuli, and think that these responses are linked to heterosexual and homosexual indexes. The interested reader, however, can obtain both sides of the argument from the current work of Dörner (1988), Gladue (1990), Gooren et al. (1990), and Meyer-Bahlburg (1984).

7. I must repeat that the evidence for most of these conclusions is derived mainly from studies of males. This is an unfortunate reflection of the present state of research.

There is some evidence that the situation in females is different (Pillard and Weinrich 1986; Eckert et al., 1986; Weinrich 1987). More ongoing research on females is needed. Whitam and I are presently replicating our study of male twins with females.

8. The importance of genetics also holds true for an individual's view of himself or herself as male or female, e.g., his or her sexual identity (Diamond 1965, 1977, 1978, 1979, 1982).

9. Several months after the presentation of this paper, a publication appeared (Gooren et al. 1990) with the title "Biological Determinants of Sexual Orientation." Several of the points covered are dealt with in the present paper with differing interpretations. The author did not at all touch on genetic evidence, which is the strongest argument for a biological bias to orientation.

10. I have previously proposed that an individual's sexual profile has five basic levels. *Sexual identity*, the core sense of being male or female, and *sexual object choice/partner preference* are two of the five. The other three are *reproduction, patterns*, and *mechanisms* (Diamond 1976, 1979, 1980, 1984). These are usually in concert but can assort independently

References

Abel, G. G., D. H. Barlow, E. B. Blanchard, and M. Mavissakalian. 1975. Measurement of sexual arousal in male homosexuals: the effects of instructions and stimulus modality. *Arch. Sex. Behav.* 4: 623–29.

Armstrong, C. N. 1964. Intersexuality in man. In *Intersexuality in Vertebrates Including Man*, ed. C. N. Armstrong and A. J. Marshall. 349–93. London: Academic Press.

Baum, M. J. 1979. Differentiation of coital behavior in mammals—a comparative analysis. *Neurosci. Biobeh. Rev.* 3: 265–84.

Bell, Alan P., and Martin S. Weinberg. 1978. *Homosexualities—A study of Diversity among Men and Women*. New York: Simon and Schuster.

Bell, Alan P., Martin S. Weinberg, and Sue K. Hammersmith. 1981. *Sexual Preference—Its Development in Men and Women*. Bloomington: Alfred C. Kinsey Institute of Sex Research.

Blumstein, Philip, and Pepper Schwartz. 1972.

———. 1977. Bisexuality: Some social psychological issues. *J. Soc. Issues.* 33 (2): 30–45.

Booth, William. 1989. U.S. probe meets resistance. *Science* 244 (April 28): 419.

Brusca, Richard C., and Gary J. Brusca. 1990. *Invertebrates*. Sunderland, Mass.: Sinauer Assoc.

Conover, M. R., D. E. Miller, and G. L. Hunt Jr. 1979. Female–female pairs and other unusual reproductive associations in ring-billed and California gulls. *Auk* 96: 6–9.

Conrad, S. R., and J. P. Wincze. 1976. Orgasmic reconditioning: a controlled study of its effects upon the sexual arousal and behavior of adult male homosexuals. *Beh. Ther.* 7: 155–66.

de Waal, Frans. 1990. Sociosexual behavior used for tension regulation in all age and sex combinations among Bonobos. In *Pedophilia—Biosocial Dimensions*, ed. J. R. Feierman. 378–93. New York: Springer–Verlag.

De Cecco, John P. 1987. Homosexuality's brief recovery: pertaining to sex research. *J. Sex Res.* 23 (1): 106–29.

———. 1990. Homosexuality: nature, nurture, or homophobia? Third International Berlin conference of Sexology. 11 July. Humbolt University, Berlin.

Demski, Leo S. 1987. Diversity in reproductive patterns and behavior in teleost fishes. In *Psychobiology of Reproductive Behavior: An Evolutionary Perspective*, ed. D. Crew. 1–28. Englewood Cliffs, N. J.: Prentice Hall.

Diamond, Milton. 1965. A critical evaluation of the ontogeny of human sexual behavior. *Quart. Rev. Biol.* 40: 147–75.

————. 1968. *Genetic-endocrine interaction and human psychosexuality*. In *Perspectives in Reproduction and Sexual Behavior*, ed. M. Diamond. 417-43. Bloomington: Indiana University Press.

————. 1976/77. Human sexual development: Biological foundations for social development. In *Human Sexuality in Four Perspectives*, ed. F. A. Beach. 22–61. Baltimore: The Johns Hopkins Press.

————. 1978. Sexual identity and sex roles. *Humanist* (March/April): 16–19.

————. 1979. Sexual identity and sex roles. In *The Frontiers of Sex Research*, ed. V. Bullough. 33–56. Buffalo, N.Y.: Prometheus.

————. 1980. The biosocial evolution of human sexuality. *Behav. Brain Sci.* 3 (2): 184–86.

————. 1982. Sexual identity, monozygotic twins reared in discordant sex roles and a BBC follow-up. *Arch. Sex. Behav.* 11 (2): 181–85.

————. 1984. *Sexwatching: The World of Sexual Behavior*. London: Macdonald Co. Ltd.

Diamond, M., and A. Karlen. 1980. *Sexual Decisions*. Boston: Little, Brown.

Diamond, M., Alfonso Llacuna, and Calvin Wong. 1973. Sex behavior after neonatal progesterone, testosterone, estrogen, or antiandrogens. *Horm. Behav.* 4 (1–2): 73–88.

Diamond, M., Roy Ohye, and Jesse Wells. In Preparation. AIDS KAP in Hawaii. *AIDS Ed. Prev.*

Diamond, M., and Frederick L. Whitam. 1987[a]. Sexuality of male twins when one or both are homosexual. Abstract, 8th World Congress for Sexology, June 17–21. Heidelberg.

Diamond, M., F. L. Whitam, and J. E. Dannemiller. 1987[b]. Homosexuality in male twins. Abstract, 13th Anuual Meeting of the International Academy of Sex Research, June 21–25, 1987. Tutzing.

————. In Preparation. Homosexuality among male twins.

Dixon, B. W., E. J. Streiff, and A. H. Brunswasser. 1991. Pilot study of a household survey to determine HIV seproprevalence. *MMWR* 40 (1): 1–5.

Dörner, G. 1983. Letter to the editor. *Arch. Sex. Behav.* 12 (6): 577–82.

————. 1988. Neuroendocrine response to estrogen and brain differentiation in heterosexuals, homosexuals, and transsexuals. *Arch. Sex. Behav.* 17: 57–75.

Eckert, Elke, Thomas Bouchard, Joseph Bohlen, and Leonard Heston. 1986. Homosexuality in monozygotic twins reared apart. *Brit. J. Psychiat.* 148: 421–25.

Ernulf, Kurt, Sune Innala, and Frederick Whitam. 1989. Biological explanation, psychological explanation, and tolerence of homosexuals: A cross-national analysis of beliefs and attitudes. *Psych. Rep.* 65: 1003–10.

Feder, H. H. 1981. Perinatal hormones and their role in the development of sexually dimorphic behaviors. In *Neuroendocrinology of Reproduction*, ed. N. T. Adler. 127–58. New York: Plenum Press.

Fieshelson, L. 1975. Ecology and physiology of sex reversal in *Anthias squamipinnis* (Peters), *(Teleostei: Anthiidae)*. In *Intersexuality in the Animal Kingdom*, ed. R. Reinboth. 284–94. New York: Springer-Verlag.

Freund, Kurt. 1963. A laboratory method for diagnosing predominance of homo- and hetero-erotic interest in the male. *Beh. Res. Ther.* 1 (1): 85–93.

————. 1974. *Male Homosexuality: an Analysis of the Pattern.* In *Understanding Homosexuality*, ed. J. A. Loraine. New York: Elsevier.

Freund, Kurt, Gerald Heasman, I. G. Racansky, and Graham Glancy. 1984. Pedophilia and heterosexuality vs. homosexuality. *J. Sex Marit. Ther.* 10 (3): 193–200.

Freund, Kurt, Hal Scher, Sam Chan, and Mark Ben-Aron. 1982. Experimental analysis of pedophilia. *Behav. Res. Ther.* 20: 105–12.

Freund, Kurt, Robin Watsons, and Douglas Rienzo. 1989. Heterosexuality, homosexuality, and erotic age preference. *J. Sex Res.* 26 (1): 107–17.

Gagnon, John H. 1987. Science and the politics of pathology. *J. Sex Res.* 23 (1): 120–23.

Gebhard, P. H. 1972. Incidence of overt homosexuality in the United States and Western Europe. In *NIMH Task Force on Homosexuality: Final Report and Background Papers*, ed. J. M. Liningood. 22–29. Rockville, MD: National Institute of Mental Health.

Gladue, Brian. 1990. Hormones and neuroendocrine factors in atypical human sexual behavior. In *Pedophilia—Biosocial Dimensions*, ed. J. R. Feierman. 274–98. New York: Springer–Verlag.

Gooren, Louis, Eric Fliers, and Keith Courtney. 1990. Biological determinants of sexual orientation. In *Annual Review of Sex Research*, ed. J. Bancroft. 175–96. Lake Mills, Iowa: The Society for the Scientific Study of Sex.

Green, Richard. 1978. Sexual identity of 37 children raised by homosexuals or transsexual parents. *Psychiatry* 135 (6): 692–97.

————. 1987. *The "Sissy Boy Syndrome" and the Development of Homosexuality.* New Haven and London: Yale University Press.

Green, Richard, and Robert J. Stoller. 1971. Two monozygotic (identical) twin pairs discordant for homosexuality. *Arch. Sex Behav.* 1 (4): 321–27.

Haeberle, Erwin. 1978. *The Sex Atlas.* New York: The Seabury Press.

Harlow, Harry. 1961. Sexual behavior in the rhesus monkey. Conference: Univ. of Calif., Berkely.

Herdt, Gilbert H. 1981. *Guardians of the Flute: Idioms of Masculinity.* New York: McGraw Hill.

Hess, E. H. 1968. Pupillometric assessment. *Res. Psychother.* 3: 573–83.

Hess, E. H. and J. M. Polt. 1960. Pupil size as related to interest value of visual stimuli. *Science* 132: 349–50.

Hotvedt, Mary E., and Jane Barclay Mandel. 1982. Children of lesbian mothers, In *Homosexuality: Social, Psychological, and Biological Issues*, ed. W. Paul, J. D. Weinrich, C. Gonsiorek, and M. E. Hotvedt. 275–85. Beverly Hills: Sage Publications.

Humphreys, R. L. 1970. *Tearoom Trade: Impersonal Sex in Public Places.* Chicago: Aldine.

Hunt, G. L., Jr., and M. W. Hunt. 1977. Female–female pairing in western gulls. *(Larus occidentalis)* in Southern California. *Science* 196: 1466–67.

Hutchinson, G. E. 1959. A speculative consideration of certain possible forms of sexual selection in man. *Amer. Nat.* 93: 81–91.

Hyman, L. H. 1951. *The Invertebrates: Platyhelminthes and Rhynchocoela, the Acoelemate Bilateria.* New York: McGraw-Hill.

Imperato-McGinley, J., L. Guerrero, and T Gautier. 1974. Steroid 5a-reductase deficiency in man: an inherited form of pseudohermaphroditism. *Science* 186: 1213–15.

Imperato-McGinley, J., and R. E. Peterson. 1976. Male pseudohermaphroditism: the complexities of male phenotypic development. *Amer. J. Med.* 61: 251–72.

Imperato-McGinley, J., R. E. Peterson, T. Gautier, and E. Sturia. 1979. Androgen and evolution of male-gender identity among male pseudohermaphrodites with 5a-reductase deficiency. *New Eng. J. Med.* 300: 1233–37.

Kallman, F. J. 1952a. Twin and sibship study of overt male homosexuality. *Amer. J. Human Genet.* 4: 136–46.

————. 1952b. Comparative twin study on the genetic aspects of male homosexuality. *J. Nerv. Ment. Dis.* 115: 283–98.

————. 1963. Genetic aspects of sex determination and sexual maturation potentials in man. In *Determinants of Human Sexual Behavior*, ed. G. Winokur. 5–18. Springfield: Charles C. Thomas.

Kinsey, Alfred, Wardell Pomeroy, and Clyde Martin. 1948. *Sexual Behavior in the Human Male*. Philadelphia and London: W. B. Saunders.

Kinsey, Alfred, Wardell Pomeroy, Clyde Martin, and Paul Gebhard. 1953. *Sexual Behavior in the Human Female*. Philadelphia and London: W. B. Saunders.

Kirsch, John A. W., and James Eric Rodman. 1982. Selection and sexuality: The Darwinian view of homosexuality. In *Homosexuality: Social, Psychological and Biological Issues*, ed. J. D. Weinrich, William Paul, John C. Gonsiorek, and Mary E. Hotvedt. 183–96. Beverly Hills: Sage Publications.

Klintworth, G. K. 1962. A pair of male monozygotic twins discordant for homosexuality. *J. Nerv. Ment. Dis.* 135: 113–16.

Lillie, F. R. 1917. The freemartin a study of the action of sex hormones in the foetal life of cattle. *J. Exper. Zool.* 23: 371.

Lorenz, Conrad. 1967. Personal communication.

Mandel, Jane Barclay, and Mary E. Hotvedt. 1980. Lesbians as parents. *Huisarts & Praktijk.* 4: 31–34.

Mandel, Jane B., Mary E. Hotvedt, and Richard Green. 1979. The lesbian parents comparison of heterosexual and homosexual mothers and their children. *Ann. Meet. Amer. Psychol. Assoc.*

Mavisskalian, M., E. B. Blanchard, G. G. Abel, and D. H. Barlow. 1975. Responses to complex erotic stimuli in homosexual and heterosexual males. *Brit. J. Psychiat.* 126: 252–57.

McConaghy, N. 1967. Penile volume changes to moving pictures of male and female nudes in heterosexual and homosexual males. *Behav. Res. Ther.* 5: 43–48.

————. 1978. Heterosexual experience, marital status, and orientation of homosexual males. *Arch. Sex. Behav.* 7: 575–81.

McEwen, B. S. 1983. Gonadal steroid influences on brain development and sexual differentiation. In *Reproductive Physiology IV International Review of Physiology*, ed. R. O. Greep. 99–145. Balitmore: University Park Press.

McWhirter, David P., and Andrew M. Mattison. 1984. *The Male Couple: How Relationships Develop*. Englewood Cliffs, N. J.: Prentice-Hall.

Meyer-Bahlburg, Heino F. L. 1984. Psychoendocrine research on sexual orientation—current status and future options. *Prog. Brain. Res.* 61: 367–90.

————. 1984. Psychoendocrine research and the societal status of homosexuals: a reply to De Cecco. *J. Sex. Res.* 23 (1): 114–20.

Money, John. 1963. Cytogenic and psychosexual incongruities with a note on space form blindness. *Amer. J. Psychiat.* 119: 820–27.

————. 1973. Prenatal hormones and postnatal socialization in gender identity differentiation. *Neb. Symp. Motivation.* 221–95.

————. 1988. *Gay, Straight, and In-Between*. New York: Oxford University Press.

Money, J., and A. Ehrhardt. 1972. *Man and Woman, Boy and Girl.* Baltimore: John Hopkins University Press.

Money, J. and P. Tucker. 1975. *Sexual Signatures: On Being a Man or Woman.* Boston: Little, Brown.

Najarian, H. H. 1976. *Sex Lives of Animals Without Backbones.* New York: Charles Scribner's Sons.

Newcomb, Michael D. 1985. The role of perceived relative parent personality in the development of heterosexuals, homosexuals, and transvestites. *Arch. Sex. Behav.* 14 (2): 147–64.

Overzier, C. 1963. *Intersexualtiy,* ed. C. Overzier. New York: Academic Press.

Phoenix, Charles H., R. W. Goy, A. A. Gerall, and W. C. Young. 1959. Organizing action of prenatally administered testosterone propionate on the tissues mediating mating behavior in the female guinea pig. *Endocrinology* 65: 369–82.

Phoenix, C. H., Robert W. Goy, and John A. Resko. 1968. *Psychosexual Differentiation as a Function of Androgenic Stimulation.* In *Perspectives in Reproduction and Sexual Behavior,* ed. M. Diamond. Bloomington: Indiana University Press.

Pillard, Richard, Jeanette Poumadere, and Ruth Carretta. 1982. A family study of sexual orientation. *Arch. Sex. Behav.* 11 (6): 511–20.

Pillard, Richard, and James Weinrich. 1986. Evidence of familial nature of male homosexuality. *Arch. Gen. Psychiat.* 43: 808–12.

Puterbaugh, Geoff. 1990. *Twins and Homosexuality: A Casebook,* ed. W. R. Dynes. Garland Gay and Lesbian Series. New York & London: Garland Publishing.

Ranier, J. D., A. Mesnikoff, L. C. Kolb, and A. Carr. 1960. Homosexuality and heterosexuality in identical twins. *Psychosom. Med.* 22: 250–59.

Ross, Robert, George Losey, and Milton Diamond. 1983. Sex change in a coral-reef fish: Dependence of stimulation and inhibition on relative size. *Science* 221: 574–75.

Rubin, Sylvia. 1983. How bisexuals face a hostile world. *San Francisco Chronicle,* 2 Sept. 1983.

Ryder, John P., and Patricia Lynn Somppi. 1979. Female–female pairing in ring-billed gulls. *Auk* 96: 1–5.

Sandfort, Theo, and G. Van Zessen. 1991. Sex and AIDS in the Netherlands. In preparation.

Schein, M.W. 1991. Personal communication.

Schiefenhovel, Wulf. 1990. *Ritualized Adult-Male/Adolescent-Male Sexual Behavior in Melanesia: An Anthropological and Ethological Perspective.* In *Pedophilia—Biosocial Dimensions,* ed. J. R. Feierman. 394–421. New York: Springer–Verlag.

Schlegel, W. S. 1962. Die konstitutionbiologischen Grundlagen der Homosexualitat. *Z. Menschl. Vererb. Konstitutionslehre* 36: 341–64.

Schmidt, G. 1984. Allies and persecutors: Science and medicine in the homosexuality issue. *J. Homosex.* 10: 127–40.

Schover, Leslie R., and Soren Buus Jensen. 1988. *Sexuality and Chronic Illness: A Comprehensive Approach.* New York: Guilford Press.

Shapiro, D. Y. 1979. Social behavior, group structure, and the control of sex reversal in hermaproditic fish. *Adv. Stud. Behav.* 10: 43–102.

Siegelman, Marvin. 1981. Parental Backgrounds of homosexual and heterosexual men: a cross-national replication. *Arch. Sex. Behav.* 10 (6): 505–13.

Sigusch, V., E. Schorsch, M. Dannecker, and G. Schmidt. 1982. Official statement by the German Society for Sex Research (Duetsche Gesellschaft für Sexualforschung e.V.) on the research of Prof. Dr. Günter Dörner on the subject of homosexuality. *Arch. Sex. Behav.* 11 (5): 445–49.

Stoller, Robert, and Gilbert Herdt. 1985. Theories of origins of male homosexuality. *Arch. Gen. Psych.* 42 (4): 399–404.

Terman, L. M. 1948. Sexual behavior in the human male: some comments and criticisms. *Psychol. Bull.* 45: 443–59.

Thresher. 1984. *Reproduction in Reef Fishes.* Neptune City, N. J.: T.F.H. Publications.

Trivers, R. L. 1971. The evolution of reciprocal altruism. *Quart. Rev. Biol.* 46 (4): 35–57.

———. 1974. Parent-offspring conflict. *Amer. Zool.* 14 : 249-64.

Weinberg, Martin S., and Colin J. Williams. 1974. *Male Homosexuals—Their Problems and Adapatations.* New York: Oxford University Press.

———. 1975. Gay baths and the social organization of impersonal sex. *Soc. Prob.* 23: 124–36.

Weinrich, James D. 1982. Is homosexuality biologically natural? In *Homosexuality: Social, Psychological, and Biological Issues,* ed. W. Paul, J. D. Weinrich. J. C. Gonsiorek, and M. E. Hotvedt. 197–208. Beverly Hills: Sage Publications.

———. 1987. *Sexual Landscapes: Why We Are What We Are, Why We Love Whom We Love.* New York: Charles Scribner's Sons.

Wellings, K., J. Field, A. M. Wadsworth, A. M. Johnson, R. M. Anderson, and S. A. Bradshaw. 1990. Sexual lifestyles under scrutiny. *Nature* 348 (22 November): 276–78.

Whalen, Richard E. 1968. Differentiation of the neural mechanisms which control gonadotropin secretion and sexual behavior. In *Perspectives in Reproduction and Sexual Behavior,* ed. M. Diamond. 303–40. Bloomington, Indiana: Indiana University Press.

Whitam, Frederick L., and R. M. Mathy. 1986. *Male Homosexuality in Four Societies: Brazil, Guatemala, the Phillipines, and the United States.* New York: Praeger.

Whitam, Frederick L., M. Diamond, and T. Vacha. 1988. *An Analysis of the Sexual Fantasies of Fraternal and Identical Male Homosexual Twins.* November 10–13.

Wilson, E. O. 1975. *Sociobiology: The New Synthesis.* Cambridge: Harvard University Press.

Yamagiwa, J. 1987. Intra- and intergroup interactions in an all-male group of Virunga mountain gorillas (Gorilla gorilla beringei). *Primates* 28: 1–30.

Zuckerman, M. 1971. Physiological measures of sexual arousal in the human male. *Psych. Bull.* 75: 297–329.

Bisexuality: A Sociological Perspective

John H. Gagnon, Cathy Stein Greenblat,
and Michael Kimmel

This paper is divided into two major parts, the first theoretical, the second empirical. The first part is itself twofold. We *first* attempt to deconstruct the conventional wisdom about "bisexuality," and *second,* propose a way of thinking about sexuality (indeed, all of social life) that takes into account that the ways in which scientists or intellectuals think about conduct and the conduct that is being thought about share a common and interactive terrain. Our goal in the theoretical segment of the paper is to offer a "temporary" or "local" theory of the variety of patterns of sexual conduct which are discussed in the second part of the paper (Geertz 1973, 1983). In the second part of the paper there is a discussion of some of the wide variety of the socially and culturally situated ways in which it is possible for persons to have sex with both men and women in the contemporary United States and the lack of fit between this variety of sociosexual practices with any unicausal or multicausal conception of "bisexuality."

We do this not because there is any particular pleasure in being a cultural or intellectual vandal, but because it is our view that the cultural constructions that we use to think about and to contain the sexual practices that are organized by the term "sexual object choice" or sexual orientation or sexual preference are profoundly coercive and profoundly muddled. If we simply substitute the term gender in each of these phrases, as in gender object choice or gender orientation and gender preference, it would provide a modicum of clarity about what it is that we choose, orient toward, or prefer in erotic relations (Gagnon 1988).

Sex with Both Women and Men as Ideology

THE CONTEMPORARY CONCEPTION of "bisexuality," here in quotes to indicate its equivocal status, is, like all scientific ideas, the result of a long process of historical and cultural construction and deconstruction. Its current status, like that of those terms that are its conceptual ancestors and which frame it like a pair of parentheses, homosexuality and heterosexuality, is the result of ongoing intellectual and sociocultural changes that have their roots in the hegemonic growth of medical, psychiatric, and sexological thought since the middle of the nineteenth century. Similarly, the collection of diverse and unlike sexual practices that we attempt to contain by uncritically applying the term bisexuality to them are the result of other social and cultural processes which are quite independent of the scientific conceptions of bisexuality.

To understand the contemporary status of the concept requires taking a few steps backward in time to try to historically and culturally situate not only bisexuality as an ideology and a practice, but "homosexuality" and "heterosexuality" as well. It is now a commonplace observation to point out that the term *homosexuality* emerged in the middle of the nineteenth century as part of the larger medicalization of the domain of the sexual (Weeks 1981). In a paraphrase of Foucault, this was one element in the medical-psychiatric occupation and reconstruction of a terrain of knowledge and practice that was previously part of the territory controlled by an alliance between the state, as embodied in the legal system, and religion, as embodied in dogma and institutional practices. This specific reconstruction was part of the general scientificization and secularization of all of social life in the nineteenth century (Foucault 1978, 1979). The "otherness" represented by the social practice of men who had sex with men and of women who had sex with women, the world of perverted biological or psychological development with a new nomenclature and practice that would reach its culmination in the diagnostic manuals of psychiatrists in the middle of the twentieth century (Bayer 1981).

The early and primitive social constructions of the unnatural or abnormal categories of the "homosexual" and "homosexuality" logically required the construction of its natural or normal opposite, the "heterosexual" or "heterosexuality" (Katz 1983; Gagnon 1992). While no one, at the time that these terms were invented, thought of themselves as heterosexuals or homosexuals, it is one of the signal successes of the medical profession that this terminology and the social practices that flow from such a dichotomy between the normal and the abnormal represent the dominant modes of discourse and practice about these matters at the present time.

Most contemporary "heterosexuals" rarely think of themselves as "heterosexuals," except in moments when they think about "homosexuals" or "homosexuality." Perhaps none conceive of the sex that they practice as a contingent domain of social practice called "heterosexuality." "Heterosexuals" simply act in a gendered sexual manner, without reflexivity, as if their gender preference in erotic relations were unproblematic. This is true despite the fact that it is clear that the "normality" of their sexual conduct is in part dependent on the abnormality of the sexual conduct of those whose have same-gender or mixed-gender sexual preferences or practices. The unproblematic or unmarked status of opposite-gender erotic preferences and the problematic or marked status or same-gender erotic prefences and practices in daily life and in science has resulted in a research program about the origins and practices of men who have sex with men and those women who have sex with women, but only a minuscule interest in the origins and practices of the majority category: persons who have sex with the opposite gender.

This massive positivist research program about homosexuality has obscured the fact that these polar categories, the heterosexual and the homosexual, are themselves based on a changing discourse and practice related to the larger set of social relations between women and men. The nineteenth century was a period in which the transformation of social life by the market, the factory, the city, and new forms of social stratification—in a shorthand phrase, the rise of hegemonic capitalism—included the transformation of all relations between women and men. Heterosexuality was the medical term which came to be fitted to the folk categories of correct sexuality that emerged in the new middle classes, folk categories that were themselves based on a newly constituted polarity (what feminists have identified as separate social spheres) between women and men. In the medicalized (and ultimately biologized and psychologized) language of gender, there emerged a newly defined dichotomy between masculinity or maleness and femininity or femaleness (Tavris 1992; Fausto Sterling 1985).

In this medicalized version of the sexual world, heterosexuality was the natural outcome of the sexual attraction between gendered opposites, homosexuality the unnatural outcome of the sexual attraction between gendered similars. Therefore, men who had sex with men were insufficiently masculine or excessively feminine, women who had sex with women were insufficiently feminine or excessively masculine. It is the conflation of these two dimensions, that of gender discourse and practice (the ideology and practice of social relations between the genders) and of gender preference in erotic relations (the ideology and practice of sexual relations between the genders) that has been the confounding element in thinking about sexuality for nearly a century.

It is this confusion between gender preferences in erotic relations and masculinity and femininity as they are constituted in gender definitions that resulted in Hirschfeld's invention of "intermediate sexual types" as a way to map "homosexuals" and "homosexuality" onto the gender continuum between completely masculine men and completely feminine women. It was a resistance to and acceptance of these typologies of gender and sexuality that led (not only in Germany) to a belief in and practice of a "classical homosexuality" in which pure masculine men would have sex with each other uncontaminated by femininity or the penetrations of the body celebrated in heterosexuality and effeminate homosexuality (Oosterhuis 1992).

Freud's observation, which is so often quoted today, represents the nineteenth-century culmination of this belief in the new dominance of gender in defining the normality of sexual relations:

> The most striking distinction between the erotic life of antiquity and our own no doubt lies in the fact that the ancients laid the stress on the instinct itself, whereas we emphasize its object. . . . We despise the instinctual activity in itself and find excuse for it only on the merits of the object. (Marcus 1975, xxvii)

The merits of the object in this case are the appropriately gendered actor with whom intercourse occurs only in marriage and with the correlative goals of reproduction and a muted pleasure. The virtuous object serves to legitimate and channel the instinct.

This conception of a polarized heterosexuality and homosexuality mapped upon a polarized masculinity and femininity became the *taken-for-granted* mode of thinking about sexual desire for the next three quarters of a century. As with all theories (scientific or folk) which succeed in becoming the dominant mode of discourse within a community (scientific of folk), this view of object choice as the central organizing feature of normal and abnormal desire organized the perceptions and research of a majority of scientists. In the usual way that science proceeds, observations were sought and techniques developed that satisfied the needs of the central scientific dogma.

This dogma was based on the existence of two opposed and completely separate essentialisms: heterosexuality and homosexuality. It was generally believed in the scientific and professional communities that had the responsibility for managing sexuality, that these two forms of behavior had separate etiologies (though only the etiology of homosexuality was ever explored since heterosexuality was an outcome which was so natural that it needed no explanation) and were the automatic outcomes of the normal and abnormal pathways of development. While it is true in Western societies that near-ly all forms of sexual expression were (and are) problematic, after overcoming these general difficulties, being heterosexual was not. In addition heterosexuality and homo-sexuality as they were thought about (rather than as they were practiced) in Western Europe and the United States between 1890 and 1950 took on trans-historical and uni-versal significance as essential features of sexual conduct in all times and in all places.

Having fixated on this dogma of the homosexual as person and personality (which was abstracted from the actual social practices of men who had sex with men and women who had sex with women) and the heterosexual as requiring no explanation (definable only by its lack of a homosexual taint) women and men who had sex with *both* women and men were a troubling anomaly, much as the advance of perihelion of the planet Mercury was to the classical physicists of the turn of the nineteenth century (Kuhn 1970). Clinical and criminological studies had early identified the existence of persons who had sex with both men and women, and such persons quickly became labeled as bisexuals, ambisexuals, or intersexuals *(bisexual* contrasted with monosexual, *ambisexual* was rooted in the idea of ambidextrous, and *intersexual* carries the resonance of being between the sexual polarities of homosexual and heterosexual) (Kinsey et al. 1948).

Traditional psychoanalysis, which had acquired the primary responsibility for the-oretically patrolling the terrain of what it labeled sexual object choice, proposed a number of solutions, the most popular of which in the United States has been to dis-criminate (in the language of psychoanalysis) between *true, obligatory,* or *exclusive* homosexuals and a number of other transitional perversities or situational practices that had different origins than "real" homosexuality (Socarides 1978). These forms of "bisexuality" were not intermediate types between the pure types of homosexuality and heterosexuality, but rather mixed practices with quite different etiologies and conse-quent character structures. The behavior of such persons was thought to be patholog-ical in its origins and expression, but often transitory (e.g., the prostitution of delin-quent boys or sexual contact among same-gender adolescents) or situational (sex between men in the military or prisons). While such sexual practices were somewhat of an embarrassment theoretically, they could be explained away in a manner that pre-served the essential differences between the homosexual and the heterosexual. In this historically and culturally situated discourse, there existed a pure or true homosexual personality type which had a common set of psychological or biological origins and a common adult character structure organized around a perverse sexual object choice.

The criminal-legal system during this period, and extending to the present moment in many jurisdictions, also patrolled the terrain between the homosexual and the heterosexual by focusing on the gender of the actors in the sex act (Gebhard et al. 1965). In such a practice those who had sex with both men and women were treated the same way as those men who had sex only with men or women who had sex only with women. While the existence of a "heterosexual" practice as evidenced by marriage or children might mitigate the offense or reduce the penalty, all persons who engaged in such acts were treated by the law as if they were "homosexual." The act is the evi-dence for the perversity, and "homosexuals" and "bisexuals" were gathered together as a single group as they are in the HIV/AIDS risk group "homosexual and bisexual men" which has been constructed by epidemiologists (CDC 1992, Openheimer 1988). In both AIDS-think and crime-think, it is easier to include men who have sex with both women and men with those men who have sex only with men than it is to create an alternative classification: "heterosexuals and bisexuals."

Kinsey, in one of the major theoretical breaks in the history of sex research, treated the "problem" of those who had sex with both men and women as unproblematic (Kinsey et al. 1948). Kinsey's treatment of bisexuality involved a radical critique of the relation between heterosexuality and homosexuality. Theoretically, he argued specifically against prior conceptions of the homosexual and homosexuality, and by creating the 0 to 6 scale (or, as it was called at the Institute for Sex Research at that time, the H-H scale) he proposed that the heterosexual and homosexual acts of persons could be best understood as the proportion of other-gender and same-gender sexual acts (here including mental acts) in which they had engaged. The relation between heterosexuality and homosexuality was to be treated as continuous rather than discrete, and individuals could move from one place to another on the continuum by adding new acts of the two different types.

What Kinsey opposed was the well-established theoretical belief that persons with substantial amounts of same-gender erotic experience represented a unitary category of persons with similar psychological or biological biographies whose lives were entirely governed, or at least strongly influenced, by the gender of the persons they sexually desired. Kinsey's theoretical counter to the biomedical-psyciatric-criminological view—that each homosexual was possessed of a defect in biology or very early education—was to take an equally strong biological line, but one that emphasized the evolutionary history of the species rather than the defective status of the individual. This is essentially the theoretical position he took about all sexual conduct, approved and disapproved. He argued that homosexuality, masturbation, and oral sex (to take the triad he most often discussed when dealing with these issues) were common activities in "the mammalian heritage" as well as among human groups where cultural repression of the sexual was not the norm. Hence, such activities repesented the diversity of nature rather than perversities and deviations from a biological or cultural standard for the sexually correct individual (Kinsey et al. 1948). This is an argument of extraordinary originality, one which allows Kinsey to bring what was thought to be unnatural under the umbrella of a larger and more copious nature. It shares with the Freudians a view that there is a severe tension between the offerings of nature and the strictures of culture; however, Kinsey's vision of what nature offers is closer to Rousseau's than it is to Hobbes's.

The moral and political legitimacy of same-gender sexual acts (whether exclusive or in some mixture with opposite-gender sexual acts) could thus be created by treating them as part of a natural world which should not be limited by the artifices of culture. Kinsey's opposition between nature and culture thus rests on a distinction between the bounty and variety of the natural world (read here the diversity of species in an unmanaged nature) as opposed to a civilized world of agriculture in which nature is pruned and limited. In much the same way as agriculture gives the fields over to monocrops, sexually repressive cultures cultivate procreative heterosexuality as their sole flower, treating all else as weeds. Kinsey remained true to his prior evolutionary and ecological concerns: It is in the biology of abundance and adaptation that he finds the template for the normal, not in the individual organismic views which character-ize the defect-finding traditions in psychiatry, psychology, and biology.

The H-H or 0 to 6 continuum rested at least in part on this understanding of nature. As Kinsey wrote:

> Males do not represent two discrete populations, heterosexual and homo-sexual. The world is not to be divided into sheep and goats. Not all things are black nor all things white. It is fundamental of taxonomy that nature rarely deals with discrete categories. Only the human mind invents cate-gories and tries to force facts into separated pigeon-holes. The living world is a continuum in each and ever one of its aspects. The sooner we learn this concerning human sexual behavior the sooner we shall reach a sound understanding of the realities of sex. (Kinsey et al. 1948, 639)

That continua are as much human inventions as dichotomies, and that there is, for certain purposes, a utility to distinguishing between sheep and goats, are reason-able intellectual responses to Kinsey's positivist view that the continua in the mind mirror the sexual facts in the world. However the important issue is Kinsey's decision to make heterosexuality and homosexuality (and hence bisexuality) a question of acts rather a question of common origins, common personalities, or common behavioral performances (in the case of males: effeminacy, artistic temperament, a broader pelvis, occupational preference, scores on Terman-Miles MF scale) (Kinsey et al. 1948, 637). It is the mixture of heterosexual and homosexual performances that impresses Kinsey; the record of "experience and psychic reactions" (ibid., 639) which fluctuates across the life course, even within a single sexual occasion.

The scale is an empirical attempt to undermine all of the usual sharp distinctions that were made between individuals who had sexual contacts with the same and the other gender. By focusing on flexibility and change in conduct across the life course, it counters arguments that same-gender erotic preferences start early in life, are fixed across the life course, and are influential in all spheres of life. By focusing on acts rather than persons, Kinsey tries to protect those who are persecuted as "homosexual" because of a few homosexual acts as well as to counter the argument that there is an essential homosexual personality. Thus, a single act or a small number of same-gender erotic acts does not a homosexual make (Kinsey did not make the corollary argument that a sin-gle or small number of heterosexual acts did not a heterosexual make). More trenchantly there is no such thing as a homosexual person, only persons with various mixtures of acts. Kinsey remains quite consistent in arguing that the intermediate numbers on the scale are not to be treated as a social type called "bisexuals," but rather represent persons with a mixture of homosexual and heterosexual acts either at that moment in time or throughout their lives. These persons were simply those who had sex both with men and women, activities that were well within the mammalian potential for sexual action.

The impact of Kinsey's theorizing and research on our thinking about the triad homosexuality-bisexuality-heterosexuality has been extraordinarily ambiguous and has come about primarily as a result of his reconstruction of ideas about homosexuality. Three separate threads can be identified—the *first* is the impact of his work on sexual reform and reconstruction of the image of "the homosexual," the *second* is the ways in which his ideas remained supportive of traditional thinking about gender and sexuality, and the *third* is perhaps a noninfluence, that is the way in which ideas which were important to Kinsey failed to have an influence in everyday or scientific thought.

Perhaps the most important impact of Kinsey's work was its role in breaking up traditional psychoanalytic and psychiatric thinking about homosexuality as a personality trait and the posing of the notion that homosexuality was both prevalent and, in some deep sense of the natural, normal. It was these conceptions that provided the scientific basis that informed the early stages of gay liberation (there are many of us and we are not crazy or abnormal) and scientific research programs that challenged the belief in the psychological and social homogeneity of the category homosexual.

However, in three important ways Kinsey's ideas on gender and sexuality remained continuous with the past: *first,* he accepts the belief that the gender of the person with whom one has sex is a centrally organizing feature of sexual conduct—it does make a difference whether one has sex with a man or a woman; *second,* mixed-gender sexual practices are viewed as being bracketed by the two poles of heterosexuality and homosexuality; and *third,* heterosexuality and homosexuality are treated as natural rather than as socially constructed categories. Each of these continuities with the past focuses our attention on gender as the pivotal element in provoking sexual desire and treats heterosexuality and homosexuality as biological essences rather than as social practices.

It is perhaps the crucial idea that gave Kinsey the ability to criticize the prior medicalized constructions of homosexuality which has had the least impact. Kinsey's view that persons are mixtures of heterosexual and homosexual acts rather than social or personality types failed to recognize that such "folk categories" were part of the individual and collective reality of everyday sexual life in the United States. Persons with same-gender erotic experiences viewed themselves, and were viewed by others, as enacting or resisting the social roles provided for the expression of same-gender desire in the then existent homosexual/heterosexual culture. Sissies, queers, dykes, fems, butches, trade, and faggots were (and are) experienced as real states of being to be embraced or denied. In gay culture today, individuals treat their sexual desires as ways of being rather than as ways of acting. Perhaps no one has ever experienced himself or herself as a person with fifty percent heterosexual and fifty percent homosexual acts. Contra Kinsey, persons with what they thought to be equal desires for or experiences with women and men have taken over the scientific nomenclature and labeled themselves "bisexuals."

Kinsey's work may be treated as the opening move in the social constructionist critique of the traditional essentialist views of homosexuality based on psychoanalytic, psychiatric, or biological beliefs. This critique was at first limited to a deconstruction of traditional perspectives on homosexuality (one end of the continuum of gender preference in erotic relations) by pointing out that the theories did not fit the facts and, moreover, that the theories were used to enforce the oppressive conditions of homosexual life. The point of this critique was to create an open space in which a new practice of same-gender desire could be fashioned or socially constructed. Willy-nilly gay male and lesbian cultures began to emerge from the ruins of nineteenth-century ideas about homosexuality (Humphreys 1972; D'Emilio 1983). What was frequently unobserved was that these new cultures were themselves socially constructed and did not represent the natural order of things any more than did the ideologies and practices that preceded them. While gay male and lesbian cultures were different and appeared to be better ways to live, they did not have any privileged status, but only a status that could be secured by continuous political self-defense.

In additon, the recognition that the ways in which homosexuality was socially constructed and practiced had fundamentally changed after the emergence of gay culture did not immediately force a recognition that the two other elements in the triad, heterosexuality and bisexuality, were themselves cultural constructions and social practices. Only a few thinkers began to consider what would happen if *what appeared to be* the most natural of all forms of conduct, the conventionalized sexual relations of women and men, was treated as problematic and the topic of history, anthropology, and sociology rather than biology, psychiatry, and individualistic psychologies. To entertain the belief that the sexual desires of the majority are as much the result of a social construction as are the desires of all sexual minorities is a classic example of what is bad (perhaps even intolerable) to think, much less to practice. As a consequence of this resistance to a "temporary existence" even within the gay male and lesbian communities, neo-essentialisms continue to flourish.

One of these neo-essentialisms has been the folk creation of a new "bisexual identity" which stands for that collection of individuals who (1) have sex with both women and men and (2) seek a subcultural identity based on the gendered aspects of their sexual practices. These developments follow from the emergence of a new social type that appeared during the liberated climate of the late 1960s, when a new ideological set of concerns about bisexuality emerged in the popular and academic literatures (Blumstein and Schwartz 1976a, 1976b). Some persons who had sex with both men and women reported that they did so because they enjoyed sex with both and that the erotic satisfactions that they recieved from one gender were not equivalent to those they recieved from the other. In the sexually experimental climate of the times, bisexuality became, at least for some persons, a way of trying our various concurrent identities (Duberman 1974).

Ideologically, this is where most theorists stand today in dealing with the historic triad of heterosexuality–bisexuality–homosexuality. Social constructionist thinking is applied only selectively to those essentialisms that seem socially regressive. While it is widely recognized that the "homosexuality" created by biology, medicine, and psychiatry is a social construction, the "gay male" and "lesbian" identities that are the products of the gay and lesbian movement are rarely treated as similarly socially constituted and historically transitory (important examples of those who recognize contemporary identities as socially constructed are De Cecco and Shively 1983–84, and Califia 1983). Heterosexuality is nearly universally treated as an essence even by those who recognize its compulsory status (Rich 1983) Finally, most scientists who study "bisexuality" and many of the better-educated persons who have sex with both men and women aspire to give bisexuality an essentialist status coequal with that of "gay men," "lesbians," and "heterosexuals."

Sex with Both Women and Men as Practices

PERHAPS THE BEST way to counter these neo-essentialist trends is to apply the strategy of those who created the social constructionist critique of the essentialist biological and medical versions of "homosexuality." This strategy involoves two concurrent arguments. The first simply points out the remarkable diversity of the forms of conduct that are labeled bisexual and the inadequecy of "bisexuality" as a simple label or as a set of theories to account for this diversity of practices. The second argument points out that the sexual desires that are evoked in the particular circumstances of any of these specific practices (e.g., swinging, male prostitution to males, sex in prisons) exists without reference to and often in spite of the gender of the sexual partner.

The sheer empirical diversity of cultural scenarios, interpersonal scripts, and intrapsychic scripts within the population of men who have sex both with women and men and women who have sex both with women and men (the population treated as "bisexual") within the United States (much less the practices in non-Western cultures, see Herdt 1981, 1984, 1985; Virulak 1989; WHO/GPA/Social and Behavioral Research Unit 1989a, 1989b) should persuade us to avoid the facile use of the term "bisexuality" and its essentialist consequences, no matter how seductive these might be. In this case, it is hoped that simple description will overwhelm the seductive delights of theory, and that paying attention to the details of difference will offer a better understanding than the search for fictive commonalities that result from the use of the narrow lens of theory.

Another support for this approach to the study of persons who have sex with both women and men is the very tiny number of persons who report such conduct at any given time. Both surveys of the general population and specialized studies of gay men and lesbians indicate that far more persons never have sex with persons of the same gender than commit to a lifelong identity as gay, lesbian, or bisexual (Lever et al. 1992; Gagnon and Simon 1973; Blumstein and Scwartz 1977). Still other surveys indicate that while many people may have had sex with both women and men at some point in their lifetime, very few report having such experiences during the year prior to the date when they were interviewed (Michael et al. 1992; Fay et al. 1989; Stall et al. 1991). The moderately high lifetime incidences of having sex with women and men are the results of quite sporadic and infrequent experiences among disparate groups of individuals with quite different scripts for the conduct.

What follows are descriptions of some (though not all) of the most common patterns of having sex with both women and men in the contemporary United States. Each of these patterns can be labeled "bisexual," though they are often quite different from each other. It is the variability in the patterns that is the most important to consider as one attempts to make sense of the ways in which sexual scripts are modified and reorganized to include partners of both genders.

Adolescent Sexual Experimentation

THE LARGEST NUMBER of people who have had sex with both women and men usually acquire that experience in early to middle adolescence and young adulthood. The United States offers little meaningful guidance about sexuality to young people during the period of transition from childhood to adulthood, and while the tilt of the society is toward increasing emotional and sexual experimentation with opposite-gender partners, there are occasions for some (or much) parallel emotional and sexual activity with persons of the same gender during adolescence (Herdt and Boxer 1990). It is thus possible for young people to develop passionate attachments (develop a "crush") to persons of the same gender during adolescence. These emotional attachments may lead to physical sexual activity, but not in all cases.

Young people may engage in a wide variety of sexual practices with same-gender partners while at the same time they are beginning to associate with members of the opposite gender and experiment sexually with them. For most young people, all early sexual experimentation, regardless of the gender of their partners, is linked to the motivational content of adolescence rather than to the more complete and fixed sexual commitments of adults. This mixed pattern of sexual commitment is vastly reduced as young people are required to choose (or drift into) a commitment to one pattern or another.

Many young people in adolescence may make a substantial commitment to affectional and sexual life with someone of their own gender, and then find that the object of their affection has fallen in love with someone of the opposite gender and begun to move toward an other-gender pattern. For a young person moving toward a gay or lesbian commitment, the loss of this adolescent lover may be deeply troubling because it may have involoved overt sexuality for both of them and deep affection on the part of at least one of them. Another pattern also occurs, though less frequently: An opposite-gender pair may break apart because of the increasing same-gender commitment of one member of the pair.

Very few young people resolve such conflicts by making a strong commitment to sex with both genders, and the capacity of these few to sustain a dual commitment is weakened by increasing social emhpasis on an exclusive gender commitment in sexual relations during young adulthood. Also, there is probably some difference in scripting for the same-gender and the other-gender commitments—one or the other can come first in time, be more important emotionally, be defined as more (or less) socially acceptable, or be largely a physical interest in contrast to an emotional one.

It is not entirely clear to what degree such experiences during adolescence with persons of both sexes might be integrated into a bisexual identity or practice later in life. It is also not known how many of the young people involved in adolescent sexuality with both genders would continue a bisexual or a major or exclusive same-gender commitment if this lifestyle were viewed to be as acceptable as an opposite-gender commitment. At present, the mixed or gay or lesbian patterns are not equally competitive with the opposite-gender pattern during adolescence.

In the last decade, a fashionable "bisexual chic" has appeared among some sophisticated urban young people who participate in the "club scene." This fashion appears to be based on the assumption that many rock stars are "bisexual," an assumption that some rock stars have deliberately fostered (e.g., Madonna and David Bowie). This is based on an assumption that bisexuality is a measure of sexual freedom in the pop music world (particularly among "new wave" groups). The existence of role models as well as participation in the "dance club scene" that exists in many large cities provides an opportunity for young people to drift through transitional bisexual practices or identity. Some will even reverse traditional patterns and claim a bisexual "identity" without actually engaging in sex with both women and men.

The Hustling World

AMONG ADOLESCENTS, both delinquent and nondelinquent, youthful members of the military, and young men detached from family life who largely prefer sex with women, there are some who have sex with men for favors (Boles 1989). Such favors can involve money, housing, food, drink, or any other thing which men often need. At no point before, during, or after the sexual act do these young men define themselves as homosexual or as experiencing or performing a homosexual act. Even though they become erect and ejaculate (following all the events of the sexual response cycle), they do not consider that they are responding to a homosexual stimulus.

There are a number of symbolic revisions of script elements that allow these young men to define their experience in this way. The first is that the act may occur only a few times, with different men, and for money—the activity is "playing the queers," not bisexuality or homosexuality (Reiss 1961). Even when they are involved over a longer period with a number of people or a number of experiences with the same persons, other script modifications are possible to make the conduct congruent with their self conception as "straight." Commonly such young men refuse to allow hugging or kissing or anything sexual above the waist. As long as the partner's head is below the belly button and contact is solely on the penis, it is the other person who is *being* homosexual. Without affection (such as there might be in sex with a woman) and reciprocity (the young man does not define what he is doing as active) there is no reason to define the self as bisexual or homosexual. The money, the genital focus, the lack of affection, and the physical "inactivity" are all components which offer the young man a heterosexual script for the act. Further, it is possible for the young man to think about his girlfriend or other women while the act is going on—some do, in fact, report that they cannot become aroused unless they have an opposite-gender fantasy (an intrapsychic script) in their heads.

The person having sex with such a young man may run a grave personal risk since not all young men have the scripting skills to protect their heterosexual self-conception. Some of them, particularly those with little experience with other men, may find it very difficult to manage the sexual experience in these limited and neutral terms. This response is sometimes labeled a "homosexual panic," because the young men feel that their identity as a "man" is threatened. As a consequence, they may feel the need to beat up or rob their customer in order to bolster their belief in their own masculinity and heterosexuality. In other cases, the customer makes a mistake by trying for more than a purely genital relationship and seeks a more affectional contact. This sometimes provokes a violent reaction on the part of the young man, who has defined the situation differently.

These reactions suggest a basic theme in such encounters. The young man is able to revise the script because he believes that "homosexuals" are or have the attributes of women. They are defined as weak, inferior, and submissive. If a person is active in certain sexual acts (fellatio), or passive in others (the object of anal intercourse), or responds to the sexual acts that are being performed, he violates the masculine image. To do these things indicates that a person is weak and therefore homosexual. The boundary being defended is the boundary between brave, strong, violent men and cowardly, passive, weak men, the boundary between "heterosexual men" and "homosexual men," and ultimately the boundary between women and men. Symbolic manipulations are required for *why* the sex goes forward, *who* the other person is defined to be, and *what* the permitted sex acts are.

There are probably many young men who have had this kind of sexual experience one or two times in their lives. Some of them may do it more frequently and earn the label "male prostitute" or "hustler." Such young men seek the bright lights of the major cities (Times Square in New York, for example), or hang around the hotels of small cities and towns offering their services to other men. They often act and look conventionally masculine, perhaps even tough and delinquent, for this version of "machismo" has a certain appeal to some clients (who have also been taken in by the imagery of masculinity).

Such young men are often called "trade" or if they look particularly tough, "rough trade." There is a saying in the gay community that "this year's trade is next year's competition"—meaning that the "heterosexual" young man you pay this year will want to pay another man for sex next year. What this suggests is that the protective script breaks down, that the continued contact with homosexual acts and experiences is seductive, and that young men who begin to have sex with men for money will eventually continue for pleasure. Given the usually transitory nature of the male prostitute role, however, it is unlikely that this happens to many young men. What may contribute to this impression is that some of the young men who hustle actually have same-gender sexual preferences but conceal their same-gender desires because many clients want "real" heterosexuals as well as masculine-appearing young men. As these young men move into more open sexual relationships with other men, they may produce the impression of a regular movement of young men from heterosexual to homosexual lifestyles.

The contemporary hustling world is complex. It is composed of these "straight" young men who may have sex with a man for money or favors once or twice, as well as "straight" young men who may have such sex frequently, neither of these two groups conceives of itself as gay.[1]

Each of these two groups represents a "bisexual" adaptation. At the same time there are hustlers who are themselves gay and work the streets, the escort services, and the telephone lines in much the same manner as do women sex workers. At any given moment most of the actual paid same-gender sex is probably being performed by these more or less professional sex workers, but on any given day there are probably more "straight" young men having sex with men for money than there are gay-identified young men.

Gender-Isolated Groups

GROUPS OF HEALTHY and active people of one gender who prefer sex with persons of the other gender may sometimes be effectively isolated from these partners. Such groups may contain a mix of people with histories of sex with and erotic interests in women and men. When the isolation involves a great deal of effort and commitment (an army in combat), a relatively brief separation (a submarine cruise or an expedition to climb a mountain), or starvation and forced labor (a concentration camp, a penal colony, or a prisoner of war camp), sexual activity of any kind is probably rare. However, in peacetime armies, in single-gender schools, and in prisons, gender segregation can result in both short-term and long-term contacts with persons of the same gender by both women and men.

Prisons are probably the exemplary institutions for the study of mixed-gender sexual practices of those who usually have sex only with opposite-gender partners. Same-gender sexual activity occurs fairly often in some prisons and less often in others. Everyone does not engage in such sexual relationships, even in loosely administered institutions where cliques and even subcultures that foster same-gender sex have existed over a number of years. Even among serious offenders serving long sentences only about half have had overt sex with other men, and this experience tends to be sporadic rather than frequent and continuous. Interviews with seven hundred men prisoners by members of the Insitute for Sex Research showed that, adding together all sources of sexual activity (masturbation, orgasm during dreams, sex with other men), very few of the prisoners had levels of sexual activity that reached even ten percent of what they usually experienced outside prison (Gebhard et al. 1965).

The prison is usually an antisexual environment for both women and men, and it is so by design. Prisons are environmentally dull, behavior is regulated by the clock, many movements from one place to another are performed in groups. Individuals have limited opportunities for personal privacy, and there are programs of active surveillance to reduce or eliminate close personal ties (including sexual ties) between prisoners. While some prisons allow conjugal visits for some prisoners (the rules for sexual encounters between men and women prisoners and their spouses vary from state to state and prison to prison) and some prisons for men allow men's magazines such as *Playboy*, the denial of sexual expression is usually seen as one of the normal punishments visited on those who have violated the law and who have been sentenced to prison. Sexual deprivation is part of the general deprivation of liberty.

The lack of erotic stimuli in prison is not solely the absence of a sexual partner of a preferred gender, but the lack of the social situations that are associated with the experience of desire in the free community. The search for a sexual partner outside of prison involves both activities (going out on the town, drinking, hanging out, chatting up prospective sexual partners) as well as everyday erotic stimuli (seeing attractive women or men) that keep sexual interest alive. Sex does occur among prisoners, but among men it may occur without choice and in violent circumstances (Sykes 1958).

The problem of sex in prison is not one of orgasms or sex acts, but rather of the meanings of the sex acts. Many heterosexual male prisoners view the sexual world very much as do the heterosexual male prostitutes described above and they often share common social attitudes toward gender and sex. That is, the sexual act between men in prison is defined as being heterosexual for one person and homosexual for the other. One man is defined as masculine, strong, powerful, and controlling, while the other is feminine, weak, subordinate, and controlled. The stronger inserts his penis into the weaker—the act of penetration parallels the act with women, and assures a symbolic continuity with experiences in the world outside the prison.

These patterns begin in reform schools and other institutions for young men in which the stronger and more powerful induce or threaten the physically weaker or more feminine appearing into sexual activity as the "female" partner. Once this process of seduction or coercion has occurred, the "female" partner can go from relationship to relationship with older boys or men (and from institution to institution) having been categorized and defined as a "punk" or "sissy" by the other men in the institution. In come cases men with same-gender preferences find themselves in this role in prison and are coerced into sex by aggressive males (see Giallombardo 1974; Linder 1946).

The majority of sexual encounters between men in prison do not involve affection. They are more often motivated by aggression, violence, and control, and are often less important in terms of the ejaculation they produce than the way they enhance the dominant partner's masculinity. The ability to dominate and control, to make someone else do what you want is extremely important in most male status rankings. Sexual coercion is one of the few ways for prisoners to achieve status in prison. Many men in prison are aggressive and assertive outside, but in prison their capacity to be aggressive or assertive is highly restricted. The guards, walls, guns, marching, working, eating, and showering to the ringing of bells deny them the freedom to affirm their masculinity in the ways they are used to: with sex and aggression. By including sex in their domination of other men (becoming "wolves" or "jockers"), they give a different meaning to sexual acts between men and make them serve the same purposes as sexual acts between men and women.

The men who are coerced have a very different experience. Some of them, because they are fearful and physically weak, drift into a transitory adaptation for the sake of protection by their lovers from other aggressive men. Men with either same- or other-gender preferences may be forced to comply in order to protect themselves from rape. Such men often suffer the same degradation as women who are raped: because they are unable to protect themselves sexually, prison officials see them as weaklings, as not "manly" enough to protect themselves. Sharing the attitude that masculinity requires a capacity for physical violence, prison officials and guards do not do much to safeguard the peaceful, weak, and unprotected.

Affectionate relationships are possible in male prisons, but they are not as frequent as they are among men in the outside community. The submissive member of the pair may develop an emotional commitment to the dominant one, but this pattern is often not reciprocated. Emotional misunderstandings can occur when one man with causal emotional standards has had sex with someone who wants love, and violence can occur when the dominant male changes sexual partners. In long-term prisons, the release of a man who has developed a long-term relationship with another can result in a period of emotional crisis for the man who remains.

Women also respond to prison life by having sex with each other, but where men model themselves on the sexual dimension of the man–woman couple, the women often recreate the family dimensions of the same social relationships. Women inmates tend to develop sexual relationships within the context of a complex quasi-kinship system (Giallombardo 1966, 1974; Ward and Kassebaum 1965). In adolescent institutions, this may mean recreating the extended family. Where the dominant, sex-initiating men are called jocks and wolves and their submissive partners are called punks and sissies, the female parallels are "poppas" and "mamas." In adolescent institutions, there are even brothers and sisters, aunts and uncles, imitating the traditional kinship patterns of the family.

Prison sexuality among women appears to be slightly less common than it is among men, but it does tend to involve much higher levels of emotional commitment. Since women's prisons contain women with extensive criminal histories as well as women who have committed serious offenses but who lack a prior criminal career, prior sexual histories are mixed. Getting an affair started may take a long courtship, both because this is what most women expect and because they have limited practice in initiating sexual contact of any kind. If the prison population includes women who have had sexual experience with other women in the community, starting up an affair is easier. The amount of sex in these relationships is often minimal, out of preference or lack of privacy, but they may be quite emotional and long-term, which produces trauma when one partner is released.

Many women and men in prison are attempting to resist the institution and trying to maintain their identities, despite all the coercive forces around them. Their sexuality in prison can thus be interpreted as a form of social and psychological resistance to a threatened destruction of identity. They fight the prison's efforts to drive individuals apart, by attempting to form sexual relationships. For men, this often means exploiting and using other men, creating an informal status ladder which the institution says should not exist. For women, it means attempting to create a family where one does not exist. For both, sex becomes a vehicle of resistance to depersonalization.[2]

Most prisoners involved in such contacts who did not have prior strong sexual commitments to others of the same gender apparently do not continue their prison adaptation in the outside community. It is less clear whether the prison experience can move male adolescents toward an easier acceptance of same-gender identifications or hustler roles in the outside world. Prisoners who have sex with persons of the same gender only in prison do not commonly seek to imitate their prison experience in the outside community; they return to the sexual lifestyle scripts they had outside. In these cases, the gender preference is substituted into their existing model of sexual relationships. The script is kept as unchanged as possible while it is applied to a new situation, and is still available when they are freed.

Cultural Variations in the United States

AS THE UNITED STATES has become a more multicultural society, patterns of having sex with both women and men that have their origins in other societies have been transferred along with other cultural practices (e.g., food, religion, languages) to the United States. The best-studied of these sexual practices is a pattern observed among men who have come to the United States from the Spanish-speaking areas such as Mexico, Central and South America (Carrier 1976, 1980, 1989; Magana 1989; Shifter 1989). Other studies have identified similar patterns in Brazil (Parker 1987, 1990). Among most Latin (ultimately Mediterranean) cultures there is a sharp division between the genders, with clearly exclusive cultural and behavioral territories reserved for men and women. This includes the expression of sexual desire.

In this cultural world, particularly in the countries of origin, men who have sex with women are "men," and men who have sex with other men are defined in some significant ways as being like women, but with one major exception. Normatively, though not always in practice, the masculinity of a man who has sex both with women and with other men can be defined by his role in the sexual act, the one who always is the inserter is defined as masculine, the one who is inserted into is the "women." The former is *activo*, the latter is a *passivo*. This well-defined cultural pattern allows some men, how many is unkown, to have sex with other men without thinking of it as homosexual or feminine or passive. Analogical symbolic definitional strategies can be found in prison populations, though it is important to note that they do not have the same cultural origins, nor are they culturally persuasive. It is important to emphasize that these script changes are not considered definitional strategies by the actors themselves, but as part of the natural order of things (see Carrier 1985).

The existence of AIDS has been the motivation for recent studies of bisexuality in African-American communities in the United States. Peterson (1989, 1992) interviewed African-American bisexual men about their sexual behaviors and AIDS-related attitudes and beliefs. He found that the bisexual men he studied had a higher number of sexual partners and higher frequency of unsafe sexual practices with both primary and secondary partners than did those African-American men who had only men or only women partners. Unsafe sexual activity was positively correlated with a low percieved susceptibility to HIV infection, high enjoyment of the sexual activity, and a low level of awareness of AIDS. What is driving these patterns of sexual acitvity, the scripts that are involved, and the relationship to the larger African-American sexual culture is currently obscure.

The Heterosexually Coupled Person with Same-Gender Desire

AS A RESULT OF THE heterosexual tilt of the culture of the United States, some people may find themselves in a heterosexual marriage that does not satisfy their desires for affectional and sexual relations with persons of their own gender. In some cases, people who have strong sexual desires for persons of the same gender may marry because "it is what is expected of them" or because they think marriage would "cure" them of their "homosexuality." Indeed, some therapists have recommended heterosexual marriage to their patients as a way out of the conflict between the social expectations and the individual's own desires. In other cases, people, perhaps more often women, have married and in the process of the marriage discovered that they want the emotional and erotic company of persons of the same gender. In both of these cases, the people involved may have children, and resolving the conflict between their sexual desires and the obligations to their spouses and children produces profound personal conflicts.

In some cases, these individuals define themselves as really "homosexual" and may sustain their marriages, sexually and socially, to meet the needs of social convention. This was a very common pattern in the past, though more and more often at the present time, marriages and families are being dissolved in order to realign the sexual desires of the individual and his or her social arrangements. More recently, at least some of these men have worked out new adjustments—some joining the gay community while attempting to continue to have social relations with former or current wives and children. Few studies of this latter population exist. It is reasonable to expect these practices to exist in minority communities as well as among whites, but it is only in the latter population where research has been conducted.

Before gay liberation, those women and men who were married who felt truly homosexual shared "the closet" with those who did not define themselves as something which they would call "really homosexual," but reported that they felt uneasy, unhappy, or unable to deal with the demands of heterosexuality without some sort of same-gender attachment. Both of these groups wanted to have sex with persons of the same gender, but many did not do so because of the fears of social ostracism, loss of family connections, being fired from work, and being persecuted by the police. Such closeted individuals who have rare or intermittent sex with persons of the same gender still exist (Ross 1971, 1972).

Most of the people we *know about* in this situation are men. Such men may feel a strong need for some homosexual experience—it is often such men who have same-gender contacts away from home or in public rest rooms and parks (Humphrey 1970). Their sex with men is a source of guilt and fear, and they wish to keep it secret from their wives and children, who are unlikely to understand. Because the man does not have extensive experience with conventionally scripted man–man relations, his sexual conduct with men is larely impersonal. These men have not historically participated in the gay community, except when out of town, and then only as sexual transients. They occasionally surface on the police blotter and in little scandals that break up families or result in therapeutic interventions, and more recently, they have been the subject of concern as their clandestine sexual behavior was thought to be a route by which AIDS might be carried into the heterosexual population (Randolph 1988; Mayo and Doll 1990).

The sex that many of these men have with other men tends to have a genital and impulsive focus, and it seems to the man to be a force, or power, or compulsion (many other socially unsupported strong feelings have this aspect) over which he has limited control. For many of these men, there is considerable risk of discovery and exposure, for they are caught not merely between two sexual preferences, but also between two social preferences (Hays and Samuels 1989). They are similar in some ways to heterosexual men who go to prostitutes or one-night stands, and who are thus risking marriage and family. The latter's risk is smaller in terms of social stigma, but many of the psychological problems remain the same. In the case of bisexual men, it is not clear that they prefer homosexual acts to heterosexual acts; rather the two domains seem to be serving different purposes for the sexual.[3]

In more recent years, there is evidence that there have been greater attempts to keep these woman–man relationships together, and that these attempts are important in forging a "bisexual identification" on the part of one or another of the partners (Coleman 1985; Wolf 1985; Brownfain 1985). Most of the persons who fall into these studies come from therapeutic or convenience samples and are middle class in origin. One element in sustaining many of these relationships may be the therapeutic intervention which involves identity work on the part of the couple. Many of the convenience samples have found their subjects in "swinging" or other alternative lifestyle groups in which some identity work has already occurred, at least in the form of more liberal sexual values and practices (D. Dixon 1985). At the same time, many of these relationships break up because of the deep sense of betrayal that women feel when they discover their partner has been having sex with men during their relationship (Hays and Samuels 1989). How much this sense of betrayal is exacerbated by the risk of HIV infection in recent years is recorded only in the popular literature.

Women who have sex with other women while staying married seem to bring different meanings to the experience (the search for emotional connection rather than sexual outlet) (Blumstein and Schwartz 1976b). This may reflect women's higher likelihood to disclose their activity more readily and openly than men. It is likely to be true that there are married women who have an interest in having sex with women who are more deeply closeted than are men. Such women are not looking solely for sexual release, but for emotional contact and an enduring relationship (J. K. Dixon 1985). At the same time they have a strong commitment to their children and conventional marriage. Many such women express their same-gender erotic desires only after a divorce.

The Indifference to Gender

THERE ARE SEXUAL situations in which people are not aware of or interested in the gender of who is doing what to whom sexually. This is usually a result of either heightened excitement, the legitimating context of group sex, or a focus on orgasm without reference to other aspects of the sexual encounter. Much of group sex in society continues to involve either opposite-gender couples or all-male sexual groups. In group sex with a mixture of women and men and gender contact, anxieties often arise—more commonly with men than with women—about the meaning of same-gender sexual contact. Women seem to be better able than men to manage the changes in sexual script that are involved. For some women it may be doing what men want to see that produces rescripting; for others it may be an autonomous interest in finding out what happens.

In such group-sex situations, people find themselves touching others of the same and opposite sex with equal interest. For some participants it turns out that some skin is hairy, and some is not, that mouths are often very similar, and that the general excitement of the activity subdues the differences in gender. Such rescripting is often transitory, lasting only during the event and not transferring to other circumstances. Only a few people use the occasion to begin a longer-term sexual commitment.

Another form of gender indifference is more individual and less contextual. As we argued above, there are people who have sex with both women and men, and who do not care much about gender. It is not that they are positively attracted to both, but rather that their script requires just another body. They will do very much the same things with both women and men; the rescripting is private and the critical element becomes the activity, not the gender. This adaptation is more common among men than among women, although it is rare among both. It is as if the script did not contain a gender differentiation. Sometimes other usual script elements may be reduced in significance as well.

Another pattern that occurs nearly exclusively among men is what might be described in the words of the participants, as "messing around." There is an indifference to the gender of the sexual partner under various conditions which include drinking, drug use, and feeling "horny." After an evening of unsuccessful sexual pursuit or when sexual pursuit is restricted by fatigue, lack of time, or income, any sexual partner will do. Women are preferred, but men are acceptable under certain conditions. "Getting your rocks off" or "getting your ashes hauled" are traditional male argot for sexual contacts which do not involve interpersonal involvement and which are motivated by a desire indifferent to its object (Peterson 1989). Often such activity is promoted by the participation of groups of men in which the sexual activity of the individuals is strongly influenced by the willingness of other men to go along with whatever sexual opportunities that present themselves.

Gender Ideology and Sexual Practice

FINALLY, WOMEN AND men engage in same-gender sexual experimentation as an outgrowth of a specific ideology. Of paricular importance are two ideologies: feminism and sexual libertarianism. For some women, a consequence of feminist ideology is the belief that sexual relationships with men are, by definition, occasions for domination and oppression (Rich 1983). Some of these women consciously choose to become "political lesbians" and cease sexual activity with men because they will not "sleep with the enemy." A more common pattern is that the intense emotional ties that arise among members of a social movement are broadened to include sexual activity, thus resembling the first route identified above (similar escalations of personal ties also occur between women and men in revolutionary groups, or political campaigns).

As a result of the increased emotional warmth that women experienced with each other in the feminist movement and as a result of intellectual persuasion, a number of women have undoubtedly tried sexual/affectional relationships with other women. Some have discovered that they preferred contact with women, others have maintained a partial commitment to both women and men, while still others did it only as an experiment. For many lesbians, this experimentation was an affront, since they felt they were being exploited by people without a true commitment to a lesbian identity.

Sexual libertarianism is the other ideological commitment that would encourage people to experiment sexually—the desire to be open to new sexual experience is a key element in this ideology. In the libertarian tradition there is focus on expanding an individual's social acceptance of "nontolerated" forms of conduct and "nontolerated" persons. In many cases the goal is to go well beyond "toleration" to acceptance, understanding, and sharing. In this circumstance, the ideology could justify same-gender sexual experimentation.

A more complex version of ideological work is involved in creating communities of desire based on nongendered attributes. Thus, Califia has argued that sex between gay men and lesbians is a form of "gay sex" that is neither "homosexual" nor "heterosexual" in the traditional sense.

> I live with my woman lover of five years. I have lots of casual sex with women. Once in while I have casual sex with gay men. I have a three year relationship with a homosexual male who doesn't use the term *gay*. And I call myself a lesbian. . . . I call myself a fag hag because sex with men outside the context of the gay community doesn't interest me at all. In a funny way, when two gay people of opposite sexes make it, it's all gay sex. (Califia 1983, 25).

Constructing the Bisexual Identity

OUT OF THIS welter of different practices there are some people whom ideological bisexuals prefer to call "true" bisexuals. These are people emotionally and sexually attracted to both women and men, and who have relations with them accompanied by all the "correct" emotions when having sex with either. Unlike the person who has sex with women or men without focusing on gender, there is among the "true" bisexual a positive response to women and men in their gendered difference, one that is affectionately caring and desiring. It would appear that such people are rarer than most other kinds, even given the prestige offered to people who can define the world in such terms.

In the 1950s, Ellis argued that people unable to have sex with both genders were being psychologically and sexually rigid and cutting themselves off from half the world (Ellis 1962). Bisexuality was not only psychologically healthy, but exclusive homosexuality and heterosexuality appeared to be compulsive, perhaps illnesses, or at least less healthy. Ellis has since changed his views in this matter and now regards exclusive homosexuality as an illness, but there are people still committed to his earlier line of reasoning. They believe, and announce, that the capacity for such bisexual experiences is the mark of mental health and that bisexuality is the normative sex of the future. Such a prescription for sexual health seems similar to the heterosexual prescriptions of the past: tyranny masking as freedom. However many such people there are, they represent a minority of all people who have had sex with both genders.

A less prescriptive stance has been adopted by a number of researchers and advocates who have adpoted the political stance that bisexuality is an "identity" in the same way that being "gay" or "lesbian" is an identity (Klein 1978; Fox 1992). Many of these advocates have affiliated with gay and lesbian creating organizations that are labeled "Gay, Lesbian, and Bisexual" Alliances. These groups are largely composed of middle-class persons, and the bisexuality that they espouse is unlike the bisexuality of prisoners, hustlers, or any of the other groups that we have described above. In part, such labels indicate that a "bisexual" identity is in the process of construction, at least for those who have the appropriate social and psychological responses when they have sex with both men and women. Linking bisexuality with gay men and lesbians does differentiate it from the heterosexual majority and, by indicating its presence as more than a behavior, may become an opportunity for creating a new and well-defined sexual minority (Paul 1984).

At the same time as bisexuality is becoming an identity, many people who have sex with both women and men continue to find themselves under pressure to "be one thing or the other." This is not so true of people who maintain secret or sequential commitments, or whose mixed-gender sexual patterns are transitional and impersonal, but it is true of those whose sexuality is marked by emotional or ideological commitment. In these cases, there is great pressure from same-gender partners on the one side and other-gender partners on the other to make up their minds.

This occurs for a number of reasons. If a person is likable, affectionate, and a decent lover, then most people whom he or she is with will want to have him or her around most of the time. The pressure on them is similar to that on a person with two lovers of the same sex. There is insistence that the person choose one or the other. The fact that the other lover or lovers are of the opposite sex merely provides a greater incentive for complaint. Accusations of not really being heterosexual or of not really being homosexual abound from both sides (Blumstein and Scwartz 1977). The preferential bisexual makes everyone nervous because he or she is not in anyone's camp. Such an independent sexual posture makes people with fixed positions uneasy.

Bisexuality and AIDS

WITH THE ONSET of the AIDS epidemic, men who had sex with both men and women very quickly became identified as a potential bridge for infection from the gay community (Rogers and Turner 1991; Mayo and Doll 1990). The concern for disease transmission required that the research pose questions in the usual epidemiological form: How many bisexual persons were there? Whom did they have sex with? How often? How many were currently infected? Did they engage in those behaviors that have been identified as risky? Such questions quickly melded into a concern for behavioral change: How could such groups be identified? Were there different channels of education that needed to be accessed for different groups of bisexuals? How secret were these practices and how difficult would it be to locate such persons?

But questions posed in this form assume the existence of either one or perhaps a couple of "bisexual" categories of persons. Many epidemiological studies have been based on an essentialist model, looking for a unitary category of persons called "bisexual" rather than at (1) the important discrepency between the number of people who engage in bisexual activities and the number of people who label themselves bisexual (Lever et al. 1992), and (2) perhaps more important, the variety of scripts that exist in order to facilitate different forms of having sex with both women and men.

However, even simple recognitions of differences in behavioral patterns are important if successful intervention is to be made among those men who have sexual contact with other men as well as with women. For example, unsafe sexual practices are more common among married, closeted, bisexual men than among openly gay men. Since many bisexual men are closeted, they are not reached by traditional sources of safer-sex information in the gay community. However, bisexual men who are socially and sexually active in the gay community are at less risk than bisexual men who self-identify as heterosexuals. Thus, the female partners of those bisexual men who self-identify as heterosexual are at greater risk for HIV infection than those females whose bisexual male partners actively participate in gay community life (World Health Organization 1989a).

Conclusion

THE LESS CULTURALLY structured a particular sexual practice is, the greater the variety of scripts that will begin to emerge around it. Thus, sex between men and women may be more constrained in its expression because it is locked into so many conventional social contexts and institutions. Sex between men and men, or women and women, is less so, but "homosexuality" or "gay and lesbian sex" have a long and complex social history and a chain of subcultural institutions which structure sexual scripts. Those who have sex with both women and men represent a great variety of practices and scripts and "bisexuality" as an ideology and practice is only now beginning to receive both publicity and support. As a consequence, "bisexual" scripts show great variability. They illustrate that sexual scripts can be modified in many ways to justify sexual contact. Because the variations include changes in the reasons (the why of the script) for doing sex (for love, lust, or resistance to social pressure) and in the person (the who of the script) (by using partners in a sequence of symbolic substitutions), it is clear that sex serves many purposes and motives.

Most persons who have sex with both women and men do so without much ideological work. They do what they do without much reflection or symbolic manipulation. However, there are some persons who have sex with both women and men that are looking for social and psychological identities to match up with their practices. Such sense-making activities are the source of new social identities and practices and will become the *taken-for-granted* realities of future generations if they succeed. There is a certain irony in this process since the major activity of the social constructionists has been to deconstruct such matches between identity and practice in same-gender sex—perhaps in opposite-gender sex as well (Gagon 1992). It is unlikely that all of these different practices will find a common script or definition, but it will not be for the want of scientific and ideological trying.

Endnotes

1. The widespread character of these practices is indicated by recent news reports of a man in Philadelphia who had paid very large numbers of young men for oral sex and articles of their clothing. The social networks through which young men in their midteens came to know of this man and engage in the "bisxual" practices were stable for nearly twenty years. Most of the boys attended a church-related high school in a working class area of the city while the man lived in an exclusive residential district (Hinds 1992).

2. A similar situation may develop among women who work in the sex industry as prostitutes. Since the nineteenth century, there has been evidence that some women prostitutes had extensive same-gender sexual experiences and desires (Thomson 1991). Often these women are referred to as "lesbian prostitutes," but the order of events for the majority is likely to have been from prostitution to same-gender sexual experiences and sometimes preferences. Clearly these women had sex with both women and men, but the motivations for each practice were quite different. Were (are) such women bisexual?

3. We have not treated the important category of men who have sex with women and men whose most important social anchor is in the gay community. Such men are quite different from the men discussed in this section. Most of these men have sex with women quite intermittently, though long-term relationships are not unknown. A more detailed consideration of these men will appear in a later publication. It is these men who have elicited the most concern in terms of HIV transmission.

References

Bayer, Ronald. 1981. *Homosexuality and American Psychiatry: The Politics of Diagnosis.* New York: Basic Books.

Blumstein, Philip and Pepper Schwartz. 1976a. Bisexuality in men. *Urban Life.* 5: 339–58.

———. 1976b. Bisexuality in women. *Archives of Sexual Behavior.* 5: 171–81.

———. 1977. Bisexuality: Some social psychological issues. *Jounal of Social Issues.* 33(2): 20–45.

Boles, J. 1989. Bisexuality among male prostitutes. A paper presented at a Workshop on Behaviorally Bisexual Men and AIDS sponsored by the Centers for Disease Control. 18–19 October. Atlanta, Ga.

Brownfain, John J. 1985. A study of the married bisexual male: Paradox and resolution. *The Journal of Homosexuality.* 11 (1/2): 173–88.

Califia, Pat. 1983. Gay men, lesbians, and sex: Doing it together. *The Advocate.* July 7: 24–27.

Carrier, J. M. 1976. Family attitudes and Mexican male homosexuality. *Urban Life.* 5: 359–75.

———. 1980. Homosexuality in cross cultural perspective. In *Homosexual Behavior: A Modern Reappraisal,* ed. Judd Marmor. New York: Basic Books.

———. 1985. Mexican male bisexuality. *The Journal of Homosexuality.* 11 (1/2): 75–85.

———. 1989. Sexual behavior and the spread of AIDS in Mexico. *Medical Anthropology.* 10 (2–3): 129–42

Centers for Disease Control. 1992. HIV/AIDS Surveillance Report. July. 1–18.

Coleman, Eli. 1985. Integration of male bisexuality and marriage. *The Journal of Homosexuality.* 11 (1/2): 189–207.

De Cecco, John and Michael Shively. 1983–84. From sexual identity to sexual relationships: A contextual shift. *Journal of Homosexuality.* 9 (2/3): 1–26.

D'Emilio, John. 1983. *Sexual Politics, Sexual Communities. The Making of a Homosexual Minority in the United States, 1940–1970.* Chicago: University of Chicago Press.

Dixon, Dwight. 1985. Perceived sexual satisfaction and marital happiness of bisexual and heterosexual swinging husbands. *The Journal of Homosexuality.* 11 (1/2): 209–22.

Dixon, Joan K. 1985. Sexuality and relationship changes in married females following the commencement of bisexual activity. *The Journal of Homosexuality.* 11 (1/2): 115–33.

Duberman, Martin. 1974. The bisexual debate. *New Times.* 28 June. 34–41.

Ellis, Albert. 1962. *The American Sexual Tragedy.* New York: Lyle Stuart.

Fausto Sterling, Ann. 1985. *Myths of Gender: Biological Theories about Women and Men.* New York: Basic Books.

Fay, R. E., C. Turner, A. Klassen and J. H. Gagnon. 1989. Prevalence and patterns of same gender sexual contact among men. *Science.* 243 (4889): 338–48.

Foucault, Michel. 1978. *The History of Sexuality. Vol. 1, An Introduction.* New York: Pantheon.

———. 1979. *Discipline and Punish: The Birth of the Prison.* New York: Pantheon.

Fox, Ronald A. 1992. Bisexuality and sexual orientation self-disclosure. Paper presented at the Society for the Scientific Study of Sex, Western Regional Conference. Palo Alto, Calif.

Gagnon, John H. 1988. Gender preference in erotic relations, the Kinsey scale and sexual scripts. In *Heterosexuality, Homosexuality and the Kinsey Scale*, ed. D. McWhirter, S. Sanders, and J. Reinisch. Oxford: Oxford University Press.

———. 1992. The social construction heterosexuality. A paper presented at the meetings of the Society for the Scientific Study of Sex, Western Regional Conference. Palo Alto, Calif.

Gagnon, John H., and William Simon.1973. *Sexual Conduct.* Chicago: Aldine.

Gebhard, Paul H., John H. Gagnon, Wardell B. Pomeroy, and Cornelia Christensen: *Sex Offenders: An Analysis of Types.* New York: Harper.

Geertz, Clifford. 1973. *The Interpretation of Cultures.* New York: Basic Books.

———.1983. *Local Knowledge.* New York: Basic Books.

Giallombardo, Rose. 1966. *Society of Women: A Study of a Women's Prison.* New York: Wiley.

———. 1974. *The Social World of Imprisoned Girls: A Comparitive Study of Institutions for Juvenile Delinquents.* New York: Wiley.

Hays, Dorotha, and Aurele Samuels. 1989. Heterosexual women's perceptions of their marriages to homosexual men. *Journal of Homosexuality.* V7: 81–100.

Herdt, Gilbert. 1981. *Guardians of the Flute.* New York: McGraw Hill.

———. 1984. *Ritualized Homosexuality in Melanesia.* Berkeley: University of California Press.

Herdt, Gilbert, and Andrew Boxer. 1990. Sexual identity and risk for AIDS in Chicago. A paper presented at the International Union for the Scientific Study of Population Seminar on Anthropological Studies Relevant to the Sexual Transmission of HIV. 19–22 November. Sonderborg, Denmark. 34 pp.

Hinds, Michael D. 1992. Two neighborhoods linked in shame. *New York Times.* Wednesday, 8 April. A18.

Humphreys, Laud. 1970. *Tea Room Trade: Impersonal Sex in Public Places.* Chicago: Aldine.

———. 1972. *Out of the Closets: The Sociology of Homosexual Liberation.* Englewood Cliffs, N. J.: Prentice Hall.

Katz, Jonathan. 1983. *Gay/Lesbian Almanac: A New Documentary.* New York: Harper and Row.

Kinsey, Alfred, Wardell Pomeroy, and Clyde Martin. 1948. *Sexual Behavior in the Human Male.* Philadelphia: Suanders.

Klein, Fred. 1978. *The Bisexual Option.* New York: Arbor House.

Kuhn, T. S. 1970. *The Structure of Scientific Revolution.* 2d ed. Chicago: University of Chicago Press.

Lever, J., D. E. Kanouse, W. H. Rogers, S. Carson, and R. Hertz. 1992. Behavior patterns and sexual identity of bisexual males. *The Journal of Sex Research.* (May) 29(2): 141–67.

Magana, Raul. 1989. Latino sexual behavior and AIDS in California. A paper presented at a Workshop on behaviorally Bisexual Men and AIDS sponsored by the Centers for Disease Control. 18–19 October. Atlanta, Ga.

Marcus, Steven. 1975. *Introduction to Sigmund Freud, Three Essays on the Theory of Sexuality.* New York: Basic Books.

Mayo, Donna, and Linda Doll. 1990. Behaviorally bisexual men and AIDS. Exexutive Summary of a Workshop sponsored by the Centers for Disease Control. 18–19 October. Washington, D. C.: American Institutes for Research.

Michael, Robert T., Edward O. Laumann, and John H. Gagnon. 1992. *Reported Sexual Behavior and Partners: Recent Evidence from the General Social Surveys, 1988–91.* 12th International Sunbelt Social Network Conference. February. San Diego, Calif.

Openheimer, Gerald F. 1988. *In the Eye of the Storm: The Epidemiological Construction of AIDS: The Burdens of History.* Berkeley: University of California Press.

Oosterhuis, Harry, ed. 1991. Homosexuality and male bonding in pre-Nazi Germany. *Journal of Homosexuality.* 22 (1/2): (entire issue).

Parker, Richard. 1987. AIDS in urban Brasil. *Medical Anthropology Quarterly.* 13(1): 160–72.

———. 1990. Male prostitution, bisexual behaviour, and HIV transmission in urban Brasil. A paper presented at the International Union for the Scientific Study of Population Seminar on Anthropological Studies Relevent to the Sexual Transmission of HIV. 19–22 November. Sonderborg, Denmark. 34 pp.

Paul, J. P. 1984. The bisexual identity: An idea without social recognition. *The Journal of Homosexuality.* 11: 45–65.

Peterson, John L. 1989. Dangerous liaisons: Risky sexual Bbehaviors and predictors among black bisexual men in the San Francisco Bay area. A paper presented at a Workshop on Behaviorally Bisexual Men and AIDS sponsored by the Centers for Disease Control. 18–19 October. Atlanta, Ga.

Peterson, J. L., T. J. Coates, J. A. Catania, L. Middleton, R. Hilliard, and N. Hearst. 1992. High risk sexual behavior and condom use among African American gay and bisexual men. *American Journal of Public Health.* In Press.

Randolph, Laura B. 1988. The hidden fear: Black women, bisexuals, and the AIDS risk. *Ebony.* 43: 120, 122–3, 126.

Reiss, A. J. 1961. The social organization of queers and peers. *Social Problems.* 9:102–20.

Rich, A. 1983, *Compulsory Heterosexuality and Lesbian Existence,* San Francisco: Antelope.

Rogers, Susan and Charles Turner. 1991. Male-male sexual contact in the USA: Findings from five sample surveys. *Journal of Sex Research.* 28: 4, 491–519.

Ross, H. L. 1971. Modes of adjustment of married homosexuals. *Social Problems.* 18: 385–93.

Shifter, Jacobo. 1989. Report prepared for the Conference on Bisexual Men and HIV Transmission at Utrecht, The Netherlands. Presented at the WHO/GPA/Social and Behavioral Research Unit/ Technical Working Group on Bisexuality and AIDS. 3–5 November. Utrecht, the Netherlands.

Socarides, Charles W. 1978. *Homosexuality.* New York: Aronson.

Stall, Ron, Robert Pierce, Joseph Catania, and John H. Gagnon. 1991. The prevalence of male-to-male sexual behavior, the national AIDS behavioral surveys. A Paper presented at the Annual Meetings of the American Psychological Association. August. San Francisco,Calif.

Sykes, Gresham. 1958. *The Society of Captives: A Study of a Maximum Security Prison.* Princeton: Princeton University Press.

Tavris, Carol. 1992. *The Mismeasure of Woman.* New York: Simon and Schuster.

Thomson, Richard. 1991. Images of the maisons closes. In *Toulouse Lautrec,* Catalogue of the exhibition at the Hayward Gallery, 10 October 1991–19 January 1992. 403–461.

Virulak, Surapone. 1989. Bisexuality and AIDS: Thailand country report. Presented at the WHO/GPA/Social and Behavioral Research Unit/Technical Working Group on Bisexuality and AIDS. 3–5 November. Utrecht, the Netherlands.

Ward, David and Gene Kassebaum. 1965. *Women's Prison: Sex and Social Structure.* Chicago: Aldine.

Weeks, J. 1981. *Sex, Politics, and Society: The Regulation of Sexuality since 1800.* London: Longmans.

WHO/GPA/Social and Behavioral Research Unit. 1989a. Report of the Technical Working Group on Bisexuality and AIDS. 3–5 November. Utretch, the Netherlands.

WHO/GPA. 1989b. Guidelines for qualitative research on sexual behavior and life-style changes of gay and bisexual men. Manuscript. December. 53 pp.

Wolf, Timothy J. 1985. Marriages of bisexual men. *The Journal of Homosexuality.* 11 (1/2): 135–48.

Paradigmatic Changes
in the Understanding of Bisexuality

Eli Coleman

Several important paradigmatic changes in our understanding of bisexuality have taken place. The first modern paradigm recognized dichotomous and trichotomous distinctions of sexual orientation. An underlying assumption in the creation of this construct was the nineteenth-century view of sexuality: Inherent or "normal" sexuality was rooted in the drive toward reproduction. Any deviation of sexuality which was not directed toward that purpose was viewed as pathological. The second paradigm shift began with Kinsey's view of sexuality. While sex leads to reproduction in many cases, Kinsey found that sexuality was expressed in many other forms. There was no one "natural" way of expressing sexuality. "Bisexuality" was much more common than anyone had ever thought. The third paradigm shift has questioned the basic assumption that sexual orientation is determined by one's gender or genitalia and the gender of genitalia of the individual one is attracted to. This new paradigm assumes that many individuals are attracted to other individuals for reasons other than biological gender. The meaning of sexual behaviors has gone beyond nineteenth-century biological deterministic understandings. This new paradigm has the potential of dominating research in sexual orientation into the next century.

There have been several important paradigmatic changes in our understanding of bisexuality which I would like to review in this paper. First of all, it is important to remember the dichotomous and trichotomous distinctions of sexual orientation were constructs developed by sexologists at the turn of the century. John Boswell, the contemporary historian of sexology, has reminded us that there was a time that "homosexuality," "heterosexuality," and "bisexuality" were not "marked." Other dimensions of an individual were more salient than their sexual orientation.

So, the first modern paradigm shift was to view sexual orientation as three distinct "conditions." An underlying assumption in the creation of this construct was the nineteenth-century view of sexuality. Inherent or "normal" sexuality was rooted in a drive towards reproduction. Any deviation of sexuality which was not directed toward that purpose was viewed as pathological. Even though some viewed homosexuality as a "normal" variation, something had to go wrong to produce this variation. This view of sexuality—and homosexuality—touched off a drive toward the search for causes and cures for homosexuality. Biological, psychodynamic, and learning explanations—based upon the pathological model—have dominated the thinking of the twentieth century.

The second paradigm shift began in the mid-twentieth-century and has dominated thinking until recently. Kinsey revolutionized our view of sexuality by recognizing that while sex did lead to reproduction in many cases, sexuality was expressed in many other forms. There was no one "natural" way of expressing sexuality. While sex was a biological phenomenon, it could take various forms.

Kinsey astonished the world by describing how relatively commonly homosexual behavior took place. "Bisexuality" was far more common than anyone had ever thought. He noted that the world was not divided into sheep and goats. Consistent with this view of sexual orientation, Kinsey and his associates developed a seven-point scale to describe the continuum of sexual orientation. Individuals were placed on this continuum based on their sexual behaviors and erotic attractions. Zero represented exclusive heterosexuality and six represented exclusive homosexuality. Three on this continuum indicated equal same-sex and opposite-sex responsiveness.

Although this continuum notion better represented the realities of the world, the Kinsey scale has many limitations for accurately describing an individual's sexual orientation. First, the scale assumes that sexual behavior and erotic responsiveness are the same within individuals. In response to this criticism, Bell and Weinberg (1978) utilized two scales in their extensive study of homosexuality. They rated their subjects on two scales: one for sexual behavior, and one for erotic fantasies. Their research revealed discrepancies between the two ratings.

While this two-dimensional and continuous view of sexual orientation represented an improvement in assessment of sexual orientation, several clinicians and researchers have recommended additional dimensions. Klein (1978) and Klein, Sepekoff, and Wolf (1985) went further in outlining other dimensions of sexual orientation. In addition to scales describing sexual behavior and fantasies, Klein added other dimensions such as emotional preference, sexual attraction, social preference, self-identification, and heterosexual/homosexual lifestyle preference. Therefore, individuals rate themselves on a seven-point scale for seven different dimensions. Klein also contended that sexual orientation is not fixed or permanent. Therefore, the Klein Sexual Orientation Grid requires a subject to provide twenty-one Kinsey-type ratings in a seven-by-three grid. This grid shows the seven dimensions of sexual orientation and provides ratings for the respondent's past and present (as defined by the preceding year) and the individual's ideal choice.

However, the previous methods still all make some basic assumptions—which until recently have not been questioned. The basic assumption is that sexual orientation is determined by one's own gender or genitalia and the gender of genitalia of the individual to whomone is attracted. However, many individuals are attracted to other individuals for reasons other than biological gender.

Another significant development at this time was the result of the psychoendocrinological studies of John Money, who evolved the concept of gender identity and gender role. These concepts were found to be distinct from an individual's physical or biological gender. Money showed us that biology was not destiny. An individual's "lovemap" was developed through a complex interplay of biological and environmental factors (Money 1986).

The assumption of biological gender as the critical variable in determining sexual orientation is based on the biological and deterministic viewpoint that our attractions serve biological purposes. However, humans—and many animal species too—have shown that attraction can be based upon many other dimensions. Therefore, a number of researchers have suggested a shift from defining orientation based upon one's genitalia to choices that are reflections of one's personal attitudes and expectations. Ross (1984), for example, believes there are a number of social and demographic variables, such as class, race, income, and religion, which may be of equal or greater importance in the analysis of sexual relationships. He believes that any of these variables could be of greater importance in partner choices, but as yet they have not been adequately researched.

Furthermore, Shively and De Cecco (1977) have broadened the notion of sexual identity to include four distinct components; sexual orientation is only one of the four dimensions. Before considering a person's sexual orientation identity, one's *biological sex* needs to be considered. However, Shively and De Cecco also identified two other important variables: *gender identity* and *social-sex role identity.* Gender identity refers to the individual's basic conviction of being male or female. This conviction is not necessarily contingent upon the individual's biological gender, as in the case of transsexuals. So, the question arises as to whether a biological male with a female gender identity, who is attracted exclusively to males and with male gender and social-sex role identities, is a heterosexual, homosexual, or bisexual individual, and whether it matters that this transsexual is preoperative or postoperative. According to the *Diagnostic and Statistical Manual* of the American Psychiatric Association *(DSM-III-R)*, this individual would be classified as a homosexual transsexual. This does not make much sense pre- or postoperatively. It has questionable diagnostic utility and seems only to reflect the historical reproductive bias in understanding sexuality. It is the author's belief that gender identity can equally serve as the main criterion variable of sexual orientation. This is reflected in the author's clinical tool in assessment of sexual orientation (Coleman 1987). This is also reflected in the author's studies of female-to-male transsexuals who adopt a "homosexual" orientation following sex reassignment surgery (Coleman and Bockting 1988).

Moreover, a person's social-sex role is an important aspect of his overall identity. Is the biological female with a male gender and social-sex role identity who is attracted to biological males with male gender and social-sex role identities a homosexual, heterosexual, or bisexual individual? Social-sex role could also be used as a criterion variable and might be more important for the individual than the other components. This also is easily demonstrated in the complex relationships of female-to-male transsexuals and their partners. Looking at these relationships, we can see the various components of sexual identity and how easily they can be orthogonal—but there are even more dimensions to consider to understand a person's sexual orientation.

The greater complexity again comes from the author's research (Coleman, Colgan, and Gooren 1987). In Myanmar (formerly Burma), there are men who engage in what appears to be cross-gender behavior. If we look at these men from our Western eyes, we start labeling them as transvestites or possibly transsexuals. Why else would they be wearing female clothing? To understand this phenomenon in Mynamar, we need to appreciate the cultural, and in this case, the religious heritage of this country. The centuries-old beliefs of this culture are deeply rooted in animism—that there are spirit gods which influence various aspects of daily life. The female spirit god, Manguedon, possesses a child to become her "husband." The child is then drawn to the power of Manguedon and becomes married in spirit to her. Once married, the person is called an *acault* and assumes an important position in

Burmese society. Because Manguedon is the spirit who controls success and good fortune, the acault become an important intermediary between those seeking good fortune and success and the spirit god. The acault wears female clothing mostly in religious ceremonies honoring Manguedon as a symbol of the presence of Manguedon—that the acault is her representative. The clothing says nothing about gender or sex-role identity. In fact, we can see how some acaults make transitions in and out of gender roles rather fluidly.

It is a narrow definition of sexuality, based upon knowledge from reproductive biology, that tends to view the world in its dichotomous ways or even in continuum, but our end points on those continua are still very much bound in this narrow understanding of sexuality. The Kinsey scale, for example, broadens our understanding of sexuality, but severely limits it as well. As William Simon (1989) pointed out:

> The Kinsey homosexual-heterosexual scale in its uses so often became discrete categories as if delineating sub-species—describing individuals by the number of their position on this continuum as if this were expressive of some basic characterological attribute. And similarly, much of the continuing quest for origins of homosexuality assumed a singular source—the naiveté of assuming that a homogeneity of acts implied a corresponding homogeneity of actors. In effect, we transformed what were little more than intellectually convenient and shallow typologies into oppressive taxonomies; the multiple meanings of all sexualities were dissolved into global identities that often obscured more than they revealed. (pp. 13–14)

So we have men and women. And if they are not men and women in the reproductive sense, then some consider them to be gender transpositions—labeled as transvestite, transsexual, bisexual, or homosexual (Money 1988; Pillard and Weinrich 1987). This is the heritage that nineteenth-century views of sexuality have bestowed upon us. We know that these are Western constructions based on certain perspectives or assumptions. The Burmese, who have some knowledge of Western cultures, say they do not have homosexuals in their culture. And, given the structure of their culture, they do not. Do the Burmese people reproduce? Yes. Physical males and females mate and produce offspring. Do men have sex with other men? Yes, and it is quite common. But they *don't* reproduce. So what is the purpose of their behavior? If we use a reproductive biological viewpoint of sexuality, we would say it is abnormal. If we recognize that there are other purposes of sexuality, we must evaluate the behavior with other criteria. In Burmese society, the meaning of the behaviors may be better understood as having spiritual or economic purposes. If we use this broader understanding of sexuality, we can better understand the many variations of sexual behavior and their purposes.

But, we see this dominant paradigm eroding and a new one emerging. The boundaries of what constitutes sexuality are expanding. The meaning of sexual behavior has gone beyond nineteenth-century biological deterministic understandings. William Simon (1989) has called this period "the postmodern period of sex research."

What a postmodernist perspective requires and promises is the development of a conceptual apparatus that can mirror shared collective and individual experiences in what will necessarily be recognized as imperfect and
temporary ways, that will move us closer not to the truth as such, but closer to finding broadened explanations for behavior and an understanding
of its meaning; moving us from an arithmetic of behavior to a literacy of
behavior. It requires that we place all sexual behavior in the larger context
of the lives lived by those having these experiences. (p. 34)

So the most significant paradigm shift has occurred since sociologists, psychologists, and anthropologists have studied human sexual behavior outside the psychiatrist's office. The research of Bell and Weinberg (1978) was groundbreaking. We were
forced to look at homosexualities—the diversity and lack of cohesion of individuals
who were called "homosexuals." We realized that many of these people were really
bisexual, given even their paradigmatic definition. The research by Bell, Weinberg, and
Hammersmith (1981) disproved many of the theories of psychosocial development of
different sexual orientations. One conclusion could be that no cause could be found
because the discrete categories didn't really exist.

The third paradigm shift has questioned the basic assumption that sexual orientation is determined by one's gender or genitalia and the gender of genitalia one is
attracted to—or even one's gender identity. This new paradigm assumes that many
individuals are attracted to other individuals for reasons other than biological gender.
While biology plays an important role in physical or reproductive dimorphism, this
biological dimorphism is playing less and less a role in today's culture. Obviously,
many still define their sexuality in the old paradigmatic ways. Others are now defying
these categories. The meaning of sexual behaviors has gone beyond the nineteenth-
century biological deterministic understandings. This new paradigm has the potential
of dominating research in sexual orientation into the next century.

References

Bell, A. P., and M. S. Weinberg. 1978. *Homosexualities: A Study of Diversity among Men
and Women.* New York: Simon & Schuster.

Bell, A. P., M. S. Weinberg, and S. Hammersmith. 1981. *Sexual Preference: Its
Development in Men and Women.* New York: Simon & Schuster.

Coleman, E. 1981/82. Developmental stages of the coming out process. *Journal of
Homosexuality.* 7: 93–103.

———, ed. 1987. *Psychotherapy for Homosexual Men and Women: Integrated Identity
Approaches for Clinical Practice.* New York: Hayworth Press.

Coleman, E., P. Colgan, and L. Gooren. 1987. Cross gender behavior in Burma: A
description of the acault. Paper presented at the International Academy of Sex
Research. June. Tutzing, West Germany.

Coleman, E., and W. O. Bockting. 1988. "Heterosexual" prior to sex reassignment—
homosexual afterwards: A case study of a female-to-male transsexual. *Journal of
Psychology and Human Sexuality.* 1(2): 69–82.

Klein, Fred. 1978. *The Bisexual Option.* New York: Arbor House.

Klein, Fritz, B. Sepekoff, and T. J. Wolf. 1985. Sexual orientation: A multi-variate dynamic process. *Journal of Homosexuality.* 11(1/2): 35–49.

McWhirter, D., and A. Mattison. 1984. *The Male Couple.* New York: Prentice-Hall.

Money, J. 1980. *Love and Love Sickness: The Science of Sex, Gender Difference, and Pair-Bonding.* Baltimore: Johns Hopkins University Press.

———. 1986. *Lovemaps: Clinical Concepts of Sexual/Erotic Health and Pathology, Paraphilia, and Gender Transposition in Childhood, Adolescence, and Maturity.* New York: Irvington.

———. 1988. *Gay, Straight, and In-Between.* New York: Oxford University Press.

Pillard, R. C., and J. A. Weinrich. 1987. The periodic table of the gender transpositions: Part I—A theory based on masculinization and defeminization of the brain. *Journal of Sex Research.* 23: 425–54.

Ross, M. W. 1984. Beyond the biological model: New directions in bisexual and homosexual research. *Journal of Homosexuality.* 10(3/4): 63–70.

Shively, M., and J. De Cecco. 1977. Components of sexual identity. *Journal of Homosexuality.* 3: 41–48.

Simon, W. 1989. Commentary on sex research: The postmodernization of sex research. *Journal of Psychology and Human Sexuality.* 2(2): 9–37.

Bisexuality: Historical Perspectives

Gert Hekma

In recent anthropological and historical literature, interesting perspectives have been developed on sexuality. Sex is no longer considered a biological drive, but a cultural artifact. What is considered to be "nature" can only be seen as such through the looking-glass of culture.[1] This perspective had important consequences for defining sexuality in other cultures and historical periods. The research of Gilbert Herdt on male initiation in Papuan cultures;[2] of various authors (Bernard Sergent, Michel Foucault, and David Halperin among others)[3] on Greek pederasty; and of others (among them Randolf Trumbach)[4] on early modern sodomy has especially changed our ideas on homosexuality—and thus sexuality—in history.[5]

Homosexual behavior in these cultures and periods had a very different structure from modern homosexuality as we know it. It had little to do with concepts as identity, minority status, or gender-deviance. So it is impossible to put the homosexual behavior of the Papuans or Greeks on a par with modern homosexuality. Several authors have been inclined to replace the homosexual with the bisexual label, but this is not a good solution either. With Greeks and Papuans, the kind of sexual behavior is restricted to certain age groups: homosexual behavior is the rule till adulthood, while heterosexual conduct (and marriage and propagation) are more or less the norm after reaching adulthood. And the sodomitical rake of early modern Europe was usually married, but evaded his marriage obligations with prostitutes as well as ganymedes.

In none of these cases is the definition of the behavior as "bisexual" satisfying, since the term bisexuality is used to mean that the two kinds of sexual preference are interchangeable throughout one's lifetime. This is certainly not the case. The problems loom still larger when bisexuality refers not only to a double sexual object-choice, but also to the androgynous habitus of individuals, their subject-status. In this article, I will go into the problems of using this polymorphous label of bisexuality. I want to suggest a solution to overcome the terminological problems connected with bisexuality and give thereby some directions for future research in social and historical sciences.

The Terminology

THE TERM *bisexual* was used in Dutch for the first time in 1877 (whereas the term *homosexual* was introduced only fifteen years later). Bisexual referred in this case to a hermaphrodite who started her sexual career as a heterosexual woman in Germany and who continued his career as a heterosexual man in America. In this first case, it is not clear in which sense the adjective was used, but most likely it referred to passing through both sexes: to being a woman with her menses and later being a man with ejaculation, and not to having both sexual object-choices.[6] It was still a time when the attribution of gender could be done on the basis of sexual object-choice: loving a man meant being a woman, and so the reverse. We can also recall the case of Herculine Barbin, published and commented upon by Ambroise Tardieu and later by Foucault.[7] Her desire for women was used as a proof she was a man.

Many authors used and still use the term *bisexuality* for both phenomena: double sexual object-choice as well as androgyny. Especially the Freudians confused the two phenomena consequently because they saw a relation between them. And indeed, in those times gender roles and sexual identities were often mixed up, as in the founding work of sexology by Karl Heinrich Ulrichs. He defined the real homosexual as a female mind in a male body, in his famous Latin formula: *anima muliebris corpore virili inclusa.*[8] The professor of forensic medicine in Berlin, J. L. Casper considered, before Ulrichs, pederasty already as a hermaphroditism of the mind.[9] For bisexuality in the sense of a double object-choice, Ulrichs coined the word " *Uranodionäismus.*"[10] To make the confusion complete, Krafft–Ebing used the term "psychosexual hermaphroditism" to indicate the double sexual object-choice. This was, according to him, the first stage of inborn homosexuality whereas the fourth and last stage should be androgyny. The last stage of acquired homosexuality was *metamorphosis sexualis paranoïca.*[11] Before Ulrichs, the gender-status could be determined by the sexual object-choice; after him, the homosexual object-choice was explained by a gender-deviant habitus. In this strange mixture, bisexuality got also its own, very peculiar place.

Problems only increased when again and again new sexological terms were coined which sometimes also interfered with the term bisexuality. To cite two of the most extraordinary: H. Rohleder coined *trisexual* for persons who fell in love not only with individuals of both sexes, but also with themselves, so bisexuality plus narcissism;[12] and the Dutch clergyman H. J. Schouten spoke of homosexual men who married women as *Vaginalmasturbanten,* a certain kind of bisexual.[13] The terminology has remained diffuse up till now. This term is therefore rather difficult to use for historical and anthropological research because of its imprecision and lack of clarity. It is not the lack of a theory, nor the marginalization of the subject, but, to the contrary, these polymorphous theoretical interventions which make the term bisexual unworkable for historical research. It is not too virginal, but too promiscuous a label. And is also rather impossible to clean up the terminology, as John Money proposed in the conference, because the production of terminologies is a social, and not a rational process, even in universitarian circles.

I will give two examples from historical research, Greek pederasty and eighteenth-century sodomy, to indicate the problems of referring to forms of sexual behavior as bisexuality.

Greek Pederasty

GREEK PEDERASTY RESEMBLED to a certain degree Papuan initiation, which Herdt discussed. *Eros* was a word mostly used for the love relations between men and boys, and rarely for relations between men and women. The Dutch historian of Greek antiquity Van Limburg Brouwer stated with horror already in 1838: " . . . in a hundred cases where eros is mentioned, never even once is it thought of a woman."[14] Love was a male affair with strong pedagogical implications. In the context of a male society where women had little to say, marriage or relations with prostitutes had a less prominent place in the cultural life of men. Severe limits nevertheless were placed on the sexual bonds between men and boys. A boy had to always take the passive role and he could not incite his lover to sexual acts: he should remain as chaste as possible. On the other hand, the lover also had to restrain himself. Apart from this male eros, love for women came in second place. Love and sexuality had a clear hierarchy: the love for boys and that for women were separate spheres, with the first more highly regarded than the second. Also, there was a life cycle involved in both loves: pederasty was more for the sake of youth and young men, whereas responsible older men had less to do with it and more with marriage. So, to use the label of bisexuality for this system of sexuality and gender is to simplify it beyond scholarly standards. Of course, there were many variations in sexual styles and certainly there were men and women whom we could label with a certain reserve bisexual, or homosexual, or "queer," but to use the container term of "bisexuality" for this system of boy-love and marriage is doing great damage to its complexities and blindfolds us for the intricacies of Greek eros.[15]

Marriage and Sodomy

SODOMY IN EARLY MODERN Europe is vividly discussed. According to Randolph Trumbach, before 1700 the sodomite was a married man who had sex with prostitutes as well as with ganymedes. No one should doubt his gender-identity as a man. His male sexual ideal was an androgynous boy, as Philippe Ariès stated.[16] After 1700, with the alleged sexual and gender revolution in the times of the Enlightenment and with the rise of sodomites' subcultures, the role of the sodomite became more exclusive and his identity was more on the female side. The "mary-ann" or "queer" was now himself more or less androgynous. Before 1700, the complaints of femininity in males referred to men who indulged too much in affairs with women, whereas after 1700, the same complaints of femininity in males referred to sodomites, lovers of men who preferred a passive sexual role. The sexual system of early modern Europe before 1700 more or less resembled the Arabic one, about which Arno Schmitt spoke in the conference.[17] It was a system of shame and honor in which homosexual behavior was not a scandal as long as the males took the active role, or as long as they could keep their passive habits a secret. They were often married, in addition to their pederastic pleasures. But after 1700, many sodomites were married as well. For a long time, sodomitical behavior and marriage obligations were not opposed. Only slowly did the acceptance of a homosexual role become incompatible with the sexual plights of a marriage. This is an interesting point for future research: the gradual diminution of the number of married sodomites and homosexuals. Again, we can label the sexual system of early modern sodomy as bisexuality, but if we do so, we completely negate the sexual and gender revolution of 1700. The sodomite before 1700 was a staunch male who fell in love with a feminine youth, and after 1700 he was an effeminate fop who looked for manly young men. Before and after 1700 he was very often married. But notwithstanding the continuation of a bisexual object-choice, gender-identifations and ideals of beauty were inverted. The word *bisexuality* has too many meanings to use it for this transition: There are too many rings around Rosie.

Proposals for Further Research

To OVERCOME THE PROBLEMS inherent in the use of the concept of bisexuality, I would propose to skip it for historical and anthropological purposes, or to go into the different forms of bisexuality: there are many bisexualities.[18] A third possibility is to research the historical and social formation of bisexualities and the terminology of bisexuality. For other research, the label bisexual poses too many problems: first of all, it is a very time-bound mixture of gender-bending and the double sexual object-choice, and moreover it refers to sexuality and identity which remain time-bound perspectives. Bisexuality is a hodge-podge of too many possibilities of sex and gender which it is better not to integrate. After the polymorphous possibilities of childhood, sexual desire gets only more specific. It is this specifity of desire which is negated in the concept of bisexuality. The Greeks did not fall in love arbitrarily with both genders, and neither did the Papuans. We have even to question as to how far their behavior can be termed sexual desire. Even nowadays, people do not fall in love indiscriminately with both genders. To negate this specificity of sexual desire and erotic experience poses problems for scholarly research. It is extremely difficult for historians to say anything about the sexual life of their subjects, be it alone for the scarcity of material on this topic, even in famous examples as the duke of Orléans, brother to the Sun-King; or King William III of England, stadtholder of the Netherlands; or Oscar Wilde. But to completely pass over the bisexual label is to deny the specifities and intricacies of erotic pursuits. The interesting point for historical research is precisely to unravel these specifities and intricacies of erotic experiences and sexual desires in the individal as well as in the social system.

Endnotes

1. For example, J. H. Gagnon and W. Simon, *Sexual Conduct: The Social Sources of Human Sexuality* (Chicago 1973); M. Foucault, *Histoire de la sexualité 1. La volonté de savoir* (Paris 1976).

2. G. H. Herdt, ed., *Ritualized Homosexuality in Melanesia* (Berkeley 1984) is his most important contribution in this field, among many others.

3. See for example, K. J. Dover, *Greek Homosexuality*, (New York 1978); H. Patzer, *Die Griechische Knabenliebe* (Wiesbaden 1982); G. Koch-Harnack, *Knabenliebe und Tiergeschenke. Ihre Bedeutung im päderastischen Erziehungssystem Athens* (Berlin 1983); B. Sergent, *L'homosexualité dans la mythologie grecque* (Paris 1984); id., *L'homosexualité initiatique dans l'Europe ancienne* (Paris 1986); M. Foucault, *Histoire de la sexualité 2: L'usage des plaisirs* (Paris 1984); C. Reinsberg, *Ehe, Hetärentum und Knabenliebe im antiken Griechenland* (München 1989); D. M. Halperin, *One Hundred Years of Homosexuality and Other Essays on Greek Love* (New York/London 1990); D. M. Halperin, J. J. Winkler, and F. I. Zeitlin, eds., *Before Sexuality: The Construction of Erotic Experience in the Ancient Greek World* (Princeton 1990).

4. R. Trumbach, "Gender and the Homosexual Role in Modern Western Culture: the 18th and 19th Centuries Compared" in *Homosexuality, Which Homosexuality*, D. Altman et al. (Amsterdam/London 1988), which is his most provocative essay in this regard. See also K. Gerard & G. Hekma, eds., *The Pursuit of*

Sodomy: Male Homosexuality in Renaissance and Enlightenment Europe, (New York 1989) (also a special issue of the *Journal of Homosexuality* 16: 1/2).

5. Research on the concept of sexuality itself has been more limited, see for example, the articles of A. Béjin in the special issue of *Communications* 35 (Paris 1982): *Sexualités occidentales* which he edited with Philippe Ariès; A. I. Davidson, "Sex and the Emergence of Sexuality" in *Critical Inquiry* 14 (1987), pp. 16–48 and my article "A History of Sexuality: Social and Historical Aspects of Sexuality" in *From Sappho to De Sade: Moments in the History of Sexuality,* J. Bremmer, ed. (London/New York 1989).

6. *De Lancet,* N. S., Jg. 10 (1877), pp. 294–295. The case was cited from an article by Dr. Lutaud in the *Journal de médecine, de chirurgie et de pharmacologie* of July, 1877. On the next page the neologism "exhibitionist" by Lasègue was mentioned for the first time in Dutch.

7. A. Tardieu, *Question médico-légale de l'identité dans les rapports avec les vices de conformation des organes sexuelles* (Paris 1874), and *Herculine Barbin dite Alexina B.,* présenté par M. Foucault (Paris 1978).

8. The 12 publications of Ulrichs on uranism appeared between 1864 and 1880 and were re-edited by M. Hirschfeld as *Forschungen über das Räthsel der mann-männlichen Liebe* (Leipzig 1898, New York 1975). This formula he used for the first time in Memnon (1868, 1975), pp. 193–195.

9. J. L. Casper, *Handbuch der gerichtlichen Medicin,* Bd. II, (Berlin 1858).

10. Ulrichs, o. c., Formatrix (1865, 1975), p. 59.

11. R. von Krafft-Ebing, *Psychopathia sexualis mit besonderer Berücksichtigung der conträren Sexualempfindung,* Stuttgart, 5. (Auflage 1890), pp. 79–96.

12. In: *Verhandlungen des I. Internationalen Kongresses für Sexualforschung,* Bd. II, (Berlin/Köln 1928), p. 158.

13. In "Ueber falsche oder missverständliche Sprachgebräuche..." in *Sexual Probleme* Jg. 8 (1912), p. 861.

14. P. van Limburg Brouwer, *Histoire de la civilisation morale et réligieuse des Grecs,* T. 2,2, (Groningen 1838), p. 236.

15. See note 3 above.

16. P. Ariès, "Réflexions sur l'histoire de l'homosexualité" in *Communications* 35, special issue *Sexualités occidentales,* A. Béjin and P. Ariès, eds. (Paris 1982), pp. 56–67.

17. G. De Martino and A. Schmitt, *Kleine Schriften zu zwischenmännlicher Sexualität und Erotik in der muslimischen Gesellschaft,* (Berlin 1985).

18. See Neil McKenna, *On the Margins: Men Who Have Sex with Men and HIV in the Dveloping World,* (London 1996), ch. 4; and Rommel Mendès-Leité, *Bisexualité, le dernier tabou,* (Paris: 1996).

Homosexuality: Bipotentiality, Terminology, and History

John Money

John Money

PART I: THE SEXOLOGICAL CONCEPT OF
BIPOTENTIALITY IS FOUND FIRST IN ULRICHS

The sexological principle popularized by Ulrichs in 1864—namely, that sexual differentiation is bipotential until it yields to female primacy—remained conjectual until 1852, the year when Thiersch published his experimental findings. As early as 1813, however, Tiedemann (quoted by Neumann 1990, 136) had anticipated such a possibility in his book *Anatomie der koflosen Missegeburten*. Tiedemann wrote:

> I maintain that the genitals are initially as soon as they appear, female and that the female genitalia are transformed later in several embryos to male genitalia. The reason for these phenomena, that most freaks and most embryos lost through abortion are of the female sex, appears to me to be that all human embryos have only female sexual organs in the first few months of pregnancy. It can therefore justifiably be said that the female genitals are male genitals which have not started to develop. They have remained stuck at a lower stage which is normal to the embryo in an earlier period. If one compares the physique of the man and the woman with that of the fetus, then it is seen that the woman obviously resembles the fetus much more closely than does the man and that, consequently, the woman is a lower stage of development than man.

Karl Heinrich Ulrichs (1825–1895), a jurist by training, has become recognized posthumously as the pioneer of sexual law reform in Christendom. It is not yet recognized that he was also the pioneer of modern sexological biological science, insofar as he believed (in vain) that a rational embryological explanation of the origin of sexual love between men like himself, whom he named *urnings*, would lead rationally to an increase of societal tolerance and reform of sexual laws. His scientific expanation was based on his knowledge of the then new (1852) findings of the primordial hermaphroditism or sexual bipotentiality of the mammalian embryo in the differentiation of its internal genitalia (Adelman 1966). In his first publication, *Inclusa* (1864), Ulrichs wrote of a woman's mind included or entrapped in a man's body *(anima muliebris corpore virili inclusa)*, a saying that originated in the diary of the Swiss author, Jacob Stutz (1801–1877). "Perhaps," Ulrichs conjectured, "the place where sexual love might be found is entirely elsewhere than in testicles, ovaries, or any other sexual parts, namely in the brain."

Ulrichs did not speculate on how the "feminine generative principle" responsible for "a womanly sense of sexual love" might gain entry into a male brain. For the next half century, the answer was supplied from the psychiatric doctrines of the day, all of which shared the common denominator of attributing all types of madness, criminality, and perversion, sexual and otherwise, to degeneracy, hence the derogatory, contemporary term, "sexual degenerate." Degeneracy theory had been stamped with the seal of medical approval by Simon André Tissot in his 1758 treatise on onanism (Tissot 1832) in which he was diffusely searching for the cause and cure of the "social disease," a term that did not differentiate syphilis and gonorrhea. Degeneracy caused by loss of semem has extremely ancient origins in the doctrine of semen conservation (Money 1985). This doctrine, found in the earliest Sanskrit and Chinese medical writings, as well as in preliterate folk medicine, specifies that semen is the most precious of all the vital fluids or humors, and the source of all strength and health. It specified also that degeneracy from masturbation is greater than from copulation, as there is an exchange of vital force between the copulating pair. Even so, copulation should be as infrequent as possible, and for procreation, not recreation. The possibility of an exchange of vitality between two partners of the same sex was circumvented by Tissot and his nineteenth-century successors. They referred to homosexuality mostly as two males masturbating, especially an older male teaching a younger one to masturbate.

In late nineteenth-century sexology, degeneracy theory expanded. In addition to semen loss, the sources of degeneracy included heredity, which was virtually all-inclusive as there was no limit to what could degenerate a pedigree, generation after generation, insofar as Lamarckian inheritance of acquired characteristics was widely accepted. In the wake of evolutionary theory, a new principle of degeneracy appeared, namely evolutionary atavism or reverse Darwinism. According to this principle, homosexuality represented a reversion or backtracking to the primitive evolutionary stage of the hermaphrodite or androgyne.

So long as degeneracy theories held sway, Ulrichs's pivotal concept of sexuality bipotentiality fell into neglect and disuse. Ulrichs himself did not use the term bisexual, nor homosexual, nor heterosexual. Although homosexual had been coined (see below) in 1869 by Kertbeny, Ulrichs's contemporary in sexual law reform, it remained dormant until Magnus Hirschfeld republished Kertbeny's original newspaper article in the 1905 *Jahrbuch für Sexuelle Zwischenstufen*, vol. 5. *Homosexual* then very rapidly replaced the term *sexual inversion* in all European languages.

Incorporated into theory to explain homosexuality, the concept of bipoteniality was revived as a psychological concept, bisexuality, by Wilhelm Fliess. From Fliess, libidinal bisexuality was taken over by Sigmund Freud to become, at the end of the last century, a basic principle of psychoanalysis.

By 1912, Eugen Steinach had experimentally masculinized the mating behavior of female guinea pigs, and likewise feminized the mating behavior of males, by castrating them as newborns, and transplanting heterotypic gonadal tissue into them (Steinach 1940, 239–40). Steinach had, in fact, demonstrated for the first time the prenatal hormonal control of the adult behavioral outcome of prenatal male/female bipotentiality. Since Steinach, the role of prenatal sex hormones on the outcome of male/female bipotentiality has been incontrovertibly confirmed, though typically reported as unipolar (hetero- or homosexual) and seldom as mixed or bisexual. By contrast, the attempt to prove the continuity of sex-hormonal bipotentiality into adolescence and maturity, as in the attempt to change homosexuality by treatment with sex hormones, has incontrovertibly been disconfirmed.

Prenatal sex hormones influence, but do not totally preordain, the long-term outcome of prenatal bipotentiality of male/female. They do so by, first of all, influencing the brain, which in turn influences sexuoeroticism as either bisexual or as monosexually heterosexual or homosexual (Money 1988). Experimental analysis of neuroanatomical bipotentiality is barely twenty years old. Thus, a century went by before the wheel of Ulrichs's prediction turned full circle.

The brain's male/female bipotentiality does not terminate at birth, but continues to be resolved into heterosexual, homosexual, or bisexual, especially during the early childhood years of cognitional assimilation and learning, and during the course of juvenile sexual rehearsal play. In the final analysis, there is no irreconcilable adversarialism between those who, according to today's sexological vogue, are named essentialists and social constructionists, respectively. To pit them against each other is as pointless as to reincarnate Ulrichs, and the sexual biological scientist doing battle with Ulrichs, the sexual law reformer. The two are a unity for those who have eyes to see them whole.

Ulrichs had faith that a biological explanation of men like himself whom he called *urnings* would entitle them to greater judicial tolerance, but his faith was misplaced. It proved only that neither tolerance nor intolerance is grounded in science and reason, but they are themselves acts of faith grounded in social custom and the politics of expediency and power. That is why, in the politics of today's gay movement, whereas Ulrichs himself is venerated as the first political gay activist, his theory, being biomedical, is heresy, spurned by many as politically incorrect. The current politically correct explanation of erotic orientation is that it is a civil right, based not on biology but on preference and moral choice. However, moral choice offers erotic minorities no more protection against the persecution of their enemies than does explanatory biology.

PART II: THE TRANSFORMATION OF THE TERMINOLOGY OF HOMOSEXUALITY IN SEXOLOGICAL HISTORY

What formerly was known as the sociology of knowledge has returned, and is in vogue today, as the social constructionist view of history and science. The new vogue is expressed in sexology in the doctrines of the social construction of gender; the social construction of sexuality, homosexuality and heterosexuality; and the social construction of deviancy, and so on. Some constructions are politically correct, some are not. Correct or incorrect, all social constructs have a history. To paraphrase Santayana: Not to know this history is to condemn one to repeat it. Part II is about the social construction of homosexuality and its changing names throughout history from classical times to the present.

Paiderastia and Pederasty

IN CONTEMPORARY VOCABULARY, the word is *homosexuality*. But in earlier vocabularies it did not exist. In the age of Aristophanes, Xenophon, and Plato, the term was *paiderastia* (*pais*, boy + *erastes*, lover). In classical Greek usage, the term signified the ideologically admired sexual and pedagogical bonding of an adolescent youth with his mentor.

Although they did not idealize paiderastia as did the Greeks, the Romans of antiquity were not by any means averse to the sexual practice of anal intercourse between two males, with the older man inserting, and the younger receiving. The Latin word *Catamitus* (English, *catamite*) referred to an effeminate youth who regularly took the womanish copulatory role. Catamitus is the Latinized form of Ganymedes (Ganymede), reputed in Greek mythology to have been the most beautiful of all mortals, carried off by an eagle to be the cup bearer and the beloved favorite of Zeus.

In modern usage, *pederasty*, far from being ideologically admired as in ancient Greece, is despised as synonymous with the Biblical sin of Sodom.

Sodomy

THE LANGUAGE OF the Hebrews had no one-word term corresponding to the Greek *paiderastia*. When the entire male population of Sodom (Genesis 19:1–11) demanded of Lot that he hand over the two messengers of the Lord "that we may know them," their demand signified male-to-male carnal knowledge (Spong 1988). Thus, did the Biblical town of Sodom become, in ensuing centuries, the eponym for *sodomy*, a term which has persisted in legal and media usage until the present. Its meaning has become confusingly expanded to signify not only engaging genitally with a same-sex partner, but also engaging anogenitally or orogenitally with a partner of either sex, or engaging in any kind of sexual practice with an animal.

Buggery

IN CONTEMPORARY BRITISH legal usage, a synonym for the sin of Sodom is *buggery*. In British vernacular usage, to call someone a bugger is a curse or an insult, whereas in American usage it is an endearment applied, for example, to a cute infant. It shares its etymology with *Bougie*, a creole term for a nose-picking, and with *bougie man* or *bogey man*. Its original etymology is *Bulger*, or *Bulgarian*. In the eleventh century, the medival church of Rome attributed the heresy of Catharism, also know as Albigensianism, after the Provençal city of Albi in southern France, to a revival of the earlier Manichean heresy. The Bulgars of the Balkan peninsula to the east were held responsible for the revival and spread of the heresy. Their name, corrupted to Bugger, became the eponym for the triad of heresy, sodomy, and treason, any one of which was held to predicate the other two, and to justify being burned alive at the stake. This triad exists still today, except that sodomy and buggery have become interchangeable, and heresy and treason have been transformed into, respectively, the sin of nonbelief and moral subversion of the social order. In the prudishly evasive language of the law, the *abominable and unspeakable crime against nature* is a euphemism which, in its explicit meaning, requires the actual practices subsumed under the term sodomy or buggery, to be quite literally unmentionable in a court of law.

Berdachism

SODOMY AND BUGGERY both pertain to sexual acts without distinguishing, when two men are together, whether their roles are interchangeable, or whether one has stereotypically a more feminine, and the other a more masculine role than the other. By the end of the fifteenth century, however, if not earlier, a new word for a male simulating the copulatory role of a female entered the European languages by way of Arabic from the Persian *bardaj*. In Spanish it became *bardaxa* (alternative spelling, *bardaje*); in Italian, *bardasso*; and in French, *bardache*. In English, *berdache* is an adaptation from the early colonial Spanish and French names for native American Indian shamans and healers who were natal males in the role of the female (Williams 1986).

Williams (p. 9), relying on the linguistic research of Claude Courove, writes regarding the definition of *bardache*:

> The 1680 edition of Dictionnaire français, gives this definition: "a young man who is shamefully abused (Caesar was the bardache of Nicomedes)." The 1718 edition of P. J. LeRoux's Dictionnaire Comique defines it more explicitly: "A young man or boy who serves another's succubus, permitting sodomy to be committed on him. These abominations are so common in France that women have rightly complained of them, and I could even name several individuals who keep bardaches, generally beautiful boys, as others keep courtesans." This dictionary offers as a synonym for bardache the term ganimede, after the boy who was the lover of Zeus in Greek mythology . . . both bardache and ganimede refer to the passive partner . . . bougre was used for the active male partner.

In English, *berdache* did not pass into general usage, but became specific to American Indian anthropology.

Urningtum (Uranism)

A NEW ADDITION to the nomenclature was devised by Karl Heinrich Ulrichs (1828–1895). It was derived from the Greek myth of the birth of Venus according to which, without a mother, Venus was generated from the sea foam stirred up by her father Uranus after his own son, Cronos, had castrated him and cast him into the ocean. Ulrichs's terms, Germanicized from Uranus, were: *Urning* for the male whose love is for another male; *Urningin* for the female whose love is for another female; and *Urningtum* (Anglicized to *Uranism*) for the condition of those whose love is for someone of the same sex. The new terminology made it semantically possible for Ulrichs to formulate a typology, the first of its kind, and a theory of causation that was unique in being compatible with the medical science of the day, and in particular with recent advances demonstrating bipotentiality in the embryology of sexual differentiation (Ulrichs 1864; see also Money 1980).

Ulrichs applied his new theory politically by drawing the conclusion that same-sex love, which he defined as innate, was natural and not criminal (Kennedy 1988). Although this conclusion was not acceptable to the moral and forensic establishment of the day, Ulrichs's typology and theoretical insights were acceptable, but only under the disguise of different names. Ulrichs's terminology became neglected and fell into total disuse.

In Germany, Karl Friedrich Otto Westphal (1833–1890), a psychiatrist who was familiar with Ulrich's writings, renamed Urningtum as *contraere Sexualempfindung* (contrary sexual feeling) in a paper published in 1869. This term fell into disuse by the end of the century. In the English translation of the writings of Richard von Krafft–Ebing (1840–1902), it became *antipathic sexual instinct*, another term that fell into disuse except in reissues of his *Psychopathia Sexualis*.

Sexual Inversion

ACCORDING TO HAVELOCK Ellis (1859–1939), Westphal's term was first translated into English as *inverted sexual proclivity* (Ellis 1942) when his 1869 paper was reviewed in 1871 in the British *Journal of Mental Science*. *Inversione sessuale* appeared in Italian in 1878, and *inversion sexuelle* in French in 1882.

The term *sexual inversion* served to separate the phenomenon conceptually from the category of sexual perversion, in which it had been included. In 1893, inversion was the word used by John Addington Symonds (1840–1893) in the privately printed, and limited, first edition (twelve copies) of his book republished in 1901: *A Problem in Greek Ethics, Being an Inquiry into the Phenomenon of Sexual Inversion*. It was Symonds who contributed the title *Sexual Inversion* to Havelock Ellis for what was to become the first published volume of Ellis's *Studies in the Psychology of Sex* (1936). Symonds died suddenly at the outset of what would otherwise have been a joint authorship.

Homosexuality

IN SUBSEQUENT VOLUMES and revisions, Ellis adopted also the term *homosexuality*. This word had first come into existence as early as 1869 in a pamphlet addressed to the Prussian Minister of Justice on sexual law reform. Though published anonymously, it was ultimately attributed to Karl Maria Kertbeny (1824–1882) who was born Karl Maria Benkert, son of the writer Anton Benkert and the painter Charlotte Graf (Herzer 1985).

As early as 1864, Kertbeny and Ulrichs knew of each other's political commitment to sexual law reform on behalf of men persecuted for their attraction to other men. They corresponded sporadically until 1869, if not longer. Not enough of their correspondence has survived to indicate why neither adopted the other's terminology. Kertbeny kept a draft of an 1868 letter to Ulrichs in which he said he had "a thick manuscript divided into four principal sections: *Monosexuality; Homosexuality; Heterosexuality;* and *Heterogenit*"—meaning self-sexual (autoerotic), homosexual, heterosexual, and heterogeneous (cross-species), respectively (Kennedy 1988). Unpublished, this manuscript has apparently been lost.

The terms *homosexual, heterosexual, homosexuality,* and *heterosexuality* were quoted by Gustave Jager, and attributed to an unidentified author, in the 1880 edition of his book, *The Discovery of the Soul* (Herzer 1985). It was not until after 1905, however, that the terms *homosexual* and *homosexuality* became widely publicized. In that year, Magnus Hirschfeld (1868–1935), founder of the Institute for Sexology in Berlin, republished Kertbeny's 1869 pamphlet in the *Jahrbuch für Sexuelle Zwischenstufen (Yearbook for Sexual Intermediate Stages)*. Obviously, the new terms filled what had been a linguistic and syntactical void, for they rapidly entered the international vocabulary of the twentieth century, as also did *heterosexual* and *heterosexuality*.

In today's usage, *homosexual* derives its meaning directly from its etymology, namely form Greek, *homos*, same + Latin, *sexus*, sex + *-alis*, pertaining to. By itself, the etymology gives no indication of what it is that pertains to the same sex. Thus, homosexual may be used as a synonym for isosexual in cases with a diagnosis of *pubertas precox* (precocious puberty) to signify matching or sameness between the hormonal sex and the genital sex, whereas heterosexual precocity signifies mismatching, as in a girl with masculinizing or a boy with feminizing precocious pubery. In such cases, masculinization and feminization apply only to body morphology and the procreative organs, not to relationships with other people, male or female.

By contrast, in everyday usage, it is taken for granted that the etymology of *homosexual* indicates that whatever it is that pertains to the same sex, it pertains very much to a relationship. The relationship may be genital, or it may not be. There are many and varied nongenital relationships with other people of the same sex, all of which should, according to the canons of strict logic and language, be labeled homosexual. The would-be escape from the confines of this strict logic has been to give the Latin root, *sexus*, double duty. Thus it has become acceptable in everyday usage to take for granted that a homosexual relationship is not simply any type of relationship between two people of the same sex, but, redundantly, a same-sex sexual relationship.

Homophilia

EARLY IN THE 1950s, the term *homophile* entered the vocabulary as a synonym for *homosexual.* Derived from same and love, *homophilia* was politically a more expedient term than homosexuality, as also was *homosocial.* Political expediency was imperative in the 1950s, the decade which saw the founding of the Mattachine Society and the Daughters of Bilitis, and the beginning of what would become the gay liberation movement in America. In 1952, William Dorr Legg founded the magazine *One Inc.*, which marked the beginning of the gay liberation press and provided a voice for the ONE Institute of Homophile Studies in Los Angeles. In contemporary usage, *homophile*, like *homosocial*, is still used, but has largely been replaced by *gay*.

Tribadism

WHEN THE TERM *homosexual* entered the language, it was used to apply to women as well as men. There were two preexisting terms, *tribadism* and *lesbianism.* Tribadism derives from the Greek *tribein*, to rub, and thus signifies mutual friction of the genitals between women. The *Oxford English Dictionary* identifies *tribade* as a sixteenth-century French word borrowed into English, and quotes it as having been used by Ben Jonson in 1601. The word was also used by Havelock Ellis in a sexological sense in 1890. In *Dorland's Illustrated Medical Dictionary* (26th ed. 1974), tribadism is equated with the simulation of heterosexual intercourse, possibly with the use of an artificial penis. *Blackiston's New Gould Medical Dictionary* (2d ed. 1956) applies the term *tribade* only to the woman "who plays the role of the male in homosexual practices." *Longman's Dictionary of Psychology and Psychiatry* (1984) goes so far as to say that a tribade usually has a large clitoris (which is manifestly in error) and plays the male role.

Lesbianism

IF IT EVER was recorded, the historical record of who coined the term *lesbian* is apparently lost. According to the *Oxford English Dictionary*, the word entered the vocabulary in 1870, and spread into general usage in the 1890s. Etymologically it derives from Lesbos, the Greek island and home, around 600 B.C., of the poetess Sappho. Her love poems celebrated love between women, and her name became the eponym, Sapphic, by which to name that love, and also the verse forms in which it was expressed.

The word *homosexuality* did not eclipse *lesbianism* in general usage, but with the militancy of reverse stigmatization, *homosexuality* was itself eclipsed by *lesbianism*. When *gay* became the liberating term in gay rights for men, *lesbian* became the liberating term for women.

Gay

THE TRANSFORMATION OF the meaning of the word *gay* from *merry* and/or *licentious* to *homosexual* may have begun in the "gay nineties" of the nineteenth century. The term "gay people" is recorded in the 1890 court transcript of Jack Saul, who gave evidence in connection with the Cleveland Street male brothel scandal in London (Weeks 1980/81, 126). Himself a professional "Mary-Anne," Saul said that he partly supported himself by doing odd jobs, mainly house cleaning, for gay people, meaning prostitutes (younger women, and perhaps males impersonating women) on the beat.

It is within living memory that, in the United States in the 1920s, *gay* was already in use as a self-labeling neologism for *homosexual*. In the 1940s, it was self-satirizing and flippantly campy, and used primarily as an adjective.

In the late 1960s, *gay* became standardized as a political term, with no burden of sex in its etymology, that signified a community of people with a shared lifestyle, and a shared legal and societal agenda for gay rights and gay liberation, freed from both medical and criminal stigmatization. The new meaning of the term spread rapidly throughout the English-speaking countries, and *gay* was either borrowed into other languages or replaced with an indigenous alternative that carried the same meaning—for example, *schwul* (Herzer 1985), in Germany.

Gay is not simply a synonym for *homosexual*, but a term that signifies a radical transformation of a phenomenon of human existence from a sin, and then a sickness, to a social status. Being gay means, like being left-handed or color-blind, being a citizen of a minority group and, irrespective of the cause of being gay, of being entitled to share equality of privilege with the majority.

Transvestite

TRANSVEST, THE VERB that derives from the Latin meaning to cross-dress, existed in 1652, according to the *Oxford English Dictionary*, and had a theatrical meaning of dressing or disguising in other garments, for example, those of the other sex. The nouns *transvestite* and *transvestism* are not even entered in the *O.E.D.* According to Havelock Ellis (1936), they were coined as sexological terms by Magnus Hirschfeld, who used them in 1910 in his book *Die Transvestiten*. Hirschfeld distinguished transvestism from the sexual inversion (already at that time renamed as homosexuality) under which rubric it had formerly been subsumed. On the criterion of whether a transvestite was erotically attracted to a male or a female partner, Hirschfeld subdivided transvestism into four subtypes: heterosexual, bisexual, homosexual, and asexual. To these he added a fifth subtype, the narcissistic, in which femininity enhances a man's masculinity.

Eonism

AS DID HIRSCHFELD himself, Havelock Ellis (1936) recognized the challenge of taking into account the multivariate nature of transvestism in devising a classification of subtypes—taking into account garment fetishism, for example, or aesthetic idealization of femininity or masculinity. In recognition of this challenge, Ellis, following the nomenclature of *sadism*, from de Sade (1740–1814) as the eponym, and of *masochism*, from von Sacher Masoch (1836–1895), proposed the term *eonism*, from the Chevalier d'Eon (1728–1810). D'Eon was celebrated in French and English eighteenth- and early nineteenth-century society as a cross-dresser. Ellis first proposed *eonism* tentatively in 1913, and again more seriously in 1920.

Despite its advantage of being conceptually more inclusive than Hirschfeld's *transvestism*, Ellis's *eonism* lost out to its rival which had the advantage of priority. The disadvantage of *transvestism* is that it signifies both the ephemeral social act of being cross-dressed, even for fun at a party, and the condition of having a persistent sexological syndrome of which being cross-dressed is only one of its characteristics.

Transexualism and Gender Dysphoria

EONISM, AS PROPOSED by Havelock Ellis, was conceptually broad enough to have encompassed a range of phenomena (including cross-cultural phenomena) for which the shared common factor is cross-dressing. In particular, eonism encompasses that phenomenon in which cross-dressing is only the surface evidence of a complete crossover of the entire image of the body, male to female, or vice versa.

The phenomena of changing sex was given literary recognition first in the Greek myth of Tiresias. Characters who cross-dressed and lived as members of the other sex were described in eighteenth- and nineteenth-century literary writings before they appeared in clinical case reports in the sexological literature toward the end of the nineteenth century. Diagnostically, the terminology progressed from contrary or antipathic sexual instinct to sexual inversion, to transvestism.

The term *transexualism* first appeared in 1949 in a short article entitled "Psychopathia transexualis" by D. O. Cauldwell, in the now defunct *Sexology* (vol. 16:274–80), a sex education magazine for the blue-collar readership, subsidized by the enlightened publisher, Hugo Gernsbach. Subsequently, Harry Benjamin settled on the spelling *transsexual*, with the double "s" (Money 1981, 104). His book *The Transsexual Phenomenon* (1966) established the term *transsexualism* (or *transexualism*) in medical nosology as the name for the syndrome of sex crossing, that is of changing from the natal sexual status to that of the other sex.

In addition to naming a syndrome, *transexualism* also is the name for the procedure of rehabilitation by means of surgical, hormonal, and social sex reassignment.

Dissatisfaction with naming a syndrome on the basis of its behavioral manifestations and its treatment, led eventually to the proposal by Fisk (1974) of the term *gender dysphoria* as the name for the underlying psychic pathology. Gender dysphoria was conceptualized as a generic state of which there are different expressions, some of which culminate in sex reassignment. In current usage, *gender dysphoria* has become virtually a synonym for *transexualism*. It has been criticized by transexuals themselves, who maintain that their dysphoria pertains to their genital sex, not their gender identity.

Mimesis: Gynemimesis and Andromimesis

MALE DOMINANCE AND female submission in the procreative relationship is endemic to all Indo-European cultures and their derivatives. The same imbalance has long been a stereotype of male/male and female/female relationships. The catamite was stereotyped as the feminine partner of a pederast, and the berdache likewise of the bugger. Ulrichs subdivided *urnings* into the *wiebling* (feminine) and the *mannling* (masculine) types. After the term *homosexuality* became established, homosexuals were subdivided into passive and active, effeminate and noneffeminate, respectively. The symmetry of this simple dualism fails in the case of transvestism, insofar as the winner of the prize for the most perfect feminine appearance may be coitally heterosexual. Similarly, in the case of transexualism, the most convincingly transformed male-to-female may settle into a lesbian lifestyle with another female.

These apparent discrepancies become resolved if the concept of simple masculine/feminine dualism is replaced by the concept of multiaxial dualism. Then the central spindle is pierced by multiple measuring rods, graded from feminine on one end to masculine on the other—one for genitoerotic orientation, and others for vocational, educational, and recreational orientation, and still others for fashion in clothing and body adornment, legal status, and so forth.

On the basis of multiaxial dualism, it is possible to construct various permutations and combinations of gynemimesis (woman-miming) in men, and andromimesis (man-miming) in women (Money and Lamacz 1988). For example, one combination is found in those gynemimetics who are natal males, who live their lives permanently and consistently as women, who take female hormones to feminize the body, but who do not undergo elective feminizing sex-reassignment genital surgery. They are ladies with penises. Their counterparts are men with vulvas.

The classificatory value of gynemimesis and andromimesis extends beyond the confines of Western sexology to the far reaches of ethnographic sexology and the study of ethnic sexological phenomena that are related to our own, but not identical with them. One example is that of gynemimesis among the *hijra* of India (Nanda 1990), which resembles both transvestism and transexualism in our own culture, but is identical with neither.

Gynemimesis and andromimesis both are terms that allow one to take account of similarity manifested in the midst of diversity. They are phenomenological and descriptive terms. They imply nothing with respect to origins or causes of the phenomena they name. Causal explanations of these phenomena are contingent upon scientific discoveries that await new investigative technology, especially in sexological neuroscience.

Conclusion

WHEREAS MALE/MALE AND female/female sexual erotic relationships have changed in name from classical times to the present, two constants have survived the name changes. One constant pertains to the criterion of effeminacy in the male, or in at least one of a male/male pair, and conversely, the criterion of virilism (or masculinity) in the female, or in at least one of a female/female pair. Specific names have been coined for the effeminate male, more than for the virilistic female, whereas specific names for the noneffeminate male and the nonvirilistic female have been lacking, except perhaps in vernacular slang.

The second constant pertains to social tolerance and intolerance. After the period in which pederasty (meaning not pedophilia but ephebophilia, i.e., a sexual erotic relationship between an adolescent youth and his mentor) was the approved norm, all the terms for male/male and female/female relationships carried the stigma of social, religious, and legal disapproval and punishment. The exception is the twentieth-century term *gay* as in gay male, and the recent affirmation of the term *lesbian* as its politically correct counterpart.

Causal explanations of homosexuality (another twentieth-century term) pertain to mythology in the classics; demonic possession and sin in Christian doctrine; criminology in secular law; biomedicine or psychiatry in science; and personal preference or moral choice in contemporary gay male and lesbian political dogma. Causal explanations have, throughout history, had absolutely no influence on the social, political, and legal tolerance or intolerance of homosexuality. The tyranny of power is the determinant of intolerance, which has prevailed over tolerance. Intolerance has been curtailed only by the political assertiveness and power of the modern gay male and lesbian movement.

Bibliography

Adelman, H. B. 1966. *Marcello Malpighi and the Evolution of Embryology.* Ithaca N. Y.: Cornell University Press.

Benjamin, H. 1966. *The Transsexual Phenomenon.* New York: Julian Press.

Ellis, H. 1936. *Eonism and Other Supplementary Studies.* Vol. 2, Part 2 of *Studies in the Psychology of Sex.* Reprint, New York: Random House, N.p. , n.d. (copyright renewal date, 1936)

————. 1942. *Sexual Inversion.* Vol.1, Part 4 of *Studies in the Psychology of Sex.* Reprint, New York: Random House, N.p., n.d. (copyright renewal date, 1942).

Fisk, N. M. 1974. Gender dysphoria syndrome. In *Proceedings of the Second Interdisciplinary Symposium on Gender Dysphoria Syndrome,* ed. D. R. Laub and P. Gandy. Stanford: Division of Reconstructive and Rehabilitative Surgery, Stanford University.

Herzer, M. 1985. Kertbeny and the nameless love. *Journal of Homosexuality.* 12: 1–26.

Kennedy, H. 1988. *Ulrichs: The Life and Works of Karl Heinrich Ulrichs, Pioneer of the Modern Gay Movement.* Boston: Alyson Publications.

Krafft-Ebing, R. von. 1965. *Psychopathia Sexualis.* New York: Bantam Books.

Money, J. 1981. Paraphilias: Phyletic origins of erotosexual dysfunction. *International Journal of Mental Health.* 10: 75–109.

————. 1985. *The Destroying Angel: Sex, Fitness, and Food in the Legacy of Degeneracy Theory, Grahm Crackers, Kellogg's Corn Flakes, and American Health History.* Buffalo: Prometheus Books.

————. 1988. *Gay, Straight, and In–Between: The Sexology of Erotic Orientation.* New York: Oxford University Press.

————. 1990. Androgyne becomes bisexual in sexological theory: Plato to Freud to neuroscience. *Journal of the American Academy of Psychoanalysis.* 18: 392–413.

Money, J. and M. Lamacz. 1988. Gynemimesis and gynemimetophilia: Individual and cross-cultural manifestations of a gender-coping strategy hitherto unnamed. *Comprehensive Psychiatry.* 25: 392–403.

Nanda, S. 1990. *Neither Man Nor Woman: The Hijras of India.* Belmont, Calif: Wadsworth.

Neumann, F. 1990. Effects of antiandrogen on sexual differentiation. In *Psychoendocrinology of Growth and Development,* ed. A. K. Slob and M. J. Baum. Rotterdam: Medicom Europe.

Spong, J. S. 1988. *Living in Sin? A Bishop Rethinks Human Sexuality.* San Francisco: Harper and Row.

Steinach, E. 1940. *Sex and Life: Forty Years of Biological and Medical Experiments.* New York: The Viking Press.

Symonds, J. A. 1901. *A Problem of Greek Ethics, Being an Inquiry into the Phenomenon of Sexual Inversion, Addressed Especially to Medical Psychologisyts and Jurists.* London. One hundred copies only of this book have been printed for Private Circulation, and the type has been distributed.

Tissot, S. A. 1832. *A Treatise on the Diseases Produced by Onanism.* Translated from a New Edition of the French, with Notes and Appendix by an American Physician. New York. Reprint, 1974. *The Secret Vice Exposed! Some Arguments against Masturbation,* C. Rosenberg and C. Smith-Rosenberg, advisory eds. New York: Arno Press.

Ulrichs, K. M. (Numa Numantius). 1864. *Forschungen über das Räthsel der mannmännlichen Liebe* (Inquiry into the enigma of man-to-man love). Vol. 2, *"Inclusa": Anthropologishe studien über mannmännliche Geschlechtsliebe, Naturwissen schaftlicher Theil: Nachwies das einer Classe von männlich gebauten Individuen Geschlechtsliebe zu Mäennern geschlechtlich angeborn ist* ("Inclusa": Anthropological studies of man-to-man sexual love, natural science section; proof of a class of male-bodied individuals for whom sexual love for men is sexually inborn). Leipzig: Selbsverlag der Verfassers. In Commission bei Heinrich Matthes.

Weeks, J. 1980/81. Inverts, perverts, and Mary-Annes: Male prostitution and the regulation of homosexuality in England in the nineteenth and early twentieth centuries. *Journal of Homosexuality.* 6: 113–34.

Westphal, K. F. O. 1869. Die Contraere Sexualempfindung. *Archiv für Psychiatrie und Nervenkrankheiten.* 2: 73–108.

Williams, W. L. 1986. *The Spirit and the Flesh: Sexual Diversity in American Indian Culture.* Boston: Beacon Press.

San Francisco's Bisexual Center and the Emergence of a Bisexual Movement

Jay P. Paul

Introduction

The history of San Francisco's Bisexual Center is a story that reflects much of the discourse around sexuality and the organized struggles for the rights of so-called sexual minorities that began in the 1970s in the United States. The evolution and eventual closing of the Bisexual Center is best understood within that historical context. It emerged in a significant decade in the development of the gay, lesbian, and bisexual communities, marked at one end by the uprising of New York City bar patrons against police harassment (thereafter known as the Stonewall riots), and on the other end by the emerging threat posed by AIDS to that nascent community. While not the first bisexual group in the United States—it was preceded by the Bisexual Forum in New York City (founded by Chuck Mishaan)—it was the first organization to have its own center offering a variety of services, and served as a model and springboard for further organizing of a bisexual movement.

The Bisexual Center of San Francisco was cofounded in 1976 by Maggi Rubenstein and Harriet Leve, and it closed in 1985. In that span of time, it had a profound impact: it created a sense of a bisexual community, educated the general public and professionals about bisexuality, confronted the gay and lesbian communities about the tendency to render the bisexual invisible, spawned several organizations (including political action groups), and changed the lives of many women and men who had felt marginalized by both the heterosexual and homosexual communities. Its history is a story of community organizing and mobilization by a relatively small group of individuals who were deeply committed to generating a sense of bisexual community akin to earlier political efforts by the gay community.

The 1970s: A Decade of Discourse on Sexual Mores and Lifestyles

THE 1970S SAW the flowering of a more visible gay[1] movement. The image of the "gay world" was replaced by the expanded concept of a "gay community" with its own culture, history, social organizations, and politics. The early gay liberation movement was strongly influenced by the discourse of previous social movements, including the women's movement. Early anticipations were that a major social revolution was under way, which would lead to a more socially conscious, androgynous individual, who was not defined in terms of limits, but in terms of expanded potentialities. Altman (1971) expressed a notion that was typical in the early 1970s: "To talk of gay liberation demands a broader examination of sexual mores than merely the attitudes towards homosexuality, for the liberation of the homosexual can only be achieved within the context of a much broader sexual liberation" (p. 70).

The women's movement had helped to raise questions about the organization of Western society around the masculine/feminine dichotomy of gender roles. The sexual revolution—fueled in part by technological advances in birth control—had led to debate about the meaning and integration of the erotic and sexual into daily life. The gay liberation movement in the initial years after Stonewall followed upon both of these arguments, and highlighted the link between gender roles and social acceptance of homosexuality. The initial ideal was that all people would be liberated sexually, freed from categories of gender and sexual orientation to behave and love as they chose (Orlando 1984). Activists anticipated that the categories of heterosexual and homosexual would lose their power to polarize actions, feelings, and people, and would cease to be considered mutually exclusive conditions. The use of the term "gay" was therefore distinct from the preexisting concept of "the homosexual," as reflected in the following:

> Homosexual is the label that was applied to Gay people as a device for separating us from the rest of the population. . . . *Gay* is a descriptive label we have assigned to ourselves as a way of reminding ourselves and others that awareness of our sexuality facilitates a capability rather than creating a restriction. It means that we are *capable* of fully loving a person of the same gender. . . . But the label does not limit us. We who are Gay can still love someone of the other gender. (Clark 1977, 103–6, original emphases)

In contrast to this early ideology, gay men and lesbians came to be conceptualized as a distinct disenfranchised minority group as the decade progressed. Along with a broader set of nonsexual attributions to being "gay," came a diminishing emphasis on broad, sweeping changes to cultural constructions of sexuality and eroticism. The issue of sexual orientation was pushed into the public domain; however, the discourse on sexual choices impacted but did not change much existing ideology. The gay man or woman was reconstructed as a member of a distinct minority group, which led to an embrace of old essentialist constructs of homosexuality. This led to notions of homosexuality as a basic invariant aspect of self fixed at an early age (Malyon 1981) which may seem to emerge at various points over the lifespan only because it has been repressed or denied (Ross 1971; Voeller and Walters 1978; Bozett 1980; Malyon 1981).

Notions of an inherent "gayness," and the return to a conception of heterosexuality and homosexuality as two mutually exclusive conditions, forced a new invisibility to those who were bisexually active. Discounting bisexuality affirmed the absolute and exclusive nature of the heterosexual/homosexual dichotomy. Thus, public images of bisexuality were mostly disparaging, with a trivialization of "bisexual chic" (Avicolli 1978). Individuals found that their claims to being bisexual were often met with suspicion and ambivalence in the gay community (Altman, 1981; Blumstein and Schwartz 1974; Bode 1976; Klein 1978). In the lesbian community, bisexuality had a special negative charge, as lesbian-feminism

> argues that lesbianism is a political choice having little to do with sexual desire *per se*. From this point of view, a bisexual woman "still define[s]

herself in terms of male needs" (Loretta Ulmschneider of the *Furies*) rather than, as she herself might argue, in terms of her own desires. Since lesbian-feminism equates meeting male needs with supporting male supremacy, it considers bisexual women traitors by definition. (Orlando 1984, 1)

Nonetheless, the proliferation of discussions of sexuality and sexual orientation in the news media, as well as in literature and film, meant that bisexuality also received a higher public profile. This public openness is reflected in the trend in the early 1970s for more androgynous images among rock stars—extending to outright "drag" (Avicolli 1978)—and public notoriety as bisexual (e.g., David Bowie, Elton John). However, by 1974, there were attacks on bisexuality in the American press, with two news magazines running articles on bisexuals that trivialized it as a "chic" or trendy aberration. But there were also more balanced portrayals, as well as the beginning of more searching, scholarly discussion of bisexuality in professional publications (Blumstein and Schwartz 1974; Bode 1976; Falk 1975; Klein 1978; Wolff 1977). Television shows and films began to focus more on gay themes and gay characters. Science fiction—works that describe the concerns and intellectual questions of the day in futuristic metaphors—showed an increasing curiosity about the malleability of sexual roles and norms in the 1970s (Barnes 1982).

In the rapid growth of the gay community in this decade, San Francisco became highly visible as a major American urban gay center. It is estimated that several thousand men flocked to the city each year from the mid-seventies to the early 1980s, which "gave substance to the early myths that in San Francisco, gay people had personal, social, and political power, and it was a place where one could be perceived as a human being regardless of sexual orientation" (Peyton 1988, 4). By 1972, there existed a gay political club; a second was organized in 1976. By 1977, San Francisco had elected an openly gay city official, Harvey Milk. Election by district, combined with the city's rich diversity of ethnic neighborhoods, allowed the creation of a distinct gay political bloc along with voting blocs determined by ethnic groups. Given its apparent openness to the gay community, the city of San Francisco appeared to be a fertile birthplace for an organized bisexual community. David Lourea, a key person in the creation of the center, moved to San Francisco in 1973 from Philadelphia, as he felt that "if a bi movement was going to happen, it would begin in San Francisco" (Personal communication 1991).

The Founding of the Bisexual Center

THE STORY OF the founding of the Bisexual Center must be seen within the historical context of the emerging gay movement, and the development of San Francisco as a major urban center of the gay community, but it is also a story of individuals. Perhaps the one person most vital to the genesis of the Bisexual Center was Maggi Rubenstein. Born and raised in San Francisco, Rubenstein was trained as a nurse. She first came out as a bisexual in her early thirties while working at the Center for Special Problems, an agency that works with a variety of clients, including sexual minority groups. She credited the women's movement as giving her the sense of strength and courage to come out as bisexual. Her personal odyssey for others who could validate her sexual and emotional feelings for both sexes, and the "immense sense of relief" that she felt when she found other self-identified bisexuals, led her to conceive of "a community center for bisexual people so that others would not have to struggle alone" (Rubenstein 1983).

The vision of starting a bisexual organization that would counter the lack of visibility of bisexually identified women and men began years before the actual founding of the Bisexual Center. Rubenstein left the Center for Special Problems in 1972. Her activities over the next few years helped her to consolidate a core of bisexually supportive friends and acquaintances who would assist in realizing the dream of a bisexual community center. In 1972, Rubenstein helped to found the San Francisco Sex Information hotline (a switchboard where the public could call in and get clear, nonjudgmental information about sexuality) with Margo Rila. She also assisted in beginning the University of California Medical Center's program in sex counseling. The National Sex Forum was also begun by an overlapping group of individuals, and an adjunct school for training sexologists, The Institute for Advanced Study of Human Sexuality, was founded in 1976.

It came to the point where opening the center simply hinged upon getting some financial backing. Rubenstein, Lourca, and Rila initially tried to get seed money to open up the Bisexual Center in 1974 from the owner of the local paper, *The Berkeley Barb* (which was closing); this failed. In 1975, Jeanne Paslé-Green introduced Harriet Leve to Rubenstein, and Leve supplied some of the financial support and additional energy to fuel this vision of a center that would draw together a bisexual community. Thus it happened that, in 1976, Rubenstein and Leve finally gathered together a group of twenty other like-minded people in Rubenstein's attic to formally plan how to open a community center that would be supportive and celebratory of people's bisexuality.

Many of the others involved from the onset of the Bisexual Center were also psychotherapists, counselors, and sex educators, including David Lourea, Margo Rila, Alan Rockway, Evelyn Hoch, Hogie Wycoff, Jeanne Paslé-Green, and Vicki Galland. They were drawn to the notion of an expanded and inclusive notion of human sexuality that avoided dichotomization of sexual orientation.

Rubenstein came out publicly as bisexual on local television; on August 24, 1976, a small notice was placed in the local newspaper *(The San Francisco Chronicle)*, and another notice was placed in a national feminist magazine. This led to hundreds of interested phone calls, and the formation of an ongoing bisexual "rap group" in September. The first general meeting of the Bisexual Center was held on November 7, 1976, at the National Sex Forum, with over eighty people in attendance. One week later was the first "potluck" social event, and the center was launched.

The Philosophy and Concerns of the Bisexual Center

FROM THE BEGINNING, there was a concern about the philosophy behind the Bisexual Center and a desire to influence the debate on sexuality and lifestyles. The original philosophy and objectives statement noted:

> We have been caught on both sides and in the middle of the homosexual–heterosexual polarity. We feel we have a unique contribution to make toward unifying polarities, equalizing relationships, and understanding the cycles of human sexuality.

Both the parallels and the connections between conceptions of bisexuality, feminist theory, and theories of androgyny were raised consistently in the initial meetings and early issues of *The Bi-Monthly*. The Bisexual Center also supported and welcomed the transgender community; its board of directors, newsletter, and philosophy reflected the value placed in their representation. In the second general meeting, held on January 16, 1977, concern was raised about the stands that the Bisexual Center would take in the broader social/political struggles occurring in American society. Fears were expressed that the Bisexual Center would be little more than a "hedonist club," an escape for those unwilling to deal with larger social issues. This led to revisions in the philosophy and objectives statement, allowing it to note that the organization had stands on sexism, racism, classism, and ageism, and supported the women's movement and the gay movement. The alterations also emphasized the center's philosophy of self-definition as bisexual, lesbian, gay, or heterosexual, and its support for all consensual sexual and sensual activities. The revised version read as follows:

> We are people seeking to love and share intimately with both women and men. Self-defined as bisexuals (although such labels are limiting) we are working to create for ourselves and others a strong sense of community.
>
> • The Bisexual Center is united in struggling for the rights of all women and men to develop as whole, androgynous beings.
>
> • We support relationships between persons of the same and other sex. These relationships may include relating spiritually, socially, emotionally, sensually, sexually, and intellectually. We also support persons choosing a celibate lifestyle.
>
> • We support people who have been oppressed because of sexual preference, gender, age, or ethnic group.
>
> • We encourage and support people struggling (a) to bring about equality in areas of employment, housing, medical care and complete sexual information; (b) for the right to engage in the free expression of consenting sexual activity.
>
> • We support the open expression of affection and touch among people, without such expression necessarily having sexual implications.

From the beginning, it was intended to be more than simply a social group; as David Lourea (1983) put it:

> I knew that the one thing we had all agreed upon was that none of us had the time, interest or energy to devote to an organization that was primarily a place to party. . . . More importantly, we had all experienced the rage of being discounted, invalidated, taken as insincere individuals incapable of any degree of integrity, because of the biphobic notion held by many monosexuals. . . . Dispelling that image was one of our priorities, yet we did not want our existence to be based in reaction to the anti-bi feelings of the

gay, straight and lesbian communities. . . .[S]ince we were likely to be the only safe place that served the bisexual community we needed to provide a safe, supportive haven for people to celebrate being bisexual. . . . (p. 3)

Within a few months, the center provided a variety of "rap groups," workshops, and trainings for interested members of the community (e.g., "Coming Out Bi"; "How to Survive the Loss of a Lover"; "Confronting the Last Taboo"(S/M); "Open Relationships Workshop"; "I Want to Be Close—Wait, Not That Close!" Intimacy Workshop; "Loving Both"). It served as an information clearinghouse, and as a source of public outreach and education. People from all across the country wrote and phoned in, seeking information, support, crisis intervention, and referrals. The center supported a number of research projects, both by doctoral candidates and professionals, to increase the knowledge base on bisexuality. It created a strong local bisexual presence, with many of its board members appearing repeatedly on both television and radio talk shows over the nine years of the center's existence. The Bisexual Center's Speakers Bureau also provided in-service trainings and presentations to a variety of agencies, educational institutions, and health workers, ensuring that bisexuality was discussed as a topic distinct from homosexuality. Once the Bisexual Center found its permanent space in a flat on Hayes Street, it also held a variety of art shows, performances, and exhibits by bisexual artists or with bisexual themes.

From its inception, the Bisexual Center also took stands on a variety of political and social issues that helped heighten its public profile. In its first year, it sent out press releases and held press conferences against the antigay efforts of Anita Bryant and her Miami "Save Our Children" crusade. The first press conference (June 30, 1977) brought together Dr. Benjamin Spock as an expert in child care, Dr. Claude Steiner (as a therapist who was noted for his work, *Scripts People Live)*, Ruth Falk (a feminist writer who authored *Women Loving*) and Dr. Phyllis Lyon, as codirector of the National Sex Forum and lesbian activist—and was aired on the evening news on local television and radio stations. The center had a booth at the National Women's Conference in Houston, Texas, in November 1977, and its representative supported the Equal Rights Amendment, and resolutions concerning sexual preferences, child care rights, and reproductive freedom. In late 1977, there was also a battle closer to home, in joining the Bay Area Coalition against the Briggs Initiative (a California state senator's initiative mandating that all homosexually active or supportive teachers be fired from public schools). At the same time, members acknowledged that it was early in the creation of a bisexual movement, and that much consciousness raising and self-discovery were crucial before bisexuals could hope to be a viable political group (Monty 1977).

Changes over Time at the Bisexual Center

WITHIN A YEAR of its founding, the center had almost 400 paid members; by spring of 1978, it claimed about 550 members.[2] Over the first few years of its existence, the center supported the efforts of others to get bisexual groups going in a variety of areas across the country. This may explain why membership dipped, and then stabilized by early 1980 with about 330 paid members. However, there continued to be an increasing demand for services, reflected not only in the increasing number of social events, but the switch to open "rap" groups on two nights a week at the Center in 1980. (An additional group, for women only, began on a biweekly basis in the summer of 1981.) Many of those who had been involved in the coordinating of bisexual events and services from the first years of the Bisexual Center started to drop out by 1982. To help provide services for all those coming to the Center, the Bisexual Counseling Services (run by David Lourea) began an internship program with graduate students in fall of 1982.

Despite all those who made use of its services, the Bisexual Center never became financially stable. Many of those who came through its doors were either young or earning marginal livelihoods. The center was committed to providing services, but was never more than minimally solvent. The center's board of directors was unsure about being able to continue after a fiscal crisis in 1980, and to ensure its survival, some board members gave not only of their time, but of their money. Efforts to gain nonprofit status as an educational community organization—which began in 1979—did not bear fruit until April 1983, when it was recognized as such by the State of California. Repeated entreaties to its membership were printed in *The Bi-Monthly* over the course of the years, but failed to change the financial health of the organization. The members of the board were not professional fundraisers, but counselors, educators, and community activists. Circumstances forced the board to regularly expend its energy on problem–solving around how to pay bills and maintain the status quo in services, rather than focusing on what they knew best: providing vision for the future of the Bi Center. (Some of those concerned about maintaining a bisexual activist presence would eventually form BiPOL, a bisexual political group, in May of 1983.)

Given this fiscal instability, the Bisexual Center was vulnerable to a crisis that would wound it further: the AIDS epidemic. On July 15, 1982, Bobbi Campbell, a gay nurse with AIDS who had become an AIDS educator and activist came to the Bisexual Center to discuss the new (and as yet unnamed) epidemic that had begun to afflict increasing numbers of gay men. The AIDS epidemic would be felt on two levels: (a) its contribution to increasing conservatism in sexual mores and an emphasis on monogamy—in contrast to the decade before, where alternative forms of relationships were seen as inevitable and perhaps preferable (Francoeur and Francouer 1974; O'Neill and O'Neill 1972; Ramey 1976); (b) its demands upon the energy and attention of the Center's leaders. The increasing conservatism of the times contributed to a slowing of the numbers of people going through the Bisexual Center, and perhaps an increasing reluctance on the part of the public to celebrate sexuality of all kinds. Membership dropped. In addition, several of the leaders of the center committed themselves to working in the field of AIDS. Rubenstein and Lourea worked with the Committee to Preserve Our Sexual and Civil Liberties from 1984 on; Rubenstein was a founding member of Mobilization against AIDS and co-chaired it from 1985–1986; both worked as sex educators with a variety of organizations, including the Women's AIDS Network, the AIDS Health Project, and the San Francisco AIDS Foundation. With its founding members moving on to other things, and under continuing financial pressures, the Bisexual Center floundered. It lost some members to a nonactivist organization which ran sex and intimacy "feel-good" workshops, and eventually closed its doors.

The Bisexual Center had been an ambitious venture, trying to be all things to bisexual people. As an early community organization that managed to last for nine years, and played a part in supporting the growth of other groups, it filled a significant need in a community that felt marginalized by the more narrowly defined "gay and lesbian community" and invisible within the larger heterosexual culture. It empowered those who came in contact with it to choose their own sexual labels, showed them that there were many others who shared their bisexual sensibilities, and affirmed the artificiality and restrictiveness of the common "either/or" perspective of sexuality. It gave rise to variety of efforts at increasing bisexual visibility on a number of fronts, not the least of which was political.

The Future of the Bisexual Movement

THE BISEXUAL COMMUNITY that coalesced around the Bisexual Center did not end when the Center closed. BiPOL continued to be an active political group, and in May 1987, another bisexual organization in the San Francisco area (known as Bay Area Bisexual Network) was begun. May of 1987 was also the time when the East Coast Bisexual Network held its Fourth Annual Conference on Bisexuality (having invited former members of the Bisexual Center to participate). Bisexuals also marched as a distinct national contingent on October 11, 1987, in the March on Washington for Lesbian and Gay Rights (following the United States Supreme Court decision in the Hardwick case, upholding state laws against sodomy even between two consenting adults in the privacy of their homes). The networking that led to this national contingent in the March also led to the formation of a National Bisexual Network. San Francisco's significance was also reflected in its choice as the site of the 1990 National Bisexual Conference, attended by over four hundred people representing twenty-two states and five countries.

Despite the way in which AIDS has served reactionary, moralistic, and religious groups who view the epidemic as validating their restrictive, sex-negative perspective, it has also forced many in the United States to acknowledge the diversity of sexual patterns and preferences that exist. This has included a renewed attention to bisexuals (if only in a negative sense, as potential vectors of transmission of HIV to the heterosexual population), with two national news magazines covering the issue of bisexuals and AIDS (Gelman, Drew, Hager, Anderson, Raine, and Hutchison 1987; Smilgis 1987). The heightened visibility of bisexuals within the United States gay community has continued in coverage by gay-identified periodicals (e.g., Wofford 1991), the publication of new books (Geller 1990; Hutchins and Kaahumanu 1991), and the establishment of a bisexual magazine, *ATM (Anything That Moves)*. Overall, the Bisexual Center helped to create a sense of bisexual community that has extended beyond its own lifetime. The "second-generation" bisexual organizations that have emerged can be thankful for its ground-breaking efforts.

Endnotes

1. For brevity, the term "gay" will be used on occasion in its more inclusive sense, referring to homosexual and bisexual men and women, rather than its more restrictive use to refer to homosexual men (particularly homosexually active men who identify as

"gay"). When intended to be used more restrictively, this article will refer to "gay men" or "gay and lesbian."

2. These numbers are based upon figures reported in *The Bi-Monthly.*

References

Altman, Dennis. 1971. *Homosexual Oppression and Liberation.* New York: Avon Books.

Avicolli, Tommi. 1978. Images of gays in rock music. In *Lavender Culture,* eds. Karla Jay B. and Allen Young. 182–194. New York: Jove Publications.

Barnes, Jim. 1982. Options unlimited: Bisexuality in science fiction, part II. *The Bi-Monthly.* 8(6): 3–6.

Blumstein, Philip, and Pepper Schwartz. 1974. Lesbianism and bisexuality. In *Sexual Deviance and Sexual Deviants,* eds. E. Goode and R. Troiden. New York: William Morrow.

Bode, Janet. 1976. *View from Another Closet: Exploring Bisexuality in Women.* New York: Hawthorn Books.

Bozett, Frederick W. 1980. Gay fathers: How and why they disclose their homosexuality to their children. *Family Relations.* 29: 173–179.

Clark, Don. 1977. *Loving Someone Gay.* Millbrae, Calif: Celestial Arts.

Doress, Hannah. 1987. Maggi Rubenstein: Bisexual rights activist. *Plexus.* August: 6–7,13.

Falk, Ruth. 1975. *Women Loving: A Journey towards Becoming an Independent Women.* New York: Random House.

Fasteau, M. F. 1975. *The Male Machine.* New York: Delta Books.

Francoeur, Robert, and Anna Francoeur, eds. 1974. *The Future of Sexual Relations.* Englewood Cliffs, N. J.: Prentice-Hall.

Geller, Thomas. 1990. *Bisexuality: A Reader and Sourcebook.*

Gelman, D., L. Drew, M. Hager, M. Anderson, G. Raine, and S. Hutchison. 1987. A perilous double love life. *Newsweek.* 13 July: 44–46.

Hutchins, Loraine, and Lani Kaahumanu. 1991. *Bi Any Other Name: Bisexual People Speak Out.* Boston: Alyson.

Klein, Fred. 1978. *The Bisexual Option.* New York: Arbor House.

Kleinberg, Ira. 1985. Sexologist speaks for bisexual rights. *Sentinel USA.* 28 March: 4.

Kohn, Barry, and Alice Matusow. 1980. *Barry and Alice: Portrait of a Bisexual Marriage.* Englewood Cliffs,N. J.: Prentice-Hall.

Leve, Harriet. 1978. Bisexual Center. *New Directions for Women.*

Lourea, David. 1983. The Bisexual Center: More than a social club. *The Bi-Monthly.* 7(1): 3–4, 8.

Maylon, Alan. 1981. The homosexual adolescent: Developmental issues and social bias. *Child Welfare.* 60: 321–30.

Monty, Barbara. 1977. Toward a bisexual self-knowing. *The Bi-Monthly.* 1(6): 6–7.

O'Neill, Nena and George O'Neill. 1972. *Open Marriage: A New Life for Couples.* New York: Evans and Co.

Orlando, Lisa. 1984. Loving whom we choose: Bisexuality and the lesbian/gay community. Where we stand. *Gay Community News.* 11(31): 1, 14.

Peyton, H. Hackson. 1988. AIDS prevention for gay men: A selected history and analysis of the San Francisco experience 1982–1987. Unpublished manuscript.

Ramey, James. 1976. *Intimate Friendships*. Englewood Cliffs, N. J.: Prentice-Hall.

Ross, H. L. 1971. Modes of adjustment of married homosexuals. *Social Problems*. 18(3): 385–93.

Rubenstein, Maggi. 1983. A bisexual perspective: An interview with Maggi Rubenstein. *The Bi-Monthly*. 7(5): 8.

Smilgis, Martha. 1987. The big chill: Fear of AIDS. *Time*. 16 February: 50–53.

Voeller, Bruce, and J. Walters. 1978. Gay fathers. *The Family Coordinator*. 37: 149–57.

Wofford, Carrie. 1991. The bisexual revolution: Deluded closet cases or the vanguard of the movement? *Outweek*. 6 February: 33–39, 70, 80.

Wolff, Charlotte. 1977. *Bisexuality: A Study*. London: Quartet Books.

Bisexuality in Early Imperial China:
An Introductory Overview

Joseph Wong

Introduction

Very little scholarly work has been done on the history of sex in China, let alone on homosexuality or bisexuality.[1] An obvious reason is that in China open discussion of sex has long been regarded as an immoral act, if not exactly a taboo, although the situation is changing gradually among Chinese communities, some faster than others.[2] It is not that the *Standard Histories*, well known for their comprehensiveness on the political aspects because of their official nature, were devoid of such records, but such writings have long been neglected, overlooked, or misinterpreted, whether deliberately or subconsciously. There are, of course, unofficial historical writings in China as in other countries, which often shed a different light on our understanding of the past. However, as a preliminary survey, this paper will deal only with the *Standard Histories*, which are better organized and systematic.[3] As I am a historian by training, my main purpose will be to identify the relevant sources and hope the information I extract below can allow us a glimpse of the topic we are dealing with and hopefully provide some clues for further research.

A few more remarks before we probe into these sources. The words *homosexuality (toxinglian)* and *heterosexuality (xiangxinglian)* in Chinese are both coined in the modern period as the result of the impact of science from the West. There were a number of words denoting such activities, but they were not often used and, when they were, it is arguable whether they were used in the modern sense of the word. Unfortunately, we have to confine ourselves to male bisexualism because basically all the historical writings were written by males for males, although they did include chapters on virtuous and, in particular, chaste females as models for others to follow. It is unlikely, therefore, that we can ever have a meaningful discussion on female bisexualism in Chinese history unless we move to a much later period. In a similar manner, readers are also reminded that since our sources were written by and for the ruling classes, there must be some reservations as to whether they could be taken as wholly representative of the Chinese people, since in the case of the females in Chinese history and elsewhere, what those being ruled did and thought would hardly ever come to light.

The Han Dynasty (202 B.C.–A.D. 189)

THE EARLIEST AND perhaps the most studied of the *Standard Histories* is the *Shiji*, of the Records of the Historian of China by Sima Qian (186–45 B.C.). It was the first conscious attempt by a historian to compile a history of the Chinese from the earliest times to his own day,[4] but it is to one of the least discussed chapters that we will turn our attention. This is chapter 125, "The Biographies of the Emperor's Male Favorites." In the first paragraph it states,

> . . . it is not women alone who can use their looks to attract the eyes of the ruler; courtiers and eunuchs can play at that game as well. Many were the men of ancient times who gained favor in this way.

While later scholars might like to broaden the definition of "gaining favor" here, it is obvious that the point that Sima Qian tries to make here by a comparison of courtiers and eunuchs with women is that many of the former group gained their influence by their sexual appeal more than anything else.

This interpretation is substantiated by the records which follow.

> When the Han arose, Emperor Gaozu . . . was won by the charms of a young boy Qi, and Emperer Hui had a boy favorite named Hong. Neither Qi nor Hong had any particular talent or ability; both won prominence simply by their looks and graces. Day and night they were by the ruler's side, and all the high ministers were obliged to apply to them when they wished to see the emperor. As a result, all the palace attendants started wearing sashes of seashells and painting their faces, transforming themselves into a veritable host of Qis and Hongs. . . .

> The gentlemen who enjoyed favor in the palace under Emperor Wen included a courtier named Deng Tong and the eunuchs Zhao Tan and Beigong Bozu. Beigong Bozu was a worthy and affectionate man, while Zhao Tan attracted the emperor's attention by his skill in observing the stars and exhalations in the sky; both of them customarily rode about in the same carriage with Emperor Wen.

A more detailed description of the intimate relations of an emperor and his eunuch, however, is saved in the part on Deng Tong:

> Deng Tong does not seem to have had any special talent. He was a native of Nan'an in the province of Shu (present Siquan). Because he knew how to pole a boat he was made a yellow-capped boatman in the grounds of the imperial palace. . . .

> Deng Tong for his part behaved with great honesty and circumspection in his new position. He cared nothing about mingling with people outside and, though the emperor granted him holidays to return to his home, he was always reluctant to leave. As a result, the emperor showered him with gifts until his fortunes mounted to tens of billions of cash and he had been promoted to the post of superior lord. The emperor from time to time even paid visits to Deng Tong's home to amuse himself there.

> Deng Tong, however, had no other talent than that of entertaining the emperor and was never able to do anything to advance others at court. Instead he bent all his efforts toward maintaining his own position and ingratiating himself with the emperor. . . .

Once Emperor Wen was troubled by a tumor, and Deng Tong made it his duty to keep it sucked clean of infection. The emperor was feeling depressed by his illness and, apropos of nothing in particular asked Deng, "In all the empire, who do you think loves me most?" "Surely no one loves Your Majesty more than the heir apparent!" replied Deng Tong. Later, when the heir apparent came to inquire how his father was, the emperor made him suck the tumor. The heir apparent managed to suck it clean, but it was obvious from his expression that he found the task distasteful. Afterward, when he learned that Deng Tong had been in the habit of sucking the tumor for the emperor, he was secretly filled with shame. From this time on he bore a grudge against Deng. . . .

There is no explicit or vivid description of sexual scenes, nor should there be any, for such was not the way the Chinese wrote. It might be noted that Emperor Gaozu (reign 202 B.C.–195 B.C.) was supposed to be the son of a dragon, who has intercourse with his mother during a time of thunder and storm. The scene as witnessed by Gaozu's father, however, was simply that "there was a dragon on top of her" (chapter 8, *Shiji*). Thus when Sima Qian wrote that Deng "bent all his efforts toward maintaining his own position and ingratiating himself with the emperor," what was implicitly implied was clear to his contemporaries. Sex was not mentioned, but it was there. This is perhaps the most important point to note for those interested in extracting information on the history of sex in premodern China.

While the historian Sima Qian was a castrated person, he apparently found fault with Deng and others not in their homosexual relations with the emperor, but in the fact that these people were not talented, as in the case of Deng, who "was never able to do anything to advance others in court," in spite of their influence. Since Deng was a courtier rather than a eunuch, he was unlikely to be a homosexual. In an unquoted passage, we find that Princess Zhang, showing a fair degree of compassion, provided him with food and clothing after the emperor had died and was succeeded by the heir apparent, who had borne a grudge against Deng. What we are certain of, however, is that the Emperor Wen (r. 180–157 B.C.) was a heterosexual person, as were Emperors Gaozu and Hui (r. 195–188 B.C.), who all had empresses and sons.

The first three emperors of the Han were not alone. The *Shiji* continued with their successors, Emperors Jing (r. 157–141 B.C.) and Wu (r. 187–41 B.C.), in whose time Sima Qian lived. Apparently, Emperor Jing did not have any particular male favorites, though there was one who enjoyed more favor than others. But the records on favorites of Emperor Wu are again worth noting.

Among the favorites of the present emperor (i.e., Wu) were the courtier Han Yan, the great grandson of Xin, the King of Han, and the eunuch Li Yanlian. When the present emperor was still king of Qiaotong, he and Yan studied writing together and the two grew very fond of each other. Later, after the emperor was appointed heir apparent, he became more and more friendly with Yan. Yan was skillful at riding and archery and was also very good at ingratiating himself with the emperor. . . . Yan had soon advanced to the rank of superior lord and received as many gifts from the ruler as

Deng Tong in his days of honor. At this time, Yan was constantly by the emperor's side, both day and night. . . .

Because he attended the emperor, Han Yan was allowed to come and go in the women's quarters of the palace and did not have to observe the customary prohibitions against entering them. Some time later, it was reported to the empress dowager that Yan had had an illicit affair with one of the women there. She was furious and immediately sent a messenger ordering him to take his life. Although the emperor attempted to make apologies for him, he was able to do nothing to change the order, and in the end Yan was forced to die. His younger brother Han Yue, the marquis of Antao, also managed to win great favor with the emperor.

Here we have an unmistaken case of a heterosexual official. But there is a slight problem of credibility here. Emperor Wu was about four when he was given the title king of Qiaotong, and became the crown prince three years later before ascending the throne at about sixteen years of age. It is doubtful that the kind of fondness that he had for Han Yan that we are interested in started in childhood, and if it had, the historian would propably have known, as they lived at about the same time. The point the historian is trying to make here is probably that the close relationship started early in life.

The case of the other favorite of Emperor Wu is equally if not more remarkable as we appear to have a heterosexual eunuch.

Li Yan'nian was a native of Zhongshan. His mother and father, as well as his brothers and sisters, were all originally singers. Li Yan'nian, having been convicted of some crime and condemned to castration, was made a keeper of the dogs in the palace. Later the princess of Pingyuan recommended his younger sister Lady Li to the emperor because of her skill in dancing. When the emperor saw her, he took a liking to her and had her installed in the women's quarters of the palace, at the same time summoning Li Yan'nian to an audience and appointing him to a higher post.

Li was a good singer and knew how to compose new tunes. At this time the emperor wanted some hymns set to music and arranged with string accompaniment to be used in the sacrifices to Heaven and Earth which he had initiated. Li accepted the task and performed it to the emperor's satisfaction. . . .

Li, by this time, wore the seals of a two thousand picul official and bore the title of 'Harmonizer of Tunes.' Day and night he was by the emperor's side and his honor and favor equaled that which Han Yan had formerly enjoyed. When some years had passed, he began to carry on an affair with one of the palace ladies[5] and becoming more and more arrogant and careless in his behavior. After the death of Lady Li, the emperor's affection for the Li brothers waned and he ended by having them arrested and executed.

There is some argument about whether it was Li Yan'nian or his brother Li Ji who actually had an affair with one of the palace ladies. What is unfortunate for us is that very little is known about Li Ji. One wonders if he was not another eunuch, which explains that he was allowed to enter the palace and commit the offense, and that his rise was altogether different from that of the Han brothers, Yan and Yue, mentioned earlier.

The Lis in fact had another brother, Guangli, a general well-known for his battles against the northern barbarian intruders,[6] a feat which accounts for his exclusion here because, as noted, this chapter was reserved for those untalented and useless, and music was never recognized as a respectable trade in the Han. It is not far-fetched, however, if we suggest that Li Guangli might also have had as close relations with the emperor as his brothers. At the end of this chapter, the historian noted that from this time on, those who enjoyed special favor with the emperor were for the most part members of the families related to the emperor by marriage, but they were not worth discussing here, for their advancement was due primarily to their talents and abilities. Two examples were given, those of Wei Qing and Huo Qubing, who had chapter 111 of the *Shiji* completely devoted to them.

As far as the advancement of these two generals is concerned, Sima Qian could be right in only one place. According to his own biography in chapter 111 of the *Shiji*, Wei was a rider in the household of marquis Hou and later served in the palace, where his sister won favor with the emperor. Wei was sent to prison when a Princess Chang heard that his sister was pregnant, but was rescued by a palace horseman and a band of young men. When the emperor heard of the incident, he summoned Wei and made him superintendent of the guards at the palace. His brothers were also appointed to high positions and, in the course of a few days, they were showered with gifts amounting to a thousand pieces of gold. Later Wei was advanced to the rank of palace counselor before embarking on his campaigns against the northern intruders. Until this juncture, there was nothing exceptional about the career of Wei. To employ Sima Qian's own words, he was not unlike the others in the "Biographies of the Emperor's Male Favorites" in that he had "no particular talent or ability," and one cannot help but wonder if he was not "ingratiating himself with the emperor" before he and his brothers received the exceptionally large amount of gold.

As for Huo Qubing, the son of Wei Jing's elder sister, it is clearly recorded in his biography that at the age of eighteen, he was favored by the emperor and made an attendant of the emperor.[7] In short, it is highly likely that both Wei and Huo were some sort of male favorites of the emperor in their career, and if not for their brilliant military career in their later lives, they would either have been included in the chapter for male favorites or completely omitted from the records. The later was probably the fate of those palace horsemen who saved Wei and perhaps from whom the emperor heard of the story, and who probably shared a similar relationship with the emperor.

In many ways, the *Shiji* set a model for later Chinese historians to follow, and the same can be said of the "Biographies of the Male Favorites." Chapter 93 of the *Hanshu*, which contains a more complete record of the Han dynasty (202 B.C.–A.D. 6), is a case in point. While it copies the *Shiji* for the earlier periods, it also offers its own material for later periods. Although the writing style changed somewhat, there are still some interesting cases. Shixian was castrated in his youth, became Director of the Eunuch Secretariat and was trusted by the Emperor Yuan (ruled 49–33 B.C.). There is no clear evidence to suggest that he was physically intimate with the emperor, although the emperor did again send him a large amount of presents, apparently without adequate reasons. The same is true for Chunyu Chang, who, adroit in handling internal court relations, was again rewarded lavishly. In fact, he is recorded to be not as in favor as Zhang Fang, who always went to bed and rose together with the emperor, and together they would dress in plain clothes and travel incognito.

Yet the most famous example is no doubt Dong Xian. It is claimed that when he was about two years old, his cuteness attracted the attention of the Emperor Ai (ruled 7–1 B.C.). Again, he was awarded large numbers of gifts and would go to bed and rise together with the emperor. Accordingly, they once had an afternoon nap together, and when the emperor awoke, he found Dong lying on him. Trying to get up without waking Dong, the emperor eventually cut his sleeves, leaving not only Dong fast asleep but also thereafter the expression "cutting the sleeves" in the Chinese classical world as a code word for male homosexual relations. Dong was heterosexual, as he had a wife, who the emperor allowed to stay at the palace in order to save Dong from making his difficult trip home. By the age of twenty-two, he was one of the Three Excellencies, a top position in the government.

So far we have examined the records of the "Biographies of the Male Favorites," but it would be misleading to infer that no records of heterosexuality are found elsewhere in the *Standard Histories*, though they are understandably fewer. In the *Hanshu*, the biography of Huo Guang, the younger brother of Huo Qibing whom we met earlier, records that Quang loved a slave superintendent by the name of Fang Zudu. Fang often discussed matters with Huo, regent from 86 to 66 B.C., and was pardoned by Huo after committing offenses on a number of occasions. Fang and Wang Zufang, another of Huo's slaves, paid no attention to the imperial chancellor when Huo was in power. Although we know little of Wang, it is noteworthy that Fang had an illicit affair with Huo's wife, Xian, when she became a widow.[8] In another case recorded in the *Huo Hanshu*, the "beloved superintendent male slave" Qin Gong of Liang Ji was equally influential. He reached the post of prefect of the grand granary, and could go into the place where Liang's wife, Shou, lived. When seeing Gong, Shou always dismissed her attendants, pretending to discuss affairs, and had illicit relations with him. Being in favor both within and without, Gong's power shook the world. All the inspectors and 2,000-picul officials visited him to bid him farewell when they left. We are uncertain whether the several thousand persons seized and turned into male and female slaves by Liang had sexual relations with their master; whichever was the case, both Liang and Qin were most likely to have been heterosexuals.[9]

The Sui and Tang Dynasties (A.D. 581–907)

THE SUI AND TANG dynasties are generally regarded as another glorious period in the Chinese history. After the Han, China disintegrated into a number of smaller states for a number of centuries, and areas north to the Yangtze River were often occupied by nomadic non-Han peoples, the Han being those who have long lived in central China around the two basins of the Yellow River and the Yangtze River, and whose customs and lifestyles were significantly different from the Chinese at the beginning of the period of disunion. But by the time Sui once again united China under one rule and a centralized government, many of these nomads had already been much sinicized. In fact, neither the imperial household of the Sui nor the Tang were of purely Han lineage, and consequently some nomadic customs and traits could be traced.[10]

Whether bisexual practices were part of the Han-Chinese or non-Chinese legacy, however, is open to question. What is certain is that such practices continue to appear in the *Standard Histories*, although not as directly or easily discernible as before. It is important to note that the tradition of compiling biographies of the emperor's favorites in the *Standard Histories* ended in the Tang, when six such histories were compiled, and none of them contained such biography.[11] While this does not necessarily mean that bisexual activities actually disappeared, it probably implies that such activities were not regarded as respectable or morally accectable; consequently, even their inclusion in the *Standard Histories* as counterexamples was no longer tolerated. We are not aware of any law denouncing such deeds openly,[12] but they were certainly discouraged.

A few cases would serve to illustrate these points. An interesting example is Zheng Yi, an official who served both in the Northern Zhou Dynasty (550–577) and the Sui (581–618) and subsequently has a biography in both chapter 35 of the *Zhou Shu* and chapter 38 of the *Sui Shu*.[13] It is noted in the latter that when he was more than ten years old, an official tried "to have some fun" with him, but was rejected by Zheng, who told him solemnly that such "intimate play" was an immoral act. Perhaps because of his rectitude, Zheng was trusted by the emperor and it was even arranged for him to marry a princess after his wife died. Yet when Zheng later became an official under the crown prince, he began to develop intimate relations with the prince, so much so that when the emperor knew of this he was stripped of his post to become a commoner. But he was soon recalled by the prince, resumed their relations, and took part in the coup d'état that led to the establishment of the Sui dynasty later.

If the Han examples of bisexuality are found mostly among the emperors, those of the Sui and Tang are more to be known among the princes. The first crown prince of the Sui, Yang Yong, for instance, was no doubt a bisexual, although this act was recorded not in his own biography but in that of one of his officials, not one who tried to curry his favor, but one who had the courage to speak against the undesirable act, and even took to court a guardsman whose laughter during his intimate play with the prince was so loud that it could be heard outside the room of the prince. From what is recorded, the prince had no fewer than four male lovers, and he also had ten sons from at least four wives.[14]

Li Chengqian, eldest son of the famous second emperor Taizor of the Tang, was perhaps better known as a homosexual, if not heterosexual. Accordingly, he loved a young musician who was goodlooking and danced well. The emperor was furious when told of the affair, and ordered the musician to be killed together with a couple of others. Li Chengqian expressed his grief by designating a room in his residence for his lover, ordered his subordinates to offer sacrifices, and eventually buried him within the prince's residence, bestowed him with posthumous titles, and erected a stele, usually reserved for respectable officials. Moreover, the crown prince excused himself from attending court affairs for months. Because his misconduct included the rejection of Han Chinese costume and hairstyle in favor of Turkish decor,[15] it had been suggested that his sexual propensity also had its origin in the Turks.[16] Given the many examples both before and after him who had little evidence of Turkish influence, this hypothesis is highly dubious.

Yet Chengqian was by no means the only member of the imperial house to have displayed bisexual behavior—two of his brothers were likely to have had a similar trait: one was recorded to have had close relations with archers under him, and the other is unknown, partly perhaps because his record has been under some later embellishment.[17] Two grandsons of Taizong, including Zhongzong, who ascended the throne at the beginning of the eighth century, were probably also bisexual. In fact, the reign of Zhongzong (705–10) was a period in which bisexual activities were most active because of the participation of the emperor himself. Zhongzong was succeeded by his son, Xuanzong Li Longji, better known as the Minghuang, or the Brilliant Emperor.

The Brilliant Emperor was so called because it was during his time that the Tang empire reached its zenith, and he was well remembered because his long reign (712–56) ended sadly by the eruption of an internal rebellion that forced him first to abandon his lover and eventually abdicate the throne. His romance with the Lady Yeng is well known, but the Emeror's male lovers have been completely neglected. Three of them are found in chapter 106 of the *Jui Tang Shu* or the Old Tang History. We Know little about one of them except that he "bent all his effort to serve the emperor." Another distinguished himself in "minor arts" such as that of brewing medicine, and the emperor often "summoned him to the imperial residence until late at night. . . . Eunuchs were sent to call him to court during rest days. He participated and heard of the big affairs, and was called the 'internal minister' by his contemporaries." The third was the bodyguard of the emperor from his days as a prince. "Whenever the emperor failed to see him for a time, he looked quiet as if he had missed something, but when the emperor saw him, they would have a happy time throughout the night, sometimes until the sun rose high." What is more important to note, that is at the end of the chapter where historians left their own remarks and comments, the three were compared to Deng Tong and Hong Ru of the Han dynasty.[18] Hong Ru refers to Hong, favorite of Emperor Hui of the Han, and about Deng Tong we have quoted at length. In short, for the historians of the day, they were well aware of the relationship of these three officials of the Brilliant Emperor. These three men were put together with the biographies of two other officials who had great influence during the reign because of the trust they gained from the emperor, but they were generally blamed for the decline of the dynasty. The two were probably not involved with the emperor physically, but if not for the change in the format of the *Standard Histories*, this chapter of these five officials would certainly have been categorized and labeled as a chapter on the emperor's male favorites.

Yet the Brilliant Emperor's male relations probably were not confined to the three mentioned. It might be suggested that a fair number of his subordinates during his days as a prince, which started during the reign of Zhongzong, had undeniably and inexplicably close relations with him that were not appropriate for an emperor and an official. One, for instance, refused to follow the rites of the day to sit with the brothers of the emperor, who tried to inhibit him from leaking happenings of the court to outsiders. Whatever these happenings might have been, they were likely to be scandalous. Interestingly enough, one of the scandals in the early Tang was caused when one of Taizong's sons, usually stationed in the provinces, made a visit back to the capital and stayed with his brother. The necessity to embellish the record by later historians[19] further strengthens the suspicion that the scandal was related to male relations. It might be noted that male prostitutes for the consumption of the same sex were found in the capital in the eighth century.[20]

That it was the trend to avoid directly mentioning homosexuality is best manifested by the memoirs submitted by the advisors of princes who were known to have such traits. At least two examples are extant: one sent to Li Chengqian, the other to Li Xuan, son of Gaozong, the third Tang emperor. One could hardly sense by reading the memoirs that they were indeed remonstrating against the acts of the princes.[21] In another case, one prime minister Li Yifu in the reign of Gaozong (649–84) was criticized by one of the censors in the government, and the first item mentioned was that Li attained his position by acts of "dividing the peace" and "cutting the sleeves." We have already mentioned the origins of the latter expression, and the former was another equivalent of the same act.[22] Even though such euphemism was used, the emperor was furious. The censor was demoted to the provincial areas, apparently for using such vulgar language, and the accusation was never followed up.[23] Whether the emperor was trying to protect his prime minister or was really angry is difficult to say because of the nature of the subject, but the fact that the censor was demoted with such an excuse suggests that open male relationships had already become a taboo in the early Tang.

This officially hostile attitude towards relationship between males meant increased difficulty of straightforward recording by historians and had induced a modern scholar to note that records of homosexual acts disappear in the *Standard Histories* from the Tang onwards.[24] The above examples have already contrasted this claim, and indeed if we are allowed to ponder deeply into some texts and interpret them imaginatively, some interesting results are to be found.

I have suggested, for instance, that both the first and second emperors of the Tang could have been bisexual. The puzzling close relationship of Li Yuan, the founder of the Tang, and one of his brothers-in-law, Dou Kang, could be understood in this light. His son Taizong not only shared similar relations with another relative of the imperial household, but also showered gifts on some musicians and presumably slaves looking after horses in the court without adequate reasons, leading to caution from one of his advisors. Whether or not Taizong, long regarded as one of the exemplary emperors in Chinese history, was a bisexual will probably remain a mystery. But if indeed he had been one, then it certainly revealed a double standard on his part, since he was probably responsible for the omission of biographies of male favorites from official *Standard Histories*, and since he was strongly against his son Chengqian who, as noted above, had a deep interest in the same sex.

Some Observations

CHINESE HISTORICAL RECORDS clearly note that there was no abscence of bisexual cases in Han and Tang China, although the style of writing and also the content did not remain unchanged. At the beginning, these materials confined themselves to happenings in the court, focusing on the emperors' favorites. But by the mid seventh century, when China was under the Tang, the tradition of such writings with an increasingly didactic overtone was discontinued, reflecting a less tolerant, if not hostile, attitude toward bisexual behavior in general. Though records of such nature become scarce though not extinct, there are many fewer cases of triangular relationships between one male and a married couple.

As far as our cases in court are concerned, adolescence seems to be the age when a bisexual relationship was most likely to develop, though such a relationship probably could develop whenever someone is sexually active. The partner in an intimate relation with the emperor or the prince was often someone who had been close to him for a relatively long period of time, and inevitably someone of much lower social class: a eunuch, a slave, a bodyguard, or a musician. Such relationships sometimes began, and were often accompanied or followed by a high degree of trust, allowing many, in particular those in the Han, to play a prominent role in politics. Fewer such cases are found in the Tang, but we have not examined the latter half of the Tang when imperial power declined and more room was allowed for officials and others to manipulate the political scene.

Many more studies have to be done if we want a better understanding of bisexual activities, and for that matter, the history of sex in China in general. More sources need to be identified, and more cases recovered. Many more biographies of the male favorites can be studied in more detail, and perhaps the question of the eunuchs in the the Tang, which this paper has not covered, should be looked into. Given the vastness of traditional Chinese historical records, both on an official and unofficial basis, it is perhaps not far-fetched to suggest that there is a wealth of information left to be mined. Such work would require the tools and skills of a historian not only well versed in the traditional area, but also with an open and imaginative mind. And once extracted, the materials should provide useful information for comparison with scrutinized theories more familar to the modern social scientist. The subject is an interdisciplinary one, and it is hoped that more joint efforts are to be carried out in the future.

Endnotes

1. R. H. van Gulik's *Sexual Life in Ancient China: A Preliminary Survey of Chinese Sex and Society from ca. 1500 B.C. till A.D. 1633*, E. J. Brill, Leiden, 1974, is the most scholarly survey of its subject in any language, but does not discuss homosexuality in length. Bret Hinsch's recent work *Passions of the Cut Sleeve: The Male Homosexual Tradition in China*, University of California Press, Berkeley, 1990, focuses on the subject utilizing western anthropological theories and using mostly second-hand literary sources. Though some of its conclusions are very tentative, it covers a longer period (with a brief appendix on lesbianism) and should be useful to those interested in the subject. Two Chinese works provide the richest source material, but do not critically examine these sources: Weixing Shiiguan Zhaizhu, *Zhongguo Tongxingren Mishi* (The secret history of homosexuality in China), Xiangkang Yuzhou Chubanshe, 1964; and *Xiaomingxiong, Zhongguo Tongxingai Shilu* (A history of homosexuality in China), Fenghongse Sanjiao Chubanshe, Hong Kong, 1984.

2. See, for instance Jiang Xiaoyuan, *Zhongguoren de xing shenmi* (The chinese

mystery of sex), Kexue chubanshe, Beijing, 1989.

3. See chapters V to VII in D. Leslie, C. Mackerras, Wang Gungwu, eds., *Essays on the Sources for Chinese History*, Australian National University, Canberra, 1973

4. This has been translated into English by Burton Watson, *Records of the Grand Historian of China*, 2 vols., New York, 1961. There is also a major translation by Edouard Chavannes, *Les memoires historiques de Se-ma Ts'ien*, 5 vols., Paris, 1895–1905; reprinted Leiden, 1967. Unless otherwise stated, extracts from the work will be from Watson's translation. I am, however, substituting the pinyin system for the Wade-Giles system used by Watson, and shall provide notes wherever necessary.

5. Watson did not think this was possible and has followed the *Hanshu* in attributing the event to his younger brother Ji.

6. See *Hanshu* (The history of the Han Dynasty), Zhonghua Shuju edition, Beijing, 1962, chapter 97a, pp. 3951–52.

7. Biographies of the two generals are in chapter 111 of *Records of the Grand Historian*, v. 2.

8. See *Hanshu*, ch. 68, pp. 2950, 2953, 2955. See *Han Social Structure*, trans. & ed. Jack L. Dull, Seattle and London: University of Washington Press, 1972, pp. 154, 353.

9. *Hou Hanshu* (The history of the later Han), Zhonghua Shuju edition, Beijing, 1965, chapter 34, pp. 1180–81. I am following the translation of J. Dull here, *Han Social Structure*, pp. 381–82.

10. For a general survey of the Sui and Tang, see the session on "the establishment of national

11. There was *Liang Shu, Chen Shu, Zhou Shu, Bei Zhou Shu, Sui Shu*, and *Jin Shu*. In its present form, *Bei Zhou* has no chapter about favorites, yet it is not the original that is at issue here, which has been lost, but a compilation of other texts, primarily the *Nanshi*, which was compiled during the early Tang Age, although not by official order. These six books, though, were not the first ones that excluded such chapters. Precedence is provided by *San Guo Ji*, which reports about an earlier time. But the *San Gou Ji* was not compiled in a single work until the Tang Dynasty.

12. *Die Allgemeinen Prinzipien der Tang-Gesetze* (The general principles of the Tang laws) have been translated into English by W. Johnson, *The T'ang Code*, Princeton University Press, 1979. Further below, though, we have an additionnal example in which someone actually was appointed to the [royal] Court for this reason; see note 14.

13. His biography is also in chapter 35 of the *Bei Shi*, but it is more or less a combination of both.

14. See *Sui Shu*, Zhonghua Shuju edition, Beijing 1973, chapter 62, p. 1478. For information about the prince's family, see also chapter 45, p. 1238.

15. See his biography in the *Jiu Tang Shu* (An ancient chronicle of the Tang) Zhonghua Shuju edition, Beijing 1975, chapter 76, p. 2648.

16. *Xiaominxiong*, ibid., p. 105

17. See my Chinese article "Tang Taizong yu aizibing" (Tang Taizong and AIDS) in: *Mingbao Yuekan*, Hong Kong, July 1990, pp. 99–102. The following discussion without notes is based on this article.

18. *Jiu Tang Shu*, pp. 3247–56.

19. See the biography of Prince Yuanzhang in *Xin Tang Shu* (A new chronicle of

the *Tang)*, Zhonghua Shuju edition, Beijing 1975, chapter 79, p. 3549. The section concerning the scandal does not appear in *Jiu Tang Shu*, chapter 64, p. 2425. Although the former work was compiled later, the material is probably from an original source such as the *True Report* (Shilu).

20. See *Kaihuan Tianbao Yishi*, Shanghai Guji edition, Beijing 1985, p. 81.

21. See *Wen Yuan Ying Hua*, Zhonghua Shuju reprint edition, Beijing 1960, chapter 60, "The Writings of Li Baiyao," pp. 271–73. The name is mentioned in *Jiu Tang Shu*, chapter 72, p. 2657, where it is remarked that memory protests against the prince's "licentious games."—The other name is in *Jiu Tang Shu*, chapter 88, p. 2863 ff. as counsel against "close reations" between the prince and his slave(s).

22. See *Shi Ji*, chapter 63, p. 2154.

23. *Cefuyuangui*, Zhonghua Shuju reprint edition 1960, chapter 520, p. 6211. *Jiu Tang Shu*, chapter 82, p. 2676 again revises the choice of words.

24. *Pan Guangdan: Zhongguo wenxian zhong tongxingren quli* (Instances of homosexuality in Chinese writings), an article that accompanies his translation of Havelock Ellis's *Psychology of Sex: A Manual for Students*, Chinese: Xing Xinlixue, reprint by Sanlian Shuden, Beijing 1987, p. 532.

The editors also call attention to Man-Lun-Ng's German-language work, *Sexualität in China* in: *Sexualwissenschaft und Sexualpolitik. Spannungsverhältnisse in Europa, Amerika und Asien* (Sexology and sexual politics: Tensions in Europe, America, and Asia). From the series *Sozialwissenschaftliche Sexualforschung* (Sociological sexology) volume 3, pp. 359–76, Rolf Gindorf and Erwin J. Haeberle eds., Berlin and New York: W. de Gruyter 1992.

Notes 11–14 and editors' note
translated by Lance W. Garmer

Bisexuality and Discretion:
The Case of Pakistan

John P. De Cecco

This last spring, for my class "Variations in Human Sexuality," I invited a woman to speak on bisexuality. Through donor insemination, she recently had become a mother. She has been married several years to a man who had been a transvestite. Her husband decided a year or two ago to be treated with hormones in order to feminize his appearance. He has stopped short of any surgical alterations of his anatomy. He now wears dresses, silk-stockings, high-heeled shoes, and so forth. Throughout their marriage, both husband and wife have had sex with each other, sometimes acting as each other's exclusive partner. The speaker called this "being monogamous." Most of their married life has included other female and male partners.

A question-and-answer period followed the speaker's presentation. To my surprise, instead of being curious about her stunning *vita sexualis* and the man's cross-gender behavior, most of the students' questions were about the child's welfare. Would the mother tell the child that the parents are bisexual? Yes, there is nothing bad to hide. When would they do this? When the child showed some curiosity about their friends. Is the child deprived by not having a father, a male role model? Perhaps, but then he has two mothers. How would the child be able to explain his domestic arrangement to playmates and others? When the time came they would share that responsibility with him in dealing with peers and adults. What would she think if the child turned out to be bisexual? That would indeed be fortunate, and so on.

A few months after that class meeting I received an article on homosexuality in Karachi, the largest city in Pakistan, which the Haworth Press hopes to publish in a book on Islam and homosexuality, edited by Arno Schmitt and Jehoeda Sofir, for a new series devoted to Gay and Lesbian Studies. The author of the article noted that the central institution of Pakistani society is the biological family. He wrote, "The purpose of life, and its meaning, is rooted in loyalty to family, in procreation, in protecting its honor and stature, and in caring for children." Childbearing and childrearing are the highest social goals. Those men who do not marry are expected to live with parents even into middle and old age.

That part of sexuality that is devoted to pleasure rather than procreation is left to individual discretion, at least for the men of Pakistan. There is familial and public indifference to recreational sex in either its heterosexual or homosexual form, but there are limitations on the indulgence of either. First, family obligations must take precedence over recreational experiences and nonmarital relationships. It is generally expected that men will marry and father many children. It would be unspeakable to place more value on an extramarital relationship than on family. Second, traditional decorum requires that any homosexual dalliance never bring shame upon the family by coming under public scrutiny. Although homosexual behavior is silently tolerated, its practice must remain private and anonymous because it is publicly and religiously condemned. It is ironic, however, from a Western point of view, that the husband's involvement with a woman is considered a greater threat to the family than his relationship with a man, since it is inconceivable that the latter would lead to a stable arrangement that would compete with marriage.

It is easy to find male partners because Karachi society is very homosocial. Men congregate in parks, by the beach, and on street corners. The observance of decorum means that individuals of the same sex do not set up their own households, even though they may have long-standing sexual and romantic relationships. Even though sex may occur in one partner's home, afterward the other is expected to return to his own home, as in the following incident which commences in a car after a young man is picked up at a bus stop:

> He lived on the other side of town near Malir, and everyone at home was going to be out. I was already hot, and when he reached down and stroked my cock, I just pushed the accelerator down all the way. There was nothing to talk about. He took me to his bedroom (which he shared with his brother) and we started embracing before he locked the door. He wanted to be kissed, caressed, and fucked, and he was not bashful about it. I stroked him, we embraced with much affection, on the bed, on the floor. I fucked him while he jerked off, and then we cuddled for a while. I reached home in time for bed.

Since domestic privacy is hard to come by for the rich as well as the poor, most homosexual behavior occurs in public toilets or wherever a little privacy can be found, indoors or out.

The pattern of homosexual behavior that occurs in Pakistan, I suspect, is common today throughout the Islamic world, much of southern Europe, Mexico, Central and South America, and parts of Asia and the Pacific Islands. It exists wherever the prevailing ideology is sex for procreation and the family is the presiding social institution. Since most of the men who engage in homosexual behavior are also husbands who have intercourse with wives, in sexual behavior they are clearly bisexual. Exclusive homosexual behavior as the dominant sexual pattern is a practice unique to northern Eurpean and North American cultures and there probably only within the last one hundred years.

Let's now return to my students, whom we left agonizing over the possibly horrendous consequences of the speaker's bisexuality for her newborn child. The students, you will recall, viewed her bisexuality as a dire threat to her son's sexual development (would he too become bisexual, or worse, gay?), to his gender development (could he become a real man with two mothers?), and to his future reputation (would he be the object of ridicule if knowledge of this cozy familial arrangement were to be leaked to the public?).

It is hard to believe that the Pakistani would be troubled by any of these concerns, of course, without the added wrinkle of a transvestite–transsexual parent. They would hardly worry about the child's becoming bisexual, since his future homosexual behavior, under the conditions I have described, is of no familial or public importance. They would hardly worry about gender issues since heterosexuality is not linked to masculinity, nor homosexuality to femininity, as they are in Northern societies, except for very visible subgroups such as the *hijras*.

Moreover, the male relationships in societies that incorporate this pattern of bisexuality depart from Western male gender stereotypes in two ways. First, there is an absence of the fear that Western men have of physical proximity and emotional intimacy with other men. Rather, affectional relationships between men are treasured. It is not uncommon to see men walking arm-in-arm and embracing in public. I once observed in a straight porn theater in Rome, young men sitting thigh-by-thigh in a row, and masturbating themselves with fierce concentration on the screen. Second, the affection and openness of Pakistani male relationships are carried over into the sex that men have with each other so that, if circumstances permit, contact can include kissing and hugging as well as good, hard North American fucking.

As Lawrence Stone (1977, 686), the historian of the English family, has pointed out, what holds the modern Western couple together is the emotional and sexual satisfaction they can get from each other. This occurs for many reasons. The marriage is inspired by the romantic belief that, although friendships may fail, the couple will always have each other, a castle in the storm. Couples have their first child after several years of premarital and marital companionship so that for prolonged periods attention can be centered solely on their own needs. Spouses can expect to go on living together about thirty years after the children depart the home. These factors combine so that marital partners expect and even demand much personal satisfaction from each other. Even as parents they head a nuclear family that is isolated from external ties— friends, neighbors, village, church, and school. The dependency and intensity of the parents' relatationship with the children mirrors their own relationship.

Such expectations for the companionate marriage and devoted parentage were reflected in the questions the students asked the speaker on bisexuality. To seek sexual satisfaction outside the marriage seemed to be an implicit threat to the marital bond of the two adults and, by extension, seemed to threaten the bond they had to their child. In a panel on sex and marriage, when I asked student wives what they would do if they discovered that their husbands had sex with another woman, the answers ranged from castration to murder. The students' questions addressed to the bisexual speaker about providing the child suitable models, besides reflecting the gender concerns I referred to earlier, grew out of their fears that the model of marriage and family that was being presented to the child ignored the requirements of the long-term companionate marriage.

Because the Pakistani marriage and family is part of an extended family and community, it is spared the isolation and the emotional and sexual demands of Western counterparts. Since husband and wife do not have to be all things to each other and their children, extracurricular sex does not pose the same threat for the Pakistani that it does for Western couples. As long as family purposes and priorities are clear and respected, some extramarital recreational sex, diplomatically ignored by the spouse, could add stability to marriage and family. The husband can have his cake—a stable domestic and community life—and eat it too, in the occasional sexual romp. The wife is spared the responsibility of being her husband's sole source of sexual pleasure and can concentrate more on caring for children and home. Unfortunately, the specter of the double standard hangs over this whole edifice since the most recreation the women can enjoy is occasionally being free of their husbands' immediate material demands.

Gay liberationists would find the Pakistani model of homosexuality troublesome for several reasons. First, at the personal level, they would be enraged that they could not live openly and alone with lovers. The basis for their anger is clear when we recall that their movement has flourished in northern Europe and North America, exactly where the companionate marriage is most popular, and the movement has had little or no success in those places where the extended family, with its devotion to children, is entrenched. In the family cultures, as I have already noted, it would be considered a scandalous rebuke of family for lesbian and gay lovers to live together. The companionate marriage has prevailed in capatalist and democratic societies that are commited to the principles of individual freedom and personal satisfaction. These are exactly the societies in which the gay liberationist movement has attracted most of its followers.

There is a second objection by gay liberationists to the Pakistani pattern of bisexuality. Homosexual behavior in Pakistan appears to be practiced through a veil of hypocrisy and deceit. Since they assume that the men who engage in such behavior are doing what love and desire dictate, to gay liberationists it appears that Pakistani men are masquerading as heterosexuals when they are really homosexuals. By failing to disclose their true identity to the public, they perpetuate a heterosexism that blindly assumes that only heterosexual behavior and institutions prevail and they fail to enroll in the battle against homophobia that treats homosexuality as sin, crime, and illness.

In the United States, there have been efforts to build gay and lesbian communities that have some aspects of the extended family. They include political leadership, neighborhoods, meeting places, friendship networks, churches, bookstores, and even subcommunities of lesbian and gay parents and their children. In places like San Francisco, the gay community has virtually erected an independent health care system to respond to the AIDS epidemic. Yet, in my experience, as remarkable as these efforts have been over the past two decades, these communities lack the cohesiveness of family cultures because they find it difficult to maintain a stable balance between personal needs, pleasures, and ambitions and commitment to the community.

Professor Stone has observed how marriage and the family are being torn apart in Western society as our aspirations for love and material comfort clash with economic and political realities. In the West, as marriages of sentiment replace marriages of accomodation, bisexuality looms as a threat to the couple's emotional and sexual satisfaction. With the AIDS epidemic it presents the danger of infecting the spouse. A parent's homosexual practice, if it becomes known to the neighbors' children, provides a basis in a growing list of occasions for them to reject the parental value of sexual fidelity along with other parental values in a rapidly changing society.

What the Western mind—and particularly in its Protestant avatar—compels is an obligation to tell the truth at all costs, both personal and social. This is matched in the family societies by the equally serious obligation to observe the rules of decorum even at the price of personal gratification. In the family societies, bisexuality becomes a practical accomodation for meeting both personal need and social obligation. With their overarching concern for children's welfare, bisexuality is simply irrelevant to family life and poses no concern.

In the coming decades, it may be the task of the industrial nations of the West and East to teach the rest of the world about capatalism. One of the propositions of capatilism, according to Professor Blinder (1987), a leading American economist, is that "for most of the goods and services produced and sold in the market economy, more is better than less"(p. 16). Wise teachers, however, also learn from their students. From the family cultures we may learn that in sexual matters sometimes less is better than more—less Western truth and moral righteousness. Surely the family societies should be spared the annoying Western inclination to preach to the rest of the world about what constitutes proper and improper sexual conduct. From the family societies we might learn that their practical sexual arrangements, as in the case of bisexuality, although twisting and tormenting our fastidious sexological categories, are the means for humankind to maintain delicate balances between competing needs, as for example, the responsibility to care for children and to keep ourselves from becoming bored in the process.

Bisexuality and the Causes of Homosexuality: The Case of the Sambia

Gilbert Herdt

Introduction

The causes of bisexuality are well known; however, they keep changing daily. The reasons for this enigma have to do with the dual status of *homosexuality*. It is a concept in popular culture, as well as a social category in Western science and medicine. Attitudes and ideas in the popular sphere affect the scientific, because science and medicine are part and parcel of our culture (Weeks 1985). For the better part of a century, popular and scientific views have alternated between seeing the causes being in nature, or the causes being located in culture. Of course, nature/nurture or biological/social dichotomies are present in arguments regarding anything of importance in human life; homosexuality is no different. What seems distinctive, and what the nineteenth-century Oscar Wilde poked fun at, were the strong and even exaggerated views of homosexuality, which suggested "naturalism" (inversion), from medicine, and "enviromentalism" (degeneracy of the morals), from popular culture.

It is perhaps audacious to address the causes of bisexuality and homosexuality. After all, experts and laymen alike worry justifiably that talk of causes leads quickly to isolation, cure, or eradication. Such concerns are not without substance, because of the Western historical tradition of associating sodomy with sin, the Devil, and criminal subversion. And one worries over the 4% (Kinsey) or 10% of recent estimates of the population who have, once again, to hide their copies of the books by Kinsey, Bob Stoller, or Dick Green under their beds at home or bus seats to work. Thus, while it is audacious, it is also timely to address the causes of homosexuality so much in evidence today in discourse from science, popular culture, and politics. Sometimes this is overt, sometimes it is hidden agenda. By addressing this matter, I do not mean to diminish the political realities associated with discourse on etiology—fears of homophobia and discrimination; rather, I want to tackle them directly, by examining what I regard as the main event in discourse on homosexuality: cultural conceptions of the nature of human nature.

FOR A VERY long time homosexuality has been a prime challenge, as a mover and shaker, in the Western liberal democracy views of human nature. Do intrinsic biological mechanisms determine human behavior? Or are extrinsic factors—such as social institutions and roles—the key determinants? Yes, there have been other targets of the human nature controversy, among which aggression, intelligence, schizophrenia, racism, motherhood, the Oedipal complex, and more recently, child abuse and violence are prime candidates. In each of these issues a debate exists regarding how much the individual's success or failure to conform to social laws rests upon the nature of the lone individual or upon the conditions of social development that create and maintain that individual, or to a cause oscillating somewhere in between the individual psyche and collective body. In these domains, I would argue that causation is neither entirely intrinsic nor extrinsic, nor one of complete success or failure in social adjustment. What troubles us most, I believe, are those areas of "problem" behavior in which there is freedom and choice: the choice not to conform to social laws or mores, where control is vested more in the person. Here, individual action does truly matter. Thus, the liberal democracies of the West have had increasingly to live with the notion of cultural variation, including in matters sexual (D'Emilio and Freedman 1988; Foucault 1980); that is, the claims and entitlements of cultural minorities that they are neither uniform nor homogeneous in fitting into the mainstream (Adam 1978; Murray 1984). To put it simply: the law is based upon a theory of human nature that does not include them in its conception of things.

However, of all these cases homosexuality is special, its claimants and constituencies—either for or against the liberalization of homosexuality—are more visible, and invisible, than in the others. Success and failure are difficult to define here. Can someone be completely normal and successful in all regards, but still have an aberrant sexual nature? Yes, the gay movement has said, pointing to such diverse figures as Michelangelo and, now, Malcolm Forbes. Homosexuality is thus a special claimant on our theory of human nature because of such successes; because of the increasing difficulty of locating the victims of consenting adults; because homosexual behavior occurs in many places and historical times; and because, the critics say, in some cultures it is even institutionalized.

Medicine and culture represent two divergent perspectives on the cases of homosexuality. Religious values and criminal laws against sodomy historically led to the trend in medicene to see homosexuality as a disease. The legacy of medicine is its classification of homosexuality (as well as masturbation and prostitution) as diseases of the nineteenth centruy. Everyone knows this; I find no pleasure in pointing it out (Foucault 1973, 1980). The Victorians, no less than their Puritan ancestors, were attempting to locate, in one segment of the social body, an abcess: individuals who seemed driven to find pleasure in the disease of same-sex eroticism. (H. L. Mencken: The Puritans were haunted by the fear that somewhere, somehow, someone was happy.) The trial of Oscar Wilde, in the 1890s, became a celebrated cause in the name of someone famous who dared to thumb his nose at the social conventions of propriety. He was crucified because the diagnosis of sodomy as a disease did not prevent him from going to prison (Ellman 1988). The trial of Wilde is suggested by social historians as the watershed in the perspective of culture as well. I want to go further and suggest that in Wilde we find the first expression of a homoerotic desire that is flaunted.

There are two dimensions of culture study, sexual science and popular culture. With the rise of anthropology and comparative sexology at the turn of the century, the history of homosexuality began its reconstitution—to alter from physical disease to social illness, and finally to become a lifestyle (Greenberg 1988). The causes were no longer attributed always to disease and fixation of the instincts. New speculative theories in culture and medicine emerged, informed more by sociocultural factors (Mead 1961). These began to recognize sexuality in general as a social category independent of disease and psychiatric symptoms. That story, and its cast of characters, such as Freud, and later Kinsey, is well known. It led to great change in social attitudes about homosexuality (Herdt and Stoller 1990).

And yet, how little our theory of the cause of homosexuality *has* changed. Consider the following quotations:

> 1894: Men have a "natural instinct" which "with all conquering force and might, demands fulfillment" in the natural object of the opposite sex. (Krafft–Ebing quoted in Weeks 1985, 69).

> 1908: Homosexual practices are due sometimes to instinctive preferences, sometimes to external conditions unfavorable to normal intercourse (Westermarck 1917, 465).

> It appears that homosexual practices are very frequently subject to some degree of censure, though the degree varies extremely. . . . On the other hand, where special circumstances have given rise to widely spread homosexual practices, there will be no feeling of disgust, even in adults. . . . (Westermarck 1917, 483–84).

Forty years later, we find Kinsey (1948, 660) concluding "The very general occurrence of the homosexual in ancient Greece, and its wide occurrence today in some cultures in which such activity is not taboo suggests that the capacity of an individual to respond erotically to any sort of stimulus, whether it is provided by another person of the same or opposite sex, is basic in the species." Many other examples from David Greenberg's (1988) recent study magnify the same point: a long historical drift in conceptions of homosexuality shows structural continuities. Bisexuality shows a parallel historical course.

We know that the term *homosexuality* was coined in 1869 by Kertbeny to find a neutral term for same-sex love and the concept of *heterosexuality* was constructed even later, in the 1890s, some would say by Havelock Ellis, for a similar purpose: Both concepts assume that sexual identity and attraction are grounded in human nature. That is, when you peel away the layers of culture you reach a core of sexuality (cf. Geertz 1965).

Take note: in the more than one hundred years since that time, a bifurcation in sexual science research has emerged. Rarely have the causes of heterosexuality been questioned. Like Krafft–Ebing, we assume that heterosexuality is human nature. Alternatively, numerous studies of the effects of heterosexuality, in investigations of marriage, gender, dating, high school achievement, and so forth have been undertaken. The very opposite is true of homosexuality. The interest in homosexuality has been solely in its causes; seldom has a study of the effects or outcomes of homosexuality in adult lives been investigated; that is, how are lives lived as gay or homosexual after age five (Reviewed in Gagnon 1971, 1989; Boxer and Cohler 1989).

And still we are fascinated by the developmental question: Is mental conflict the cause or the result of homosexuality? Beginning at least as late as the 1880s, homosexuality was pinpointed as a major cause of psychic distress and illness in the person. Freud's (1905) influential view in *The Three Essays* suggested as much in Western culture, though he recognized that the gender of the sex object choice was not conflictual for the ancient Greeks, or for primitive peoples. Subsequent psyhoanalytic models, and psychiatric work up to the *DSM-II* and the reclassification of homosexuality as a lifestyle in *DSM-III* in 1972, suggested intellectual and cultural ambivalence regarding whether the mental conflicts associated with homosexuality are the cause or outcome of sexual development (see Stoller 1985, 1973; Bayer 1982). Recent works on homosexuality and gay identity development, including Richard Green's (1987), suggest that mental conflict (either biosocial or psychological in origin) causes homosexual feelings.

A different view, however, is suggested by recent anthropological work in the Pacific. Distress related to homosexual behavior may be the by-product, rather than the cause, of social adjustment. That is, a product of strong developmental discontinuity between childhood and adult experience. In this view, homosexual behavior *is* conflictual, but not because of intrinsic mechanisms (Oedipal conflict, abnormal hormones, absent fathers or dominating mothers: too much of this, too little of that). Rather it is due to the demands of cognitive category change (from heterosexual to homosexual identity) and social adjustment imposed upon the person by social structure, much as Ruth Benedict once suggested (1938). It is, then, not homosexuality *per se*, that is conflictual, but rather the discontinuities of change from heterosexual to homosexual self-representations and relationships, that causes distress.

In such ways, the entity "homosexuality" has long been in dispute. Some believe that it is a single essence—inside the body—or, say, a construct—in the mind, or a role outside in "society"—that vitalizes it. But the anthropologist questions: Is it valid to represent these essences or constructs through the concepts of Western cultural traditions?

It is of course central to these debates to question whether there *is* a single "it entity" or a plurality of them. Theorists of the universalist/teleological persuasion generally subscribe to the position that there is a single "it entity." Freud, for instance, generally did; many but not all Freudian theorists still do so. Stage model theorists, writing about the development of homosexual identity and lifestyles, generally do so also. Cultural relativists such as anthropologists, however, seem to subscribe to the plurality model, in which it is argued that there are divergent "homosexualities." For instance, by suggesting that the North American Indian category *berdache* is an essential type distinctive from others, some authors nominalize the "it entity" as "berdachehood" (Williams 1986; Whitehead 1981). Kinsey is interesting in this regard, because although he suggested that sexuality exists on a continuum of homosexual/bisexual/heterosexual, he believed that there were common biosocial origins to them all (Kinsey et al. 1948). The later Freud is similarly reviewed in Herdt (1989). Thus, some psychiatrists and biologists have joined anthropologists, sociologists, and historians who apparently hold a divergent view of homosexualities. In fact, though, a close reading suggests that culturual relativists have not often disagreed with the human nature claim that there is an "it entity," only that its shapes and sensibilities belong in social reality.

Anthropologists have thus joined others in the social sciences in pluralizing the "it entity" into divergent types of homosexualities. Typologies of homosexualities, in complex and simple societies, now abound. They owe their modern history to sexologists, such as Havelock Ellis. A set of prototypic forms has thus emerged regarding historical/cultural category differences between the plural entities across time and space. Thus, a growing consensus is emerging about a set of four categories of same-sex erotic relationships. I label these: "age-structured," "gender transformed," "class or role specialized," and "the modern gay/lesbian" categories have evolved as divergent entities of this nature (Herdt 1988, 1987). These categorical types assume a distinction between "identity" and "behavioral form," with lifelong habitualized preferences for the same sex indicative of identity.

But how do these "culturally constituted" homosexualities relate to Western constructs, such as homosexual "sexual identity," and bisexual "sexual orientation," and underlying factors of social classification (e.g., race, gender, age, class) which predicate sexual developement ?

The representation of these cultural prototypes suggest that a conundrum of comparison is at stake. One sign of this is a tendency to nominalize cultural contructs as entities beyond the boundaries of the culture of origin. For example, we talk of age-structured, North American Indian *berdache* homosexualities, as if their application to over one hundred divergent cultural groups implied the same feelings, identities, and eroticism for all persons across these tribal groups. But there is more at stake than the matter of nominalization.

The comparative study of sexuality across cultures is, as in so many other of anthropological research, saddled historically with the problem of situating entities, objects (e.g., roles, institutions), and meanings between universal processes and particular situations. Sexuality research, however, has long been entangled in another, parallel debate—actually a discourse held over by popular demand from the Victorian era —regarding biological social theories of causation. Many authorities now believe this conceptual polarity to be outmoded, and I am one of them (Herdt and Stoller 1990). In short, both social and biosocial factors are necessary to interpret crosscultural studies, with the general proviso that one's research interest determines which elements, in what combinations, are significant for the provision of understanding. The study of different types of social homosexualities is particularly useful here, enabling us to see around the edges of the biological versus social causes of dichotomy.

Models of divergent cultural homosexualities are simultaneously lumping and splitting strategies in cultural comparison. On the one hand, they split up the cultures of the world via one basic trait—homosexuality—into multiple types of roles, identities, and relationships; while on the other they lump together traditions that seem to "fit" into the same type across time and space. That is, the homosexuality form is subsumed into a particular type of human nature.

The new typologies of crosscultural homosexuality have thus far skirted the fundamental issue of their ontologies. Local theories of being and metaphysics of the world constitute ontologies. Folk models of ontology are concerned with the nature of being a person and of being in the time/space world with such a nature. Such local theories implicitly ask: What drives, intentions, desires, and developmental pathways characterize the nature of a person? Are these characteristics found also in other persons, in entities (such as spirits), and the social and physical surround? The genius of culture is to create an ontological system so compelling that what is inside and outside of a person are viewed as of a piece, no seams and patches noticeable (Shweder 1990). And thus it is with the ontology of sexuality. Our American folk model of sexuality, for instance, emphasizes the lone individual, whose sexual nature is borne in the flesh, apart from other entities of social and spiritual sort, and which seems unchangeable across developmental time. For various reasons homosexuality has always been problematic in our Western ontological folk theory. The emergence of a new ontological category—gay/lesbian—has shifted our discourse and representations here. Homosexual and gay are now distinctive cultural systems in our society, largely age-stratified. The older generation self-identifies as closet homosexuals; the younger generation as gay.

In short, our theory of the human nature of homosexuality lumps everyone into a single type. Many anthropologists and more psychiatrists today believe, however, that there is no such thing as "homosexuality." Unlike our own theory of human nature, they suggest that there are many kinds of homosexuals and homosexualities. And Bob Stoller suggests that if you look inside the heads of everyday average people, neither does the thing "heterosexuality" exist. These are normative fictions, born of a strong collusion between the popular culture theory of human nature and medical and sexual science. Or, to paraphrase John Gagnon, there are as many ways to get to be homosexual as there are the many paths to heaven.

Let me illustrate by briefly contrasting the two best known forms of institutionalized same-sex practices in the tribal world: gender-reversed homosexuality and age-structured homosexuality. Their divergent principles are simple to outline. In gender-reversed homosexual practices, someone takes on the dress, social role, gestures, tasks, and erotic position of the other sex. The North American Indian *berdache* is the best known tradition. It occurred in approximately 113 different tribes; in two-thirds of these cultures, there were only male *berdaches*, whereas in the other third there were both male and female *berdaches*. Thus, a biologically normal Indian male would turn to the *berdache* role, dress as a girl and then a woman, and simulate menstruation and pregnancy. For males, the gender-reversal type resulted in their feminization; and this was a life-long role (reviewed in Nanda 1989; Williams 1986).

In the second type, age-structured homosexuality, males of different ages, never equals, engage in homosexual practices for a period of years, usually in adolescence for at least one of them. This is the form of the ancient Greeks' practice (Dover 1978). The age-structured form occurs in many places and times, such as the Japanese samurai, archaic societies, as well as in the Southwest Pacific, and parts of Africa. The Sambia of New Guinea, whom I have studied, have this type of homosexual ontology. It co-occurs with warriorhood cults of masculinity, sexual antagonism between the genders, and strong developmental discontinuity in sexual life (Herdt 1981).

Take note that these two types of homosexuality occur in different geographic areas. They are mutually exclusive. *Berdaches* and age-structured homosexual practices do not occur in the same premodern cultural tradition. Note that with regard to male development, the *berdache* feminizes males, whereas age-structured homosexuality masculinizes them. Note further that the *berdache* role never alters for the life of the persons; whereas in age-structures, the male is first passive, then active; will later marry; and may or may not be required or desire later to engage in sexual relations with younger males.

Now I want to introduce a further distinction in my analysis. I believe that social and cultural factors very broadly channel and limit sexual variation in human populations. Sexual laws, codes, and roles *do* restrict the range and intensity of sexual practices, as far as we can judge from the crosscultural literature (Herdt and Stoller 1990). Kinsey lent his support to this view; Ford and Beach (1950) documented it in surveys; and Margaret Mead (1961) did so in her ethnographic studies. But biosocial, genetic, and hormonal predispositions also broadly limit and channel. Each culture's theory of the combination of these social and biological constraints we could call its theory of human sexual nature. Yet none of these broad principles, nor the local theory of human sexual nature, entirely explains or predicts a particular person's sexual desires or behaviors. A sexual behavior, that is, does not necessarily indicate an erotic orientation, preference, or desire. The homosexual is not the same as the homoerotic; whether in our society or one very exotic, I will claim, we can distinguish the homosexual from the homoerotic, as Oscar Wilde's case first hinted.

To illustrate now, I must return to the Sambia of New Guinea. By an example of the strange, I do not expect necessarily to find the familiar. Rather, I want to show that when one begins with a different local theory of human nature, you end up with a different analysis of the causes of homosexuality in a society where "it" is institutionalized.

Sambia males undergo a dramatic form of developmental discontinuity in their sexual/gender growth. Ritual initiation procedures fully institutionalize same-sex erotic contact between the seven- to ten-year-old boys and adolescent unmarried youths. This homosexual contact focuses upon beliefs about the power of semen transmission. Semen is an elixir, a growth stimulant, in the eyes of many tribal peoples (Herdt 1984), but here, insemination functions like an externally introduced androgen to secure male maturation. Sambia believe the male body by nature is incapable of spontaneously producing semen. Boys begin as semen recipients, until their midteens. Successive initiations transform them at third-stage (social puberty) rites into semen donors, inseminators. Only oral sexual intercourse is permitted among Sambia. Masturbation to orgasm is absent. Homosexual contacts between females are believed to be absent. After first initiation, strict avoidance taboos, and strongly sanctioned premarital heterosexual and adultery rules, make contact between males and females extremely rare. Not until their late teens, and the formation of marriage alliances (by politics, not personal choice), are youths able to resume male/female interactions or contacts, even with their mothers or sisters. After the marriage ceremony, but before their wives' first birth, males begin heterosexual development, first in fellatio with their wives, and later in missionary-position genital intercourse. These youths are behaviorally bisexual until fatherhood, because same-sex contacts with boys are permitted as usual. After fatherhood, however, homosexual activities for adults are prohibited. My research suggests that 95% of all Sambia males go through these stages of sexual and erotic development. The 5% of males who continue to have only homosexual behavior or who are behaviorally bisexual are different from them (Herdt and Stoller 1990). In a word, Sambia males universally engage in homosexual behavior, whereas 5% of them are homoerotic.

I must pause parenthetically to mention the incidence of this form of ritual homosexual practices in other cultures. My exhaustive review of the Pacific literature, published in 1984, has identified over fifty distinct societies reported to practice this form of homosexuality. This represents somewhere between 10 and 20% of all existent Pacific socities. The term "age-structured homosexual practice" thus captures the asymmetric older/younger character of the rites, which must never occur among equals (Herdt 1988). If it *were* practiced between consenting adults, it would make them homoerotic, not just homosexual. But it is not.

What I want to consider now is the theoretical understanding of the causes of Sambia sexual development. Is the concept of homosexual *sexual preference* applicable to a non-Western society such as Sambia? Many assume so; I do not. Robert Stoller and I have written of the theories of origins of homosexuality, which we believe overemphasize individual behavior change through social learning and underestimate the importance of subjective factors (such as desire and fantasy) and cultural context (Stoller and Herdt 1985). The construct "sexual orientation" has a nefarious history, and we should note the problematic nature of the linking concepts of "sexual object" from Freud (1905) and sexual orientation from Kinsey (et al. 1948). Margaret Mead's (1961) work implied that the cultural classification systems, economic roles, social status position, and kinship relationship—alongside of sex-assignment at birth—were so powerful in the regulation of sexual and gender behavior that they could alter sexual preference from one life stage to the next, creating more fluidity and sexual-object seeking in development than we allow in our Western conception of human nature.

The problem of the causes of homosexuality among Sambia for Western science is with how their same-sex behavior and other-sexed behavior fit into the *same* normative lifecourse design. Sambia do not think of their taking in semen as being concerned with an *exclusive and habitualized preference* for males at the childhood stage. But, in fact, the practice *is* exclusive, and it becomes habitualized: no one questions the logic of seeking semen only from males, or its sublogic, that one must ingest semen to become manly. These criteria of homosexual sexual preference in our own society are, therefore, largely fulfilled by the Sambia developmental pattern. But, then, so too are the requirements of the heterosexual pattern. After the midteens, males seek and find exclusive, habitualized, other-sexed contacts, in their wives. Thus, they fulfill our own definition of normative heterosexual orientation after the onset of young adulthood. This view of the Sambia developmental system is subject to misunderstanding.

Although it will be obvious to many, it is worthwhile to repeat the *cultural/linguistic* definition of the scientific and medical categories of aetiology and classification that we use. Sambia do not have a noun category either for *homosexual* or for *heterosexual.* They do not recognize in their history or culture that someone can be exclusively homosexual in partner selection, or exclusively heterosexual either throughout their whole life. All humans are sexual creatures, as they see it; they see no necessary contradiction in the person's having sexual contacts with both males and females, provided they do so at the right stage, and in the culturally appointed manner. Sambia cannot imagine a boy who lacks a male sexual partner, or an adult man who has one. These distinctions were more or less true for the ancient Greeks as well, as they are for other cultural populations around the world (Herdt 1988). These categories profoundly shape child development and sexual subjectivity. The ritual origin of these practices does not preclude their being pleasurable in varying degrees of erotic response, according to the particular individual, situation, and sexual encounter, just as it is for us. It would be empirically wrong to suggest that the theoretical construct "sexual preference" does not apply to Sambia development simply because sexual pleasure is not involved; on the contrary, pleasure *is* involved powerfully so.

The difficulty with our bisexual construct is that it locates the origin and meaning of preference too much inside the lone individual and not enough in the social surround. The notion of sexual preference, with its linking conception "sex object choice," requires an individual difference psychology of choice and free will that may correspond to the reality of philosophers, but seldom does for ordinary mortals. Our sexual development is driven and regulated by extraordinary forces, intrinsic and extrinsic, which include our genes, hormones, early parental relationships, peer pressures, cultural training for categories and language, and out-and-out social sanctions and physical force. We seldom are free to choose freely, but entertain the enchantment that we can. The Sambia pattern of ritual homosexual activity is simply a more extreme form of the many social influences that regulate sexuality across all socities, ours included; perhaps especially ours, with our strong ideas of individualism, romantic love, and the right to orgasm.

The higher-order theory problem with homosexual orientation is not that it is culturebound, though it is, or that we think and work scientifically with categories that are not universal, which we do; but rather that in *normative human development* sexual orientation embraces an ontology that is far too restricted in scope to account for crosscultural variations in the human condition. Our normative idea begins with sexual orientation being "naturally" inclined to the opposite sex. This contemporary conception differs from Freud's (1905) famous "polymorphous perverse" orientation in the anlagen of sexual development, which he believed was biologically bisexual. Kinsey et al. (1948) and subsequent workers could not embrace this bisexual conception, mainly, I think, because it was so far at odds with our own cultural model of human nature (Herdt 1990).

But if the anthropology of sexual development in its total scope teaches us anything, it is that the sexual dimension of the human animal must begin with a broad, generalized range of sexual response, that is narrowed only across developmental time in a society. The restriction of the scope of sexual function (and, by implication, preference and sexual selection) are strongly regualted by culture and society, with early sensitive learning in the first few years of life anticipating subsequent continuities and discontinuities, such as those of the Sambia. Our Western *normative pathway* theory of sexual development is far too heterosexist in its leanings, and not open-ended enough to encompass the human record. When we discuss aberrant pathways, however, as in the course of homosexual or gay development, we begin with the same assumption of "natural" heterosexuality, but invoke mechanisms (usually of a deficit nature) to explain why the normative development (phylogenetic) outcome in sexual orientation did not occur.

What the New Guinea material advises—and that from other crosscultural and historical periods too—is that sexual function and development are under greater social and cultural regulation, even at the organismic level, than we once believed. In culture theory terms, if you want to change the direction of sexual function and outcome, you must implement broad behavioral controls and social reinforcements, and the earlier the better in development. However, these social directives will *not* produce homosexuals or heterosexuals; those outcomes are obviously ontogenetically regulated at other levels, at least for some indivduals, such that strong desires for same- or opposite-sexed partners are felt to be a part of their deepest human nature. (Remember the phenomenology of the primary male transsexual in this regard: Stoller 1986.) With the decrease in social regulation we would expect to see, then, earlier developmental variation, and more random variation in sexual behavior, with more same-sexed and bisexual behavior, for the broad middle of the bell-curve distribution of populations, ours included.

IN THE MORE than a century of debate on the causes of homosexuality, medicine, sexology, and popular culture have agreed with each other more often than not regarding its form of human nature. From sin to sickness, criminality to moral degeneracy, and now to a contested lifestyle, our culture holds a rationalist view that all same-sex attractions or behaviors denote the same kind of nature. And yet there are many forms of socially constituted homosexualities around the world. These peoples too have their own theories of human nature, and while they explain why and how people of the same biological sex should have sexual intercourse, they have not normalized the phenomenon into a category type as much as we have. There are many factors that explain this crosscultural difference, but one above all impresses me: sexual desire.

I do believe that there is a kind of human nature related to this thing we call "homosexuality." I do not know how much it is born in the flesh or bred in psyche; I suspect it is often of both. What is distinctive of this Western form of human nature is a relatively exclusive and lifelong preference for certain members of the same sex. This is not, however, our homosexuality; it is homoeroticism. It should not be confused with transient, casual, experimental same-sex activity; that occurs most everywhere. Neither should it be confused with institutionalized homosexual practices in New Guinea. Some individuals among Sambia ever and always prefer sex with boys; they, too, are homoerotic, not homosexual. The sexual desire is by far the more powerful indicator of their distinctive human nature. Oscar Wilde's life insinuated this as a new idea long ago.

And it follows, *pari passu*, that our highly complex, individualized Western society has also many persons who seldom or never feel sexual attraction for the same sex, but only for certain members of the opposite sex. It is in their deeper nature, their cultural ontology, to feel only those desires. They are, most properly, not heterosexual, but heteroerotic.

Now, to reframe my opening question, I should ask: What are the causes of homosexuality and homoeroticism? Why should our species have evolved individuals of different sexual nature? Are the differences negligible in the history of culture?

The answers to these questions take us back to the basic perspectives of Western sexologists a century ago. Freud's view is the most catholic: Homosexuality arises in part from biosocial predispositions, and in part from the accidents of the individuals' developmental history. But neither of these control dimensions alone will suffice to produce erotic desire for the same sex across time and space. For that, the person supplies intentions and agreement: the willingness to be homoerotic. That form of sexual nature is neither sin nor sickness, but the expression in society of a deep form of sexual nature, one that I suspect is probably panhuman.

Bibliography

Adam, Barry D. 1978. *The Survival of Domination*. New York: Elsevier.
Bayer, R. 1987. *Homosexuality and American Psychiatry*. New Brunswick, N.J.: Rutgers University Press.

Benedict, R. 1938. Continuities and discontinuities in cultural conditioning. *Psychiatry.* 1: 161–67.

Boxer, Andrew, and Bertram Cohler. 1989. The life course of gay and lesbian youth: An immodest proposal for the study of lives. In *Gay and Lesbian Youth*, ed. G. Herdt. 315–55. New York: Harrington Park Press.

Carrier, J. 1980. Homosexual behavior in cross-cultural perspective. In *Homosexual Behavior: A Modern Reappraisal*, ed. J. Marmor. 100–122. New York: Basic Books.

Dank, B. 1971. Coming out in the gay world. *Psychiatry.* 34: 100–197.

D'Emilio, J., and E. Freedman. 1988. *Intimate Matters.* New York: Harper and Row.

Dover, K. G. 1978. *Greek Homosexuality.* Cambridge, Mass.: Harvard University Press.

Ellman, Richard. 1988. *Oscar Wilde.* New York: Alfred A. Knopf.

Ford, C. S., and F. A. Beach. 1951. *Patterns of Sexual Behavior.* New York: Harper and Bros.

Foucault, Michel. 1980. *The History of Sexuality.* Trans. Robert Hurley. New York: Vintage Books.

Freud, S. 1905. *Three Essays on the Theory of Sexuality. S. G.* 7: 125–245.

Gagnon, John H. 1971. The creation of the sexual in early adolescence. In *Twelve to Sixteen: Early Adolescence*, ed. J. Kagan and R. Coles. New York: Norton.

———. 1989. Disease and desire. *Daedalus.* 118: 47–77.

Geertz Clifford. 1965. The impact of the concept of culture on the concept of man. In *New Views on the Nature of Man*, ed. John R. Platt. 93–118. Chicago: University of Chicago Press.

Green, Richard. 1987. *The "Sissy Boy Syndrome" and the Development of Homosexuality.* New Haven: Yale University Press.

Greenberg, David. 1988 *The History of Homosexuality.* Chicago: University of Chicago Press.

Herdt, G. 1987. *Sambia: Ritual and Gender in New Guinea.* New York: Holt, Rinehart, and Winston.

———. 1984. Ritualized homosexuality in the male cults of Melanesia, 1862–1982: An introduction. In *Ritualized Homosexuality in Melanesia*, ed. G. H. Herdt. 1–80. Berkeley: University of California Press.

———. 1988. Cross-cultural forms of homosexuality and the concept "gay." *Psychiatric Annals.* 18: 37–39.

———. 1989. Introduction: Gay and lesbian youth, emergent identities, and cultural scenes at home and abroad. *J. Homosex.* 17: 1–42.

———. 1989. Father presence and ritual homosexuality: Paternal deprivation and masculine development in Melanesia reconsidered. *Ethos* 18: 326–70.

Herdt, G. and R. J. Stoller. 1990. *Intimate Communications: Erotics and the Study of Culture.* New York: Columbia University Press.

Kinsey, A., W. Pomeroy, and C. Martin. 1948. *Sexual Behavior in the Human Male.* Philadelphia: W. B. Saunders.

Mead, Margaret. 1961. Cultural determinants of sexual behavior. In *Sex and Internal Secretions.* 1433–79. Baltimore: Williams and Wilkins.

Murray, S. 1984. *Social Theory, Homosexual Realities.* New York: Gai Sabre Monographs.

Nanda, Serena. 1990. *Neither Man Nor Woman*. Belmont, Calif.: Wadsworth Publishing Co.

Shweder, Richard A. 1990. Cultural psychology—What is it? In *Cultural Psychology*, J. Stigler, R. A. Shweder, and G. Herdt, 1–46. New York: Cambridge University Press.

Stoller, Robert J. 1968. *Sex and Gender*. New York: International Universities Press.

———. 1985 Psychoanalytic "research" on homosexuality: The rules of the game. In *Observing the Erotic Imagination*, R. J. Stoller. 167–83. New Haven: Yale University Press.

Stoller, Robert J., and Gilbert Herdt. 1985. Theories on the origins of homosexuality. *Arch. Gen. Psychiatry*.

Weeks, Jeffrey. 1985. *Sexuality and Its Discontents*. London: Routledge and Kegan Paul.

Westermarck, E. 1917. The *Origin and Development of the Moral Ideas*. Vol. 2, 2d ed. London: MacMillan and Co.

Whitehead, Harriet. 1981. The bow and the burden strap: A new look at institutionalized homosexuality in Native North America. In *Sexual Meanings*, ed. S. B. Ortner and H. Whitehead. 80–115. Cambridge: Cambridge University Press.

Williams, Walter. 1987. *The Spirit and the Flesh*. Boston: Beacon.

Becoming and Being "Bisexual"

Martin S. Weinberg, Colin J. Williams, and Douglas W. Pryor

This essay explores the process by which people come to adopt the label *bisexual* as their sexual identity. Becoming bisexual involves a special problem of meaning and adjustment. It requires the rejection of not one, but two recognized categories of sexual identity: heterosexual and homosexual. Most people settle into the status of heterosexual without any struggle over the identity. There is not much concern with explaining how this occurs. That people are heterosexual is simply taken for granted. To those who find heterosexuality unfulfilling, however, the development of a sexual identity is more difficult. Our point of departure is the work of researchers who focus on the process through which people become "homosexual." This approach to sexual identity describes the individual as moving through a series of stages. Three basic process models in relation to homosexual identity have been formulated (Cass 1984; Coleman 1982; Ponse 1978; Troiden 1988).

While each of the models involves a different number of stages, there are three common elements among them. The process begins with the individual in a state of identity confusion—feeling different from others, struggling with the acknowledgment of same-sex attractions. Then there is a period of thinking about possibly being homosexual—involving associating with self-identified homosexuals, sexual experimentation, and forays into the homosexual subculture. Last, is the attempt to integrate one's self-concept and social identity as homosexual—acceptance of the label, disclosure about being homosexual, acculturation to a homosexual way of life, and the development of love relationships.

According to these models, not every individual will follow through each stage. Some will remain locked in at a certain point. Others will move back and forth between stages. Troiden (1988, 59), whose model is the most sociological, emphasizes how the process of acquiring a homosexual identity varies with the social context. On the one hand, he suggests that during a period of social tolerance toward homosexuality, passage through the different stages may be faster and less problematic than at other times. On the other hand, because of the AIDS situation, it may be that progress through the stages will become increasingly difficult.

To our knowledge, no model of *bisexual* identity formation exists. In this paper, we present such a model. There is some overlap with the basic process involved in becoming homosexual. But there are differences which require modifications of that model. For example, the label *bisexual* is not widely recognized and is not readily available to most people as an identity. Also, the absence of a bisexual subculture in most locales means a lack both of information and of support for sustaining a commitment to the identity. Thus, with our subjects, there seem to be four distinct stages: problems with finding the label, understanding what the label means, dealing with social disapproval from two directions, and continuing to use the label once it is adopted.

Method

THE DATA REPORTED here are part of a wider study of bisexuals conducted in San Francisco during the mid-1980s. This part involves in-depth interviews conducted with 93 self-defined bisexuals (49 men and 44 women). The sample all were members of an organization for bisexuals called the Bisexual Center. The wider study also includes comparable samples of self-defined heterosexuals and homosexuals and will appear as a book, *Dual Attraction: Bisexuality in the Age of AIDS.*

THE STAGES
Initial Confusion

MANY OF OUR respondents said they had experienced a period of considerable confusion, doubt, and struggle regarding their sexual identity prior to self-defining as bisexual. This was ordinarily the first step in the process of becoming bisexual. Our respondents described a number of sources of early confusion in relation to their sexual identity. For some, it was the experience of having strong sexual feelings for both sexes that was unsettling, disorienting, and sometimes frightening. Often, these were sexual feelings that, according to the respondents, they did not know how to easily handle or resolve:

> I was confused because of being attracted to members of both sexes and not feeling okay about it. (F)

> In the past, I couldn't reconcile different desires I had. I didn't understand them. I didn't know what I was. And I ended up feeling really mixed up, unsure, and kind of frightened. (F)

> I couldn't see how I could like men and women. It just didn't make sense to me. I couldn't merge my religious background with my feelings of wanting to put my arms around another man. . . . (M)

> I thought I was gay, and yet was having these intense fantasies and feelings about fucking women. I went through a long period of confusion. (M)

Others explained having been confused because they thought strong sexual feelings for, or sexual behavior with, the same sex jeopardized or meant an end to their long-standing heterosexuality:

> When I first had sexual feelings for females, I had the sense I should give up my feelings for men. I think it would have been easier to give up men. (F)

> I can remember after having my first sexual contact with a man that I felt, because I had a nice sexual contact, that I had to go live with him and not

be with . . . [my female partner]. It was very, very confusing. I soon discovered that a contact with a man not only didn't take away from my other relationship, but enhanced it. (M)

A third source of confusion that characterized this initial stage of the process stemmed from attempts by respondents trying to categorize their feelings for, and/or behaviors with, both sexes, yet not being able to do so. Being unaware of the term *bisexual*, some tried to formulate and organize their sexuality through recourse to readily available labels of *heterosexual*, or *homosexual*—but these did not seem to fit. Thus, there was a period of time in which no sense of sexual identity jelled. It was an aspect of themselves that remained unclassifiable:

I was not sure in the past if I was gay or not. I did not feel straight or gay. More just like me. (F)

It was confusing trying to figure out if I was homosexual or heterosexual. (M)

When I was young, I didn't know what I was. I knew there were people like Mom and Dad—heterosexual and married—and that there were "queens." I knew I wasn't like either one. (M)

I thought I had to be either gay or straight. That was the big lie. It was confusing. . . . That all began to change in the late 60s. It was a long and slow process. . . . (F)

Finally, others suggested they experienced a great deal of confusion because of their "homophobia." This was more commonly the case with the men than the women, but not exclusively so. It was difficult for some of the respondents to face up to the fact of the same-sex component of their sexuality. The consequence was often one of long-term denial:

I was still relating to women and had a couple of relationships, but I had my first relationship with a man. I was so devastated by the experience. It was a year before my next experience with a man. . . . It really destroyed my identity. I felt very guilty. I couldn't come to terms with the fact that I had attractions to men. So, as a result, I stayed away from them. (M)

Very early on . . . I was afraid that maybe I really was homosexual, and that . . . the first stirrings or erotic fantasies I had about men . . . was really the first little indicator. I was also disturbed by the types of fantasies. . . . I didn't have emotional loving feelings for men, but rather the feeling that I wanted to be fucked by them. (M)

Finding and Applying the Label

FOLLOWING THIS INITIAL period of confusion, which often spanned years, was the experience of finding and applying the label. We asked our respondents for specific factors or events in their lives that led them to self-define as bisexual. There were a number of common experiences.

For many who were unfamiliar with the term *bisexual,* the discovery that the category in fact existed was a turning point. This happened by simply hearing the word, reading about it somewhere, or learning of a place called the Bisexual Center. The discovery provided a means of making sense of long-standing feelings for both genders as the label seemed to readily fit:

> Early on I thought I was just gay, because I was not aware there was another category, bisexual. I always knew I was interested in men and women. But I did not realize there was a name for these feelings and behaviors until I took Psychology 101 and read about it, heard about it there. That was in college. (F)

> The first time I heard the word, which was not until I was 26, I realized that was what fit for me. What it fit was that I had sexual feelings for both men and women. Up until that point, the only way that I could define my sexual feelings was that I was either a latent homosexual or a confused heterosexual. (M)

> Going to a party at someone's house, and finding out that the party was to benefit the Bisexual Center. I guess at that point I began to define myself as bisexual. I never knew there was such a word. If I had heard the word earlier on, for example as a kid, I might have been bisexual then. My feelings had always been bisexual. I just did not know how to define them. (F)

In the case of others, the turning point was their first homosexual or heterosexual experience coupled with the recognition that sex was pleasurable with both sexes. These were people who already seemed to have knowledge of the label *bisexual* yet, minus experiences with both men and women, could not label themselves accordingly:

> The first time I had actual intercourse, an orgasm with a woman, it led me to realize that I was bisexual, because I enjoyed it as much as I did with a man, although the former occurred much later on in my sexual experiences. . . . I didn't have an orgasm with a woman until 22, while with males, that had been going on since the age of 13. (M)

> When I had my first same-sex encounter at 21, I realized that it could happen and that sex with men felt good, guilt notwithstanding. I knew then [I was bisexual]. . . . I could have sex successfully with a man or a woman . . . both felt good. . . . It was not necessary to limit myself to one gender. I realized that making love to a man or a woman was the same thing. (M)

> At about 23, when I made love to a female high school friend for the first time, that's when I began using the term bisexual. (F)

Still others reported not so much a specific experience as a turning point, but emphasized the recognition that their sexual feelings for both sexes were simply too strong to deny. They eventually came to the conclusion it was unnecessary to choose between them:

Realizing that I wanted sex with both women and men and realizing that I have feelings for both as well. Realizing that I am not willing to make a choice between the two as an overall pattern. When I learned the term bisexual I felt validated. (F)

Politically, being gay seemed desirable, but I had no inclination to give up males. So it was impossible to be gay. I realized that just because I had some strong negative feelings about males does not make me gay. I also had some strong positive feelings for men. So I had to identify myself as bisexual. After all, I was in a gay chorus and my lover was male. (F)

At 24, when I began relating to men on a consistent basis, one of my thoughts was, do I have to choose between heterosexuality and homosexuality? And I came to the decision that I did not because I was attracted to both and there was no reason I could not have both. . . . (M)

The last factor that was instrumental in leading respondents to initially adopt the label *bisexual* was the encouragement and support of others. Encouragement sometimes came from a partner who already defined as bisexual:

Encouragement from a man I was in a relationship with. We had been together two or three years at the time—he began to define as bisexual. . . . [He] encouraged me to do so as well. He engineered a couple of threesomes with another woman. Seeing one other person who had bisexuality as an identity that fit them seemed to be real encouragement.

Another source of encouragement was forthcoming from sex-positive organizations in San Francisco, primarily the Bisexual Center, as well as places like San Francisco Sex Information (see Weinberg, Williams, and Pryor 1987), the Pacific Center, and the Institute for Advanced Study of Human Sexuality:

At the Gay Pride Parade, I had seen the brochures for the Bisexual Center. Two years later I went to a Tuesday night meeting. I immediately felt that I belonged and that if I had to define myself that this was what I would use.

Through SFSI [San Franciso Sex Information] and the Bi Center, I found a community of people . . . [who] were more comfortable for me than were exclusive gay or heterosexual communities. . . . [It was] beneficial for myself to be . . . in a sex-positive community. I got more strokes and came to understand myself better. . . . I felt it was necessary to express my feelings for males and females without having to censor them, which is what the gay and straight communities pressured me to do. (F)

Thus our respondents became familiar with and came to the point of adopting the label bisexual in a variety of ways: e.g., through reading about it on their own, being in therapy, talking to friends, experience with sex partners, involvement with sex-positive organizations, and so forth.

Settling into the Identity

USUALLY IT TOOK years from the time of first sexual attractions for, or behaviors with, both sexes before people came to actually think of themselves as "bisexual." The next stage then was one of settling into the identity, which was characterized by a more complete transition in self-labeling.

Most reported that this settling-in stage was the consequence of an increase in self-acceptance. It involved being less concerned with the negative attitudes of others about their sexual preference:

> I just decided I was bi. I trusted my own sense of self. I just stopped listening to others tell me what I could or couldn't be. (F)

> I decided I would do what I wanted. This was me. It would be part of my life. . . . So I accepted it. (F)

> Coming to grips with the fact that that's who I am and learning just to accept myself and love myself because I am bisexual. (M)

> I learned to accept the fact that there are a lot of people out there who aren't accepting. They can be intolerant, selfish, shortsighted, and so on. Finally, in growing up, I learned to say "So what, I don't care what others think." (M)

The increase in self-acceptance was often attributed to the continuing support from friends, counselors, and the Bi Center, through reading, and just being in San Francisco:

> Fred Klein's *Bisexual Option* book and meeting more and more bisexual people. It helped me feel more normal. . . . There were other human beings who felt like I did on a consistent basis. (M)

> Exposure to other bisexuals. Well, San Francisco is an oasis for that kind of freedom to be what you are. . . . Knowing I can be what I want to be. . . . Knowing there are lots of other people like me. (F)

> I think going to the Bi Center really helped a lot. I think going to the gay baths and realizing there were a lot of men who sought the same outlet I did really helped. Talking about it with friends has been helpful and being validated by female lovers that approve of my bisexuality. Also the reaction of people who I've told, many of whom weren't even surprised. (M)

> The therapy and rap groups at the Bi Center and making friends with people who were going through the same thing that I was. (M)

The majority of the self-defined bisexuals we came to know through the interviews seemed settled in their sexual identity. We tapped this through a variety of questions. First was asked, "Do you think you are currently in transition from being homosexual to being heterosexual or from being heterosexual to being homosexual?" Ninety percent of the sample answered no. This was followed by two series of related items directed only at those who said they were not in transition. One group of questions focused on self-definition, and asked, "Is it possible, though, that some-day you could define yourself as either lesbian/gay or heterosexual?" Here, 59% answered no. Of the remaining 40% who answered yes, about two-thirds (63%) indicated the change could be in either direction, while one-quarter (26%) saw themselves as more likely becoming heterosexual, and the rest (11%) homosexual. However, 69% said such a change was not probable, 20% somewhat probable, and only 11% very probable.

The possibility of someday undergoing a change in self-definition did charac-terize *some* in our sample. We asked what it might take to bring about such a change. The most common response referred to becoming involved in a meaning-ful relationship that was monogamous or very intense. Often the sex of the hypo-thetical partner was not specified, underscoring that it was the overall quality of the relationship that really mattered:

> Love. I think if I feel insanely in love with some person, it could possibly happen. (M)

> If I should meet a woman and want to get married, and if she was not open to my relating to men, I might become heterosexual again. (M)

> Getting involved in a long-term relationship like marriage where I wouldn't need a sexual involvement with anyone else. The sex of the . . . partner wouldn't matter. It would have to be someone who I could com-mit my whole life to exclusively, a lifelong relationship. (F)

> I suppose one strong relationship with one person that would obviously be either gay or straight. I do not think I would give up my bi-ness even for that. To me, being gay or straight means restricting myself to only half the people that I meet. (F)

A few mentioned the breaking up of relationships and how this would incline them to look toward the other sex from the partner with whom they were involved:

> Steve is one of the few men I feel completely comfortable with. If anything happened to him, I don't know if I'd want to try and build up a similar relationship with another man. I'd be more inclined to look towards women for support. (F)

Changes in sexual behavior seemed more likely for our respondents than changes in self-definition. Similar to the previous set of questions, we asked "Is it possible that someday you could behave either exclusively homosexual or exclusive-ly heterosexual?" To this, 82% answered yes. This is over twice as many as who saw a possible change in self-definition. Of this particular group, the majority (57%) felt there was nothing inevitable about how they might change, indicating it could be in either a homosexual or heterosexual direction. Around 28%, though, said the change would be to exclusive heterosexual behavior and 15% to exclusive homosex-ual behavior. There was a sex difference, however, in this regard. More women than men answered either direction (69% versus 48%). Twice as many women noted the homosexual direction (22% versus 10%). But many more men than women said the heterosexual direction (43% versus 9%): 41% responded that a change to exclusive heterosexuality or homosexuality was not very probable, 32% somewhat probable, and 27% very probable.

Again, we inquired about what it would take to bring about such a change in behavior. Once more the answers centered around achieving a long-term monogamous and involved relationship, often with no reference to a specific sex:

> For me to behave exclusively heterosexual or homosexual would require that I find a lifetime commitment from another person with a damn good argument of why I should not go to bed with somebody else. (F)

> I am a romantic. If I fell in love with a man, and our relationship was developing that way, I might become strictly homosexual. The same possibility exists with a woman. (M)

Thus "settling into the identity" must be seen in relative terms. Some of our respondents do seem to accept the identity completely, which solves many of their problems. However, compared to models of homosexual identity formation, we were struck by the absence of closure that characterized our bisexual respondents, even those who appeared most committed to the identity. This led us to posit a final stage in sexual-identity formation that seems quite unique to bisexuals.

Continued Uncertainty

THE BELIEF THAT bisexuals are often confused about their sexual identity is quite common. This conception has been promoted especially by lesbians and gays who see bisexuality as being in and of itself a pathological state. From their point of view, "confusion" is literally a built-in feature of "being bisexual." As Cory and LeRoy wrote (1963, 61):

> While appearing to encompass a wider choice of love objects, . . . [the bisexual] actually becomes a product of abject confusion; his self-image is that of an overgrown young adolescent whose ability to differentiate one form of sexuality from another has never developed. He lacks above all a sense of identity. . . . [He] cannot answer the question: What am I?

The issue was addressed directly in the interviews. Two questions read: "Do you *presently* feel confused about your bisexuality?" and "Have you *ever* felt confused?" For the men, 25% and 84% answered "yes," respectively. For the women, it was 23% and 56%. Also, there was the question: "Have there been any factors or events that led you to call your bisexual identity into question?" Again, 59% of the men and 57% of the women replied "yes."

When asked to provide details of what was involved, the respondents primarily conveyed that *even after having discovered and applied the label "bisexual" to themselves, and having come to the point of apparent self-acceptance, they still experienced continued intermittent periods of doubt and uncertainty regarding their sexual identity.* One reason was the lack of social validation and support that came with being a self-identified bisexual. It was the social reaction people received that made it difficult to sustain the identity over the long haul.

While the heterosexual world was said to be completely intolerant of any degree of homosexuality, it seemed that the reactions of the homosexual world mattered more. Many bisexuals referred to the persistent pressures they experienced to relabel as "gay" or "lesbian" and to engage in sexual activity exclusively with the same sex because no one was really "bisexual" and that calling oneself "bisexual" was a politically incorrect and inauthentic identity. Given that our respondents were situated in San Francisco (which has a large homosexual population) and that they frequently moved in and out of the homosexual world (to which they often looked for support) this could be particularly distressing:

> Sometimes the repeated denial the gay community directs at us. Their negation of the concept and the term bisexual has sometimes made me wonder whether I was just imagining the whole thing. (M)

> My involvement with the gay community. There was extreme political pressure. The lesbians said bisexuals didn't exist. To them, I had to make up my mind and identify as lesbian. . . . I was really questioning my identity, that is, about defining myself as bisexual . . . . (F)

For the women, the invalidation carried over to their feminist identity (which most had). They sometimes felt that being with men meant they were selling out the world of women:

> I was involved with a woman for several years. She was straight when I met her, but became a lesbian. She tried to "win me back" to lesbianism. She tried to tell me that if I really loved her, I would leave Bill. I did love her, but I could not deny how I felt about him either. So she left me and that hurt. I wondered if I was selling out my woman-identity and if it [being bisexual] was worth it. (F)

Lack of support also came from the absence of bisexual role models, no real bisexual community aside from the Bisexual Center, and nothing in the way of public recognition of bisexuality, which bred uncertainty and confusion:

> I went through a period of dissociation, of being very alone and isolated. That was due to my bisexuality. People would ask, well, what was I? I wasn't gay and I wasn't straight. So I didn't fit. (F)

> I don't feel like I belong in a lot of situations because society is so polarized as heterosexual or homosexual. There are not enough bi organizations or public places to go to like bars, restaurants, clubs. . . . (F)

> It took me a long time to understand myself. The fact that you don't have to be either a sheep or goat. There's not much support or encouragement for being bisexual . . . . It is a matter of having to break your own sense of self without much help from others. (M)

For some, continuing uncertainty about their sexual identity was related to their inability to actually translate their sexual feelings into sexual behaviors (Some of the women had *never* engaged in homosexual sex):

> Should I try to have a sexual relationship with a woman? . . . Should I just back off and keep my distance, just try to maintain a friendship? I question whether I am really bisexual because I don't know if I will ever act on my physical attractions for females. (F)

> I know I have strong sexual feelings towards men, but then I don't know how to get close to or sexual with a man. I guess that what happens is I start wondering how genuine my feelings are. . . . (M)

For the men, their confusion stemmed more from the practical concerns of implementing and managing multiple partners or from questions about how to find an involved homosexual relationship and what that might mean on a social and personal level.:

> I felt very confused about how I was going to manage my life in terms of developing relationships with both men and women. I still see it as a difficult lifestyle to create for myself because it involves a lot of hard work and understanding on my part and that of the men and women I'm involved with. (M)

> I doubted its existence. At times, I thought, well, I must be gay or I must be straight, that even if I had those feelings it was an unworkable reality. By that I mean it would be impossible to maintain . . . more than one relationship. (M)

Many men and women felt doubts about their bisexual identity because of being in an exclusive sexual relationship. This is comparable to what many have predicted in response to our hypothetical questions earlier. After being exclusively involved with an opposite-sex partner for a long period of time, some of the respondents questioned the homosexual side of their sexuality. Conversely, after being exclusively involved with a partner of the same sex, other respondents called into question the heterosexual component of their sexuality:

> Since most of my enduring relationships have been with males, and since I am not doing much with females, I question sometimes whether I am really "bi". . . . (F)

> When I'm with a man or a woman sexually for a period of time, then I begin to wonder how attracted I really am to the other sex. (M)

> In the last relationship I had with a woman, my heterosexual feelings were very diminished. Being involved in a lesbian lifestyle put stress on my self-identification as a bisexual. It seems confusing to me because I am monogamous for the most part, monogamy determines my lifestyle to the extremes of being heterosexual or homosexual. (F)

There were also others who made reference to a lack of sexual activity with or to having weaker sexual feelings and affections for one sex. Such leanings did not fit with the perception that bisexuals should have balanced desires and behaviors. The consequence was doubt about "really" being bisexual.

> That most of my behavior has been with males makes me wonder sometimes if I am really bisexual. (F)

> On the level of sexual arousal and deep romantic feelings, I feel them much more strongly for women than for men. I've gone so far as questioning myself when this is involved. (M)

> I thought it had to be 50% male and 50% female, but it wasn't so for me. (F)

> For years I was only sexual with women and for years I was only sexual with men. . . . Sometimes I have desires only for women . . ., other times I have desires only for men. (M)

Just as "Settling into the Identity" is a relative phenomenon, so too is "Continued Uncertainty," which can involve a lack of closure as part and parcel of what it means to be bisexual.

Summary and Conclusion

THIS ESSAY EXAMINES how people made sense of their sexual feelings and behavior through the adoption of a bisexual identity. We identify four major stages that seem to characterize the experiences of the majority of our respondents during this period: initial confusion, finding and applying the label, settling into the identity, and continued uncertainty.

Like the extant models of homosexual identity formation, our first stage—*Initial Confusion*—shows many of our respondents experiencing strong feelings of confusion regarding their sexual identity. These are associated with the inability to make sense of their sexual feelings, the difficulty of fitting themselves into existing sexual categories, the threat to an existing heterosexuality, and homophobia directed toward the self. The experience of the bisexual differs from the homosexual in that a dual attraction is present, giving rise to feelings of marginality or of belonging nowhere.

Similar to the homosexual models as well, our second stage—*Finding and Applying the Label*—shows that bisexuals are able to work through their feelings of confusion. This comes from discovering the label *bisexual*, continued positive sexual experiences with both sexes, accepting that the attraction to both sexes is genuine, and receiving social support from others. Again, though, there are some conditions that make the identity-formation experience different in the bisexual case.

First, finding a label to organize their sexuality is more difficult for those who become bisexual. As a social category, the term *bisexual* is not as pervasive nor as visible as the terms *homosexual* or *heterosexual*. Second, introduction to and support for initially accepting a sexual identity comes mostly through interaction with other persons. Because the bisexual world is smaller and less visible than the homosexual world, with less-developed (or absent) subcultural institutions, assistance from others in adopting and experimenting with the label is less available.

These factors affect the third stage of identity acquisition, *Settling into the Identity.* Compared to the experience of the homosexual, settling into an identity seems more of a relative phenomenon in that even though the identity "bisexual" is accepted, for many bisexuals an absence of closure on this point seems evident. That is, they see the possibility of future changes in their sexual preferences as a likelihood.

Part of the reason for this is that even though the identity of bisexual may be accepted, it does not provide a solution in the way the homosexual label does. The homosexual label tends to more fully prescribe what homosexuals do, viz.: increase contacts with other homosexuals and decrease them with heterosexuals, develop same-sex intimate relationships, subscribe to the gay subculture and its ideologies, and so forth. The label *bisexual,* in contrast, does not provide such a clear message. There are no informal rules about how much same-sex versus opposite-sex interaction one should have, whether relationships should be simultaneous or sequential, or generally how to relate and interact with both men and women in a sexual/affectional way. Nor are there role models or folk heroes that structure "how to be bisexual" for the bisexual as there are for the homosexual.

Thus we have proposed a fourth stage for bisexual identity formation— *Continuing Uncertainty*—that does not exist in the homosexual models. Not only does the meaning of the label remain somewhat unclear, and social support precarious, but the very nature of bisexuality seems to subvert a stable identity for the bisexual. For the homosexual there is ordinarily a finality to the acceptance of a sexual identity. It is defined as a core part of the personality, (i.e., "I *am* a homosexual") and is accomplished through an acculturation into the homosexual world and a corresponding withdrawal from those heterosexual interactions and institutions that are deemed unnecessary. In short, homosexuality becomes a way of life as much as an identity. And it is sustained by more or less exclusive social, emotional, and sexual interactions with persons of the *same sex.* It is such exclusive involvements that seem to present a problem for the bisexual—being involved with a person of the same sex may lead to questioning their heterosexual interests while being involved with a person of the opposite sex may call into question their homosexual interests. At the same time, the lack of social support for bisexuality and the belief that bisexuality is "transitional" may further erode the acceptance of a completed identity. And, it should not be forgotten, bisexuals do not want to cut off their relationships with the heterosexual world. In fact they may be more integrated into this world (through, for example, marriage and children) than is generally considered.

Despite this, however, nearly all our respondents have accepted their bisexuality and do not see themselves as in "transition." But, just as in the past, future considerations of whether their bisexual definition *may* undergo change are related to whether or not they anticipate becoming involved in a long-term relationship. Thus, like the homosexual, social arrangements fill in the meaning of sexual identity. But, as noted, unlike the homosexual's experience, accepting the identity is more problematic due to the special social and sexual character of bisexuality itself. Especially for bisexuals who engage in sequential relationships, to be able to solidify a bisexual identity means learning that being bisexual is something more complex and that lack of closure is part of what accepting such an identity entails.

We do not wish to claim too much for our model of bisexual identity formation. There are limits to its general application. Our respondents are unique in that not only do *all* the respondents self-define as bisexual (a consequence of selection criteria), but they are all members of a bisexual social organization in a city that perhaps more than any other in the United States at the time could be said to provide a bisexual subculture of some sort. Bisexuals outside of San Francisco surely must move through the early phases of the identity process with a great deal more difficulty. Many probably never reach the later stages.

Finally, the phases of the model we present are very broad and somewhat simplistic. While the particular problems we detail within different phases may be unique to the type of bisexuals in this study, the broader phases can form the basis for the development of more sophisticated models of bisexual identity formation given that there are none we know of elsewhere. Not all bisexuals will follow these patterns. Indeed, given the relative weakness of the bisexual subculture as compared to the social pressures toward conformity exhibited in the gay subculture, there may be more varied ways of acquiring a bisexual identity. Also, the involvement of bisexuals in the heterosexual world means that various changes in "heterosexual" patterns (e.g., the decision to get married) will be a continuing (as yet unexplored) influence on bisexual identity. Finally, wider societal changes, notably the AIDS situation, may make for changes in the overall identity process. Being used to choice and being open to both sexes can make for a range of adaptations in the sexual life of the bisexual that are not available to others.

References

Cass, V. C. 1984. Homosexual identity formation: Testing a theoretical model. *Journal of Sex Research.* 20(2): 143–67.

Coleman, E. 1982. Developmental stages of the coming out process. *Journal of Homosexuality.* 7(2/3): 31–43.

Cory, D. W., and J. P. LeRoy. 1963. *The Homosexual and His Society.* New York: The Citadel Press.

Ponse, B. 1978. *Identities in the Lesbian World: The Social Construction of Self.* Westport, Conn.: Greenwood Press.

Troiden, R. R. 1988. *Gay and Lesbian Identity: A Sociological Analysis.* New York: General Hall, Inc.

Weinberg, M., C. Williams, and D. Pryor. 1988. Telling the facts of life: A study of a sex information switchboard. *Journal of Contemporary Ethnography.* 17(2): 131–63.

The Acquisition of Sexual Identity: Bisexuality

Pepper Schwartz and Philip Blumstein

Conceptual Background

Sexuality may be the most intensely personal subject sociologists have ever studied. No matter how much sex researchers try to depersonalize sexuality, part of its intellectual appeal—and much of its intellectual stigma—is due to its intimate place in people's lives. One way to depersonalize sex research has been to seek only the causes of sexual behavior, defined as a set of objective acts that can be counted and placed in unambiguous categories. But the temptation remains also to understand the very causes of sexual *experience* as both objective and subjective reality. The temptation is particularly great among sociologists, for what better vindication of the sociologist's vision than to be able to show that even the most intimate, personal, private, and "basic" of human experiences is as much a product of social forces as are the less exotic subject matters. Only recently has it become legitimate to treat sexual experience (the experience of oneself, events, stimuli, and meanings as sexual) as a crucial part of the scientific study of sexuality. Indeed the study of sexual *behavior* is giving way in some circles to the study of *sexual conduct* (Gagnon and Simon 1973, resurrecting the early formulation of F. W. Burgess 1949), with an emphasis on the construction and application of sexual meanings.

According to this approach, in trying to render sexuality meaningful for themselves, actors impose structure on their physiological and emotional symptoms, and create order in their erotic careers, past, present, and future. Sociologists, likewise, bring an orderliness to the picture by developing concepts and schemata to stabilize meanings and careers. Because of the common cultural backgrounds of lay actors and sociologists, and because of the conceptual immaturity of sex research, it is not surprising that the conceptual activities of the two groups do not differ greatly. Among the numerous categories they share are *gender, sexual orientation,* and *sexual identity.*[1] These concepts reflect, and at the same time reinforce, the ways persons are organized into social categories based on significant criteria of differentiation in Western culture, and at the same time represent the culture's more essential understandings of sexuality. Taken together, they provide the following schema which is *generally accepted uncritically by sociologists:*

1. Gender is dichotomous. It is also a master-status in the sense that perception and evaluation of persons use gender as a major organizing frame.

2. Gender is constituted by a presumed consistency of factors, including in various formulations: chromosomal aspects, hormonal aspects, primary and secondary anatomy (particularly genital), and many aspects of behavior and temperament.

3. Sexual orientation may be inferred on the basis of the *object* toward which a person's *energy* is directed. The purposely ambiguous word *energy* is used because there

is little clarity or consensus concerning this aspect of sexuality.[2] Under many circumstances sexual orientation is inferred from the gender of the actor's sexual partners. But this simplistic inference rule is forced to encounter empirical anomalies which then have to be dealt with on an *ad hoc* basis. The fact that the empirical usually are ignored suggests the operation of a number of simplifying premises. For the most part, sociologists have adopted uncritically the lay simplifiers which are outlined below. There are an enormous number of imaginable ways to categorize people's sexuality, and the small number of ways that become institutionalized are culturally idiosyncratic. In the present cultural contest there are the following elements:

3a. Sexual orientation derives from the *object* of erotic energy, rather than some other quality. Thus we have hetero- and homosexuals, rather than daylight versus nighttime sexualists, or standing-up versus lying-down sexualists.

3b. An important way to differentiate sexual objects is through their gender. So again we have homo- and heterosexuals, but not tall- versus short-partner sexualists or soprano-partner versus contralto-partner sexualists.

4. The complications in this scheme, as noted earlier, derive from the ambiguous concept we have termed *erotic energy*. Sexual orientation is, after all, an ontological category, and there is no perfect practical methodology for making any concrete ontological determination. Some would argue that sexual *behavior* must be at the foundation of sexual orientation, and so genital contact with a person of the opposite gender could constitute *heterosexual behavior*, and with a person of the same gender, *homosexual behavior*. This is certainly the preferred route of sexual bookkeepers who argue that behavior must and can be unambiguously counted and catalogued (observation of such cataloguing would surely reveal many departures from this simple methodology).

But sexual behavior is not the same as sexual orientation. In practical reality, both lay and scientific observers reference to other factors in determining *who a person "is" sexually.* So "sexual energy" may mean more or less than genital contact; it may mean sexual fantasy directed at a person of one gender or the other, or simply sexual desire so directed. Of course, these are both private experiences, and as such are subject to private processes about which we know very little.

5. Sexual orientation is an abstraction designed to make simple a complex social reality. In designating someone's sexual orientation, i.e., indicating who he or she "is" sexually, one imputes to that person a *sexual essence.* While not the most felicitous terminology, sexual essence is meant to convey (following Katz 1975, 1371) a conception of "inherent qualities which may be manifested, reflected, indicated, or represented by, but [which] do not exist in, conduct." In reference to sexuality, Katz comments that "persons who cannot be identified as having broken sexual rules may be identified as latent perverts; thus latent homosexual orientations are commonly imputed to religious celibates as well as to actively heterosexual people."

"Sexual orientation" is the term used by lay and scientific observers to capture part of an individual's sexual essence. Its increasing popularity as a construct reflects the pervasiveness of essentialist imagery. In practical reality, locating a specific person in a specific sexual orientation may be a difficult process where rules of placement might have to be violated. While specific cases may thus create ambiguities and untidiness, nevertheless, sexual orientation or some similar essentialist concept is understood unambiguously, and its legitimacy as an organizing principle is unchallenged. It thereby possesses an "objective" reality which guides perceptions of others and of oneself. From the standpoint of the sociology of knowledge, the critical question of sexual orientation becomes: *What is the formula by which actors arrange information of various sorts in order to construct a sexual essence for classifying other persons?*

The only sociological study to address this question outright was by Kitsuse (1962) who focused on homosexuality. He observed that respondents used four kinds of information to label someone *homosexual*: behaviors "which everyone knows" homosexuals to engage in (e.g., talking about homosexuality in "inappropriate" settings); failure to engage in behaviors "which everyone knows" heterosexuals engage in (e.g., pursuing members of the opposite gender); behavior interpreted as sexual advances; and behaviors and physical appearance perceived to violate gender-role norms.

6. Implicit in the judgments of Kitsuse's respondents was the notion that sexual orientations are dichotomous and mutually exclusive: homosexuality was inferred from lack of heterosexual interest. Most psychogenic theories of homosexuality are also predicated on the notion that hetero- and homosexuality have incompatible causes (e.g., Bieber 1965), while many other social scientists assume the two sexual orientations to be mutually exclusive without ever treating that presumed dichotomy as problematic and therefore worthy of scientific investigation.

7. Sexual behavior freely chosen from a number of possible courses of action is more indicative of a sexual essence than is sexual behavior caused by duress, "deprivation," or nonerotic incentives. An example of a "scientific" version of this feature is the distinction between *facultative* and *obligative* conduct, which is most often applied to homosexuality. Much research has been done on the facultative type, with the focus being on male and female correctional institutions (e.g., Gagnon and Simon 1973, 235–59; Giallombardo 1966, 1974; Kirkham 1971; Lindner 1948; Sykes 1958; Ward and Kassebaum 1965), and some treatment of male prostitutes (e.g., Reiss 1961). Homosexual behavior in prison is viewed as facultative if it is discontinued after leaving the institution. If it is not discontinued, then the same prison behavior was obligative "all along." A return to exclusively heterosexual conduct makes the prison homosexuality irrelevant for the imputation of a homosexual essence, while failure to engage in postincarceration heterosexual behavior allows the prison experience to be a legitimate datum in deriving a homosexual essence.

8. Sexual behavior that invites condemnation or stigma is more informative for imputing a sexual essence than is unstigmatized behavior. Presumably there are costs, both psychological and interpersonal, for pursuing lines of action that incur negative sanctions. Hence simple notions of hedonism suggest that such behaviors would be avoided unless they were overwhelmingly attractive or compelling. If they are so seductive, then they certainly must say something quite fundamental about the individual's essential sexuality. It has been shown in other areas of research (e.g., Jones, Davis, and Gergen 1961) that "when a person willingly incurs negative sanctions to pursue his aims, he seems to become a source of causal dynamism, a locus of causality, in the eyes of others" (Alexander and Epstein 1969, 381).

9. *Sexual identity* is the subjective manifestation of sexual essence, just as sexual orientation is its public manifestation. Because sexual identity is subjective, it can never be *ultimately* known by anyone other than the actor, and so there is always the possibility of a hiatus between a projected sexual identity and a sexual essence. That is one reason that the latter construct is "more real" epistemologically. Because stigmatized sexual conduct is implied by certain sexual essences, it is widely assumed that actors have a great deal at stake in obscuring or dissimulating in matters of sexual identity. Therefore other cues must be adduced to make an essential imputation.

10. Sexual essence is "more real" than sexual identity, not only because actors often have an investment in keeping the subjective reality private or falsely reporting it, but because one can have a sexual essence *without knowing it.* This is a key element in our cultural and professional schemata for understanding sexuality: that one's sexual essence has a reality independent of one's self-identity or self-awareness. Moreover, sexual essence, rather than projected sexual identity (even if sincere), is the true core used by others in orienting their behavior toward the individual. Many sex researchers also tend to believe in the reality of sexual essence without a subjective component: for example, psychiatrist Martin Hoffman (1968, 135) reports on an individual who "did not *realize* he was a homosexual until he was 27" as an illustration of "repressive forces [of society] that prevent people from *knowing what their real sexual feelings are,*" (emphasis added). The tenacious psychoanalytic concept of *latent* homosexuality provides an important example of this aspect of essentialist thinking.

Although not all sex researchers are guilty of this uncritical perspective, there seems to be very little recognition of the phenomenological dilemma posed by essences existing in counterposition to the actor's subjective reality.[3] This dilemma is a common feature of lay notions of sexuality. It is particularly apparent from even the slightest ethnographic aquaintanceship with the homosexual subculture in Western societies. There, it is routine to hear discussions of people who are "unaware" of their homosexuality. Indeed some people are believed to be homosexual "deep down" even though they have never engaged in a genital contact with a person of the same gender, and some are expected never in their lifetime to "realize" their homosexuality. It is also common for homosexual men and women to say in retrospect that they *were* homosexual prior to any awareness of the "fact." Some event might have precipitated a person's homosexual self-definition, but it is rarely said to have "caused" one to *be* homosexual. Rather earlier events or feeling states can be reconstructed and recalled which *should have* alerted one to his or her homosexual essence:

> . . . . it was completely brought home to me that I was what I was by nature. . . . How clearly I can now see every act and friendship of my boyhood interpreted from my proper sexual temperament. . . . (Hyde 1978).

11. Sexual essence is indeed a dominating typification of persons. As far as we can specify (following Kitsuse 1962), a sizable array if ambiguous factors may lead observers to impute a sexual essence to an individual. Once the essence is assigned, however, its implications for predicting the actor's behavior are a good deal less ambiguous. Clear stereotypes concerning the gender-role behavior of persons with given sexual essences (especially stigmatized ones) are very common (Rooney and Gibbons 1966; Simmons 1965). What is even more taken for granted are the stereotypes concerning sexual

behavior derived from imputations of sexual essence, e.g., that bisexuals are *equally* drawn to members of both sexes (Warren and Johnson 1972, 75). Sexual essences clearly serve, for better or worse, to render more predictable the behaviors, intentions, and feeling states of individuals.

12. Sexual essences are core features of individuals and are not subject to modification. When a sexual identity or sexual orientation changes in the course of a lifetime, this is simply a superficial transformation in an *apparent sexual essence*, while the real essence "was there all the time," and retrospection will always succeed in recreating events of experiences to verify the continuous existence of the essence.

13. The antecedents of sexual orientation can be located in factors occurring during the first several years in the life of the individual. The antecedents of sexual identity are seldom considered separately from those of sexual orientation, and little attention has been directed toward the question of how a person acquires a sexual identity from a social constructionist perspective (exceptions include Dank 1971; Plummer 1975; Ponse 1978; and Weinberg 1978). Even less attention has been given to the influence of retrospection in this process; if actors routinely accept the premise that sexual identity is ordained by factors in early childhood, and if such factors are amenable to subsequent reconstruction, then surely the autobiography that one creates is likely to further confirm the premise.

If the prime question concerning sexual orientation focused on the processes by which actors construct sexual essences for others, then in the case of sexual identity the focus turns inward and the question becomes: *What is the process by which an actor arranges information in order to construct a sexual essence for herself or himself?* [4] While the two processes are surely quite different, both must be significantly shaped by the cultural understandings outlined above. The question of acquisition of sexual identity is not one to be answered in a single paper. It is our purpose simply to report some observations from an exploratory study of the *sexual identity of bisexuals* (Blumstein and Schwartz 1976*a*, 1976*b*, 1977).

Bisexuality Study

IN ORDER TO deal with the acquisition of a bisexual identity it has been necessary to contrast it with the homosexual identity and the heterosexual identity. Since we know precious little about either of these, we will need to rely quite heavily on our own data in all three cases. Wherever possible we try to restrict our discussion of the latter two identities by simply focusing on their quality as *nonbisexual identities* and using them as contrasts to the bisexual. Surely the processes for acquiring the three identities differ in many critical respects. Among these let us focus simply on the following premises:

1. Heterosexual identity, by not transgressing any culturewide norms, is for the majority of people an ordinary essence, and its development goes largely ignored. That is not to say its acquisition is not problematic for some persons, and it is these, of course, who are most important in our discussion, since by virtue of the culture's dichotomous prejudice in matters of sexual orientation and identity, problems in development of heterosexuality invariably invoke homosexuality or bisexuality. But for the nonproblematic majority, the imputation of heterosexuality to oneself and to others is a product of "nothing being out of the ordinary" and therefore deserving of no attention, either psychic or interpersonal. In this regard homosexual and bisexual

Table 1
AGE AND EDUCATION DISTRIBUTIONS OF RESPONDENTS

	Males	Females
20 years or less	7%	4%
21 to 25	19	22
26 to 30	20	28
31 to 35	18	22
36 to 40	11	10
41 to 45	9	4
46 to 50	5	4
51 to 60	8	4
61 years or more	3	0
Total	100%	100%
Mean (years)	34	31
Did not complete high school	1%	2%
Completed high school	5	9
Completed some college	37	41
Bachelor's degree	34	26
Master's degree or higher	23	21
Total	100%	100%
<u>N</u>	76	80

identities are very different and are subject to all the phenomena that accompany deviance (see Plummer 1975 on deviance in sexuality).

2. Homosexuality and bisexuality differ from one another in that the present socio-historical context provides a subculture of meanings and social organization for persons with homosexual identities, but hardly anything of that sort for those with bisexual identities (Blumstein and Schwartz 1974, 1975*b*; Hooker 1965; Leznoff and Westley 1956; Plummer 1975; Warren 1974). Therefore the advantages of interpersonal support and lifestyle models derived from subgroup membership are nearly absent for persons with a bisexual identity. In addition, the homosexual subculture is not routinely and consistently receptive to bisexuality or to bisexuals. Indeed, it often fosters an ideology that denies the possibility of a bisexual essence (Blumstein and Schwartz 1974, 1976*b*).

Our data comes from lengthy semistructured interviews with 156 people who volunteered to participate in a study requiring them to have had "more than incidental sexual experience as adults with both men and women." The interviews were conducted predominantly in Seattle, New York, Berkeley, and San Francisco in 1973 and 1974. Respondents covered a wide variety of ages, educational levels, and sexual histories (see Table 1). Most were recruited through signs in taverns, restaurants,

	Males	Females
Table 2		
GENDER AND SEXUAL IDENTITY OF RESPONDENTS		
	Males	Females
Heterosexual identity	18%	24%
Bisexual identity	41	41
Homosexual identity	37	28
Refused an identity	4	7
Total	100%	100%
N	76	80

churches, universities, voluntary associations, and even a few newly formed bisexual "rap groups." A large number of respondents were from a "snowball sample" or were personal contacts of the authors. The respondents were a very heterogeneous group, but they are not really representative of anything but themselves. We reject the idea of random sampling from a specifiable universe when dealing with unorganized aggregates of persons, many of whom have a great stake in remaining invisible to social researchers. Indeed the goal of research on such persons should be diversity, which we achieved in some measure, rather than random sampling.

Early in the interview, respondents were asked the term they found most comfortable when *thinking about themselves sexually*. From the context of the question, most of them showed little hesitation in characterizing themselves as heterosexual, homosexual, or bisexual. Some tried to hedge with such statements as "heterosexual with a small amount of homosexual" but these were quite rare and they would usually settle on something distinct ("homosexual") upon being probed to make it clear we were not asking them to capture their sexual histories, but rather their sexual identity. While respondents indicated in one way or the other a distaste for labels, only a small number (6%) refused to state a label after being probed. Table 2 presents the distribution of respondents' sexual identities. It should be recalled throughout that *all* respondents had what they had considered more than incidental sexual experience with both men and women.

Given this baseline it should be noted that the sample is atypical in a number of respects, but how atypical is difficult to evaluate. First, the typicality of those with bisexual identities is totally impossible to assess given the absence of earlier studies. Second, in the case of the heterosexuals and homosexuals, there are two kinds of relevant data: (1) Kinsey's data on prevalence are quite old and have been seriously criticized, but are in our judgment the best available (Kinsey, Pomeroy, and Martin 1948, 650–51; Kinsey, Pomeroy, Martin, and Gebhard 1953, 473–74). They found that 15% of the male population in the mid-1940s had more than incidental homosexual and heterosexual experience or reactions for at least three years between the ages of 16 and 55.[5]

For women between the ages of 20 and 35 the findings range from 1 to 8% depending on age and marital status. These are people who would have fit the criteria for inclusion in our study if it had been conducted thirty years earlier.

Of course the Kinsey study provides no data on sexual identity, so we can only make some very tentative inferences from it. If *all* of the Kinsey respondents with *no* homosexual experience are assumed to have heterosexual identities (a great unlikelihood), they would outnumber the respondents relevant to our sample criteria (hetero- and homosexual experience) by more than four to one in the case of males, and by approximately between ten to twenty-five to one for females. So even by tempering the assumption of all having heterosexual identities, it becomes quite likely that our heterosexual respondents are quite atypical of people with that identity. On the other hand, if all the Kinsey respondents with some homosexual but no heterosexual experience were assumed to have homosexual identities (probably a lesser distortion of the data), they would be outnumbered by those relevant to our sample criteria (both kinds of experience) by almost four to one for males and approximately two to one for females. So it seems our homosexual respondents are probably less atypical of homosexuals. This issue can be addressed more directly by smaller-scaled studies of self-identified homosexual men and women which, while more recent, are much less representative than Kinsey's. It appears that the majority of homosexuals have experienced heterosexual coitus.[6] These are the group whom our homosexual respondents might represent.

What is most striking about the data in Table 2 is that a large number of persons with identities other than bisexual (53%) were able to fit the criteria for inclusion in the study).

In order to begin to focus on the process of acquiring a sexual identity, it is necessary to distill those events that are relatively common in the biography of persons with the same identity and different from with other identities. Because of the selection of respondents in this study, the bisexual identity is the most amenable to generalization. The first place to look might be the sexual histories of respondents, working, for the moment, on the premise that actors form hypotheses about their sexuality which they set against various elements of their sexual histories. Unfortunately sex research has not provided any clear set of parameters for characterizing or abstracting details of a person's sexual history. One aspect of sexual history which actors might evaluate in evolving a sexual identity is the number of sexual experiences they have had with men and with women. Table 3 summarizes data on this question, characterizing persons of each sexual identity on the basis of whether there were more or fewer than five sex partners of each gender in their sexual histories. These findings show quite a gender difference consistent with everything we know about male and female sexuality in our culture: no matter what the gender of one's sexual partner, males have more partners than females. Otherwise, very little is happening in the table, and indeed for neither gender is there an association between number of partners and sexual identity. For our respondents, a tabulation of sex partners seems not to predict the acquisitions of a sexual identity.

It must be recalled that the data we are reporting here are cross-sectional and are limited by the age and retrospection of respondents. How many of them will have a future sexual experience with males and females, and how many will modify their current sexual identity is impossible to know.[7] But clearly the temporal patterning of sexual relationships must be considered in examining the impact of sexual behavior on sexual identity acquisition. First it is necessary to modify the premise that actors make imputations about

	Table 3 RESPONDENTS WITH FEWER OR MORE THAN FIVE SEX PARTNERS OF EACH GENDER					
	Male Respondents			Female Respondents		
	Heterosexual Identity	Bisexual Identity	Homosex. Identity	Heterosex. Identity	Bisex. Identity	Homosex. Identity
Fewer than 5 of each gender	36%	29%	14%	57%	52%	64%
Fewer than 5 of same gender; More than 5 of opposite gender	21	13	11	21	21	9
More than 5 of same gender; Fewer than 5 of opposite gender	29	35	61	11	12	18
More than 5 of each gender	14	23	14	11	15	9
Total	100%	100%	100%	100%	100%	100%
<u>N</u>	14	31	28	19	33	22

their sexual essence by examining their sexual histories. What is more likely is that sexual histories are examined in light of other relevant information in arriving at an imputed sexual essence. While this examination is in progress, the actor may choose to test a tentative imputation by some form of experimentation. Once a sexual identity has been firmly acquired, then one would expect the ensuing sexual history to reflect the change.[8] Table 4 presents findings relevant to this discussion, the percentage of respondents whose sexual experience before and since becoming firmly committed to their current identity included persons of both genders. Table 4 also shows the percentage with both kinds of sexual experience in the twelve months preceding the interview. For most respondents, commitment to their current identity had occurred more than one year before the interview, with most exceptions being among lesbians and bisexual women, for whom 33 and 15%, respectively, had changed identities during the previous year.

If it were true that past experience is a partial guide in acquiring a sexual identity which, once assumed, has implications for subsequent sexual behavior, then we might expect a number of findings. First, there should be no heterosexuals in our sample

Table 4

RESPONDENTS WITH HETEROSEXUAL AND HOMOSEXUAL EXPERIENCE BEFORE AND
SINCE ACQUIRING CURRENT SEXUAL IDENTITY AND THOSE WITH BOTH TYPES OF
EXPERIENCE DURING THE TWELVE MONTHS PRECEDING INTERVIEW

	Before Identity	Since Identity	Before Only	Since Only	Before and Since	Preceding 12 months	N
Heterosexual males	*	86%	*	86%	*	57%	14
Heterosexual females	*	84	*	84	*	42	19
Bisexual males	81%	94	6%	19	75%	84	31
Bisexual females	73	91	9	27	64	61	33
Homosexual males	82	39	61	18	21	29	28
Homosexual females	91	23	77	9	14	32	22

*All but 14% of males and 16% of female heterosexuals had never had anything but a heterosexual identity. All of the remainder had had both kinds of sexual experience prior to assuming their current identity and none had had both since.

because they would not have qualified for the study. Second, we would expect all of the heterosexual experience of homosexual respondents to have occurred prior to the development of their current identities. Neither of these seems to be reflected by the data in Table 4. Almost all of the heterosexual respondents have had homosexual experiences while being firmly committed to a heterosexual identity, and indeed 48% had such experience within the year preceding the interview. Interestingly, in the case of homosexual respondents, for many their heterosexual experience terminated when they acquired their current identities, and yet a sizable number (39% of males and 23% of females) have had sexual relationships with men and women since their identity commitment. Moreover, 18% of the homosexual males and 9% of the lesbians had more than incidental heterosexual experience *only after* becoming committed to their homosexual identity.

Turning to the bisexual respondents, indeed most had sexual experience with males and females subsequent to bisexual identity acquisition. It should be noted, too, that 19% of the males and 27% of the females had not had experience of both kinds prior to the adoption of a bisexual identity. Clearly some other form of information must have been present besides sexual experience for self-imputing a bisexual essence. Bisexuals *without* prior relevant sexual experience reported strong erotic attraction or fantasies directed toward members of both genders (16% of the male and 21% of the female bisexuals, with both types of sexual experience prior to acquisition of the identity). An interpretation for these findings is that for at least some bisexuals, internal events, in the absence of actual erotic experiences, provide a basis for an identity, while for others actual experience, in the absence of enduring internal events, has the same outcome. By way of contrast, among the homosexuals with subsequent though no prior relevant experiences, only two out of seven (both males) reported more than very

Table 5
RESPONDENTS WITH DIFFERENT PREVIOUS SEXUAL IDENTITIES

Previous Identity	Male Respondents			Female Respondents		
	Heterosexual Identity	Bisexual Identity	Homosexual Identity	Heterosexual Identity	Bisexual Identity	Homosexual Identity
Heterosexual	--	58%	32%	--	67%	55%
Bisexual	7%	--	18	0%	--	18
Homosexual	7	16	--	11	18	--
None	86	26	50	89	15	27
Total	100%	100%	100%	100%	100%	100%
N	14	31	28	19	33	22

occasional current attraction to both genders. Their heterosexual experiences after commitment to a homosexual identity occurred without a foundation of relevant fantasies or erotic attractions, but rather for some nonerotic reasons. For those with relevant experience *before and since* identity acquisition, three out of six males and two out of three females reported such attraction. While these numbers are quite small, they suggest that sexual experience prior to adoption of a homosexual identity has some effect on the arousal basis for heterosexual behavior after identity adoption.

The data summarized in Table 4 have only limited utility for examining the acquisition of bisexual identity. While informative in showing the sometimes complex relationships between sexual histories and sexual identity, they obscure differences in the routes to various sexual identities as well as the events which actors feel punctuated their identity transformation. First let us consider the identities respondents had prior to those they currently reported. Table 5 presents data on identity changes. While there are a few exceptions, the only heterosexuals we have enough cases to discuss are those who have viewed themselves as heterosexual throughout their lives. Some may have wondered if they were homosexual or bisexual, but only 12% ever assumed one of these identities. We have suggested elsewhere how these people maintain a heterosexual identity and yet have homosexual relations (Blumstein and Schwartz 1976a, 1976b, 1977). Most of the bisexuals moved from a heterosexual identity, while approximately equal numbers changed from a homosexual identity as those who report never having any commitment to an identity other than bisexual.[9] Among homosexuals, twice as many males as females passed through no other identity in becoming homosexual. Among those who did, it was equally likely for males and for females to have once considered themselves heterosexual. These gender differences probably reflect the general tendency for males in this culture to develop their sexuality through adolescent fantasy and masturbation, which occurs prior to the age when events channel the individual into a heterosexual commitment (dating, marriage) or when others impute to him a heterosexual essence. Females, on the other hand, tend to learn their sexuality at a later age, within the context of courtship and marriage, where a strong heterosexual commitment is likely to be formed and a heterosexual essence imputed by others (Gagnon and Simon 1973). It is for these reasons, probably, that lesbians, in this study and others, are more likely than homosexual men to have had sexual experience with the opposite gender.

Respondents were asked about a number of events suggested by the literature as possibly important in the development of sexuality and were further requested to assess their impact on their own sexual biographies. Their responses are summarized and tabulated in Table 6 (on pages 194–97). Respondents were organized according to their current sexual identities and then further divided in terms of the sexual identities they had before coming to their current status. This reflects the cross-classification in Table 5. Respondents with currently heterosexual identities are not relevant to the discussion here, and so are omitted from the table. Respondents whose former identity was heterosexual and those with no reported former identity are combined.

Before turning to these findings, it would be useful to discuss the mean ages for respondents' current identity acquisition (bottom row of table). Consistent with some of the data presented in Table 5, women seemed to arrive at their current identity a few years later than the comparable men. It should be recalled from Table 1 that the female respondents were about three years younger than the males. More interesting perhaps is the finding that bisexual identities are acquired later than homosexual identities for both men and women, and that any change from a heterosexual identity (or no identity) occurs earlier than a change from bisexual or heterosexual. The only exception is that bisexual women who had been heterosexual acquired this identity later than those who were homosexual. Even though this finding suffers from a small case base, it probably reflects the larger number of heterosexual women who reported first considering bisexual as a desirable identity as part of their feminist activities (Blumstein and Schwartz 1976*a*).

Returning to the other findings in Table 6, the first two rows report respondents' recollection of adolescent homosexual play, the first indicating those who felt their current sexual identity began as an immediate and direct result of that play. In general, few respondents made such self-imputation, but among those who did, it seemed to be mostly males, who are more likely to experiment sexually in adolescence, and among males it was more common for those whose identity was to be homosexual. This finding is particularly striking in contrast to those respondents who also engaged in adolescent same gender sex-play but did not think of it as influential in their identity acquisition until well after the fact (second row of table). Again this was a predominantly male pattern, but the difference between bisexuals and heterosexuals has disappeared or even slightly reversed. This suggests that the differences in the first row should not be taken to mean that homosexuals are more likely to have had homosexual adolescent play than bisexuals (the relevant percentages are 70 and 65 respectively), rather that among those having such experiences, homosexuals are more likely to recall them having immediate identity consequences (31% of homosexuals versus 18% of bisexuals who recall meaningful adolescent homosexual play). Of course, one explanation for this pattern of findings is that the homosexual essence is a more available understanding of sexuality for adolescents than is a bisexual identity. The latter

Table 6			
RESPONDENTS REPORTING VARIOUS PRECIPITATING EXPERIENCES IN THEIR CURRENT IDENTITY ACQUISITION			
Male Respondents			
Former Identity	Heterosexual or none		Bisexual	Homosexual
Current Identity	Bisex	Homosex	Homosexual	Bisexual
Adolescent homosexual play and immediate identity impact	11%	22%	0	*
Adolescent homosexual play used only in retrospection	54	48	3/5**	*
Homosexual fantasies	46	65	0	*
. . . with immediate identity impact	8	22	0	*
. . . with identity impact only after experimentation	38	43	0	*
Heterosexual fantasies	*	*	*	1/5**
Fell in love (same gender)	15	9	1/5	*

requires more sophistication and more willingness to maintain the ambiguity involved in denying the dichotomy of heterosexual/homosexual. Nevertheless, the adolescent sex-play could have led the eventual bisexuals to a homosexual identity, but indeed it did not. Whatever insulated them from the implications of behavior for identity at that early age may have continued to operate in later life when the bisexual identity became more readily available as a framework for packaging their prior experiences.

The next three rows of the table reflect the respondents' reports that homosexual fantasies were relevant in their coming to their current identities.[10] Because these fantasies could either be overtly sexual or sexual/romantic, females had almost the same percentages as males. When the fantasies are broken down by whether they immediately

Table 6 (Continued)				
Male Respondents				
Former Identity	Heterosexual or none		Bisexual	Homosexual
Current Identity	Bisex	Homosex	Homosexual	Bisexual
Fell in love w/ opposite gender	*	*	*	2/5
Teased for being "sissy" or "tomboy"	4	26	1/5	*
Significant other asserted respondent was homosexual	4	21	1/5	*
Serendipitous same-gender experience	19	4	0	*
Serendipitous opposite-gender experience	*	*	*	4/5
Disenchantment with members of own gender	*	*	*	2/5
Disenchantment with members of opposite gender	7	0	0	*
Feminist involvement influential	19	9	1/5	2/5
Own gender ceased being erotic	*	*	*	0
Opposite gender ceased being erotic	0	57	4/5	*
<u>N</u>	26	23	5	5
Mean age for identity acquisition (years)	24	20	23	26

* This experience is not relevant for persons with this identity pattern.
** Case base too small to percentage.

Table 6 (continued)			
Female Respondents			
Former Identity	Heterosexual or none		Bisexual	Homosexual
Current Identity	Bisex	Homosex	Homosexual	Bisexual
Adolescent homosexual play and immediate identity impact	4%	6%	0	*
Adolescent homosexual play used only in retrospection	11	11	1/4**	*
Homosexual fantasies	41	50	0	*
. . . with immediate identity impact	22	33	0	*
. . . with identity impactonly after experimentation	19	17	0	*
Heterosexual fantasies	*	*	*	0
Fell in love (same gender)	41	56	4/4	*

affected a developing identity or whether they simply created a "deviant hypothesis" in the mind of the respondent which he or she then "tested" in a sexual encounter, then gender differences begin to emerge. The fantasies of males led to an identity much more commonly only after sexual experimentation intervened, while those of females more commonly led to an identity without experimentation. This reflects the greater availability of causal sexual opportunities for males than females and their greater willingness to have sexual experiences for other than romantic reasons. Among males the fantasies were less likely to have a direct impact on identity for bisexuals than for homosexuals, probably for reasons outlined above in the discussion of adolescent play. This was also true for females, probably for the same reason. There are only a small number of persons with bisexual identities who formerly had homosexual ones. Among these eleven people only one recalled his identity transformation to have involved heterosexual fantasies.

Table 6 (Continued)				
Female Respondents				
Former Identity:	Heterosexual or none		Bisexual	Homosexual
Current Identity	Bisex	Homosex	Homosexual	Bisex.ual
Fell in love w/ opposite gender	*	*	*	5/6**
Teased for being "sissy" or "tomboy"	0	17	1/4	*
Significant other asserted respondent was homosexual	0	11	0	*
Serendipitous same-gender experience	41	11	0	*
Serendipitous opposite-gender experience	*	*	*	2/6
Disenchantment with members of own gender	*	*	*	3/6
Disenchantment with members of opposite gender	30	17	1/4	*
Feminist involvement influential	63	28	2/4	4/6
Own gender ceased being erotic	*	*	*	0
Opposite gender ceased being erotic	0	39	1/4	*
N	27	18	4	6
Mean age for identity acquisition (years)	27	22	24	25

* This experience is not relevant for persons with this identity pattern.
** Case base too small to percentage.

The factor which the literature least prepared us to expect was love. A number of respondents reported an intense relationship with a person which they came to interpret as romantic love and which caused them to embark on a sexual involvement. Sometimes the sexual involvement preceded the resultant identity transformation, but more commonly the transformation came first. Perhaps this ordering simply reflects that this was predominantly a female pattern (51% of women with bisexual or heterosexual identities claimed that falling in love with a woman was a significant factor as compared to 13% of men). For women, there was a tendency for this to be more common among lesbians, probably reflecting that other factors (e.g., not being involved romantically with a man) were occurring to make the woman more "susceptible" to homosexual romance than were bisexual women. In the case of males, the reverse was true. Bisexual men were more likely than homosexuals to report love being significant. This probably reflects the fact that the homosexual males acquired their identity at an earlier age, often when romantic scripts were less available. Among respondents moving from homosexual to heterosexual to bisexual, women again were more likely to attribute change to romantic love.

A theme in the literature on homosexuality is the stigma attached to gender-role nonconformity in childhood and adolescence (e.g., Saghir and Robins 1973). Treatment of this subject is usually unsatisfactory. The sociologically naive suggest that effeminacy in male children and masculinity in females are simply manifestations of the homosexuality that will become manifest in late adolescence or adulthood. This is just another formalization of folk wisdom as it relates to processes for imputing consistent sexual essences. The more sociological explanations argue that effeminacy and masculinity are negatively sanctioned and that punishment and teasing help transform primary deviance into secondary. This, too, is a rather unfastidious analysis, since the primary deviance involves behaviors that are clearly not erotic, while the secondary deviance—organizing one's life around a homosexual identity—has a plainly erotic component. The connection between gender-role and sexuality is never explicitly discussed. It is our suspicion that effeminacy and masculinity have little direct influence on the eroticization of other males or other females, respectively. Rather the labeling experience lowers the threshold for a homosexual or bisexual identity, among those persons who experiment with homosexual behavior, have fantasies with a homosexual component, or are at risk of falling in love with a person of their own gender. Others with the same experiences and risks have a higher threshold for identity acquisition.

In Table 6 we present data on respondents' recalling others labeling them "sissies" or "tomboys" and whether this labeling started them thinking of themselves as sexually different. This was a more common pattern among males than females. This difference reflects the more damaging stigma attached to gender-role nonconformity for males than for females. The culture seems to have a definite ambivalence toward "masculine" behavior in females, while the reverse in males is quite unambiguously condemned (Bullough 1974; Money and Ehrhardt 1972; Spence, Helmreich, and Stapp 1975). These findings are all the more impressive when it is recalled that respondents were indicating whether they had felt that their sexual identity was affected by being labeled and teased. Many others felt they had been so labeled, but that it was of no consequence for their identity (among the formerly heterosexual males, 23% of the bisexuals and 57% of the homosexuals had been teased; among the comparable females, 44% of the bisexuals and 67% of the lesbians had been teased). Clearly, teasing had a greater impact on males than on females when it occurred. It should be noted that recalling being teased for gender nonconformity was more common for homosexual men and women than for bisexuals.

Another labeling experience that has received little attention in the literature (except Goode 1978, 381) is having an acquaintance explain that one is a homosexual. This is almost invariably a person who reveals himself or herself at the same time as a homosexual and claims superior wisdom in such matters because of their identity. A small number of persons in our sample report such an event as having had an effect on their identity acquisition. It was more likely to be a male respondent or a homosexual respondent.

Bisexuals were much more likely to report an unplanned influential sexual encounter with a person of the same gender than were homosexuals. These encounters were either seductions by others or, more commonly, group-sex experiences where the individual accompanied a person with whom he or she was already romantically involved. These were more common for bisexuals, probably because it was their pre-existing heterosexual commitment that placed them in the situation in the first place. Moreover, these experiences are more likely to happen to fairly sophisticated adults who have already become committed to a heterosexual or homosexual identity at an earlier age. This is a safe introduction to a behavior that is not congruent with one's identity but can sometimes precipitate a transformation to bisexual. It should be noted that this pattern was true of homosexuals changing to bisexual as well as heterosexuals making the transformation. It is also interesting to note that this pattern was much more common among females than males. This largely reflects two factors: (1) women are less resistant to experimenting in sexual encounters where another woman in present, which in turn reflects the greater stigma and sanctions attached to homosexual conduct among males as compared to females; and (2) the group-sex episodes were very likely to be at the instigation of a male who wished to introduce a second female into an ongoing heterosexual relationship (Blumstein and Schwartz 1976*a*).

Another factor that female respondents reported was disaffection from males that led them to change their sexual identity in favor of one that would allow them to have sexual relations with women. This disaffection was usually in reaction to the termination of a relationship and was usually couched in terms of a feminist critique of gender-role constraints within traditional heterosexual relationships. There was a greater tendency for this stance to occur in the reports of bisexual women, whose feminism was more likely to antedate their identity acquisition and be bound up in it than was the case among lesbians. It is also clear in the next row of the table that feminism was a much more important feature in the identity transformation of bisexuals than of homosexuals.

The final factors that are tabulated in Table 6 are the curtailment of erotic attraction on one gender or the other. The only meaningful comparison here is between the male homosexuals and the lesbians who recalled members of the opposite gender losing erotic appeal as an indicator to themselves that theirs was no longer a heterosexual

	Table 7
	RESPONDENTS REPORTING VARIOUS CURRENT EXPERIENCES RELEVANT TO THEIR IDENTITY

Male Respondents

Former Identity	Heterosexual or none		Bisexual	Homosexual	Continuously Heterosexual Respondents
Current Identity	Bisex	Homosex	Homosex	Bisex	Male
Opposite gender not erotic	15%	61%	4/5*	1/5*	0%
Own gender not erotic	23	0	0	3/5	42
In monogamous same-gender relationship	12	17	2/5	1/5	8
In monogamous opposite-gender relationship	19	4	0	1/5	42
Could not romance same gender	19	0	0	0	75
Could not romance opposite gender	8	96	5/5	0	0
Go to gay bars, etc.	58	78	4/5	3/5	17

or bisexual identity. One interpretation is that males are more likely to appeal to such intrapsychic readings in inferring their sexual essence than are females. Another is that males do indeed stop finding women erotic upon acquiring a homosexual identity more than women cease to find males erotic. The latter interpretation is not supported by the data, however; approximately equal percentages of homosexuals of both genders currently do not find the opposite gender erotically attractive (64% of males and 68% of females).

The findings in Table 5 have addressed the question of what retrospective factors respondents point to as occurring during the period when they were acquiring their current sexual identities. But since identities are fairly modifiable, another question in understanding acquisition is what factors stabilize an identity so that it is not continually in a state of flux. In Table 7 we present some of the relevant factors that characterize

Table 7 (continued)

RESPONDENTS REPORTING VARIOUS CURRENT EXPERIENCES
RELEVANT TO THEIR IDENTITY

Female Respondents

Former Identity	Heterosexual or none		Bisexual	Homo-sexual	Continuously Heterosexual Respondent (Female)
Current Identity	Bisex	Homosex	Homosex	Bisex	
Opposite gender not erotic	19%	67%	3/4*	2/6*	0%
Own gender not erotic	15	0	0	1/6	29
In monogamous same-gender relationship	19	61	2/4	2/6	24
In monogamous opposite-gender relationship	15	6	1/4	4/6	59
Could not romance same gender	11	0	0	0	47
Could not romance opposite gender	11	78	4/4	0	0
Go to gay bars, etc.	37	39	2/4	1/6	24
N	27	18	4	6	17

* Case base too small to percentage.

the respondents at the time of the interview. We have already discussed the data in the first row of the table, i.e., that most homosexuals in the sample no longer find the opposite gender erotically appealing. What is quite interesting (second row) is that 29% of bisexual males and 15% of bisexual females do not find their own genders erotic. It should be recalled that the question was framed in the abstract, i.e., whether the respondent thinks erotically about males or females. How is it that persons can hold a bisexual identity without homosexual attractions? Two typical responses to that question (paraphrased) would be that (1) previous positive homosexual experiences show that the possibility for such a response always remains and is therefore a part of one's sexual essence, and (2) every person has the potential for bisexuality, and since that is a highly desirable potential, one should be actively open to any opportunity that might arise. Since it is a "natural" part of everyone's sexuality which civilization has caused to atrophy, then by recognizing it as part of one's sexual essence, one increases the chances of being able to act upon it in the future.

It is interesting that the largest number of persons unable to eroticize their own gender are the heterosexuals and yet 48% of these respondents have had homosexual experiences during the year prior to the interview (Table 4). This apparent incongruence reflects the fact that a sizable number of continuously heterosexual respondents engage in "spontaneous" group-sex experiences in which they enjoy homosexual contacts, but report that they have no homosexual attractions outside of these restricted contexts (25% of the males and 35% of the females). It is possible that the contextual definition of the behavior acts as an insulation from either homosexual or bisexual identity acquisition (cf. Reiss 1961).

The third and fourth rows of Table 7 present the percentages of respondents currently in monogamous relationships. The most significant variation among these data is that women, no matter what their sexual identity, are more likely to be involved monogamously than men. These data can be more interestingly tabulated in terms of the percentages of currently monogamous men and women who are heterosexual, bisexual, and homosexual. For males the majority are bisexual (44%) while there are approximately equal numbers in the other categories (26% heterosexual and 30% homosexual). In contrast, the women are least likely to be bisexual (27%) and most likely to be homosexual (41%), with heterosexuals in between (32%). These differences have a clear interpretation based on the transcripts of the relevant interviews. Women were much more likely than men to say that they inferred their sexual identity from the gender the person they were currently involved with romantically: heterosexual if it were a man, lesbian if it were a woman. Several warranted this assertion by referring to the fact that although they might at some time have called themselves bisexual, it was never while they were involved in an important relationship. This type of account was less frequently expressed by male respondents, who were more inclined to base their identities on their readings of internal cognitive and emotional factors. They were more likely to label themselves bisexual despite a current restriction on sexual relations with one gender or the other.

Table 7 also presents a tabulation of respondents who felt they could not or would not become involved romantically with a man or a woman. Heterosexual males were clearly less willing to romanticize a man than were heterosexual females to romanticize a woman. This again reflects greater accompaniment of sexuality and romance for women, as well as the greater stigma for male homosexuality. Interestingly, 18% of all lesbians (as opposed to 4% of male homosexuals) felt they could under some circumstances romanticize a person of the opposite gender. Most of the lesbians were quick to indicate they did not expect it to happen and would not invest any effort in trying, but nevertheless past relationships with men allowed them to feel it was possible. Again this sex difference reflects the tendency of women to allow for environmental changes to affect their sexual behavior, suggesting that they saw their sexual essence as less prescriptive of a narrow range of sexual behavior. Males, on the other hand, were more likely to base the derivation of their sexual identity on readings of internal cues, which they then saw as implying a narrow set of sexual and emotional lines of action. For homosexual men, romantic attachment to a woman was outside the implicational boundaries of their sexual identity.

The bottom row of Table 7 presents the percentage of respondents who go to gay bars, clubs, steambaths, political meetings, or other places where homosexuals socialize.

An important feature of these environments is that by being in them one is presumed to have a homosexual essence and one is also presumed to share the values and orientations of the homosexual subculture. It has been argued elsewhere (Blumstein and Schwartz 1974, 1976*b*) that these are often mildly hostile or unaccepting environments for persons not committed to a homosexual identity, while at the same time they provide an opportunity (especially for males) to meet potential sex partners. As is commonly known (e.g., Gagnon and Simon 1973) females are less likely to frequent these kinds of establishments. Not surprisingly, males go to homosexual social establishments in direct relationship to their sexual identities: homosexuals are most likely to go, followed by bisexuals, and then heterosexuals. In the interviews about a quarter of bisexual and heterosexual men commonly felt unaccepted in these environments, although a slightly greater number of these were quite surprised that any heterosexual or homosexual " who knew the scene" would have that reaction. Females, on the other hand, were very likely to feel unwanted in lesbian establishments or other organized lesbian environments. This dovetails with what some lesbians have reported about feeling hostile to bisexual women and heterosexuals who have sexual relations with other women (Blumstein and Schwartz 1974, 1976*a*).

One feature of the perceived inhospitality of people in the homosexual community is a subcultural disbelief in the existence of bisexuality as a sexual essence (Blumstein and Schwartz 1974, 1976*b*). As Warren and Johnson (1972, 75) observe: "The test of being bisexual within the gay community is not . . . 'Would you, or have you ever, had sexual relations with members of both sexes?' Rather, it is perceived in terms of this hypothetical case: 'If a man is faced with a beautiful man and a beautiful woman, and cannot decide to which he is most attracted . . . then he is a bisexual.'" This is certainly a stringent test, one that few of our bisexual respondents would be able to pass.

The homosexual subculture is not the only source of doubt as to the reality of bisexuality (e.g., Bieber 1965). To the extent that bisexuals feel themselves a beleaguered minority they ought to develop a set of meanings for the unique opportunities a bisexual essence provides. One of the meanings they must combat is the notion that a bisexual *identity* is simply a disguise for a homosexual *essence*.[11] As part of their accounts for their bisexuality and its desirability as a way of life, respondents expressed their feelings about those features of a homosexual or heterosexual essence they found acceptable. The more common responses are presented in Table 8.

Many of these comments tend to be couched in terms of "objective" facts about being homosexual. From our point of view, that is irrelevant; rather we are concerned with how well these statements insulate and support a bisexual identity. Some males complain about the lack of warmth and intimacy in homosexual relationships, while a number of females have the same complaint about heterosexual relationships. This suggests that the complaint is directed toward males as relationships partners rather than the sexual essence of the partner—even though respondents often focus on sexual essences for their discussion. The possibilities for a family are certainly a critical factor expressed by respondents as disposing them toward bisexuality, as is the ability to avoid the stigma of living a homosexual lifestyle. It is also interesting to note that for one-quarter of the bisexuals, the sexual essence of homosexual implies violations of gender-role norms, and that for 17%, relationship instability accompanies a homosexual essence.

For the most part, bisexual women report more consequences keep them from being heterosexual than do males, at least in terms of a lexicon of distancing complaints. The most common is a distaste for the "sexual politics" involved in heterosexual courtship and romantic relationships. This is consistent with the findings in Table 6 that bisexual women credit their feminist involvement with preparing them for the acquisition of a bisexual identity. Again, here is an environmental factor that affects sexual identity choice in women. Both males and females have complaints about the limitations of the opposite gender in the erotic realm and use this as a clear justification for choosing the same gender. Both are about as likely to say that one has to be of the same gender to know how to provide sympathetic sexual pleasure. But apart from this comment, women are likely to complain of men being sexually clumsy and self-indulgent, while men complain that women cannot be found for quick impersonal sexual encounters. These comments tend not to justify a bisexual essence directly. Rather they justify sexual relations with both men and women, and thereby imply the legitimacy of the essence implied by the behavior.

Discussion

WE RETURN TO the question that oriented the presentation of findings: *What is the formula by which an actor arranges information in order to construct a sexual essence for him- or herself?* We are far from having a definitive answer, but we have some suggestions that stem from the differences among men and women with bisexual, homosexual, and heterosexual identities. These suggestions can serve to guide future systematic research.

Several interwoven themes have run through the findings presented. These include: (1) the mutability of sexual identity in adulthood, (2) the relationship between sexual conduct and sexual identity, (3) the differences in sexual careers and the acquisition of sexual identity among men and women, (4) the admixture of recent experience, current interpretations of past experience, and the anticipation of future experience in the acquisition process, and (5) the interplay of cultural understandings of sexuality and sexual identity development.

It is probably true that most individuals in American society acquire only one sexual identity in the course of their lives, and for the most part that acquisition is unproblematically heterosexual. Our data characterize the sizable minority for whom this is not true. All of the bisexual and homosexual respondents have experienced acquisition processes that were out of the ordinary and therefore allowed us to focus more attention on the contributing events. This was also true for a number of the heterosexual respondents. Moreover, the majority of respondents experienced a transformation from one definite sexual identity to another. Just as the existence of bisexuals contradicts one element of our cultural understandings of sexuality (that sexual essences parallel the gender of one's sex partners and are hence dichotomous), so too transformations of sexual identity contradict another element of the schema (that sexual essences are immutable).

On the matter of sexual essences, the logic of this paper implies that sociology ought to remain neutral. Essences are defined as having observable consequences (from a lay perspective), but are themselves inherently unobservable. *Essence* is a concept

Table 8
BISEXUAL RESPONDENTS' REPORTS OF UNDESIRABLE CONSEQUENCES OF
BEING EXCLUSIVELY HOMOSEXUAL OR HETEROSEXUAL[*]

	Males	Females
Consequences of being exclusively homosexual		
Not enough intimacy in homosexual relationships	16%	0%
No possibility for a family	52	64
Stigma and discrimination	48	33
Homosexual relationships are unstable	19	15
Homosexuals are repugnant because of behavior counter to gender-role norms	32	18
Consequences of being exclusively heterosexual		
Not enough intimacy in heterosexual relationships	0%	21%
Resent the "sexual politics" of heterosexual relationships	19	58
Sex with the opposite sex inadequate (clumsy, inhibited, requiring preliminary romance, technically deficient)	26	30
N	31	33

[*]Percentages do not add to 100% because respondents were allowed to offer as many responses as they wished.

with analytic utility for sociologists attempting to understand how sexuality is socially constructed, but should be inadmissible as a scientific term. This is not just because essences are not empirically real; sexual identities have similar problems and yet sexual identity is a valid scientific concept. Rather it is because sexual identity is a "fact" from the point of view of the actor (just as sexual orientation is a "fact" from the point of view of the observer), while essence is a "fact" from the point of view of some "objective truth," and this is what must be rejected.

It is undeniable that sexual conduct and sexual identity affect one another, but certainly it is in a complex manner which has only been rudimentarily addressed. If sexual conduct is construed narrowly as sexual behavior, without reference to its environmental, biographical, and motivational contexts, then it has some impact on the acquisition of sexual identity, but a rather small and uninformative impact. It is clear from our findings that one can arrive at a given sexual identity with many different kinds of biographies. At the same time, people can have quite similar histories and yet acquire different sexual identities. Our failure to find clear predictors of sexual identity in respondents' sexual conduct may mean we did not choose the appropriate aspects of sexual history, but we chose those features which ought to be most useful if sexual conduct were to be a *parsimonious* predictor.

The usual critique of this observation is that one must not construe sexual conduct narrowly, but indeed look at it in its environmental, biographical, and motivational contexts, i.e., consider its full meanings. Broadly speaking, this is a valid critique, but the data also suggest that the meaning of sexual conduct before and during its occurrence is an imperfect predictor of the subsequent acquisition of identity. This reflects the fact that contemporaneous meaning is imperfectly related to the retrospective meaning of any given sexual conduct. Surely sexual meaning is a component of the acquisition process, but it too is modified as the process unfolds.

There are limitless reasons for sexual conduct. Most have nothing to do with the private deliberations by which identities are generated. But once the sexual conduct has occurred, reasons imputed to it become "data" which may play a part in the acquisition process. Other reasons for sexual conduct are more directly relevant. Our data suggests that numerous factors may cause a person to speculate or hypothesize ("suspect," from the actor's point of view) that he or she is sexually "different." Sexual conduct may be motivated by the desire to test such an hypothesis. Given the stigma and negative evaluation of being sexually different, one might imagine that a common response to the "different" hypothesis is to prefer not to know. While there seems to be some of this occurring among our respondents, the logic of sexual essences usually impels individuals to deal with the hypothesis. Since sexual essences surely exist, and have observable consequences, then one must try to discover what one is sexually, even though the signals may be temporarily inconsistent or misleading.

It is the actor's interpretation of the sexual conduct, in its relationship to the hypothesis testing that motivated it, that helps confirm or reject the hypothesis. The actor seldom realizes that the very act of hypothesis testing may affect the outcome of the experiment, not to mention the interpretations of the outcome. There are surely a number of detailed social psychological and psycho-physiological processes involved here which are barely understood (see Rook and Hammen 1977). Just as scientists' hypothesis testing is predicated on the logic of lawful empirical givens, so too the lay hypothesis testing in sexual identity acquisition is predicated on the cultural understandings of sexuality, e.g., that essences are dichotomous and immutable.

The effect of sexual identity on subsequent sexual conduct is also complex. It is important in the present discussion only because it serves to support and maintain the identity which has been hypothesized. Most striking in out data is the difference between bisexuals and homosexuals in that the latter are more likely to discontinue heterosexual conduct after acquiring their identity. But even this effect is not strong and consistent. Following the metaphor of hypothesis testing, it is not difficult to understand how, as the homosexual hypothesis begins to accumulate confirmation, it would lead to a curtailment of heterosexual conduct. We know essentially nothing concrete about how such a curtailment occurs except that it follows from the logic of dichotomous essences and further supports that logic. One should be very suspicious of the accounts respondents offer of the curtailment of heterosexual conduct after homosexual identity acquisition. Some report a reduction in erotic attraction, while others report there never to have been a "real" attraction, but rather an "imaginary" or "misguided" one. Still others report that heterosexual opportunities were too difficult to pursue compared to the case of homosexual ones.

Our data suggests that bisexuals entertain the "different" hypothesis at a later point in time in their lives. It often occurs when they are already sexually experienced, and so much of their sexual conduct has not yet been colored by the act of hypothesizing. Some may have an earlier history of sexual conduct which is "inconsistent" given the logic of essences, but that behavior did not have early identity implications because of various insulating mechanisms (e.g., the notion of adolescent "phase"). Adult events that do not fit one's homosexual or heterosexual identity occur after a strong commitment to those identities have been established. By commitment we mean being embedded in a specifically scripted lifestyle or subculture, as well as having a backlog of sexual experience whose implications for one's identity are undeniable. Therefore any hypothesizing about being different must take into consideration undeniably incompatible versions of sexual conduct. The appropriate identity modification is to be bisexual. an unexpected homosexual encounter (for a heterosexual) or heterosexual encounter (for a homosexual) would be a possible precipitating event, especially if there were other factors which could be used in retrospection to support the bisexual identity. Such factors might be adolescent homosexual sex-play or heterosexual courtship which had never before had identity implications. Others might be the romantic context of the current event or the ideological support for new forms of sexual conduct (e.g., feminism). In summary, it is not the existence of sexual conduct which might have identity implications that affects whether one assumes a heterosexual, bisexual, or homosexual identity, but rather the point in one's life where that behavior causes one to form implications for identity and what kinds of sexuality one is embedded in at that point.

Surely this differs by gender. As we noted earlier, bisexual women have consistently female sexuality, while bisexual men have consistently male sexuality. Hypothesis testing seems to be a more compelling behavior for males, and the possibility of being different seems also more prominent. Because of male adolescents' preoccupation with sexuality, difference testing is more likely to occur earlier for males and even though homosexuality is more frightening for them, they are more likely to become homosexual than are females. Females, on the other hand, are more likely not to deal with sexuality until it emerges in a romantic context. Therefore any difference hypothesizing will occur in an ongoing heterosexual script, and bisexuality is more likely to be the outcome, once differences are considered.

For males, hypothesis testing is more likely to be based on such indicators of erotic energy as sexual fantasy and attraction to strangers. Masturbation is a major step (and often the final step) in hypothesis testing. It often occurs before the male has much access to a sex partner. Sexual norms from very early adolescence impel males to resolve anything problematic in their feelings. Early reliance on internal reactions to sexual stimuli and on masturbation for one's self-knowledge seems to continue into adulthood. Our males were more likely to assert a bisexual identity even when they were sexually involved in a monogamous relationship.

Female hypothesis testing surely involves fantasy, but is more likely to stem from the implications of a relationship that takes on romantic qualities. Such relationships, of course, are much more ambiguous in their sexual implications than are masturbation fantasies. Moreover such relationships are only likely to acquire any erotic meaning after the adult female has learned, usually through heterosexual relationships, how to interpret erotic cues and responses to stimuli. This pattern also seems to continue through a woman's life, wherein she bases her self-knowledge about sexuality on a current relationship in which she finds herself sexually. So, again, our women, who might have been expected to call themselves bisexual, hesitated to do so because of their current monogamous involvement.

Bisexual identity has a peculiar place in the cultural logic of sexuality that was discussed earlier. In most obvious ways it does not fit. Sexuality is based on dichotomies. We have argued that dichotomous understandings affect the acquisition of identity as well as sexual conduct. But it seems that they affect identity more than conduct. Surely behavior that could lead one to identify oneself as a bisexual is more common than people who are so identified. There is more sexual conduct that defies the sexual schema than there are sexual identities that do the same. Behavior is more perverse in its defiance of the norms of sexual packaging, while identity is itself packaging and therefore more tractable.

In the current historical context, behavior that is called bisexual is receiving greater scientific and public attention, and this presages a modification in the cultural wisdom about sexuality. Debate over the existence of bisexuality is surely a sign of this change as well as a further indication of the implications bisexuality has for the entire scheme. Of course, once the logic of sexuality begins to change, the more conservative sexual identity can follow. So the ultimate relationship between sexual conduct and sexual identity is clear in the bisexual case. The conduct begins to affect sexual understandings, and these create a niche, a new essence which people can then assign to themselves.

Endnotes

1. Without prejudging the discussion to follow, let us simply indicate a sense of the lay usage implied by these terms: *gender* has to do with a person's *being* in some sense "female" or "male"; the terms deal with the person's *being* "homosexual," "heterosexual," or some other "-sexual."

2. By *erotic energy* we do not mean sex drive. In lay terms, the referents of *erotic energy* are such things as sexual desire, erotic fantasies, or overt sexual behavior. The term is an unobservable abstraction whose purpose is to build a motivational bridge

between a person's "true" and ultimately unknowable sexuality and his or her sexuality as it is socially constructed by self and others. *Sexual drive*, a lay term that has been adopted uncritically by sex researchers (see Gagnon and Simon 1973, 11), is a motivational concept rooted in the biological imperative of the human organism which "causes" sexual behavior.

3. We readily admit there might be strong temptation to impute in many cases a sexual essence not congruent with an individual's sexual identity. Our own data certainly suggest that in many cases an actor's sexual behavior—indeed her or his entire erotic biography—would lead most reasonable observers to impute a sexual essence quite different from her or his sexual identity (Blumstein and Schwartz 1976*a*, 1976*b*, 1977). This simply indicates that actors and observers, while sharing a common cultural schema for understanding sexuality, process information differently in assigning sexual essences (Jones and Nisbett 1971). For a detailed ethnographic study of seemingly incongruous behavior and identity, see Humphreys (1970).

4. Matza (1969, 170) has posed a similar question with respect to all deviant identities: "the meaningful issue of identity is whether [an act] can stand for me, or be regarded as proper indications of my being. . . . To answer affirmatively, we must be able to conceive a special relationship between being and doing—a unity capable of being indicated. . . . It may be summarized in a single . . . word . . . : essentially."

5. The Kinsey data are actually not comparable with ours because persons were categorized on the basis of sexual experience *or reaction* and it is very difficult to disentangle the two features of the data. It is reported that 13% of the males reacted erotically (whatever that means) without overt sexual contact with other males. Comparable data for females do not seem to be reported. Another problem with the Kinsey data, as well as with any in this area, stems from the arbitrariness of the age distribution of the sample. In essence, one cannot characterize a person's sexual history until after his or her death. Hence the distribution of current sexual experiences, current sexual identities, or number of identity changes are all partially dependent upon the age at which the respondent was interviewed.

6. Saghir and Robins (1973, 88, 246) found this to be true of 48% of their male subjects and 79% of the females. The comparable figures found by Bell and Weinberg (1978:286) are 64% and 83%. Again those data suffer from the age distribution limitations mentioned earlier. This clearly exemplified by Saghir and Robins' (1973) finding that significantly *fewer* of their heterosexual women had experienced heterosexual coitus than their homosexual women.

7. Some evidence of the mutability of sexual identity comes from a moderately sized and unrepresentative number of respondents whom we were able to contact in the years following the interview. Among these were several persons who changed sexual identity and several who had romantic involvement with members of a gender which they had totally renounced in the original interview.

8. Weinburg (1978), in focusing on the relationship between homosexual behavior and the acquisition of homosexual identity among males, examined the ordering among three events: engaging in homosexual behavior, suspecting oneself to be homosexual, and labeling oneself homosexual. We prefer the terms *tentatively impute*, or *hypothesize*, rather than suspect, since the latter gives the impression of the

actor problematically discerning something that has a knowable truth to it prior to her or his thinking about it.

9. The notion of having no sexual identity is rather peculiar. Certainly adult celibates can and usually do have sexual identities. Moreover, they are seen as having sexual essences (although asexual is a possible dimension in the fabric of essences, especially for women). Because they are imputed essences by others, they are given permission to have sexual identities themselves. We take the position that children and adolescents are in an ambiguous status with respect to sexual essence. They are simultaneously treated as though they had none and as though they were heterosexual by default. This ambiguity for other-imputations is equally troublesome for self-imputation. Accordingly, some of our respondents are probably referring to their pre-essence state (before they were normatively provided or permitted to have an essence) as a period of having no sexual identity, while others equate that period with heterosexuality-by-default.

10. Here again, in discussing the effect of fantasies we are explicitly faced with the troublesome notion of *erotic energy*. It is difficult to avoid the temptation to build some kind of motivational primitive into any scheme for coming to grips with sexual conduct and identity. Surely actors themselves have such an amorphous construct. It is our feeling that there are many unexplored dimensions that characterize individuals' *subjectively perceived* erotic attractions. For example, we feel our data suggest that the acquisition of a sexual identity strongly affects subsequent erotic attractions (Blumstein and Schwartz 1977). But that is not the focus of the present paper. We also feel that much erotic attraction, especially in adolescents, is inferred by actors based on their readings of the stimuli they presume to elicit erotic responses in themselves. Surely, considerations concerning the antecedents of erotic response and how this affects the meanings actors then impute is critical to a full understanding of sexual identity. We have omitted it from our current discussion because conceptual work on this topic is only now beginning (see Gagnon and Simon 1973; Rook and Hammen 1977; Victor 1978), and relevant methodologies are seriously lacking. We assume that the universe of erotic stimuli far exceeds individual's erotic experience. This raises a question we must ignore, i.e., why some erotic responses (e.g., homosexual fantasies) never eventuate in behavior. This question is logically prior to why some erotic behaviors or attractions never eventuate in a sexual identity.

11. *The Queens' Vernacular* (Rodgers 1972, 32) provides the following characterization of the *bisexual*: "Many gays feel that bisexuals brag about their superiority to homosexuals. They reassure one another that bisexuals are but repressed faggots who simply refuse to admit defeat ('Nobody can dance at two weddings dear; you're either one or the other!')."

References

Alexander, C. Norman, Jr., and Joyce Epstein. 1969. Problems of dispositional inference in person perception research. *Sociometry*. 32 (December): 381–95.

Bell, Alan P., and Martin S. Weinberg. 1978. *Homosexualities: A Study of Diversity among Men and Women.* New York: Simon and Schuster.

Bieber, Irving. 1965. Clinical aspects of male homosexuality. In *Sexual Inversion: The Multiple Roots of Homosexuality*, ed. Judd Marmor. 248–67. New York: Basic.

Blumstein, Philip W., and Pepper Schwartz. 1974. Lesbianism and bisexuality. In *Sexual Deviance and Sexual Deviants*, ed. Erich Goode and Richard Troiden. 278–95. New York: Morrow.

———. 1976*a*. Bisexuality in women. *Archives of Sexual Behavior.* 5 (March): 171–81.

———. 1976*b*. Bisexuality in men. *Urban Life.* 5 (October): 339–58.

———. 1977. Bisexuality: Some social psychological issues. *Journal of Social Issues.* 33 (Spring): 30–45.

Bullough, Vern L. 1974. Transvestites in the Middle Ages. *American Journal of Sociology.* 79 (May): 1381–94.

Burgess, Ernest W. 1949. The sociological theory of psychosexual behavior. In *Psychosexual Development in Health and Disease*, ed. Paul H. Hoch and Joseph Zubin. 227–43. New York: Grune and Stratton.

Dank, Barry M. 1971. Coming out in the gay world. *Psychiatry.* 34 (May): 180–97.

Gagnon, John H., and William Simon. 1973. *Sexual Conduct: The Social Sources of Human Sexuality.* Chicago: Aldine.

Giallombardo, Rose. 1966. *Society of Women.* New York: Wiley.

———. 1974. *The Social World of Imprisoned Girls.* New York: Wiley.

Goode, Erich. 1978. *Deviant Behavior: An Interactionist Aproach.* Englewood Cliffs, N.J.: Prentice–Hall.

Hoffman, Martin. 1968. *The Gay World: Male Homosexuality and the Social Creation of Evil.* New York: Basic.

Hooker, Evelyn. 1965. Male homosexuals and their "worlds." In *Sexual Inversion: The Multiple Roots of Homosexuality*, ed. Judd Marmor. 83–107. New York: Basic.

Humphreys, Laud. 1970. *Tearoom Trade: Impersonal Sex in Public Places.* Chicago: Aldine.

Hyde, Louis, ed. 1978. *Rat and the Devil: Journal Letters of F. O. Matthiessen and Russell Cheney.* Hamden, Conn.: Archon Books.

Jones, Edward E., Keith F. Davis, and Kenneth J. Gergen. 1961. Role playing variations and their informational value for person perception. *Journal of Abnormal and Social Psychology.* 63 (September): 302–10.

Jones, Edward E., and Richard E. Nisbitt. 1971. The actor and the observer: Divergent perceptions of the causes of behavior. In *Attribution: Perceiving the Causes of Behavior*, Edward E. Jones, David E. Kanouse, Harold H. Kelley, Richard E. Nisbett, Stuart Valins, and Bernard Weiner. 79–94. Morristown, N. J.: General Learning Press.

Katz, Jack. 1975. Essences as moral identities: Verifiability and responsibility in imputations of deviance and charisma. *American Journal of Sociology.* 80 (May): 1369–90.

Kinsey, Alfred C., Wardell B. Pomeroy, and Clyde E. Martin. 1948. *Sexual Behavior in the Human Male.* Philadelphia: W. B. Saunders.

Kinsey, A. C., W. B. Pomeroy, C. E. Martin, and Paul H. Gebhard. 1953. *Sexual Behavior in the Human Female.* Philadelphia: W. B. Saunders.

Kirkham, George L. 1971. Homosexuality in prison. In *Studies in the Sociology of Sex*, ed. Jack M. Henslin. 325–49. New York: Appleton-Century-Crofts.

Kitsuse, John I. 1962. Societal reaction to deviant behavior: problems of theory and method. *Social Problems.* 9 (Winter): 247–56.

Leznoff, Maurice, and William A. Westley. 1956. The homosexual community. *Social Problems.* 3 (April): 257–63.

Lindner, Robert. 1948. Sexual behavior in penal institutions. In *Sex Habits of American Men*, ed. Albert Deutsch. 201–15. New York: Prentice-Hall.

Matza, David. 1969. *Becoming Deviant.* Englewood Cliffs, N. J.: Prentice-Hall.

Money, John, and Anke A. Ehrhardt. 1972. *Man & Woman: Boy & Girl: The Differentiation and Dimorphism of Gender Identity from Conception to Maturity.* Baltimore: Johns Hopkins University Press.

Plummer, Kenneth. 1975. *Sexual Stigma: An Interactionist Account.* London: Routledge and Kegan Paul.

Ponse, Barbara. 1978. *Identities in the Lesbian World: The Social Construction of Self.* Westport, Conn.: Greenwood Press.

Reiss, Albert J., Jr. 1961. The social integration of queers and peers. *Social Problems* 9 (Fall): 102–20.

Rodgers, Bruce. 1972. *The Queens' Vernacular: A Gay Lexicon.* San Farncisco: Straight Arrow.

Rook, Karen S., and Constance L. Hammen. 1977. A cognitive perspective on the experience of sexual arousal. *Journal of Social Issues.* 33 (Spring): 7–29.

Rooney, Elizabeth A., and Don C. Gibbons. 1966. Social reactions to "crimes without victims." *Social Problems.* 13 (Spring): 400–410.

Simmons, J. L. 1965. Public stereotypes of deviants. *Social Problems.* 13 (Fall): 223–32.

Spence, Janet T., Robert Hemreich, and Joy Stapp. 1975. Likability, sex-role congruence of interest, and competence: It all depends on how you ask. *Journal of Applied Social Psychology.* 5 (April–June): 93–109.

Sykes, Gresham. 1958. *Society of Captives.* Princeton, N. J.: Princeton University Press.

Victor, Jeffrey S. 1978. The social psychology of sexual arousal: A symbolic interactionist interpretation. In *Studies in Symbolic Interaction*, Vol. I, ed. Norman K. Denzin. 147–80. Greenwich, Conn.: JAI Press.

Ward, David A., and Gene G. Kassebaum. 1965. *Women's Prison: Sex and Social Structure.* Chicago: Aldine.

Warren, Carol A. B. 1974. *Identity and Community in the Gay World.* New York: Wiley.

———., and John M. Johnson. 1972. A critique of labeling theory from the phenomenological perspective. In *Theoretical Perspectives on Deviance*, ed. Robert A. Scott and Jack D. Douglas. 69–92. New York: Basic.

Weinbers, Thomas S. 1978. On "doing" and "being" gay: Sexual behavior and homosexual male self-identity. *Journal of Homosexuality.* 4 (Winter): 143–56.

Bisexualities:
Heterosexual Contacts of "Gay" Men, Homosexual Contacts of "Straight" Men

Rolf Gindorf and Alan Warran

Abstract

The findings presented are based on two very different research instruments: first, on questionnaire and interview data collected from a cohort of 172 clients, i.e., "gay" men who came to our institute for anonymous HIV-antibody testing: second, on field research data of the participating observer type among ca. 1,000 men having "gay" sex contacts in Autobahn (motorway) service and picnic areas.

Thirty-six percent of the first study group indicated to have had, over the past five years, sex also with women, partly to a large or more than occasional extent, with considerable emotional and sexual gratification, and at various ages well past adolescence. Nearly a quarter of all the self-identified "gay" men in this part of our study are, or once were, married. Of the second study group, 70% turned out to lead married "straight" lifestyles, and only rather few of them experienced emotional problems. Sexual practices (mutual masturbation, oral, and anal intercourse) are equally preferred in both groups.

The most important conclusion drawn: The widespread "essentialist" idea of sexual orientations being dichotomic, i.e., that more or less all people "are" either heterosexual or homosexual, is not supported by our data. Rather, sexual orientation and behavior, at least for a considerable number of individuals, seem to be the result of culturally and individually established social constructions which are often not handled categorically, or dichotomically. This agrees with our counseling experience over the past 20 years with more than 23,000 gay and bisexual clients.

Key Words: Bisexuality, homosexuality, sexual theory, empirical sex research, sexual behavior, essentialism/constructionism, gay counseling.

Little empirically sound knowledge is available of "bisexual" men (or women, for that matter): of their emotional, behavioral, and social make-up. Their very existence confronts us with three basic problems: of definition, of methodology, and of science theory.

First Problem: How shall we meaningfully define "bisexuality"—in terms of mere fantasies, or of types and degrees of activities, or even of possibly developed "identities"? Thus, on the definition plane alone, we have various "bisexualities"—just as there are various "homosexualities" and various "heterosexualities."

Second Problem: What do we actually know about those who—to use the broadest definition—occasionally, predominantly, or constantly feel attracted to, and/or interact sexually with persons of both the other and the same sex? And how, by which methods, do we get reliable information about these "bisexualities" anyway? The answer to this is, blunty: We know few facts, and they are hard to get. For we can neither expect complete and true answers from the usual interviews or questionnaires, nor form representative samples of "bisexuals" of whatever definition, as long as most of them carefully hide their bisexual fantasies, their bisexual behavior, and their bisexual identities, if any.[1]

Our *third problem* is even more basic, as it involves a fundamental problem in science theory: what is it that we perceive, beyond the pure behavioral or phenomenological plane, as "bisexuality," or "sexuality," for that matter? Depending on our frame of reference—for instance, "essentialist" or, more complex, "constructionist"—we look and perceive according to different patterns. Is sexuality, or rather, are all the different sexualities to be found in human beings "essential" to, or even prearranged for, the individual? Or are they instead social, or bio-psycho-social, "constructions" erected, interpreted, lived, and modified in a complex interaction process between individuals and societies (which tends to be misunderstood as "nature")?[2]

The findings presented here are based on two very different research instruments: first, on a questionnaire and interview study of a cohort of 172 clients, i.e., "gay" men who came to our institute for anonymous HIV-antibody testing; second, on a field research of the participating observer type among ca. 1,000 men having casual, anonymous male sex contacts in Autobahn (motorway) service and picnic areas.

Both samples studied share the following common features:

- They were originally assumed to consist of "homosexual," not "bisexual" men, and "bisexuality" was found, after the study was well on its way, in a considerable part of the samples;

- The men of either group live roughly within the same area and thus could, in principle, have been present in both samples.

Therefore we think that the results of both studies can meaningfully be linked, and that the results of the field study—for all its methodological characteristics—can supply important information on the "living reality" of "bisexual" men.[3]

In short, we shall be looking at straight sex of gay men, and gay sex of straight men.

Results of Questionnaire and Interview Study: Heterosexual Sex Contacts of "Gay" Men

THIS STUDY IS based on data from a cohort of 172 bi- and homosexual men. The data was collected at our institute in 1985, and evaluated under different perspectives between 1986 and 1990.

At this point I should explain that, since 1978, our institute is Germany's only specialized professional gay counseling and research organization which offers its counseling service seven days a week, from 9 A.M. to 10 P.M. It is run by, and staffed with, openly gay professionals. Principles and results of our work in gay counseling and reseach have been widely published.[4]

Now: All the 172 men of our study defined themselves as "gay" insofar as the invitation had been directed to "gay" men, and had been distributed via gay networks. All applied for anonymous counseling and HIV-antibody testing by openly gay counselors and doctors. All agreed to submit to a partly structured personal interview and answered a standardized questionnaire with 72 items relating to, among other points,

- sexual practices,

- number of different sex partners,

- lifestyles, and

- "bisexuality" in terms of "additional heterosexual sex contacts."

Of course, it cannot be assumed for a moment that our sample is truly representative, or that all pertinent information was collected. But based on our experience we have reason to assume that what we found is not too far removed from overall empirical reality.

We found we could form and compare two distinctive groups:

- a larger one of 110 men (64%) who indicated only homosexual sex contacts over the period of five years preceding the interview, against

- a smaller group of 62 men (36%) who indicated also heterosexual sex contacts for the same period. These men I shall call our "bisexuals." (Parenthetically, this percentage would no doubt have been higher than 36% if we had asked for cumulative heterosexual contacts during their entire life and not just during the preceding five-year span.)

Now mind you, I'm using the term "bisexual" merely as an abbreviation. It refers to those men who indicated to have had sex not only with men but also with women— partly to a large or more than occasional extent, with considerable emotional and sexual gratification, and at various ages well past adolescence. But for all, in their own definition, the main activities and orientation were homosexual.

The foremost result of comparing the two subgroups: they are extremely similar. Most sexual and social data shows little or no significant differences. For instance, and contrary to what might be expected, the "bisexual" experience did not influence significantly our subjects' forming, or not forming, long-term gay relationships.

The following parameters of the overall sample will give a pretty accurate picture of either group.

Age ranges from 18 to 70 years, mean being 35, median 33 years. About one-quarter live in places having a population of less 100,000; nearly one-half live in cities of more than one-half million. The age at first homosexual sex contact varies between 6 and 65 years, both modus and median being 18, the mean 20 years. By the age of 30, nearly all (93%) had experienced sex leading to orgasm with a same-sex partner.

Of the various sexual outlets, four practices take top positions:

- mutual masturbation: 97%

- oral intercourse: 98% in the "passive," or insertee, position; 94% in the "active," or inserter, position,

- anal intercourse: 80% in the "active," 72% in the "passive" position, and

- anilingus: 71% in the "passive," 55% in the "active" position.

Sadomasochist practices were reported as follows: 14% sadistic, 11% masochistic. In addition, 18% of our sample indicate sex with rent or call boys.

So much for the results applying more or less to both groups. Now to some of the significant differences:

One doesn't come as much of a surprise: More than 35% of our "bisexuals" are, or once were, married. For our gay-only group this percentage shrinks to less than half of that, viz., to under 17%.

As for the other differences, I'm afraid I have to limit myself to just three examples: in the area of sex practices—one each common and less usual—and on the number of different sex partners:

- Example one: sex with more than 50 different partners: 32% of the gay-only group, as against merely 21% of the straight-only group. Thus one third less "bisexuals" than "gays only" were found in the highest partner-number bracket.

- Example two: receptive anal intercourse with more than 10 different partners: 21% of the gay-only group, as against merely 10% of the straight-also group. Thus only half of our "bisexuals" indicated this practice with this above average number of different sex partners.

- Example three: fisting, "active" and "passive": 14% and 3% respectively of the gay-only group, as against merely 5% and 1% respectively of the straight-only group. Thus only about one-third of our "bisexuals" practiced this type of sex, in both the "active" and "passive" positions.

Let me sum up: 36% of the "gay" men of this study group indicated to have had, over the past five years, sex also with women, partly to a large or more than occasional extent, with considerable emotional and sexual gratification, and at various ages well past adolescence. Nearly a quarter of all the self-identified "gay" men in this part of our study are, or once were, married.

Furthermore, on the basis of our limited data, we can say for our cohort of "bisexuals" (viz., gay men with additional straight sex contacts during the last five years) that sexual practices, social data, and lifestyles of our homosexual men are, in general, not significantly affected by additional heterosexual experience—except in special areas, involving partner-change frequencies and certain sexual practices. In short, our "bisexuals" in this sample are, in general, not significantly different from those men with exclusive homosexual sex contacts.

"Bisexualities" on Highway Service and Picnic Areas:
Homosexual Sex Contacts of Heterosexual Men

HUMAN SEXUAL ACTIVITIES take place at many very different places: in people's own or in hotel beds, in brothels and saunas, in movie theaters and automobiles, in fields, woods, and meadows, in parks and public toilets, in offices and church sacristies—nearly anywhere.

A relatively new, and scientifically hardly researched into, place is highway service and picnic areas used especially for homosexual activities. Such places exist all over Germany. We shall describe these activities, and the men taking part in them, at ten such areas within 20 kilometers of Düsseldorf, the capital (population 600,000) of the industrial Rhein/Ruhr region.

When the weather is fine each of these areas average from about 100 to 150 participants per day, most of them after it has become dark.[5] These areas were observed by Alan Warran over a period of nearly two years.[6] Using techniques of open participating observation and interviewing, he collected data from about 1,000 men seeking anonymous sex contacts at these rest areas.[7] Through his behavior, our participating field researcher succeeded in convincing his clientele that he was one of them, and in creating an atmosphere of trust and confidence. He used a memorized interviewing grid pertaining to age, occupation, marital status, sexual orientation in terms of overall sexual activity, preferred sexual activity, age of first homosexual activity, preferred age group of men and women, openness vs. secrecy of homosexual activity in marriage, and problems (if any) in marriage resulting from bisexuality. The raw data collected was subsequently discussed, interpreted, and evaluated in our institute. For lack of time, it cannot be discussed here.

The main results: As a rule, both sexual overtures and sexal activities take place in silence, without much talking. A surprisingly high percentage of the group—about 70%—was found to be "bisexual" in terms of their sexual preferences and activities. Only a minority of them seem to experience emotional problems as a result. In terms of male-to-male sexual practices on site, these are very much alike to those of the other group, with the same distribution of preferred sexual outlets:

- mutual masturbation,

- oral intercourse,

- anal intercourse.

In addition, and with considerably less frequency, sadomasochistic actions and spanking take place.

As for the differences which we found, most practitioners in this scene are married, have children, and continue to have sexual relations with their wives (and partly with other women). As a rule, their "bisexual" behavior does not, however, lead to the development of a "bisexual identity": most men identify themselves neither as "homosexual" nor as "bisexual" but as "heterosexual" (that is "normal" or "straight" in their terms) with occasional or frequent sex contacts to men. Most of them reject the "gay lifestyle" and refuse to view themselves as part of the gay subculture, with which they have no or very little contact.

Table 1 Ten Typical "Highway Rest Stop Bisexuals"

Name	Age	Occu-pation	Marital Status	Hetero-/Homo-Prefs. % of each[1]	Sexual Practices[2]	Age of 1st Homo-Contact[1]	Preferred Age[2]	Openly Bisexual to Friends/ Wife (if any)[2]	Marital Prob-lems[3]
Hans	55	Truck Driver	Married	60/40	Fellatio Masturbation Voyeurism	18	18–40 M + F	No/No	No
Erich	38	Hair-dresser	Divorced	50/50	Fellatio Masturbation	18	18 M + F	No/—	—
Peter	50	Designer	Divorced	20/80	Fellatio Anal Coitus Masturbation	15	20–30 M 18–25 F	No/ —	—
Wer-ner	30	Truck Driver	Married	50/50	Fellatio Anal Coitus Masturbation S/M (sadomasochism)	15	18+ M 16+ F	No/Yes	No/Yes (wife has)
Heinz	50	Entre-preneur	Married	30/70	Fellatio Anal Coitus Masturbation	23	18+ M + F	No/Yes	No
Harald	42	Civil Servant	Married	60/40	Fellatio Anal Coitus Masturbation	18	20+ M 18+ F	No/No	No
Stefan	35	Nurse	Divorced	40/60	Masturbation Fellatio	20	16–20 M 16–40 F	Yes/—	—
Ansgar	45	Sales Rep	Married	50/50	Voyeurism Exhibitionism Masturbation	40	18–40 M + F	No/No	No
Otto	65	Pen-sioner	Married	80/20	Masturbation Voyeurism	55	18–30 M 18–40 F	No/No	No
Henry	60	Man-ager	Unmarried	40/60	Masturbation Fellatio Anal Coitus S/M	16	18–40 M + F	No/—	—

1. As told to researcher
2. On site, as told to reasearcher and according to field observations
3. Due to bisexuality

In conclusion, we can say for these, as it were, "highway rest stop" bisexuals (i.e. heterosexual men with additional homosexual contacts) that distribution and preference hierarchy of their homosexual acts do not differ significantly from those of our first group, viz., gay men with straight contacts. They do differ significantly, though, in the degree of separation, or split, between sex and social life, and in the much more discreet organization of their homosexual life.

General Conclusions

LET ME TRY to draw four tentative conclusions from both studies.

1. There seem to be relatively few differences between all samples with regard to the sexual behavior indulged in.

2. There seem to be no significant patterns specific only to one of the groups or subgroups, except in a few special areas. The highway rest stop bisexuals differed in two aspects of the organization of their sexuality: a stricter separation, or split, between the sexual and other apects of their lives, and a greater insistence on discreetness.

3. Most importantly, the widespread "essentialist" idea of sexual orientations being dichotomic, i.e., that more or less all men are either exclusively heterosexual or exclusively homosexual, is not supported by our data. An unknown but substantial number of adult men do, or did, obtain emotional and physical sexual gratification from both sexes.

4. These men might be tentatively classified as "bisexuals," on the understanding that their sexualities—just as those of "homosexuals" and "heterosexuals"—represent "constructed," or "virtual," rather than "essential" sexualities, similar perhaps to the "virtual realities" created by advanced computer technology.

All of this, incidentally, agrees with our counseling experience over the past 20 years with more than 23,000 gay and bisexual men.

Endnotes

1. It may be noted that there are some sexologists (especially in Germany) who bluntly deny the existence of "genuine" bisexuals, declaring them to be "actually" heterosexuals, or, more often than not, homosexuals not accepting the "true nature" of their sexual orientation. In view of the massive empirical evidence to the contrary, we venture to suggest that such views are the result of a reductionist frame of mind, or of an ideological, dichotomous skotome—a blind spot in perception ability.

2. Cf. E. J. Haeberle's introduction to this book.

3. To repeat the obvious, the methodological limitations of our research do not allow us to pinpoint our "bisexuals" as "the" bisexuals as such.

4 Specifically on gay counseling (not including gay research) cf. Rolf Gindorf (1978): Gay Counseling. Programm des Instituts für Lebens- und Sexualberatung. Düsseldorf: GFSS-Druck; excerpts in Sexualpädagogik 3 (1978) 35; 4 (1978) 35–6. See also Gindorf (1982, 1989): Der mache den ersten Schritt. Lebensberatung für homosexuell liebende Menschen. In: Homosexuelle Liebe. Für eine Neuorientierung in der christlichen Ethik, H. G. Wiedemann. Stuttgart/Berlin: Kreuz Verlag, pp. 185–202; Gindorf (1984): Hilfe, ich bin schwul! Beratung für Homosexuelle. Psychologie heute, March, p. 11; Gindorf (1986): Bisexuell, homophil, schwul.

Homosexualitäten in Theorie und Beratungsarbeit. In: Von der Last der Lust. Sexualität zwischen Liberalisierung und Entfremdung, J. C. Aigner and R. Gindorf, eds. Wien: Verlag für Gesellschaftskritik, pp. 155–73; Gindorf (1989): Sexualverhalten, Sexualberatung, Sexualideologie: Zur Situation bi- und homosexueller Männer vor und in der AIDS-Krise. In: Sexualitäten in unserer Gesellschaft. Beitrage zur Geschichte, Theorie und Empirie, R. Gindorf and E. J. Haeberle, eds. Schriftenreihe Sozialwissenschaftliche Sexualforschung, Bd. 2. Berlin/New York: W. de Gruyter, pp.109–24; and Gindorf (1992): Ethische Probleme in der professionellen Schwulen-Beratung (Gay Counseling). In: Sexualität, Recht und Ethik, R. Gindorf and E. J. Haeberle. In progress. Paper given at the IV. International Berlin Conference for Sexology/XI. DGSS-Congress of Social Scientific Research "Sexuality, the Law, and Ethics," on 16.–19.07.92 at Humboldt-University in Berlin under the patronage of the Senator (State Minister) for Science and Research.

5. Main areas: Bundesautobahn (Federal Motorway) number 46 (Wuppertal-Düsseldorf) and number 52 (Düsseldorf-Essen), especially Eselbach (two places), Monheim- Richrath, Kreuz Hilden, Geismühle, Ruhrtalbrücke, Cloebruch, and 5 km further—at both the right and left lanes. Also observed, but not included in this study, were four municipal parks: Grafenberger Wald, Benrather Schloßpark, Schwanenspiegel, and Hofgarten, as well as two artificial lakes in gravel pits: Kaarst and Kalkum-Angermund.

6. Warran was at this time a full-time streetworker for a local AIDS prevention organization who had received special training for field research at our institute. Before that, he had been well grounded by us in the basics of sexology, and received a weekly supervision.

7. For a description of the problems and methods, cf. Kromrey (1980): Empirische Sozialforschung, Opladen, esp. pp. 160–209: Freidrichs, J. (1977): Methoden empirischer Sozialforschung, Reinbek, esp. p. 272 f.; Aleman, H. v.: Der Forschungsprozeß. Eine Einfürung die Praxis der empirischen Sozialforschung, Stuttgart, esp. pp. 207–44.

Clinical Aspects of Bisexuality among Men

Richard C. Friedman

Introduction

In this chapter, I stress the following ideas:

1. Sexual orientation, a multidimensional construct, may be helpfully conceptualized from a clinical perspective in terms of an interaction between four specific behavioral elements that emerge during different phases of development.

2. Clinical treatment planning depends on the relationship between the lifetime history of psychiatric disorders and the lifetime history of the behavioral components that determine sexual orientation. Of the psychiatric disorders that influence the way in which patients experience sexual orientation, the personality disorders are probably the most common. I concentrate on them today.

Let me now elaborate on these two points. The term "sexual orientation" may be used to refer to four major dimensions of behavior: (1) conscious erotic fantasies, (2) sexual activity with others, (3) the sense of identity, (4) social role. Even though I am a psychoanalyst, I use the terms "erotic fantasy" and "sexual fantasy" synonymously to connote consciously experienced phenomena, that is, consciously experienced imagery that is associated with a feeling of sexual desire or lust. Erotic fantasies are experienced by most boys during childhood, well before puberty (Friedman 1988).

In a paper entitled "The Problem of Ego Identity," Erik Erikson discusses the concept of identity, and I use the term here as he does (Erikson 1959).

Erikson described identity in terms of a person's identification with the values, attitudes, and philosophy of life of a particular group—and also a person's experience of self continuity over time. The person with a sturdy sense of identity knows who he is in relation to others, and feels secure in his imagined sense of who he will become in the future. During adolescence and early adulthood, ego identity is forged as a consequence of inner synthetic and integrative capacities. When someone experiences himself as "being gay," he is referring to his ego identity, and only indirectly and inferentially to his erotic behavior. The construct "ego identity" should not be confused with gender identity, which, as we all know, differentiates in early chilhood.

In recent years, the most common system for describing sexual orientation history has been the well know Kinsey Scale (Kinsey, Pomeroy, and Martin 1948). Kinsey's emphasis was on erotic experiences/activity and not on identity/social role. The latter behavioral dimensions mandate use of a more complex model in the clinical situation than the Kinsey Scale. Although erotic experience and activity may be concpetualized as a continuum, labeling as "gay," or heterosexual ("straight"), involves assignment to categories.

In the United States and societies with similar value frameworks, one finds tendency to label the self in terms of only two categories: homosexual/gay, or heterosexual/straight, regardless of whether one's erotic history has been homo-, hetero-, or bisexual. (This is not invariably true, of course—some patients do identify as bisexual, but many—and probably most—do not.)

Self-labeling involves the subjective evaluation by a person of the significance of his sexual fantasies for his sense of identity.

Erotic fantasies are experienced well before puberty and the sense of identity as heterosexual or as "gay," or more rarely, as bisexual, coalesces in late adolescence of early childhood. Thus, during a period of ten or more years, the developing boy must place positive or negative value on his erotic fantasies, and use them as indicators that direct him toward, or away from, specific social groups.

Homosexuality and heterosexuality, although often discussed as equivalent mental constructs by researchers, are not equivalent mental constructs in the minds of many patients, or in the minds of those in their support networks.

Identity

THE SENSE OF identity in relation to sexual orientation has been the focus of clinical attention in a number of ways including:

1. The acquisition of gay identity (Cass 1984).

2. The vicissitudes of erotic fantasy and identity during adolescence.

3. The relationship between identity disturbances in the personality disorders and various aspects of sexual orientation (Friedman 1988).

In order to discuss the latter topic, I must introduce concepts of psychoanalytic diagnosis here. I preface this discussion with the qualification that most gay, bisexual, and heterosexual individuals should not be discussed in clinical terms. A sizable number of people should, however, and it is to this group of patients that I now refer.

The Sexual Orientation Diagnosis Cube

ELIMINATION OF HOMOSEXUALITY as a diagnostic category from the *Diagnostic and Statistical Manual* of the American Psychiatric Association, although a progressive step, still left certain problems unsolved concerning diagnosis and documentation of psychopathology. Because significant conflicts about sexual orientation are so common, mental health professionals still needed a way of describing sexual orientation in relation to parameters of psychopathology without suggesting that homosexuality, in itself, is inevitably pathological. To meet that need, I designed a triaxial system to describe sexuality, characterology, and psychopathology.

One axis of this cube describes an individual's erotic fantasy and activity along a seven-point scale as described by Kinsey. The remaining two axes are borrowed from recent psychoanalytic theories of characterology. The second axis of the diagnosis cube describes the *level* of a patient's character structural integration (Kernberg 1984). The central point here is that a large group of patients exist who experience fragmentation of the mental representations of self and others. These patients also experience identity disturbances which may express themselves in many different ways. Fragmentation of the internal world of these patients is associated with intense unstable relationships with others, and with emotional volatility. Because these patients were thought by many clinicians to be on the border between psychosis and neurosis, the term "borderline" came to be used to describe them. Only some patients with personality disorders are borderline, however. Many are not borderline, and *they* experience integration of the representational world and identity cohesion. These latter patients manifest what psychoanalysts have traditionally described as neurotic characters—despite inhibitions in various dimensions of their functioning, they do not "fall apart" in the way that borderline patients do (See figure 1).

Figure 1
STRUCTURAL LEVEL OF CHARACTER INTEGRATION

Highest level	*Lowest level*
Neurotic character	Borderline syndromes
Repression is core defense	Splitting is core defense, primitive idealization and devaluation occur
Representational world is stable	Representational world is unstable
Self representation is stable	Self-representation is unstable
Identity is solid	Identity diffusion is present

From R. C. Friedman, *Male Homosexuality: A Contemporary Psychoanalytic Perspective* (Yale University Press, 1988)

The traditions of descriptive sexology research exemplified by Kinsey, and of psychoanalytic characterology have long remained isolated from each other. When a Kinsey model for fantasy and activity and a psychoanalytic object relations model are used together, however, an economical construct emerges that may be applied to record sexual orientation history in clinical situations.

Figure 2 depicts two dimensions of behavior. Triangles indicate well-integrated people who are at polar opposites in the Kinsey Rating Scale. Rectangles represent poorly integrated borderline patients who are polar opposites. Open circles represent well-integrated bisexual people, and cross-hatched circles, poorly integrated bisexuals. It is this latter group, borderline bisexual patients, that I focus on today.

Although this two-dimensional model is useful, it is apparent that a third axis is necessary in order to depict personality type. Patients may differ as to level of character structural integration but have identical personality types. By personality *type*, I mean whether someone is obsessive-compulsive, hysterical, narcissistic, and so forth. Figure 3 illustrates these three axes in the Sexual Orientation Diagnosis Cube.

Figure 2
CHARACTER STRUCTURE AND KINSEY RATING

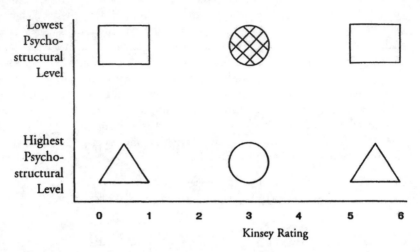

From R. C. Friedman, *Male Homosexuality: A Contemporary Psychoanalytic Perspective* (Yale University Press, 1988)

Figure 3
SEXUAL ORIENTATION DIAGNOSIS CUBE

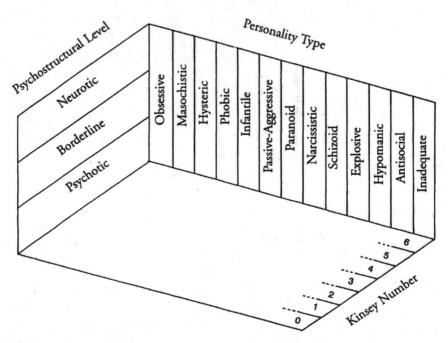

From R. C. Friedman, *Male Homosexuality: A Contemporary Psychoanalytic Perspective* (Yale University Press, 1988)

To summarize the points thus far, erotic *fantasy* differentiation in males seems to unfold as a developmental line in homo-, hetero-, or bisexual. People in all three erotic fantasy groups are distributed across the entire spectrum of psychological health and illness. The onset of most personality disorders tends to overlap the time in life when erotic fantasy differentiates. The erotic life of the person is therefore filtered through the lens of a personality disorder during that person's development, beginning years prior to the onset of adolescence. The personality disorder influences the way in which the person assesses the significance of erotic fantasies for his emerging sense of identity.

Clinical Aspects of the Bisexualities

LET ME GO ON now to address clinical aspects of the *bisexualities themselves*. Patients with bisexual fantasies/activity and coincident personality disorders often experience the need to coalesce an identity as homosexual or heterosexual, but cannot do so. The complex reasons for this are illustrated by considering bisexual borderline men whose personality type is obsessive-compulsive. Patients in this subgroup are prone to self-fragmentation as are all borderline patients. In addition, however, these patients process experience in an obsessive-compulsive manner.

The *DSM-III* criteria for compulsive personality disorder are: impaired ability to express warm feelings, perfectionism and preoccupation with detail, stubbornness, indecisiveness, preoccupation with work to the point of impairment in interpersonal relationships or in the capacity to enjoy other activities.

Contradictory and conflicting impulses are typically experienced by patients with obsessive-compulsive personality disorders. Their *ambivalence* is the reason that they are so indecisive. These patients often seem to make a decision about something only to subsequently negate it and decide on the exact opposite. Borderline patients who have bisexual erotic fantasies and obsessive-compulsive personality disorders often experience much confusion as they try to decide whether their fantasies mean that they are "truly" homosexual or "truly" heterosexual. Many of these patients, in light of the unique importance of sexual orientation in their subcultures, attribute the reasons for their identity disturbance to their bisexual fantasies. It is as if they believed that they could find their way to an integrated sense of identity if only they did not experience erotic fantasies pulling them in contradictory directions. Of course, this is not the case. Rather, they endow their bisexual erotic fantasies with unusual significance because of their underlying personality disorder.

Sometimes, borderline obsessive-compulsive bisexual patients experience a transient sense of self-authenticity—a sense of "truly being gay" or "truly being heterosexual–straight." For a variety of reasons, however, this is soon renounced and the patient then experiences himself as the opposite. Patients who previously experienced themselves as heterosexual may "come out" as gay. Patients who previously experienced themselves as gay may "decide" that they were never really gay at all, and opt for heterosexuality and marriage.

The reasons for the change over time in the way that some obsessional-borderline patients experience bisexual fantasies exceed the scope of today's talk. Often, stressful life events precede the identity crisis.

One reason that it is important to diagnose personality type is that specific medication now available for obsessive-compulsive disorder may be helpful in some subgroups of these patients. Their ambivalence about their identity as gay or straight sometimes diminishes as their obsessionalism gets treated. Generally, their bisexual fantasies remain unchanged, however.

A variety of secondary symptoms occur in obsessional-borderline bisexual patients leading to a wide array of sexual behaviors. For example, one man might repetitively enage in sexual activity with numerous women, as a reaction against unacceptable consciosly perceived homosexual feelings. Another might experience depersonalization and phobic avoidance of women in reaction to unwanted heterosexual desires which threaten his already fragile gay sense of identity.

These types of phenomena, usually of only marginal interest to most sexologists, are of great importance to clinicians who work with disturbed populations.

As I mentioned earlier, adolescence has been the focus of much clinical interest with regard to sexual orientation, since adolescence is of crucial importance with regard to the sense of identity.

A compressed vignette illustrates interactions of clinical relevance.

A sixteen-year-old patient had bisexual fantasies and had been sexually active with males and females. He experienced sex with males as more pleasurable, and was rated 4 on the Kinsey Scale. He thought he might "be gay," and sought consultation to decide if he "really was" and if so, how to tell his parents whom he loved and was dependent on, but who he feared might reject him.

This boy's father was also rated 4 on the Kinsy Scale in fantasy. He had gone through a phase of exclusive homosexual activity prior to marriage—and active bisexual activity early in the marriage. Because homosexuality was incompatible with his value system, however, he ultimately became heterosexually monogamous. This man was not overtly homophobic, but his wife, a monogamous heterosexual woman, was. Years before, she had discovered his sexual affairs with men and was unrelentingly bitter about this.

In this complex clinical situation, the designated patient was the son. The actual unit in need of help, however, was the entire family. The father was an obsessional-borderline man, whose fragile sense of identity as heterosexual was associated with many rituals and inhibitions in personality functioning. The son's sexual history was similar to his father's. He, too, had an obsessive-compulsive personality structure. His struggles with identity, however, were leading him away from his father's route, and toward a solution that his father had renounced. Both parents avoided their own sexual difficulties by worrying about this son.

The outcome of this case hinged on individual diagnosis of each family member—and assessment of the meaning of homosexuality, bisexuality, and heterosexuality in the family system. It also hinged on the therapist—myself—*not* trying to impose a solution about the desirability of a specific type of sexual orientation, either on the adolescent patient, or his father.

Because of limitations of space, I will comment on only one additional personality disorder: Self-Defeating Personality Disorder (SDPD).

This is the name given by *DSM-III* to what used to be termed Masochistic Personality Disorder. This category calls attention to the tendency that many patients have to engage in repetitive self-destructive behavior for irrational reasons (Shapiro 1981; Friedman 1988). In this age of homophobia, homoparanoia, and the AIDS epidemic, the topic of sexual self-destructiveness is especially salient. The bisexual patient with SDPD often *uses* his sexuality in a self-destructive way. Homosexual or heterosexual imagery may be experienced as a reason for attack upon the self. Because more patients come from environments in which caretakers and authority figures have antihomosexual attitudes, homosexual fantasies probably trigger self-attack more frequently than heterosexual fantasies do. In these situations, the patient internalizes negative attitudes from authority figures and then experiences shame, guilt, and the need for punishment in reaction to his sexual fantasies.

The varieties of self-attack are many and often include denial of the need for safe-sex practices.

The bisexual patient with SDPD may manifest his self-destructiveness primarily in the area of identity and social role. Among the many ways this may be expressed, one that is particularly important clinically is "coming out" as gay. Obviously, most people who come out are not self-destructive. Among self-destrcutive people, however, the sadism in the general culture directed against homosexual people unfortunately sometimes acts as an irresistible magnet. These patients, bisexual in erotic fantasy life, choose to announce that they are gay in ways that are highly self-damaging. I have described this more extensively elsewhere (Friedman 1988).

Although many patients manifest personality disorders in "pure form," many manifest mixed types with, for example, obsessive and self-defeating traits.

The types of patients described here illustrates how important it is that clinicians avoid reductionistic, dichotomous approaches when counseling patients about sexual orientation. Simple reassurance about the normalcy of "sexual preference" is not likely to be experienced as being helpful by these patients.

Moreover, patients with personality disorders tend to come from families with psychopathology. In the case of younger bisexual patients particularly, the difficulties of moving out into the world when they may be in conflict with their families' value systems generally, and sexual value systems in particular, are often formidable.

Despite a potentially bewildering array of clinical interactions, however, bisexual patients may, in fact, be approached in a systematic and clinically effective manner.

References

Cass, V. C. 1984. Homosexual identity formation testing a theoretical model. *J. Sex Research*. 20(2): 143–67.

Erikson, E. H. 1959. The problem of ego identity. In *Identity and The Life Cycle*. Psychological Issues Vol. (1): 101–64. New York: International Universities Press.

Friedman, R. C. 1988. *Male Homosexuality: A Contemporary Psychoanalytic Perspective.* New Haven and London: Yale University Press.

Insel, T. R., ed. 1984. *New Findings in Obsessive-Compulsive Disorder.* Washington, D.C.: American Psychiatric Press.

Kernberg, O. 1984. *Severe Personality Disorders.* New Haven and London: Yale University Press.

Kinsey, A. C., W. B. Pomeroy, and C. E. Martin. 1948. *Sexual Behavior in the Human Male*. Philadelphia: Saunders.

Mavissakalian, M., S. S. Turner, and L. Michelson, eds. 1985. *Obsessive-Compulsive Disorder*. New York: Plenum Press.

Shapiro, D. 1965. *Neurotic Styles*. New York: Basic Books.

———. 1981. Sadism and masochism: Central tendencies. In *Autonomy and Rigid Character*. New York: Basic Books.

Stone, M. H. 1980. *The Borderline Syndromes*. New York: McGraw–Hill.

Bisexuality during the Teenage Years: A Theoretical Model and Several Clinical Experiences in Confused Identity

A. X. van Naerssen

For most scientists knowledge is universal and objective; it is independent of personal taste, of political and religious meanings. Scientific knowledge in fact is seen as a verbal representation of reality. There is another point of view saying that theory, models, and verbal representation exist only in our heads; that is their only reality. Latour and Woolgar (1986) are outlining a third possibility. They introduce the idea of an anthropology of science. Knowledge is seen as a social construction. A forum of scientific experts decide on the rules of the game; it decides on what is accepted as knowledge.

We can look at sexuality in these three different ways: First, sexuality is a universal concept to describe and understand certain desires in people and to predict their behavior in certain situations. Second, sexuality is only in our heads: each notion of sexuality, the psychoanalytic, the behavioral, the medical, is real. Third, there must be some agreement between experts about sexuality: The social network of experts is functioning as a forum, tracing the lines between what sexuality is and what it is not.

As an example, let us look at the models on the formation of a homosexual identity (van Naerssen 1989). Becoming homosexual can be seen as a process of cognitive, emotional, and social abilities of a person. This person learns to identify, to choose, to decide. The process is divided in stages, called sensitization, identity confusion, identity assumption, and commitment.

Troiden (1990) defines commitment in the following way: "A commitment is a feeling of obligation to follow a particular course of action. . . . In the homosexual context, *commitment* involves adopting homosexuality as a way of life. . . . Entering a same-sex love relationship marks the onset of commitment." So commitment is presented as a universal, objective, reliable, and valid concept to describe the goal of a process.

Plummer (1987) defended the second point of view, as he states: "What matters in my life is not those earliest experiences but the way in which I recall them, organize them, and ultimately fashion them into my adult life." It is not the adopting of a homosexual lifestyle, not the entering of a same-sex relationship that is characteristic in the formation of a sexual identity. An adult man, happily married, with children, feeling that his romantic sexual relationship with another schoolboy years before was the most emotional and essential element in his sexual life and considering himself homosexual, is a homosexual.

The third position, defended by myself, states that speaking on homosexual identity formation is only one of the possible ways to look at the psychosexual development of persons. It is a scientific tradition, on which we agree since in 1968 Erikson's much celebrated book *Identity, Youth, and Crisis* appeared. This study was published in a time of changing sexual morality, seeing it not only as a method of reproduction but as the possibility of lustful experience of ourselves and others and as the expression of affection, of love. At the same time the religious ideas on sexuality as the expression of divine will was replaced by a more liberal idea that each person had to decide for himself how to manage his sexual desires, how to express it in a social lifestyle.

Social science accepted this idea in 1978 as Bell and Weinberg's book appeared: *Homosexualities: A Study of the Diversity among Men and Women.* It is in my opinion, not a study of sexual diversity but a study of socially accepted sexual diversity. Now, twelve years later, after a decade with AIDS, we see that which was lauded as sexual freedom in 1978, is now frowned upon as a dangerous sexual lifestyle. We have the possibility of lustful experience of ourselves and others, but the diversity of expression is limited. As a consequence, scientists have to agree on how to integrate the scientific tradition with psychosexual development on the analysis of a changing society.

Let us look now at sexual identity, especially in adolescence. Our sexual morality at this moment is still liberal, such that every person has to decide for him or herself on how to manage sexual feelings, emotions, desires. At the same time, there is a heightened awareness of sexuality and aggression, of the prevalence of incest and pedophilia, of the dangers of sexually transmitted diseases, and of addictive and obsessive-compulsive aspects of sexual expression. Young people nowadays are no longer sexually naive. We teach them, in the tradition of the sixties, how sexuality can be lustful, can be an expression of affection and love. But at the same time we teach them that gender differences are deeply ingrained in the socialization process, generating a male sexuality that is egoistic, aggressive, and domineering. We teach them not to trust adults as soon as physical contact is possible. We teach them to live in a sexually healthy way. And as Schmidt (1988), criticizing the ideas on sexual health of the World Health Organization, states: "This means pleasure instead of lust, control instead of surrender, social integration instead of breaking taboos."

As a consequence the question of sexual identity is not: How can I manage my desires to find my real self—hetero-, homo-, or bisexual? But: How can I control what I see, fantasize, feel, and experience in a socially acceptable way?

If this line of reasoning is correct, it means that we have to replace Erikson's notions of identity, youth, and crisis, with a question: Is it possible to develop a personal sexual identity in a society in which certain social sexual identities are promoted, especially sexual identities in which pleasure, control, and social integration are central concepts in the social and scientific discourse on sexuality?

Starting with this question in a discourse on bisexuality in adolescence means that we have to do ethnographic research on the incidence and prevalence of bisexual behavior in the population as a whole or in some stratified subsamples, but at the same time we have to analyze the diverse ways in which young people manage their feelings and emotions and how they experience this management. Does it lead to pleasure, control, and social integration; does it produce discomfort, subjective stress, even loneliness and despair; or does it give lust, surrender, autonomy?

I could not find this kind of research. The main reason, I suppose, is the fact that the scientific debate on bisexuality is the same as that on homosexuality: essentialism against constructivism, looking at homosexuality as a universal concept to understand same-sex relationships or seeing it as a historical idea from which we have to liberate ourselves by a subjective organization of our emotions. So the only things I have to offer you are some systematic observations of about ten males in adolescence, who all came to our clinic with extreme discomfort over their sexual cognitions, emotions, and behavior. According to Stein (1988) psychotherapy is "a process which involves a verbal interaction between two individuals, one of whom has specialized training and certification to assist the other with an emotional or mental disturbance, and both of whom have agreed to some structured arrangement in order to accomplish this task."

The extreme discomfort in these young males was, in their own words, a consequence of their hetero- and homosexual fantasies leading in most cases to masturbation fantasies. Masturbation took a lot of time, three or four hours a day at least. The content of the fantasies was not unusual, if we take Masters and Johnson's findings in hetero- and homosexual males as a criterion (1979). According to them, homosexual fantasies in heterosexual males are not unusual, nor are heterosexual fantasies in homosexual males.

The only difference in my clinical samples was that these adolescents did not know if they were heterosexual or homosexual. All of them had had female partners for more than a year and some homosexual experience in preadolescence. So, their sexual lives were not very unusual or exciting, nor were their sexual fantasies. It was the masturbation and the discomfort before, during, and after these sexual outlets that brought them to the edge of despair. It was easy to classify this autoerotic sexual behavior as compulsive, following Coleman's definition that this kind of behavior is driven by anxiety reduction mechanisms rather than by sexual desire. The question remains: what kind of anxiety?

I tried to understand this both by analyzing their life histories and by letting them talk about their discomfort in detail as long as possible. At first they spoke about themselves in a way identity theorists could easily classify in the proposed developmental stages: sensitization, confusion, and sometimes assumption and commitment. But the bridge between confusion and assumption was fragile. How can a person choose, make decisions, and act accordingly if it is not clear what the alternatives are? It is relatively easy in sociosexual research to make sensible distinctions between different sexual orientations (hetero-, homo-, or bisexual) or between different sexual lifestyles (independent, close-coupled, open-coupled). But these alternatives are not given as separate entities in a person's head. These young males tried to solve this problem by going to an expert, exposing their life histories, their fantasies, their masturbation sessions, their lovemaking before him and then asking him: Tell me what my identity is, tell me how to live in a way that is sexually satisfying. If this is the structured arrangement of psychotherapy, it is easy to say to them: "Look there are heterosexuals, homosexuals, and bisexuals. Let us try to make sense of your experiences and we will find out in the course of time, who you are, what you are."

Or I could follow Plummer's suggestion, saying: "It does not matter, tell me your earliest experiences and I will help you organize them into the adult life that is to come." This structured arrangement capitalizes not on orientations or lifestyles, but on the management of cognitions and emotions.

Both strategies are in fact, highly directive. In the first strategy, a context of orientations and lifestyles is proposed; in the second, the attention of the client is directed to his past experiences and teaches him to structure these in his life.

The third strategy, followed by myself, was to accept identity confusion as normal, confusion being the human condition. So your masturbation fantasies, your romantic, sensual, and sexual relationships, your cognitions and emotions do not tell you who you are. You *are* your fantasies, relationships, cognitions, and emotions. Life is not being a heterosexual with homosexual fantasies or a homosexual with heterosexual fantasies or a bisexual with no fantasies. Life, especially social life, expects from you that you interact with other people, feel attracted to some of them and feel repulsion, hate, or insecurity in the presence of others. Social life expects from you that you handle these situations in a certain way. So you are an adolescent male and society expects from you that you are autonomous. You have to find a partner. Now you can look at all these things as plans or scripts. The first stage is to make that plan, then choose, make decisions, and do what you want. I propose something different. You are an adolescent male and you experience a lot of things now; do not try to make plans for the future, do not look to the past, but express what you feel now, in the presence of other people, male or female. My role as a therapist is not to tell you who you are; I cannot tell you that. The only thing I can do is take your confusions as seriously as possible.

I will report briefly on the main outcome of this strategy. In my opinion, the most important finding was that all these adolescents tried to solve their sexual problems by themselves, not in interaction with others. Being a male in this society meant to them: trying to control relationships, especially emotional and sexual relationships. They were all concentrating on their social identity, seeing their personal identity as something difficult and potentially dangerous. Having a social identity as a heterosexual or a homosexual is relatively easy today. The codes and the morality are given. But making love to a person, touching him or her, being without clothes, in the presence of only one other person, who is touching you—that is different. In fact, to enjoy that is to forget your personal and social identity and to surrender yourself to the very social experiences of touch and smell. On the contrary, coming of age in this society means that you do not surrender yourself, not even in the most intimate situations.

These young males thought that what was happening in their sexual interactions was a consequence of their desires, either hetero- or homosexual. But desire is only a script in masturbation where it is possible to control excitement and orgasm. As soon as touching, smelling, and kissing are involved, the script is social, not personal. Now, we can look at this situation in two ways. First, each participant has an own inner story of desires and making love is a compromise between two lonely people. Second, making love constitutes desire and is by definition social, not personal. Just as in normal conversation a common language is necessary, making love is to invent that common spiritual and body language that each participant cannot find on his own.

Bisexuality in such a situation can be a conversation on how satisfying or dissatisfying the dimorphism of the body is, which means that the standard is your own desire. Or you make love and just see what is happening when you are not alone and in that case the question "hetero-, homo-, or bisexual" becomes relatively unimportant. So the most satisfying identity is between personal and social definitions, the relational balance that constitutes something you can only invent yourself. Society cannot invent for you, the World Health Organization cannot define it, social scientists cannot formulate the rules of the game, neither can psychotherapists. The rules of the game are invented by you and your partners.

References

Bell, A. P,. and M. S. Weinberg. 1978. *Homosexualities: A Study of the Diversity among Men and Women.* Bloomington: Indiana University Press.

Erikson, E. 1968. *Identity, Youth, and Crisis.* New York: Norton.

Latour, B., and S. Woolgar. 1986. *Laboratory Life: The Construction of Scientific Facts.* Princeton: Princeton University Press.

Masters, W,. and V. Johnson. 1979. *Homosexuality in Perspective.* Boston: Little, Brown.

Naerssen, A. X. van. 1989. *Labyrint zonder muren, analyse van het seksueel verlangen.* (Labyrinth without walls, analysis of the sexual desire.) Utrecht: Veen.

Plummer, K. 1987. Beyond childhood: organizing "gayness" in adult life. Public Lecture. International Conference: Homosexuality Beyond Disease. Amsterdam.

Stein, T. 1988. Theoretical considerations in psychotherapy with gay men and lesbians. *Journal of Homosexuality.* 15(1/2): 75–95.

Troiden, R. R. 1990. The formation of homosexual identities. *Journal of Homosexuality.* 17(1/2): 43–75.

Differences in Sexual Orientation in Relation to HIV-Risk Behavior among Intravenous Drug Addicts

Michael W. Ross, Alex Wodak, Julian Gold,

and M. E. Miller

Abstract

Injecting drug users (IDUs) play a disproportionate role in the spread of HIV, given their injecting and sexual contacts, and thereby act as conduits between these risk groups. We investigated differences in risk behavior and HIV seroprevalence in a Sydney sample of 1,245 IDUs. Significant differences were observed across sexual orientation in HIV serostatus for males, with homosexual men having the highest HIV seroprevalence rate (35%), bisexual men intermediate (12%), and heterosexual men lowest (3%). Sexual HIV risk behaviors were lowest for homosexual men, intermediate for bisexual men, and highest for heterosexual men. There were no differences across sexual orientation for either sex or injecting drug risk behaviors. Both male and female respondents reported having sex while under the influence of drugs more than half the time. This study suggests that risk reduction in the sexual domain has not generalized to the injecting risk domain regardless of sexual orientation, and demonstrates that sexual risk behaviors in IDUs are lowest in homosexual, intermediate in bisexual, and highest in heterosexual men.

Chu, Doll, and Buehler (1989) found from an assessment of CDC data in the United States that bisexual men with AIDS were more than twice as likely to have injected drugs than homosexual men (and that this did not differ significantly when adjusted for race and ethnicity). Further, Battjes, Pickens, and Amsel (1989) noted that equipment sharing by male homosexual or bisexual injecting drug users with heterosexual IDUs was a common and efficient means of introducing HIV to low-prevalence areas. These data suggest that the combination of risky sexual and equipment-sharing behaviors is a potent one for HIV transmisson.

Although sexual transmission of HIV appears to be less important than transmission by sharing of injecting equipment in IDUs, sexual behavior has been found to be more resistant to change than needle sharing (Hart et al. 1989; Donoghoe at al. 1989a). Further, a high prevalence of sexual risk behaviors has been found in this population. Donoghoe et al. (1989b) report that IDUs at a needle exchange did not use condoms for sexual activity up to 79% of the time, and Jones and Vlahov (1989) report similar figures.

This data suggests that bisexual IDUs may have a special role in the dissemination of HIV transmission, through multiple risk behaviors and multiple contacts. However, no research has been carried out on differences across sexual orientation in IDUs to confirm this. The aim of this study was therefore to investigate differences between heterosexual, bisexual, and homosexual IDUs in both sexual and injecting risk behaviors.

Method

THIS STUDY FORMED part of a national HIV-IDU research project. Respondents were obtained by three forms of advertising. First, by interviewers distributing cards with study details and the telephone and address of the interview site, and the indication that injecting drug users would be paid $20 for an anonymous interview, to injecting-drug-using contacts; second, by putting advertisements with the same message in employment and social security offices, needle exchanges, and pharmacies which sold needles and syringes; and third, by placing the same advertisement in a popular free central city magazine. Interviews took place in an unmarked building several blocks from the centre of the drug-using subculture in the Kings Cross–Darlinghurst area of Sydney, with direct access off the street into a waiting room. These interviews were conducted in an individual private cubicle by interviewers who had extensive personal or professional experience in the area of injecting drug use. A single receptionist took initials of first and surnames and date of birth and where respondents were suspected or recognized as having attended previously, this data was checked to ensure that there was no double interviewing. In addition, interviews were conducted by one interviewer in the western suburbs of Sydney to obtain a broader geographical distribution of injecting drug users: these interviews were conducted at a community health center under the same conditions. All data was entered on the interview schedule by the interviewer.

The study employed an interview schedule which had been piloted on over one hundred injecting drug users and modified as a result of this. Sections covered deomgraphics, drug use behavior, use of new equipment/reuse of own equipment, sharing injection equipment, cleaning of injection equipment, disposal of used injection equipment, social context of injecting drug use, sexual history, knowledge and attitudes about HIV/AIDS, HIV/AIDS prevention, sources of HIV/AIDS information, HIV/AIDS antibody testing, and modules on treatment and prison use if appropriate. Response possibilities ranged from closed options to open-ended questions, and all response possibilities were provided on show-cards where appropriate. A copy of the full 36-page interview schedule is available from the first author on request. The interview took on average 75 minutes to complete.

Results: Sample Characteristics

A TOTAL OF 1,245 respondents were interviewed: these included 908 males, 331 females, and 6 male-to-female transsexuals. Characteristics of the males and females are described separately (means±SDs are given where appropriate).

MALES: Mean age was 27.9±6.7, and modal highest level of education was some high school (57.2% of the sample). Modal employment status was social security benefits of pension (59.2%) with only 13.5% employed full- or part-time and 20%

unemployed. The majority (50.8%) had been on benefits or pension for over one year, and a further 38.2% for over a month. The sample was predominantly Australian-born (79.2%) with the majority of the remainder (15.5%) being born in the U.K., New Zealand, or North America. Mean number of children was 0.6±1.3, with the mean number of children financially dependent on the respondent being 0.1±0.5. The mean number of other people financially dependent on the respondent was 0.2±2.6. A majority (63.8%) had been in some form of drug treament which had ended on an average 2.3±4.6 years ago. The most common previous treatments were Methadone maintenance (19.7%), detoxification (40.1%), and inpatient rehabilitation (13%). For those currently in treatment (30.4%), the most common treatment was Methadone maintenance (39%), followed by therapeutic community (26.6%). Neraly half (45.2%) had been to prison, with a mean time of 3.6±3.8 years since release. Just over half (55.4%) had moved to Sydney from elsewhere, on an average of 4.8±7.7 years ago.

Most males were currently injecting, with the majority having injected within hours (17.2%) or days (33.9%) of the interview; only 6.7% had not injected within the year. Mean age of first injection of a drug was 18.6±4.4, and mean age of injecting drug once a month or more was 20.0±4.6 years. Average frequency of injecting (or for those not currently injecting, when they were last injecting) per typical month was 4.9±6.6 times. The drugs most commonly injected were heroin (67.1%), amphetamines (34.6%), and cocaine (13.2% of the male sample).

FEMALES: Mean age was 26.3±7.6, and modal highest level of education was some high school (53.5% of the sample). Modal employment status was social security benefits or pension (58.5%) with only 16.7% employed full- or part-time and 13.7% unemplyoed. The majority (57.6%) had been on benefits or pension for over one year, and a further 32% for between a month and a year. The sample was predominantly Australian-born (84.6%) with the majority of the remainder (12.3%) being born in the U.K., New Zealand, or North America. Mean number of children was 0.9±2.7, with the mean number of children financially dependent on the respondent being 0.6±2.1. The mean number of other people financially dependent on the respondent was 0.1±0.4. A majority (55.9%) had been in some form of drug treatment, which had ended on average 2.3±5.5 years ago. The most common previous treatments were Methadone maintenance (21%), detoxification (48.5%), and counseling (10.2%). For those currently in treatment (15.7%), the most common treament was Methadone maintenance, (49.1%), followed by therapeutic community and counseling (12% each). Less than a fifth (19.6%) had been to prison, with a mean time of 3.5±4.6 years since release. Just over half (54.1%) had moved to Sydney from elsewhere, on an average of 4.9±8.4 years ago.

Most females were also currently injecting, with the majority having injected withing hours (20.3%) or days (30.9%) of the interview: only 2.7% had not injected within the year. Mean age of first injection of a drug was 18.1±3.8 and mean age of injecting a drug once a month or more was 19±4.4 years. Average frequency of injecting (or for those not currently injecting, when they were last injecting) per typical month was 5.3±6.6 times. The drugs most commonly injected were heroin (70.1%), amphetamines (32%), and cocaine (15.1% of the female sample).

Table 1
DIFFERENCES IN SEXUAL ORIENTATION IN MALE INJECTING DRUG USERS
Percentages

Variable	Heterosexual (n=719)	Bisexual (n=117)	Homosexual (n=50)	Significance
College educated	18.7	23.1	22.0	*
Always lived in Sydney	26.7	42.1	38.0	*
Been to prison	47.5	35.7	35.4	*
Had HIV test	76.2	88.9	94.0	**
HIV seropositive	3.2	12.1	35.4	**
Changed behavior since test	45.9	60.4	59.6	**
Regular sex partners bisexual	9.1	46.4	18.8	**
Pay for sex	13.1	1.8	6.1	*
Paid for sex	4.0	33.9	32.7	**
Oral drugs used:				
Benzodiazapines	1.5	5.1	2.0	*
Ecstasy	1.5	6.8	14.0	**
LSD	6.2	8.6	16.0	*
Drugs used when having sex:				
Heroin	63.3	53.8	42.0	**
Other opiates	8.8	16.2	10.0	*
Benzodiazapines	18.5	24.8	36.0	**
LSD	7.2	14.5	14.0	*
Ecstasy	5.4	44.4	22.0	**
Alcohol	56.1	70.1	64.0	*
Sexual practices past 6 months				
Vaginal	90.4	84.8	0	**
Vaginal, withdrawal	27.4	44.7	0	**
Anal receptive, no condom	17.7	57.1	44.0	*
Anal insertive, with condom	39.6	64.5	71.9	**
Anal receptive, with condom	0	64.5	72.4	**
Anal insertive, withdrawal	16.3	42.9	46.7	*
Oral receptive with male	0	62.5	85.0	**
Oral receptive, with male, withdrawal	0	53.5	78.4	**
Oral insertive, with female	76.0	80.7	0	**
Manual, male partner	0	66.7	85.0	**

Table 1 (continued)
DIFFERENCES IN SEXUAL ORIENTATION IN MALE INJECTING DRUG USERS

Variable	Percentages			Significance
	Heterosexual (n=719)	Bisexual (n=117)	Homosexual (n=50)	
STDs:				
Gonorrhea	11.0	19.7	30.0	**
Genital warts	9.5	17.1	24.0	**
Nonspecific urethritis	11.3	19.7	26.0	**
No STDs reported	35.0	33.3	18.0	*
Sex with HIV serospositive person:				
After knowing	1.5	12.2	30.4	**
Took pecautions	72.7	68.5	92.9	**
Before knowing	1.4	12.5	44.8	**
Practice unsafe sex, past 6 months	26.8	69.2	26.0	**
	Mean			
Number of HIV tests	3.0	3.8	3.7	Bi Ho>He**
Number female partners, past year	6.1	6.2	0	Bi He>Ho**
Number male partners, past year	0	10.8	23.1	Ho>Bi>He*
% time condoms used:				
Vaginal	30.9	41.7	0	Bi>He>Ho *
Anal insertive	22.0	45.6	70.7	Ho>Bi>He**
Anal receptive	0	58.4	75.6	Ho>Bi>He *
Oral receptive	0	31.5	22.4	Bi>Ho>He *
Oral insertive	10.2	21.5	19.2	Bi>He**

*p< .05   ** p<.01

Sexual orientation was defined by sexual partners in the past five years, with bisexuals reporting at least one sexual contact with males and females in this period. Unsafe sex was defined as reporting anal or vaginal sex without a condom in the past six months *and* having more than one partner in that period. Unsafe needle-sharing practices were defined as having accepted a used needle or syringe from another person in the past six months. Analyses of variables by sexual orientation appear for males in Table 1 and for females in Table 2. Variables not included in the tables were not significantly different in sexual orientation. There were no differences in sexual orientation by use, reuse, or sharing of injecting equipment, or cleaning or disposal of equipment. There were no significant associations between those carrying out safe needle-sharing practices and safe-sex practices for either males or females, and no difference in sexual orientation on knowledge about AIDS.

Table 2
DIFFERENCES IN SEXUAL ORIENTATION IN FEMALE INJECTING DRUG USERS

Percentages

Variable	Heterosexual (n=220)	Bisexual (n=95)	Homosexual (n=10)	*Significance*
In drug treatment	52.8	71.4	57.1	**
Had HIV test	73.4	86.3	80.0	*
HIV seropositive	5.7	3.8	42.9	**
Regular partner bisexual	83.3	76.2	60.0	**
Pay for sex	0.9	4.4	30.0	**
Paid for sex	12.6	35.2	10.0	**
Drugs used when having sex:				
Opiates other than herion	8.2	20.0	0	**
Barbiturates	5.0	17.9	0	**
Cocaine	21.4	35.8	20.0	*
Sexual practices past 6 months:				
Vaginal	94.1	87.4	60.0	**
Anal insertive, without condom	5.9	27.4	20.0	*
Fellating male partner	77.7	75.8	0	**
Fellating male partner, withdrawal	59.6	65.3	0	**
Active oral sex with female partner	0	71.6	60.0	**
Receiving cunnilingus	70.5	89.5	50.0	**
Masturbating male	74.6	73.7	0	**
Masturbating woman	0	72.6	70.0	**
Being masturbated	65.0	81.1	30.0	**
STDs				
Genital warts	16.8	31.6	10.0	**
Hepatitis B	27.7	42.1	20.0	*
Pelvic inflam. disease	10.9	20.0	0	*
No STD reported	16.4	13.7	50.0	*
Unsafe sex, past 6 months	10.0	70.5	27. 7	**

		Mean		
Number HIV tests	3.4	4.1	1.9	Bi>Ho *
Male partners past year	8.1	28.1	0	Bi>He>Ho**
Female partners past year	0	4.2	4.2	Ho Bi>He**
Number regular partners	1.2	1.2	2.0	Bi>Ho He *
Number sexual partners IDUs	1.2	2.1	1.3	Bi>Ho He**
% time intoxicated during sex	53.1	66.0	54.7	Bi>Ho He**
% time condoms used, oral receptive sex	7.6	3.7	85.0	Ho> Bi He**

*p<.05 **p<.01

Mean percentage of the time respondents wre "high, stoned, or drunk" during sex was 57.9% for males, and 56.8% for females.

Discussion

IT MUST BE acknowledged that the representatives of samples of IDUs remains uncertain, as the size and characteristics of the drug-using population in a community have never been confidently defined. However, this is a large sample, containing in-treament and out-of-treatment populations recruited systematically and is comparable on many indices with another large sample of IDUs recruited from multiple sources in a city 400 kilometers from Sydney. Self-report of sexual behaviors (McLaws et al. 1990) and drug use behaviors is reported to be of acceptable reliability and validity, although this may be an additional source of error. However, such error is unlikely to be systematic.

This data indicates that differences in sexual orietation in injecting drug users is almost exclusively limited to sexual behavior, as there is little difference in type of drug administered by injection or other routes, or in injection equipment-sharing behaviors. The major drug-related differences in sexual orientation appear limited to oral drugs, with the party drugs Ecstasy (metamphetamine) and LSD being used more by homosexual men, and benzodiazepines more by bisexual men. Drugs used when having sex also differed in sexual orientation: generally, homosexual men were more likely to use benzodaizapines and Ecstasy and less likely to use heroin. Bisexual and homosexual men reported more frequent use of alchol, and bisexual men more frequent use of opiates (such as morphine, pethadine, and codeine) other than heroin, and Ecstasy. For the women, the bisexual women were also more likely to use opiates other than heroin, barbiturates, and cocaine than heterosexual or homosexual women. The fact that male and female respondents were both likely to be under the infulence of a drug or drugs more than half the time when having sex may have led to disinhibition and an increased risk of unsafe behavior.

Male heterosexuals in this study were more likely to be less well educated, to have been in prison, and to have moved to Sydney. Sexual practices, however, differentiated the three groups as would be expected. Apart from the anticipated differences between groups, STDs showed a trend toward a higher reporting as homosexual contact increased, and the same trend was apparent for having sex with an HIV-seropositive person. HIV serostatus also showed the same trend, with the probability of seropositivity increasing sharply as homosexual orientation increased. Homosexual and bisexual men were more likely to have had more HIV tests, and to have reported changing their behavior (in any way) since testing.

There is no positive transfer of modification of risk behaviors from the sexual domain to needle- and syringe-use patterns. Within the three groups of sexual orientation in males, condom use was greater among homosexual men than the bisexual men, who in turn used condoms more frequently than the heterosexual men. However, homosexual and bisexual men were more at HIV risk from sexual activity because of higher HIV seroprevalence among homosexuasl and bisexuals in Sydney, as is demonstrated by the differences in the prevalence of antibodies to HIV observed in this study.

The conclusions drawn on differences between groups of women need to be interpreted with greater caution given the small number of homosexual women in the sample. That a significant proportion of the bisexual women (over one-third) worked as prostitutes at some time adds an additional risk factor. In this study the bisexual women were found to use more opiates other than heroin, barbiturates, and cocaine during sex and to have significantly higher reported STD rates, probably reflecting their greater participation in prostitution. A significantly higher proportion of bisexual than heterosexual or homosexual women had also practiced unsafe sex in the past six months. They also reported enaging in most of the particular sexual activities on which information was requested more than heterosexual or homosexual women, as well as having more HIV tests, having more IDU partners, and being intoxicated more frequently during sex than the other two female groups.

This data for both male and female IDUs suggests that sexual orientation only influences sexual behavior of IDUs, and that a compartmentalization of risk behaviors exists with a lack of positive transfer between other risk areas. This is consistent with the risk compensation hypothesis (Weinstein 1989) which holds that taking safety precautions may increase the exposure to risk. It may be that, by taking precautions against sexual HIV transmission, homosexual and bisexual IDUs feel they are protected and that the risk from parenteral transmission is minimal. In terms of risk reduction, this data also confirms that homosexual, and to a lesser degree bisexual, men are taking precautions against sexual infection with HIV. In the case of female IDUs, the bisexual women appear to be most at risk of HIV infection or transmission because of their higher frequency of being paid for sex. However, the fact that over half of the male and female IDUs in this study were intoxicated during sex raises a major problem for the control of HIV infection not only in this population but possibly in many communities where IDU is relatively common. As yet, the influence of drug taking on high-risk sexual practices is uncertain. Future research needs to identify the degree of intoxication and links between this and sexual behavior.

References

Battjes, R. J., R. W. Pickens, and Z. Amsel. 1989. Introduction of HIV infection among intravenous drug abusers in low prevalence areas. *Journal of AIDS.* 2: 533–39.

Boles, J., M. Sweat, and K. Elifson. 1989. Bisexuality among male prostitues. Paper presented at CDC workshop on bisexuality and AIDS, Atlanta, Ga.

Chu, S. Y., L. S. Dool, and J. W. Buehler. 1989. Epidemiology of AIDS in bisexual males. Paper presented at CDC workshop on bisexuality and AIDS, Atlanta, Ga.

Donoghoe, M. C., G. C. Stimson, and K. A. Dolan. 1989a. Sexual behavior of injecting drug users and associated risks of HIV infection for non-injecting sexual partners. *AIDS Care.* 1: 51–58

Donoghoe, M. C., G. C. Stimson, K. Dolan, and L. Alldritt. 1989. Changes in HIV risk behavior in clients of syringe exchange schemes in England and Scotland. *AIDS.* 3: 261–65.

Hart, G. J., A. L. M. Carvell, N. Woodward, et al. 1989. Evaluation of needle exchange in central London: Behavior change and anti-HIV status over one year. *AIDS*. 3: 261–65.

Jones, C., and D. Vlahov. 1989. Why don't intravenous drug users use condoms? *Journal of AIDS*. 2: 416–17.

McLaws, M. L., B. Oldenburg, M. W. Ross, et al. 1990. Sexual behavior in AIDS-related research: Reliability and validity of recall and diary measures. *Journal of Sex Research*. 2: 265–81.

Marmor, M., K. Krasinski, and M. Sanchez. 1990. Sex, drugs, and HIV infection in a New York City hospital outpatient population. *Journal of AIDS*. 3: 307–18.

Maskill, W. J., C. Silvester, and D. S. Healey. 1989. Application of protein blotting to the serodiagnosis of Human Immunodeficiency Virus Infection. In *Protein Blotting: Methodology, Research, and Diagnostic Applications*, ed. B. A. Baldo and E. R. Tovey. New York: Karger.

Weinstein, N. D. 1989. Perceptions of personal susceptibility to harm. In *Primary Prevention of AIDS: Psychological Approaches*, ed. V. M. Mays, G. W. Albee, S. F. Schneider. 142–67. Newbury Park: Sage.

Williams, M. L. 1990. A model of the sexual relations of young IV drug users. *Journal of AIDS*. 3: 192–93.

EDITORS AND AUTHORS

The Editors

Haeberle, Erwin J.: Professor, Dr. phil., Ed.D., M.A. Director of the Archive for Sexology at the Robert Koch Institute in Berlin. Full Professor at the Institute for Advanced Study of Human Sexuality, San Francisco (on leave); former visiting professor at San Francisco State University, the University of Kiel, the University of Geneva, and Humboldt University in Berlin; scientific advisor to the Shanghai Sex Sociology Research Centre; former Research Associate at the Kinsey Institute for Sex Research in Bloomington, Indiana. President of the German Society for Sociological Sexual Research (DGSS). Secretary general of the European Federation of Sexology (EFS) and international advisor to the Asian Federation for Sexology (AFS). Memberships: International Academy of Sex Research; Fellow, Society for the Scientific Study of Sexuality (SSSS); Board of Examiners, The American College of Sexologists; Society for Practical Sexual Medicine. Address: Robert Koch-Institut, Archiv für Sexualwissenschaft, Hannoversche Str. 27, D-10115 Berlin, Germany. Website address: http://www.rki.de/GESUND/ARCHIV/HOME.HTM. E-mail: HaeberleE@rki.de

Gindorf, Rolf: Ph.D. candidate; Sex researcher, theoretical and clinical sexologist. Director (since 1978) of the Institute for Life and Sexual Counseling (DGSS Institute) in Düsseldorf. Scientific advisor, Shanghai Sex Sociology Research Center. Areas of concentration: theoretical principles of sexology; general sexual counseling and therapy; homosexual and bisexual research and counseling; AIDS research and counseling. Author, coauthor, and editor of more than fifty publications on sex research, including eight books and two book series. Founder (1971), chairman (until 1979), and vice president of the German Society for Sociological Sexual Research (DGSS). International activities, memberships, and honors, including: Sex Information and Education Council of the United States (SIECUS), Society for the Scientific Study of Sexuality (SSSS), editorial advisor of *Journal of Homosexuality.* After completing language studies and accompanying studies of economics, law, and sociology, he initially pursued entrepreneurial activity in developing countries and then began the study of sexology, counseling and therapy, as well as of sociology and psychology. Address: DGSS-Institut, Germersheimer Str. 20, D-40211 Düsseldorf, Germany. Website address: http://www.sexologie.org. E-mail: Rolf.Gindorf@sexologie.org

Authors

De Cecco, John Paul: Ph.D., professor of psychology. Director, Human Sexuality Studies, San Francisco State University, where he is also the coordinator of bisexual, lesbian, and gay studies. Editor-in-chief of *Journal of Homosexuality* since 1977. He has for many years had a critical interest in the concept of homosexual identity, especially of its biological foundation; recipient of the Magnus Hirschfeld Medal for Sexual Research; member of the American Psychological Association, the International Academy for Sex Research, the Society of the International Academy for Sex Reseasrch, and the Society for the Scientific Study of Sexuality. Address: Center for Research and Education in Sexuality (CERES-Psychology), San Francisco State University, San Francisco, CA 94132.

Coleman, Eli: Ph.D., director and associate professor, Program in Human Sexuality, Department of Family Practice and Community Health, Medical School, University of Minnesota, Minneapolis. Research, teaching, and clinical practice (with numerous publications): sexual orientation, gender role dysphoria, bi- and homosexuality, chemical dependency, and family intimacy; psychological and pharmacological treatment of various sexual disturbances. Partial list of publications by Haworth Press: *Chemical Dependency and Intimacy Dysfunction; Psychotherapy with Homosexuality in Men and Women: Integrated Identity Approaches for Clinical Practice; John Money: A Tribute; Sex Offender Treatment: Psychological and Medical Approaches; Sex Offender Treatment: Explanations of Interpersonal Violence, Intrapsychic Conflict and Biological Dysfunction* (currently in press). Editor of *Journal of Psychology and Human Sexuality* since its first issue in 1988. Memberships and functions: Society for the Scientific Study of Sexuality (former president), World Association of Sexology (secretary general), Harry Benjamin International Gender Dysphoria Association (board of directors), Institute for Child and Adolescent Sexual Health, International Academy for Sex Research, American Association of Sex Educators, Counselors and Therapists, Sex Information and Education Council of the United States. Address: Program in Human Sexuality, Medical School, 1300 South 2d Street, Minneapolis, MN 55454.

Diamond, Milton: Ph.D., professor, University of Hawaii-Manoa, John A. Burns School of Medicine; Department of Anatomy and Reproductive Biology, Honolulu. Director, Pacific Center for Sex and Society. Research concentrations: sexual development, intercultural sexual models, pornography, AIDS, reproduction/abortion and sex. Honors include: Lederle Medical Faculty Fellow; President of the Society for the Scientific Study of Sex Western Region; AAAS/NSF Chautauqua Lecturer. Most important publications: *Perspectives in Reproduction and Sexual Behavior* (editor, 1968), *Abortion Politics* (with P. G. Steinhoff, 1977), *Sexual Decisions* (with A. Karlen, 1980), *Sex Watching: The World of Sexual Behavior* (2d edition, London, 1992), "Homosexuality and Bisexuality in Different Populations" (in *Archives of Sexual Behavior* 22(4): 291-310, 1993), "Some Genetic Considerations in the Development of Sexual Orientation" (in M. Haug, R. Whalen, C. Aron & K. L. Olson, eds., *The Development of Sex Differences and Similarities in Behavior,* Dordrecht, 1993). Address: University of Hawaii-Manoa, John A. Burns School of

Medicine, Department of Anatomy and Reproductive Biology, 1951 East-West Road, Honolulu, HI 98682.

Friedman, Richard C.: M.D., clinical associate professor of psychiatry, College of Physicians and Surgeons, Columbia University, New York; research professor of psychology, Adelphi University, New York. Previously in the Human Sexuality Committee, *DSM-III;* consultant, The Gender Identity Committee, work group *DSM-IV;* currently chairman, Program Committee, American Academy of Psychoanalysis. Publications: *Male Homosexuality: A Contemporary Psychoanalytic Perspective* (1988) as well as more than fifty book and journal contributions on endocrinology and psychoanalysis. Address: 224 Central Park West, Apt. 103, New York, NY 10024.

Gagnon, John H.: Ph.D., professor of sociology at the State University of New York in Stony Brook. Previously senior research sociologist and member of the board of trustees, Kinsey Institute for Sex Research, Indiana University; visiting professor at Harvard, Princeton, and the University of Essex, and Overseas Fellow at Churchill College, Cambridge. Fellow, American Association for the Advancement of Science. Publications as author or coauthor include: *Sex Offenders* (1965), *Sexual Conduct* (1973), *Human Sexualities* (1977), *The Organization of Sexuality* (1994), as well as numerous other specialty publications. Address: 40 E. 19th Street., Apt. 8, New York, NY 10003.

Hekma, Gert: Ph.D. in sociology and history. Lecturer on homostudies at the University of Amsterdam, Faculty for Political and Sociocultural Sciences. Chairman of the Forum on Sexuality and editor-in-chief of its English-language newsletter *fos.* Member of the editorial board of *Journal of Homosexuality, Paidika, GLQ* and *Perversion.* Numerous publications, some of them as coauthor, on sociology and history of sexuality and homosexuality, including: *The Pursuit of Sodomy. Male Homosexuality in Renaissance and Enlightenment Europe* (New York, 1989); *De roze rand van donker Amsterdam* (Dark Amsterdam's red edge) (Amsterdam, 1992) on the history of the Amsterdam gay and lesbian bar culture from 1930 to 1970; *Als ze maar niet provoceren* (As long as they do not provoke) (Amsterdam 1994) on the discrimination of gays and lesbians in organized sports. Address: University of Amsterdam, Faculty for Political and Sociocultural Sciences, Department of Sociology, Oude Hoogstraat 24, NL-1012 Amsterdam, the Netherlands.

Herdt, Gilbert: Ph.D., professor of human development, University of Chicago. Received his doctorate in anthropology in 1978 at Australian National University with an investigation of male initiation rites among the Sambia in Papua-New Guinea. Research concentrations: cultural and psychological anthropology, sexuality and gender, erotic development, general theory of desire. Primary book publications: *Guardians of the Flutes* (1981), *Rituals of Manhood* (1982), *Ritualized Homosexuality in Melanesia* (1984, 1993), *The Sambia* (1987), *Gay and Lesbian Youth* (1989), *Intimate Communications* (1990, with Robert J. Stoller), *Gay Culture in America* (1992), *Children* *of Horizons* (1993), *Third Sex, Third Gender: Beyond Sexual Dimophism in Culture and History* (1994). Address: Committee on Human Development, University of Chicago, 5730 S. Woodlawn Blvd., Chicago, IL 60637-1603.

Money, John: Ph.D., honorary doctorates from the Institute for Advanced Study of Human Sexuality (San Francisco) and Hofstra University (New York), former professor of medical psychology and of pediatrics, director of the psychohormonal research unit, Johns Hopkins University School of Medicine, Baltimore. Born in New Zealand, emigrated to the USA when he was twenty-six and received his doctorate from Harvard in 1952 after he had already begun his teaching and research activity at Johns Hopkins a year before. Clinical and research concentrations: pediatric developmental psychoendocrinology, hermaphroditism, gender and identity, new gender assignment, paraphilias ("lovemaps"). Publications include: 350 scientific articles, 90 textbook chapters and 40 books as author or editor. His 1972 book (with Anke A. Ehrhardt), *Man and Woman, Boy and Girl,* has become a classic; *Principles of Developmental Sexology* (New York: Continuum) was published in 1997. He is the main editor of *Handbook of Sexology* (eight volumes) and author of the clinical supplementary volume *Biographies of Gender and Hermaphroditism* (Amsterdam: Elsevier, 1991). Honors and distinctions include those from the American Psychiatric Association, the Children's Hospital of Philadelphia, the Society for the Scientific Study of Sex, the American Association for Sex Educators, Counselors, and Therapists, the Erikson Educational Foundation, the National Council on Family Relations; the American Psychological Association, the Harry Benjamin International Gender Dysphoria Association, the National Institute of Child Health and Human Development, the Polish Academy of Sexological Science, the International Academy of Sex Research, the Robert Wood Johnson Medical School in New Jersey, and the New York Society of Forensic Sciences. Address: Suite LL 20, Old Town Office Center, 1235 E. Monument Street, Baltimore, MD 21202.

van Naerssen, A. X. ("Lex"): Dr., lecturer of clinical psychology and sexual psychology at the University of Utrecht. As a sex counselor, he works primarily in the fields of exhibitionism and pedophilia. He is the author of a book about sexual desire: *Labyrinth ohne Wände,* (Labyrinth without walls). Address: Rijksuniversiteit te Utrecht, Faculteit der Sociale Wetenschappen, Heidelberglaan 1, NL-3508 TC Utrecht, the Netherlands.

Paul, Jay P.: Ph.D. in clinical psychology. Lecturer at the University of California, San Francisco, where he works on several AIDS prevention studies with gay and bisexual men at the Center for AIDS Prevention Studies (CAPS). Concentration: drug abuse and the promotion of health care among risk groups. In addition, he has had a free practice as a psychotherapist primarily for gay and bisexual men for ten years. Member of the executive committee of the former San Francisco Bisexual Center and author of several articles and book chapters on bisexuality. Address: University of California, Prevention Sciences Group, 74 New Montgomery Street, Suite 600, San Francisco, CA 94105-3411.

Pryor, Douglas W.: Visiting lecturer for sociology at Wake Forest University. Coauthor, with M. S. Weinberg and C. J. Williams, of *Dual Attraction*. Presently working on a book entitled *Breaking Sexual Boundaries: Men Who Molest Children*. Address: care of Martin S. Weinberg.

Ross, Michael: Ph.D., associate professor of community medicine, University of New South Wales, Sydney; deputy director, Australian National Centre for HIV/AIDS Social Research, Sydney. Studied in New Zealand, Australia, the United States, and Sweden; degrees in psychology, sociology, health education, public health, and medicine. Author of seven books and 150 articles and book contributions. Honors: 1980 Hugo Beigel Award for Sexological Investigations; 1989 Neuman Aware for AIDS Research. Address: Albion Street AIDS Centre, 150-154 Albion Street, Surry Hills, Sydney, NSW 2010, Australia. Or: University of Texas, Houston, Center for Health Education, PO Box 20186, Houston, TX 77225, Tel. (713) 792 8540, Fax (713) 794 1758.

Schwartz, Pepper: Ph.D., professor of sociology, University of Washington, Department of Sociology, Seattle. Research concentration: male and female bisexuality. Book publications include: *Gender in Intimate Relationships* (with B. Risman); *American Couples: Money, Work and Sex* (with P. Blumstein); *Sexual Scripts* (with J. J. Laws); and journal articles. Activities and functions include: President of the Western Region of the Society for the Scientific Study of Sexuality from 1989 to 1991; Committee on the Status of Homosexuals of the American Sociological Association from 1988 to 1990; editorial board of the *Journal of Sex Research* and *Journal of Family Issues*. Address: Department of Sociology DK-40, University of Washington, Seattle, WA 98195.

Warran, Alan: Streetworker who advises on AIDS prevention; sexuality education in the home; cares for teenage male prostitutes and helps them to find new lives with the goal of their psychic and social reintegration; counsels and cares for clients with bi- and pedosexual tendencies. Address: Care of DGSS-Institut, Germersheimer Str. 20, D-40211 Düsseldorf, Germany.

Weinberg, Martin S.: Ph.D., professor of sociology at Indiana University; has been an associate at the Kinsey Institute for Sexual Research at Indiana University for many years. Author or coauthor of numerous sexological books, including: *Dual Attraction: Understanding Bisexuality*; *Sexual Preference: Its Development among Men and Women*; *Homosexualities: A Study of Diversity among Men and Women*. Address: Indiana University, Department of Sociology, Ballantine Hall 744, Bloomington, IN 47405-6628.

Williams, Colin J.: Ph.D., professor of sociology at Indiana University/Purdue University, Indianapolis; has worked at the Kinsey Institute for Sexual Research at Indiana University for many years. Author or coauthor of numerous sexological books, including: *Sex and Morality in the U.S.*; *Dual Attraction*; *Male Homosexuals: Their Problems and Adaptations*; *Homosexuals and the Military*. Address: see Martin Weinberg.

Wong, Joseph: Ph.D., (deceased), was a researcher at the Centre for Asian Studies, University of Hong Kong. First studied at International Christian University in Tokyo, where he received his B.A., then did post graduate studies at Australian National University in Canberra, where he received his M.A. and Ph.D. in East Asian studies. Research concentration: ancient East Asian studies with a particular concentration in political history and social history of the T'ang Dynasty and its relations to Japan and Korea. Recently published works (all in Chinese) include: *Studies On Relations Between China, Korea and Japan in Ancient Times*, Centre of Asian Studies, University of Hong Kong, 1987 (editor with T. W. Lin); *Studies on T'ang-Sung History*, Centre of Asian Studies, University of Hong Kong, 1987 (editor with T. W. Lin); *Selected Papers by Hong Kong and Taiwan Scholars on the History of Sui and Tang*, Sanqin Press, Xian, People's Republic of China.

Index of Names

Index of Subjects

*Index of Subjects translated
by Lance W. Garmer*

Robert T. Francoeur, Editor-in-Chief
Martha Cornog, Timothy Perper, and Norman A. Scherzer,
Coeditors
***THE COMPLETE DICTIONARY OF SEXOLGY:
NEW EXPANDED EDITION***

In paperback. "Well executed . . . a remarkable job."
— *Booklist*

Robert T. Francoeur, Editor
***THE INTERNATIONAL ENCYCLOPEDIA
OF SEXUALITY***

An indispensable three-volume set: 30 countries, 130
contributors. Recepient of the "1997 Citation of Excellence for an
outstanding reference work in the field of sexology."

Sigmund Freud
PSYCHOLOGICAL WRITINGS AND LETTERS
Edited by Sander L. Gilman

Many of the classic works on sexuality, infant sexuality, dreams,
psychological procedure, telepathy, jokes, and the uncanny — also
featuring a selection of Freud's correspondence. Available in hard-
cover and paperback.

Dalin Liu, Man Lun Ng, Li Ping Zhou,
and Erwin J. Haeberle
SEXUAL BEHAVIOR IN MODERN CHINA

"A groundbreaking study that profiles attitudes about everything
from premarital sex to extramarital affairs to divorce."
— *Time*

John Money
PRINCIPLES OF DEVELOPMENT SEXOLOGY

A seminal work. "Perhaps no one since Freud has provided us
with such a blend of biological and psychological facts, theory,
and clinical material intensively integrated into an increasingly
coherent picture of the origins of human experience."
— DR. JUNE REINISCH, former director of the Kinsey Institute

Charles Moser, M.D., and JJ Madeson
BOUND TO BE FREE: THE SM EXPERIENCE

"The first intelligent, fully informed, fact-based discussion of
what SM is. . . . The authors provide a perspective that is uniquely accurate, sensitive, and fair in its depiction and interpretation
of erotic sadomasochism."
— *Library Journal*

William E. Prendergast, Ph.D.
SEXUAL ABUSE OF CHILDREN
AND ADOLESCENTS

A thoughtful and compassionate guide for those who are touched
by sexual abuse themselves or care for others who are.

Dr. Ruth K. Westheimer and Jonathan Mark
HEAVENLY SEX:
SEXUALITY IN THE JEWISH TRADITION

In paperback. "A fresh look at sexuality from a Jewish
perspective. . . . Dr. Ruth is as wise and witty as ever, and
her earthy observations and down-to-earth advice will be
helpful to Jews and non-Jews alike."
— *Library Journal*